THE UNIVERSITY OF
WINCHESTER

Martial Rose Library
Tel: 01962 827306

To be returned on or before the day marked above, subject to recall.

AFTER WAGNER

After Wagner

Histories of Modernist Music Drama from *Parsifal* to Nono

Mark Berry

THE BOYDELL PRESS

The right of Mark Berry to be identified as the author of this work has been asserted
in accordance with sections 77 and 78 of the Copyright, Designs and Patents Act 1988

First published 2014

The Boydell Press, Woodbridge

ISBN 978 1 84383 968 2

The Boydell Press is an imprint of Boydell & Brewer Ltd
PO Box 9, Woodbridge, Suffolk IP12 3DF, UK
and of Boydell & Brewer Inc.
668 Mt Hope Avenue, Rochester, NY 14620–2731, USA

website: www.boydellandbrewer.com

A catalogue record of this publication
is available from the British Library

The publisher has no responsibility for the continued existence or accuracy of URLs for external
or third-party internet websites referred to in this book, and does not guarantee that any content
on such websites is, or will remain, accurate or appropriate.

This publication is printed on acid-free paper

Typeset by Word and Page, Chester

CONTENTS

MUSIC EXAMPLES

Ex. 6–11 (from Luigi Dallapiccola's *Il prigioniero*) are reproduced by kind permission of Hal Leonard MGB, Italy,

ACKNOWLEDGEMENTS

This book has been a good time in the making. Admittedly, its gesta-tion pales beside that of *Parsifal*; it was nevertheless quite long enough. Most books draw upon a lifetime's experience, at whatever stage that life may find itself. Perhaps, though, there is a distinction of degree to be made here; if so, then this case errs more towards the cumulative, if necessarily incomplete, synthesis than many. That is a reflection in part of the subject matter, in part of the way in which I have organised it, and in part of the way in which, for better or worse, my mind seems to work. A full list of acknowledgements, even if I were capable of pro-viding it, would therefore be absurdly long; it might even have to be my autobiography. I shall therefore restrict myself to mentioning some of the greatest obligations, and shall hope that a general acknowledge-ment of heartfelt thanks will in no way offend those who, more or less arbitrarily, are not thanked individually here. 'Virtual history' is a dubious business; 'virtual acknowledgements' would extend beyond parody. This would nonetheless have been a very different, in many ways poorer, book without contributions from people and institutions who will go unnamed.

There can be no question of failing explicitly to thank the British Academy for a Postdoctoral Fellowship and the Leverhulme Trust for an Early Career Fellowship, both of which offered me time and space to pursue the early stages of my research. In that respect, I must also thank the Master and Fellows of Peterhouse, where I was a Fellow from 2001 to 2009. Although the debts I have incurred to the most ancient of the Cambridge colleges are many, I trust that it will not go amiss if I explicitly cite but one, namely the friendship and unwavering support of the late Neil Plevy; he remains greatly missed. My relationships with other friends, colleagues, members of staff, and pupils remain cherished. I should also like to thank Royal Holloway, University of London, and specifically the Department of Music, for having appointed me to a Lectureship, for subsequent friendship and collegial support, and not least, for a term's sabbatical leave, in which a further tranche of writing took place. Thanks should go to the Arnold Schoenberg Center for making me welcome twice as a visitor, once during that period of sabbatical leave; its library and archive, as well as the generous assistance of the archivist, Eike Feß, are greatly appreciated. (It was also a splendid thing to experience the epiphanic inspiration of an impromptu visit from Nuria Schoenberg-Nono, daughter and widow to two of this book's featured composers.)

Many friends and colleagues have, of course, contributed to more informal and more general discussion, both in traditional form and – increasingly – via social media such as Facebook and Twitter. Moreover, some thornier translation problems have been more readily resolved as a result of general enquiries to Facebook 'friends'. Such contributions, almost countless, are greatly valued, but again, I must limit myself. Formal acknowledgement therefore goes to the following, who have commented on earlier versions of material published here, whether in writing or in presentation of seminar papers: Michael Bentley, Tim Blanning, John Deathridge, Alexander Goehr, Robin Holloway, John Hughes, Erik Levi, Tim Jenkins, Barry Millington, Hamish Scott, and Alice Wood. Earlier versions of material in the first two chapters appeared respectively in *The Wagner Journal*, 3/3 (2009), 29–59, and in *Music and Letters*, 89 (2008), 84–108; I am grateful to those journals and their editors for having granted me the opportunity to try out ideas further developed here. I owe much to discussion of related issues with, amongst others: James Stevens Curl, Gregory Fullelove, Hermann Grampp, Paul Harper-Scott, Gavin Kelly, Sebastian Kokelaar, Sophie Lunn-Rockliffe, Emanuel Maess, Benjamin Moore, Anna Morcom, Rowena Naciri, Anne Ozorio, Oliver Perry, Tamsin Rolls, Hugo Shirley, Michael Tanner, Nicholas Vazsonyi, David Watkin, and Ross Wilson.

Attendance at performances discussed has sometimes been at personal expense; I have also been fortunate enough to receive press tickets for some. In no particular order, I should therefore like to thank the Bayreuth Festival (2011 and 2012, for both *Parsifal* and *Lohengrin*, and Per-Erik Skramstad for supporting my application), the Southbank Centre (*Il prigioniero*), the Berlin State Opera (*Lohengrin, Lulu*), Oper Leipzig (*Lohengrin* and *Al gran sole carico d'amore*), the Opéra national de Paris (*Katya Kabanova*), RC Theatre Productions (*Don Giovanni: The Opera*), the Salzburg Festival (*Lulu* and *Al gran sole carico d'amore*), and the Young Vic Theatre (*American Lulu*). More generally, thanks go to concert halls, opera houses, orchestras, other musicians, directors, and so on, for having truly opened my eyes and ears in practice to the role of performance in broadening and questioning understanding of the 'musical work'. Pierre

Acknowledgements

Boulez, a ghostly presence throughout much of the book, deserves especial mention for a career which, like those of Wagner, Schoenberg, and others before him, has stood as inspiring witness and conscience for his strenuously held conception of new music.

At Boydell and Brewer, Michael Middeke and Megan Milan have shown great courtesy, support, and not least, patience, throughout my dealings with them. Michael's role as commissioning editor was crucial from the time when he visited me in Cambridge and encouraged me to put forward a proposal, and throughout. His suggestions for improvements were all well made and, I hope, well enough taken.

Finally, and returning to the longer *durée*, I thank my family, especially my parents, to whom this book is dedicated, for support and forbearance, both before and after my first encounter with Wagner and his works. Although the following 'must' customarily be said, necessity lessens neither its importance nor its sincerity: all errors, omissions, and other shortcomings remain my responsibility and mine alone.

Mark Berry, London
Feast of St John the Silent, May 2014

To my parents

INTRODUCTION

'AFTER WAGNER'

'After Wagner': a good many objections may doubtless be raised to this title, not least that the first chapter is devoted to *Parsifal*. That, however, is partly my point. In his final stage work, intended exclusively for the very particular stage of Bayreuth, Richard Wagner was not only writing a 'late work', not only writing the drama he had always intended to be his last, but was, to an even great extent than in his earlier music dramas, dealing with issues he had raised in previous works, or which, intention notwithstanding, those works had raised. So, as will become immediately apparent from that chapter itself, 'after Wagner' may be understood partly to denote 'after Wagner's *Ring*', or 'after Wagner's *Ring*, *Tristan*, and *Meistersinger*', although from the second chapter onwards, the original phrase will work in the chronological sense as well as any other. That holds at least until the concluding chapter, which looks back to Gluck and Mozart, as well as forward to Berg and Nono, albeit all the while from Wagnerian and post-Wagnerian standpoints.

'The chronological sense as well as any other'? What other senses, then? The English 'after' is blessed by a host of other meanings, some of greater relevance than others here: to a certain extent consonant with the German *nach* and the French *après* and *d'après*, but arguably going beyond them too. Not for nothing did Herder, to whom Wagner owed a great deal, insist upon the importance of language in forming thought, and not for nothing has that been such a preoccupation amongst philosophers and latterly historians ever since. There is certainly a sense here of enquiring after Wagner, or more to the point after his musico-dramatic principles and their after-life. 'As a result of' is another meaning of relevance to each of these chapters, in various ways and to a varying extent. Arguably the most important complementary meanings, however, are 'according to' and 'in the manner of'. For Wagner's strenuous conception of music drama as something beyond mere 'opera' haunts the following pages. More importantly, it haunts the theory and practice of those composers and, in many respects, performers to be discussed. Here is not the place to give a detailed account of Wagner's conception of music drama; to the extent that it is relevant, it will be discussed and referred to below. However, a combination of seriousness of purpose, and a broader, religious or quasi-religious, political or quasi-political, conception of art and the artwork may certainly be understood to form an integral part of this tradition 'after Wagner'.

Within the titular phrase, then, there lies a tension far from accidental. Moreover, insofar as that tension might be described as both an elision and a conflict between chronology and dialectics, it also very much informs the dramatic material and the æsthetic conception of all those works, world-views, careers, and performances to be considered. The work is, like any text, unstable, yet that 'like any text' points to a truth too readily lost or discarded, namely that instability does not imply that we should rid ourselves of the concept itself. Quite the contrary: it provides us, as historians, critics, performers, even analysts, with provocations that are at least as often opportunities as problems. Contradiction exists, as any good – or even bad – Hegelian will tell us. It is perhaps worth asking ourselves whether, in what is in many respects, whether we like it or not, a post-modernist age, we have become too accustomed to describing anything and everything as a 'text', to claiming to 'read' it, or at least whether we might consider what differences there lie between things that are more or less 'textual'.

Issues of performance, as we shall see, here fruitfully complicate, problematise, fascinate. We inevitably begin to ask, as does James Treadwell in his discussion with David J. Levin, to what extent audiences and critics 'experience the [operatic] work as a read text'.[1] Perhaps also: to what extent they 'should'. Moralism or at least moral questions intrude, irrespective of our wishes, just as we shall see them do so more explicitly in the case of Richard Strauss. Strauss indeed offers an instructive compositional comparison here; his apparent preoccupation with surface, ornament, and irony might be seen as more stylistically 'operatic' than, say, Schoenberg's quest for 'truth'. For, as Treadwell comments, 'our sense of the meaning of a production is likely to be hugely affected by its stylistic surface'.[2] Or is it? If we follow Schoenberg – Moses rather than Aron, in terms to be more fully explored in the second chapter – do we actually move closer to a distinction between style and idea, which may or may not be the same as that manifested within the work, but which probably has light to shed upon it?

[1]   James Treadwell, 'Reading and Staging Again,' in *Cambridge Opera Journal*, 10 (1998), 212.
[2]   Ibid., p. 215.

To turn to modernism, I do not wish to become bogged down with questions of definition. It is not that I think they are pointless or fruitless, but that they tend to overshadow other concerns as soon as they are voiced, and they are not really here the fundamental concern.[3] There are dangers of course in failing to attend to definition, not least that before one knows it, almost everything has become 'modernist', just as everything might elsewhere become 'Romantic' or 'Enlightened', and not even just from the period concerned. For what it is worth, it seems perfectly clear that not all twentieth-, let alone later-nineteenth-century, music is illuminated by applying the label, let alone by shoehorning it into the category of 'modernism'. By the same token, all of the works and composers studied here may in their different ways be considered to be responding to similar difficulties and opportunities. Here it may be worth recalling Hugh Honour's pointedly non-defining summary of the Romantics as 'united only at their point of departure'.[4] In crystallising the points of departure relevant in this case as coming and being 'after Wagner', that is not intended to inflate the stature of one man and his works, but simply to offer a signpost and, perhaps more important, a non-exclusive way of shaping thoughts and understanding. This history and these histories – there is again a deliberate tension in the naming, as in the recounting – might have been 'after Mozart', 'after Marx', 'after Schoenberg', 'after Adorno', even 'after Hitler', given the inevitable post-Holocaust shaping of Western political, social, and cultural experience. However, in this case, it and they are not, or at least not so strongly as it and they are placed and formed 'after Wagner'. The choice is not merely arbitrary, but equally does not claim to have been dictated by iron necessity. Necessity in any case ceases to be of interest, or indeed of meaning, when it becomes ironclad.

History, for better or for worse, is like that – and I think it overwhelmingly for the better. Like men (people) in general, from the celebrated opening to that finely crafted revolutionary drama, Marx's *Eighteenth Brumaire of Louis Bonaparte*, historians in particular 'make their own history, but they do not make it just as they please; they do not make it under circumstances chosen by themselves, but under circumstances directly encountered, given, and transmitted from the past'. And if the 'tradition of all the dead generations weighs like a nightmare on the brain

---

[3] For an excellent recent musical treatment, see Paul Harper-Scott, *The Quilting Points of Musical Modernism* (Cambridge University Press: Cambridge and New York, 2012).

[4] Hugh Honour, *Romanticism* (Harper and Row: New York, 1979), p. 19. See also Arthur Lovejoy's classic article, 'The Meaning of Romanticism for the Historian of Ideas', in *Journal of the History of Ideas*, 2 (1941), 257–78.

of the living', then inspiration can be born of nightmare too. Just as 'Luther donned the mask of the Apostle Paul [and the] ... Revolution of 1789 to 1814 draped itself alternately as the Roman republic and the Roman empire', so composers, historians, even performers, will dress themselves according to their historical memories and inclinations, without that necessarily meaning that they, as Marx perhaps unfairly alleged of the 1848 revolutionaries – one of them especially familiar to us from the Dresden barricades – 'knew nothing better ... than to parody' revolutionary experiences that preceded them. We can and at different times will conjure up 'the dead of world history', yet it will always be for different purposes, without that in any sense entailing their dishonour.[5]

Likewise, I see no point in attempting to define 'music drama' here, save to say that it is being used in a sense one might characterise as generally post-Wagnerian. It is not intended to be exclusive, and the only reason I prefer it in the title to 'opera' is that a number of the composers discussed here, in some of their works, from Wagner in his *Bühnen-weihfestspiel, Parsifal*, to Henze in his 'show mit 17', *Der langwierige Weg in die Wohnung der Natascha Ungeheuer* and Nono in his *azione scenice, Intolleranza 1960* and *Al gran sole carico d'amore*, specifically rejected the term 'opera' and thus some of its social and ideological associations. *Natascha Ungeheuer* might more readily be assimilated to the genre of 'music theatre', alongside works by, say, Peter Maxwell Davies and Harrison Birtwistle, but Nono's works would not. There is no need necessarily to abjure 'opera' when speaking specifically of such pieces – neither Henze nor Nono employed 'music drama' in any case – and there is certainly no such need in general terms; however, use of an alternative from time to time counsels that usage should not go uncontested.

Let us then adopt a somewhat different route, by assuming and questioning rather than by defining modernism, and by considering what it has asked and might continue to ask us. Especially when standing, both as political and musical animals, in the shadow of Adorno and the Frankfurt School, not the least of its overarching questions might be: is emancipation still possible? That question may be seen to stand at the core of the modernist project, though it neither defines that project nor is exclusive thereto. We should of course be wary of the almost anthropomorphistic attribution of characters, goals, and so forth to periods and

---

[5]   Karl Marx, 'The Eighteenth Brumaire of Louis Bonaparte', in Karl Marx and Friedrich Engels, *Selected Works*, 3 vols (Progress: Moscow, 1969–70), vol. 1, p. 398.

movements, yet at the same time need not entirely eschew them. That current, predominant in, yet far from exclusive to, the eighteenth century, which we have come to call the Enlightenment, would have answered yes, although it would have been slightly puzzled by the 'still', or indeed by the question itself. Of course it was possible; of course it was desirable. Was that not the very Kantian definition of Enlightenment: man's emergence from his self-incurred immaturity?[6] The pessimism voiced at the end of Voltaire's *Candide* – 'Il faut cultiver notre jardin' – is exceptional, though not unique. Indeed, it is curiously similar to the pessimism that made the proto-Romantic Rousseau break off his *Social Contract* and attend to less impossible tasks, abruptly concluding that he 'ought throughout to have kept to a more limited sphere'.[7]

The Romantics levelled all manner of charges at their eighteenth-century predecessors – and it was with respect to the eighteenth century that Romantics' much-trumpeted historicism lost out to ahistorical accusation as extravagant as anything the French *Encyclopédistes* might have hurled at the Middle Ages. Nevertheless, they shared the goal of emancipation, even if what that entailed might, according to one's standpoint, have broadened or become more diffuse. Likewise Hegel and his school, although one of his and its most signal achievements was a far more sophisticated understanding of subject, object, and their relationship: the discovery and part-rediscovery of the dialectical method so crucial to the following study. Ontology in Hegel threatened once again to challenge epistemology; it is no coincidence that it is Hegel's ontology that later readers have generally found the most difficult aspect of his philosophy to accept.[8] For Hegel himself, emancipation formed part of a greater project of reconciliation; for most of his more interesting followers, that reeked too much of compromise, even of Prussianism. Yet emancipation remained the goal, almost irrespective of from what or with which goal in mind. Move forward to the recent prevalence of post-modernism, and such attitudes would at best raise a

---

[6] Immanuel Kant, 'An Answer to the Question: "What is Enlightenment?"', in *Political Writings*, tr. H. B. Nisbet, ed. Hans Reiss (Cambridge University Press: Cambridge, 1970), p. 54.

[7] Voltaire, 'Candide, ou l'Optimisme, traduit de l'allemand de M. le Docteur Ralph', in *Œuvres completes*, vol. 15, 'Romans' (Hachette: Paris, 1859–62), p. 154; Jean-Jacques Rousseau, *The Social Contract and Discourses*, tr. G. D. H. Cole, revised J. H. Brumfett, John C. Hall, and P. D. Jimack (Dent: London, 1993), p. 309.

[8] Cf. Charles Taylor: 'While Hegel's ontology is near incredible, his philosophy is very relevant to our age.' (*Hegel and Modern Society* (Cambridge University Press: Cambridge, 1979), p. 135.)

wry smile, as if one had spoken of the possibility of 'truth' or some other such quaint Platonic remnant.

Yet, in the modernist world, although that prospect has become far more difficult to entertain, those very forces of objectivity that have engendered this difficulty have also helped to intensify the subjective insistence that emancipation might somehow be possible. However relentlessly negative (Adornian) the dialectic may have become, there must remain some chink of light, even if we ultimately fear or even believe it to be illusory. And it is worth insisting even at this point that modernism in this sense and indeed in many other senses is not dead; that, rather than grammatical ineptitude, is the reason or at least the justification for the recent persistent changes of tense. (Something similar may be seen in the third part of this book. When dealing specifically with Stefan Herheim's staging of *Parsifal*, I tend to employ the present, dealing with the production as something approaching a 'work' in itself; when constructing something approaching a history involving different productions of different works, the past is preferred.)

Such, anyway, is one way to characterise the history and histories about to be recounted. Are the stories different, parallel, or one and the same? Are there others, which concentrate on, for instance, historiography, political history, or that of the fine arts? What is to be gained from studying them in parallel or in a dialectical relationship? What lies at their intersection? Some answers will be attempted, but a running theme will be that questioning is often more important than answering, a theme that may certainly be traced back to Wagner's dramas, whatever his intentions as dramatist.

This history is necessarily partial, even eccentric; it is not complete, still less 'total'. The latter ambition represents the darker side of the Hegelian tradition – at least to the fragmented wasteland of the early twenty-first century. (That is pretty much what Adorno thought of Wagner, whom he considered to have dispensed with the antagonism between the universal and popular, 'the rebel of the particular' having become 'the executive organ of the totality'.[9]) The nature of this present attempt will have been shaped by many contingencies, foremost amongst which will have stood personal interests and aptitudes or otherwise, not least of the linguistic variety. Yet I have tried to ensure that the contingent does not harden into the exclusivity of the arbitrary. If the roots of this history lie deeper than

[9] Theodor Adorno, *In Search of Wagner*, tr. Rodney Livingstone (Verso: London and New York, 1981), p. 132.

Wagner, there remains a strong sense of treating with his legacy. That not only shapes and defines the particularity and form of the story; it also, doubtless more controversially, makes a claim for something of particular status in Wagner's œuvre, and his later œuvre in particular. I do not intend that with an unduly Romantic sense of hero-worship. For one thing, the legacy is far from unambiguously positive or un-problematical; for another, a great deal more of modern culture fed into what we have come to consider to be represented by and indeed simply to *be* 'Wagner' than even his considerable ego – in any available sense of the word – could have produced. There is no document of what we have come to call civilisation that is not, to quote Walter Benjamin, 'at the same time a document of barbarism', and a document of the 'anonymous toil' of so many others.[10]

I could readily tie myself up in knots trying to argue for my choice of composers and works; I freely own that different choices might have been made, choices at least as satisfactory. Personal inclination plays a part, of course, though not always, at least in terms of rejection. There is no twentieth-century opera I admire more than *Wozzeck*. Indeed, autobiography might itself have inclined me to include it, given the pride I have always felt that it was the first opera I saw staged, by Opera North, when I was a schoolboy in 1993. It led me into, instantly and irreversibly converted me to, an operatic world beyond and not just 'after' Mozart. Moreover, its musical form and its subject matter would be directly relevant to this book. That theatrical experience would have led naturally to the third, staging-oriented section. So there was no reason whatsoever not to include *Wozzeck*, as I had originally intended, other than the unfortunate fact that I could not include everything. I very much wanted to address the more awkward case of Strauss; indeed, I increasingly felt that the concerns I was pursuing demanded that I include him. *Wozzeck*, alas, would have to wait. Linguistic ignorance meant that Czech and Russian operas, for instance, could not be addressed; whilst happy to deal with them in passing, it would be insupportable to offer any closer reading of works whose libretti are written in languages I do not read. Farewell then, Janáček, Prokofiev, and many others.

Furthermore, it is worth reiterating that I am not principally concerned with tracing Wagner's influence, fascinating though that project would be. And so, whilst there would certainly be much to say, even from the standpoint of this book, upon Stockhausen 'after Wagner' – whether in

---

[10] Walter Benjamin, 'Theses on the Philosophy of History', tr. Harry Zohn, in Wolfgang Schirmacher (ed.) *German 20th Century Philosophy: The Frankfurt School* (Continuum: New York, 2000), p. 74.

the relatively rare overt politics of *Mittwoch*'s 'World Parliament' or the importance of *Parsifal*'s Monsalvat bells for *Samstag*'s later tale of transformation – Henze always seemed the more natural choice.[11] Moreover, in his rejection of avant-gardism, there was an interesting path to follow with respect to the prior Straussian example – an example Henze himself would doubtless have disdained or rejected. There is always room, then, for another history; indeed, an attempt at historical writing that did not open or at least reveal new doors would be a failure indeed. History, in that sense, might be seen to endorse Judit's curiosity, even in the face of Bluebeard's – and necessity's – response.

That said, it may reasonably be claimed that all of my composers shared a concern – often willingly, but on occasion despite themselves – to bear witness, a concern inescapably born of the history, the politics, the thought, of their times. Strauss is again the most obviously awkward case, but as I shall try to argue, he could not help himself either. By this, I do not merely claim a connection to social and political currents, for what music has ever been 'free' of them? Strauss's æstheticism – let alone the more obvious 'political' concerns of the other composers and indeed the stage directors considered subsequently – went beyond reflection to offer something that might, indeed should, be considered just as much a form of politico-dramatic witness as that borne by his apparent antithesis, Schoenberg, or by a 'committed', Strauss-excoriating composer such as Henze.

I stress the lack of objectivity because the nineteenth-century Rankean claim or desire to tell history 'as it really was' (*wie es eigentlich gewesen*) was always inherently a nonsense, born of a positivism it is difficult to believe ever held sway, though twentieth- and even on occasion twenty-first-century adherents have remained implacable.[12] It was a nonsense insofar as it was so clearly unattainable. A sixth-former fresh from reading, say E. H. Carr, could reel off all manner of reasons to explain the unreality of the 'really was'.[13] It was, moreover, pernicious, on account of the undesirability of the unattainable claim of 'objectivity', always a shroud for an insidious subjectivity – in the common more than the strictly philosophical sense

---

[11] On *Samstag* and the Bayreuth Bells, see Robin Maconie, *Other Planets: The Music of Karlheinz Stockhausen* (Scarecrow Press: Lanham, MD, Toronto, and Oxford, 2005), pp. 440–1.

[12] Leopold von Ranke, 'Geschichte der romanischen und germanischen Völker von 1494 bis 1535,' 2nd edn, in *Sämtliche Werke*, 54 vols (Duncker and Humblot: Leipzig, 1867–90), vol. 33, p. 7.

[13] Edward Hallett Carr, *What is History?* (Penguin: Harmondsworth, 2008).

– that either will not speak its name or has not reflected sufficiently to be able to do so. For history is or should always be a dialogue between past and present, or perhaps better, pasts and presents. Moreover, for historians, critical theorists, and performers alike – if not for logical positivists – there is 'no point of view without a perspective from which the taking of it occurs'.[14]

Performance helps bring that to the fore and, at its best, sometimes even at its worst, will engage in a dialogue so as to further our knowledge and understanding of past, present, and the multifarious paths in between. For that reason, I decided to devote the final section of this book to an exploration of different performances, with particular though far from exclusive emphasis upon stage direction. There were difficult choices to make here, of course, but none more so than the decision to forego more detailed exploration of opera following Henze and Nono; that is certainly not because I think composers and works of subsequent generations to be unimportant.

Again, however, one cannot do everything, and I wanted not only to address an aspect of musical drama that in such a treatment might readily be overlooked, despite it being overwhelmingly the way in which many people beyond the musicological fraternity – audiences, who surely matter enormously in any 'political' consideration – not only become acquainted with but also engage with artworks and their instability. It is certainly not the case that musicology, or at least an important element within, has not engaged with performance, or indeed with staging, but in many quarters at least there persists if not a conviction, then at least a tacit assumption, that performances are to be treated, to quote Carolyn Abbate, 'as way stations in a total reception history, sonic inscriptions of the work's meaning over historical time'.[15] That is not necessarily a false or even problematical assumption; it is difficult and it may well be undesirable to avoid it at some level. But it is well worth bearing in mind those problematical aspects of the seemingly ineradicable element of *Werktreue*, perhaps especially when we trumpet our suspicion or hostility towards the work as lode star. The distinction between the stage director's role and the conductor's or singer's – or, for that matter, the principal oboe's – is interesting. It is true, as Abbate says elsewhere, with reference

---

[14] Renate Holub, *Antonio Gramsci: Beyond Marxism and Postmodernism* (Routledge: London and New York, 1992), p. 74. The quotation refers to Gramsci's solidarity with the Frankfurt School in its writers' battle with positivism, but it serves well to summarise a broader solidarity, both historical and performative.

[15] Carolyn Abbate, 'Music – Drastic or Gnostic?' in *Critical Inquiry*, 30 (2004), 509.

to *Parsifal*, that there is a strong habit 'familiar in readings of operas as text: music is not subject to questions, not onstage. Though musical sounds may have shaped a whole series of beliefs, and while this fact may be openly acknowledged, they nonetheless make no appearance in the critical regimen.'[16]

That said, there are a good few examples of more 'critical' engagement in *musical* performance: Pierre Boulez, for instance, freely owns that he has sometimes conducted works in which he does not necessarily believe, from which he would not only wish to distance himself but does so through performance, and yet also which he thinks are interesting to present, distanced, as 'documents'.[17] One has the sense that, for instance, in the case of the twelve-note Schoenberg, *Moses und Aron* included, and even some neo-classical Stravinsky, the experience of performance has brought him closer to the works. Certainly Boulez's second recording of *Moses*, resulting from staged performances in Amsterdam and Salzburg, sounds more vividly in a Wagnerian-musico-dramatic tradition, perhaps partly born of the conductor's Bayreuth experience, than his first, originating in concert performances; it also seems to edge a little closer to Schoenberg's Brahmsian inheritance, always an object of suspicion for Boulez. And yet, the composer-conductor retains his distance – not entirely unlike many a musicologist. That remains different in scale, however, from the more wholesale *Verfremdungseffekt*, deconstruction, or other critical method employed by many opera directors. And of course, in some sense, the 'work' remains whilst the staging questions, accuses, or deconstructs. In Wagner's particular case, Boulez has insisted upon a 'difference between Wagner and the rest of the nineteenth century – as far as opera concerned, that is'. What has interested Boulez is that Wagner's works 'have such depth that one can return and be enriched each time'.[18]

That certainly seems to have been the case in terms of staging and audience reception too. The work criticises the performer, the director, the audience, as much as the other way round, quite irrespective of whether we wish that to happen – and often, that seems to be the last thing for which many wish. Moreover, the music – 'in itself' if we dare, or at least as it emerges from its confrontation with other aspects of the work – will often criticise the words, often confusingly described as 'the text', at least as much as the other way around. Not for nothing did Christopher Morris,

---

[16] Carolyn Abbate, *In Search of Opera* (Princeton University Press: Princeton, 2001), p. 109
[17] Jean Vermeil, *Conversations with Pierre Boulez: Thoughts on Conducting* (Amadeus: Portland, 1996), p. 52.
[18] Ibid., p. 47.

when embarking upon a project of *Reading Opera*, elect to concentrate upon the operatic interlude, and not only in such celebrated instances as *Pelléas* and *Wozzeck*, but also in the case of *Götterdämmerung*.[19]

The complication becomes greater still when we add to this particular witches' brew the mediatised experience of DVD or indeed cinema broadcasts, which are at the time of writing at least beginning to tilt the balance away from first operatic acquaintance via audio recording and thus imaginary self-staging of works in one's head. My first *Ring*, imagined to Karajan's studio recording, whilst following orchestral scores borrowed from my school music teacher, was doubtless a very different staging not only from that I saw when borrowing from a public library videos of the Boulez-Chéreau *Ring*, but from anything I should see, whether in my imagination, on screen, or on stage, following that viewing. Moreover, it is not only ironic but dialectically telling that, in *Moses und Aron*, an opera that pushes literally to the breaking-point of incompletion the idea of the possibility or impossibility of representation, a home audience seated in front of a DVD player or computer might encounter, in Reto Nickler's 2006 production for the Vienna State Opera, images of pornography, a genre or product now so intimately associated with such modes of reception as in some lives to be more or less synonymous with them, which might thereby draw that audience into Schoenberg's own interrogation of representation.[20] My own first experience of that same production was somewhat different, given that I saw it in the State Opera itself, but there the contrast and similarities between house and stage, audience and protagonists had its own tales to tell, its own resonances to provoke and to be questioned.

Performance also helps raise questions, pursued in the final section of the book, concerning the instability of the artwork, questions which will often in themselves hold interesting political as well as æsthetic implications. Such questions do not necessarily lead one to discard a strong conception of the artwork; I should not be writing this book as it stands, had that been the case. Yet the more inviolate our conception of the work, the more we should test it, both in itself, and in the revealing complexity of its relationship towards broader conceptions of history and society. Historical and societal forces certainly help to write our works of art and to mediate them, but works of art, both 'in themselves' – a chimera, but heuristically sometimes a useful one – and in performance, also help

[19] Christopher Morris, *Reading Opera Between the Lines: Orchestral Interludes and Cultural Meaning from Wagner to Berg* (Cambridge University Press: Cambridge, 2002).
[20] Arthaus Musik DVD 101259.

write history and thus the societies in which we have lived, presently live, and perhaps one day shall find ourselves living.

Should those words echo the Christian 'Sicut erat in principio, et nunc, et semper, et in saecula saeculorum,' that is no bad thing; for another theme, sometimes explicit, sometimes implicit, running through much of this book is that the religious nature of our conceptions of musical drama has too often been overlooked or downplayed. Wagner was explicit about his wish to renew the spirit of Greek tragedy in all its manifestations, a standing rebuke to the mere 'opera' of his own time. His model was *Agamemnon*: 'I declare that to be the most perfect thing in every way, religious, philosophic, poetic, artistic. One can put Shakespeare's histories beside it, but he had no Athenian state, no Areopagus as a final resort.' Pessimistically, he responded to Cosima's response that she could only put the *Ring* beside it, by saying that that was merely 'something thought up by an individual, only to be made a mess of immediately, as happened with newly established religions'.[21] The histories to be traced will help show quite how much he erred. Certainly a 'mess' might be made in many performances; yet, even if one were to accept the claim that the *Ring* had been merely 'thought up by an individual' rather than being a product at least as much of history and society, the attempt at renewal has, consciously and unconsciously, shaped more than a century of responses, compositional and performative – not to mention the echoes resounding across all manner of other manifestations of modern(ist) culture and modern history.

The lack of 'objectivity' also makes an important point concerning the 'typical' and the 'atypical', majoritarianism and its alternatives. Kant's response to that 1784 prize essay question, 'What is Enlightenment?', was anything but typical, although ultimately more influential and enduring than those of his competitors. There is much to be learned from the 'typical', or at least less extraordinarily atypical, answers; it depends what one is looking for.[22] It is, however, inverse snobbery, a conformism closely connected to the Culture Industry, to suppose that there is nothing or little to be learned from the exceptional, be that Kant or Beethoven, Adorno or Schoenberg. Canons cry out to be challenged; it does not follow that they therefore hold no meaning or value. There would of course be nothing

21 *Cosima Wagner's Diaries*, ed. Martin Gregor-Dellin and Dietrich Mack, tr. Geoffry Skelton, 2 vols (London: Harcourt Brace Jovanovich, 1978–80), vol. 2, 24 June 1880, p. 495.
22 See, e.g., James Schmidt (ed.), *What is Enlightenment? Eighteenth-Century Answers and Twentieth-Century Questions* (University of California Press: Berkeley and Los Angeles, 1996).

wrong in principle with finding what was most typical about writing and conceptions of music drama 'after Wagner'. However, it is often the case that what is most interesting, most noteworthy, most destined to last, most resistant – and those 'mosts' will often turn out to be the same – will prove to have been anything but the most 'typical' response. If more composers than not, more audiences than not, evinced little interest in Wagner's vision, that would be of relevance to some studies, yet not necessarily to this. (The matter of audiences is my concern to a certain extent, as will be argued in the third part, but even there it is not the foremost matter.)

In any case, our plight is to find ourselves immersed in a pernicious mania for measurement – and that 'we' certainly includes the academic world: 'metrics' for publication, 'league tables', the hydra-like monstrosity of a 'Research Excellence Framework', etc., etc. Modern, neo-liberal governments seem or at least act as though they are incapable of valuing – a telling word in itself – anything that cannot be economically quantified. More to the point, those governments would surely wish to prevent any form of artistic flourishing, were they to realise quite how dangerous its questioning might prove. For, as Herbert Marcuse argued, in his attempt at a critique from within of Marxist æsthetics, 'Art cannot change the world, but it can contribute to changing the consciousness and drives of the men and women who could change the world.'[23] Such is the last thing that anyone in any position of authority, political or economic, would wish, hence the enormous effort expended upon pacification by the Culture Industry – which, again, we should not anthropomorphise, for it is a far more terrifying, systemic foe than such reductionism, however tempting, would allow.

Louis Andriessen's 1994 note to accompany publication of his *De Staat* (1972–6), for four women's voices and large ensemble, is worth quoting here in full:

> I wrote *De Staat* (The Republic) as a contribution to the debate about the relation of music to politics. Many composers view the act of composing as, somehow, above social conditioning. I contest that. How you arrange your musical material, the techniques you use and the instruments you score for, are largely determined by your own social circumstances and listening experience, and the availability of financial support. I do agree, though, that abstract musical material – pitch, duration and rhythm – are beyond social conditioning: it is found in nature. However, the moment the musical material is ordered it becomes culture and hence a social entity.

[23] Herbert Marcuse, *The Aesthetic Dimension: Toward a Critique of Marxist Aesthetics*, tr. Herbert Marcuse and Erica Sherover (Basingstoke and London: Macmillan, 1979), pp. 32–3.

I have used passages from Plato to illustrate these points. His text is politically controversial, if not downright negative: everyone can see the absurdity of Plato's statement that the mixolydian mode should be banned as it would have a damaging influence on the development of character.

My second reason for writing *De Staat* is a direct contradiction of the first: I deplore the fact that Plato was wrong. If only it were true that musical innovation could change the laws of the State![24]

Plato's celebrated, indeed notorious, strictures on music should thus both strike fear into and engender hope amongst those not only involved in creation and performance of artworks – in our case, particularly opera – but also, at least according to Andriessen's persuasive view, provide an antique instance of justification for critical study of the works in question. There is surely also a utopian element to be discerned not only in the Dionysian revelry of Andriessen's work but in the words quoted above: 'if only it were true…'. Might it then yet become true? Indeed, Andriessen's setting provides an almost classic instance of Brechtian alienation with respect to Plato's warnings.[25] For it has never been clear why, save for the difficulties dealing with musical scores might present to those who cannot read them, musical works should often have found themselves less privileged by many historians than novels, verse, painting, architecture, and so forth. Yes, issues of performance and the unstable nature of the musical work muddy the waters; that is, in many respects, they make them more interesting. Yet related problems will raise themselves with respect to many non-musical artworks too. After all, the best that any of us can hope for is, with Beckett, to fail better.

In some senses, the greater problem, then, is, as moralists from at least Plato onwards have argued, one of education. Which comes first: composer or audience, consciousness or performance? In our list of moralists we might just as well include Wagner, Schoenberg, and Boulez as we might Rousseau, Marx, and Lenin. Yet prospects for education seem if anything to have receded in the neo-liberal world of 'metrics' and 'performance' in anything but an artistic sense. Consider briefly Rousseau, whose ideas of education as propounded in *Emile* offered what would later be dubbed a child-centred theory of education: let a child, indeed an adult, plot a

[24] Louis Andriessen, note to *De Staat* (Boosey and Hawkes: New York and London, 1994). On *De Staat*, see Robert Adlington, *Louis Andriessen: De Staat* (Ashgate: Aldershot and Burlington, VT, 2004).
[25] Cf. Louis Andriessen, 'Komponieren für *Die Massnahme*,' in *Brechts Modell der Lehrstücke: Zeugnisse, Diskussion, Erfahrungen*, ed. Reiner Steinweg (Suhrkamp: Frankfurt, 1976), pp. 362–82.

singular path, with the help of a tutor, and all will be well, no oppressive, objectivist diktats coming from without. Yet, just as Rousseau's political theory apparently reaches an impasse, so does his educational theory. For if no path is offered to enable us to reach the utopia in which 'true' education and citizenry may emerge, does that utopia have any role other than to shame us in our current malaise? Many of us feel that all too keenly, but it remains necessary to do something about it, to try to persuade ourselves and others that hopes invested in art and education are not in vain. (It is no bad thing necessarily to attend to nagging doubts; if we do, we might actually be able to rid ourselves of them.)

Wagner, though, like any of us, he could be given to moments of cultural pessimism, no more relinquished such hopes than he did those of socialism. Like Rousseau, he never harboured the slightest sympathy for liberalism. 'My German heart . . . swelled when we took the liberal path of "free trade"', he wrote, as Bismarck skilfully outflanked German liberals. 'Of course there was and is much poverty in the country; the worker starves and industry ails. But "business" . . . does well.'[26] Yet the more thoughtful nineteenth-century liberals – not the oxymoron it might seem today – believed and expected that free trade would lead to social and economic equality. John Stuart Mill, for one, would have given up his liberal creed for socialism had he thought otherwise. Contrast with the present day is stark; our 'neo-liberalism' evinces not the slightest interest in such fundamental issues of equality, indeed acting to uphold social inequality, save for certain matters of (middle-class) gender redress, at every juncture. Neo-liberalism – and it seems as though this will pertain for the foreseeable future as well – is not even really a political stance, at least not in the sense of the nineteenth-century liberalism Wagner and Marx opposed. It is, as David Harvey has pointed out, better understood simply as a project for a small group of extremely wealthy people to accumulate more and more capital.[27] Alberich without the political (repressed by Wotan) and psychological (rejected by the Rhinemaidens) justifications, we might say. Sadly, much of our contemporary 'anti-capital-ist' movement remains trivial, more concerned with particular instances than with a fundamental, systemic problem. Yet that in a sense provides an opportunity, not that one should ever glibly underestimate the forces involved. Art, new and/or re-imagined, may actually be better placed to

[26] Richard Wagner, 'Was ist deutsch?' in *Sämtliche Schriften und Dichtungen*, ed. Richard Sternfeld and Hans von Wolzogen, 16 vols in 10 (Breitkopf und Härtel: Leipzig, 1912–14), vol. 10, p. 53.
[27] David Harvey, *A Brief History of Neoliberalism* (Oxford University Press: Oxford, 2005).

highlight such simple crudity, not merely by agitprop, though that may also have its place, but by the rich complexity of alternatives that it can and must offer.

How is that relevant to us? Perhaps most obviously in the sense that opera audiences remain overwhelmingly drawn from a narrow stratum of society, especially in Anglo-Saxon countries with ever-decreasing or non-existent levels of public subsidy. They could barely stand further from Wagner's vision of the artwork of the future, engaged in post-revolutionary celebration of its membership of 'free humanity', a 'nobler universalism'.[28] Revolutionary experience, then, would educate – perhaps rather more than education would incite revolution. For 'a *performance* [of the *Ring*]', he wrote, 'is something I can conceive of only *after the Revolution*; only the Revolution can offer me the artists and listeners I need. The coming Revolution must necessarily put an end to this whole *theatrical business* of ours: they must all perish, and will certainly do so; it is inevitable.'[29] Wagner's practical writings on theatre reform – more often than not more pragmatic and conciliatory than his compelling vision of destruction – continue to be ignored, yet continue to speak more sense, to bear greater witness, than anything soaked in the language of 'investment', 'management', 'outreach', 'access', and so on.[30]

One of Wagner's most obvious twentieth- and twenty-first-century heirs, despite not (yet) having written an opera, is Boulez, a great interpreter and of course fellow composer-conductor-agitator. Boulez's most celebrated solution to the 'problem' of opera houses, presented in both playful and angry Wagnerian fashion, remains that voiced in a 1967 interview with *Der Spiegel*. Given the journalistic tendency to refer to his 'solution' out of context, it is worth quoting him a little more fully:

> New German opera houses certainly look very modern – from the outside; on the inside, they have remained extremely old-fashioned. To a theatre in which mostly repertoire pieces are performed one can only with the greatest difficulty bring a modern opera – it is unthinkable. The most expensive solution would

[28] Richard Wagner, 'Die Kunst und die Revolution,' in *Sämtliche Schriften*, vol. 3, pp. 23, 29.
[29] Letter to Theodor Uhlig of 12 November 1851, in Richard Wagner, *Sämtliche Briefe*, ed. Gertrud Strobel, Werner Wolf, Hans-Joachim Bauer, Johannes Forner, *et al.* (VEB Deutscher Verlag für Musik/Breitkopf und Härtel: Leipzig, 1967–), vol. 4, p. 176.
[30] See, e.g., 'Entwurf zur Organisation eines deutschen National-Theaters für das Königreich Sachsen,' in *Sämtliche Schriften*, vol. 2, pp. 233–73; 'Theater-Reform,' in ibid., vol. 12, pp. 233–6; 'Nochmals Theater-Reform,' in ibid., vol. 12, pp. 237–9; 'Vorwort zu der 1850 beabsichtigen Veröffentlichung des Entwurfs von 1848 "Zur Organisation eines deutschen Nationaltheaters für das Königriech Sachsen"', in ibid., vol. 16, pp. 86–92; 'Ein Theater in Zürich,' in ibid., vol. 3, pp. 23–57.

be to blow the opera houses into the air. But do you not think that that might also be the most elegant solution?[31]

Boulez was doubtless unduly harsh on the efforts of some German Intend-ants, for instance the Swiss composer Rolf Liebermann, who, in Hamburg, commissioned not only Henze's *Der Prinz von Homburg* (see chapter 6) but twenty-four other works, including Alexander Goehr's Brechtian drama, *Arden Must Die*.[32] Granted, few if any would have conformed to Boulez's desires and strictures, yet at least there remained possibilities for change, if not quite for transformation.

Meanwhile, proponents of what is essentially the privatisation and financialisation not only of the arts but also of education more broadly construed, seemingly lack appreciation that 'philanthropic' patronage tends to lead to a reactionary stance that would lead to a grand total of zero performances for any of the works studied in this book. (Possible exceptions would be *Parsifal* and *Capriccio*, and then only in the most 'traditional' of stagings, any semblance of resistance properly smothered.) In Levin's terms, we should replace 'reading' with 'weak enactment'.[33] Perhaps there is no such lack of appreciation and the anti-performative hegemony of 'weak enactment' is the aim; we may be reasonably certain any conceivable post-Wagnerian, post-Adornian conception of art is critical is not what our political class has in mind. For whilst Wagner at least had the cultured patronage of Ludwig II, we have 'Shell International' concert seasons, Rolex advertisements in opera programmes. Even for those who have not felt it already, composers, directors, segments of the audiences, are thereby led into a stance of inescapable opposition to the greater part of their audience and, when they think a little harder, to the foundations of the society that produces it and its expectations. That, perhaps, is a non-stylistic understanding of one aspect of what we might consider to be modernism, since, unlike post-modernist successors, it retains a belief, an imperative even, to uphold high cultural values. Adorno is not dead yet; nor is Wagner. We may find ourselves both 'after Wagner' and anything but; perhaps we languish, in what Kant would have recognised once again as humanity's self-incurred immaturity, awaiting the advent of a musical

[31] Felix Schmidt and Jürgen Hohmeyer, Interview with Pierre Boulez, 'Sprengt die Opernhäuser in die Luft!', in *Der Spiegel*, 40 (25 September 1967), 172.
[32] Liebermann would respond to Boulez: '"Opera Houses? – Blow them up!" Pierre Boulez versus Rolf Liebermann,' in *Opera*, 19 (1968), 440–50.
[33] David J. Levin, 'Reading a Staging/Staging a Reading,' in *Cambridge Opera Journal*, 9 (1997), 68.

dramatist now born more than two centuries ago.[34]

What nevertheless, I hope, binds together these different yet connected histories is a conception, in a sense post-Wagnerian though there are many other ways of characterising it, of works, reception, and performance which recognises not only that they are not autonomous, but that composers, performers, and audiences alike both work and ascribe meaning in relation to one another. In *Opera and Drama*, Wagner cites a celebrated – especially to the Young Hegelians and their successors – 1841 Potsdam production of Sophocles's *Antigone*, in Ludwig Tieck's translation, which took place at the command of Frederick William IV of Prussia.[35] The promised new dawn, political as much as æsthetic, promised by the new, mystically inclined King's accession in 1840 had not yet proved utterly false, so parallels were inevitably drawn between Creon's *polis* and hopes invested in the modern, Hegelian – in Bruno Bauer's language, the 'Christian' – state.[36] However, from the standpoint of a decade later, the standpoint of post-1849 political exile, Wagner, perhaps drawing upon Bauer via Bakunin, sees in that very Potsdam staging a prophecy of the state's destruction.[37] He treads a line between divining an aspect of the work which in a sense had always been there and recognising that its truth content, to borrow from the Adornian future, revealed itself just over time, offering his own answer to that post-Hegelian question which exercised Marx, amongst others, namely how the art of ancient Greece continued to speak to a radically different world.[38] Wagner's vision of renewal rather than restoration of Attic tragedy, whether in new productions of old works, or creation of new works, adds a crucial artistic and not only performative standpoint, which in many respects goes beyond Marx's response.[39] As we shall see in the final chapter, an avowedly political, indeed Marxist, work such as Nono's *Al gran sole carico d'amore* could, in different circumstances, convincingly take on a role, even when – particularly when – staged by a Marxist director, as commemoration of the 1989 *Wende*. As Wagner wrote of the *Ring*, albeit,

[34] See Mark Berry, 'Wagner Rescued from the Opera House?' in *The Wagner Journal*, 7/3 (2013), 3.

[35] Richard Wagner, *Oper und Drama*, ed. Klaus Kropfinger (Reclam: Stuttgart, 1994), p. 158.

[36] Bauer, writing in Arnold Ruge's *Hallische Jahrbücher*, analysed the Prussian state as the modern, transitional form of the 'Christian state'. ('Der christliche Staat und unserer Zeit,' *Hallische Jahrbücher für deutsche Wissenschafte und Kunst* (1841), 537–58.)

[37] Wagner, *Oper und Drama*, p. 199.

[38] Karl Marx, *Grundrisse: Foundations of the Critique of Political Economy*, tr. Martin Nicolaus (Penguin: Harmondsworth, 1993), pp. 110–11.

[39] See Mark Berry, 'Richard Wagner and the Politics of Music Drama,' in *Historical Journal*, 47 (2004), 663–83.

as we have seen, crucially in envisaged post-revolutionary performance, it could and did recount 'to the men of the Revolution the *meaning* of that Revolution', even if it were a different revolution from those either composer had in mind.[40] Marx knew that writing 'receipts (Comtist ones?) for the cook-shops of the future' was a utopian fool's game, which is why, good Hegelian that he was, he proved so loath to predict the form of any post-revolutionary society.[41] And yet, unpredictable though the future might be, the artwork of the present might, in terms familiar to Wagner, yet become at least part of the artwork of the future.

'Truths' remain: one of the most striking aspects of, for instance, both Wagner's and Marx's work is that some of their claims seem, if anything, still more true of the twenty-first century than of the nineteenth. That claim to prophecy is not to be disregarded entirely. Yet works and questions also change; their rewriting, reformulation, and re-presentation are both rooted in changes in production and a sign of relatively autonomous questioning and resistance in themselves. The Schillerian conception of art as both abidingly political in its concerns and abidingly human in that it shows how humans will create (and re-create) when permitted and enabled to do so, lives on through Wagner, Marx, and their successors, amongst whom we might count ourselves.[42] Neither liberalism nor neo-liberalism has ever really understood that; nevertheless, blindness and deafness born of that lack of comprehension rather than of total opposition may yet prove a saving grace, a dialectical twist which, not only in the classically Adornian formal sense, but also in subject matter, 'reading', and performance, continues to resist.

---

[40] Letter of 12 November 1851 to Uhlig, in Wagner, *Sämtliche Briefe*, vol. 4, p. 176.

[41] Karl Marx, 'Capital, a Critical Analysis of Capitalist Production,' in *Marx-Engels Gesamtausgabe*, eds various (Dietz: Berlin, 1972–), part II, vol. 9, p. 22.

[42] See Philip J. Kain, *Schiller, Hegel, and Marx: State, Society, and the Aesthetic Ideal of Ancient Greece* (McGill-Queen's University Press: Kingston and Montreal, 1982).

Part I
In the Shadow of German Idealism:
From *Parsifal* to *Capriccio*

Prelude

The first two parts of this book progress in broadly chronological fashion – though not without offering some conception of alternatives in historical writing. Straightforward narrative is far from the only form available to the historian, or indeed to the creator of the *Ring*-cosmos, but it retains an honoured place. Here, *Parsifal* is considered not only in itself but very much 'after the *Ring*' and, to a certain extent, after the Wagner of his other works too.

Yet, as we shall see, the seeds of the composer's final music drama were sown many years previously, at least as early as an 1846 visit to Marienbad. Indeed, reading during his first stay in Paris, six years or so earlier, may actually have proved an 'earlier beginning', as it were, to Wagner's conception. We are not always sure – a state of affairs which may both frustrate and incite. (Such is an issue that will also be considered in the final chapter, with respect to the instability of the musical work, to Wagner's own Zurich 'version' of *Don Giovanni* and some of its successors.) At any rate, immediately following the completion of *Tannhäuser*, that Marienbad cure afforded Wagner the opportunity to consider not only a fuller, more detailed conception of *Lohengrin* than had previously been the case, but also the dramatic sources for *Die Meistersinger* and *Parsifal*. In one sense, then, if not ultimately an especially important one, *Parsifal* may have been born before the *Ring*. Whatever the historical constructions we outline, both the 'facts' and the 'meaning' we draw from artworks always prove more complicated than the tidiness of rationalisation and schematisation would permit.

Wagner's method is born in, revels in, such complications. His tendency to 'follow on' from previous works will be discussed more fully, likewise his striking ability, less sceptical than magnificently generative, to ask questions whose scope lies not only beyond his own ability to answer them, but often beyond that of subsequent generations too. We witness both battle and cross-fertilisation between two strikingly different conceptions of history and of time, which we may broadly associate with Hegel and Schopenhauer, conceptions which shape our interpretation of the work – but which also may prove to be shaped by the work. The themes outlined penetrate the rest of this book: not, I hope, in unduly schematic fashion, but as part of a broader history that is yet not blind to the particular demands of more specific histories. On the one hand, it is almost impossible not to regard *Parsifal* as a summation; on the other, it should not be regarded *only* as a summation. The world of music drama also had to 'follow on', to attempt to deal with the questions Wagner continued to pose, and crucially, to attempt to deal with them in terms that both acknowledged Wagner's historical situation and recognised that new historical situations required different answers. For the depth and breadth of Wagner's legacy remain largely uncontested; twentieth-century culture, not just opera or music, is as inconceivable without him as that of the nineteenth century is without Beethoven. It is certainly the case that musical drama would never be the same again, whether after the *Ring*, after *Tristan und Isolde*, or after *Parsifal*.

Such is one way of understanding the following two chapters, on Schoenberg and Strauss respectively. They are not intended simply as studies in a history of Wagnerism, but nor can we ignore the 'after Wagner' dimension to those composers' dramatic and indeed non-dramatic works. No such attempt is made here, but the emphasis lies less upon Wagnerism as such than upon the process of questioning, with respect to politics, history, and æsthetics, not that those fields are distinct in the case of any of our three composers, Strauss included. Schoenberg may seem the more obvious case for such treatment; in many respects, he is. In the intellectual history traced, he moves from religious syncretism to an extreme form of negative monotheism. Yet, as with Wagner, no such journey is ever complete. The path taken is of greater importance than the destination, if indeed one may speak of a destination at all; the nature of that path may also, as we shall see, be understood in various ways, each of them shedding light upon a whole that is, as the cliché has it, greater than the sum of its parts. Such remains the case when the 'whole' remains, as with *Moses*, incomplete, even, for some at least, incapable of completion.

Modernism, like Romanticism, dies hard – perhaps better, lives hard. Schoenberg's pressing towards the very boundaries of artistic representation and his dramatisation of that testing will inform a good number of the works discussed in the second part of this book: after Schoenberg, then, as well as after Wagner. But then how could it even be possible to continue the story after Schoenberg without also continuing after Wagner? It would be perverse to dissent from Malcolm Macdonald's contention that 'there is hardly a major composer in this [twentieth] century whom contact with Schoenberg's work has not forced to reexamine the foundations of music'.[1] The same, we shall see, has continued to be true of Wagner, at first- and second-hand. Moreover, that necessity to re-examine, to question, has been far from limited to matters of allegedly 'absolute' music: not in the cases of Schoenberg and Strauss, nor beyond them.

The reader may well have expected to see Strauss placed before Schoenberg, ten years Strauss's junior. There are several reasons for having reversed that more obvious ordering. The chronology, as with *Parsifal*, is not straightforward. Whereas Schoenberg is considered on a path leading roughly from *Die Jakobsleiter* to *Moses und Aron*, origins and consequences naturally extending the chapter's purview in either direction, the path traced towards *Capriccio* concludes later than *Moses*, though also commences earlier, with Strauss's first opera, *Guntram*. The destination being what it is, however, there is historical sense in considering an opera from the time of the Second World War period later than *Moses*, on which work had halted prior to the Nazi seizure of power in 1932. There is, moreover, dramatic sense in treating our history's Aron after its Moses, though, by the same token, either might be seen as the spirit that negates. However that may be, the treatment of Strauss 'after Schoenberg' doubtless presents *Capriccio* in a different light from *vice versa*. It is not a matter of right or wrong, but of acknowledging choices made and of granting them their due as an integral part of the writing of history.

It may be pertinent here to recall that in his *Metahistory*, Hayden White convincingly reinstated the idea of writing history as a poetic act.[2] Publication of that work and the ensuing debate have coloured a great deal of historical reflection since. Other writers would soon contribute, and in many cases already had, to this renaissance of the historian as 'artist' rather than 'scientist' – if I may temporarily adopt, for heuristic reasons,

---

[1] Malcolm Macdonald, *Schoenberg* (Oxford University Press: New York, 2008), p. 299.
[2] Hayden White, *Metahistory: The Historical Imagination in Nineteenth-Century Europe* (Johns Hopkins University Press: Baltimore, MD, 1973).

a blunt and somewhat unsatisfactory dichotomy.[3] White's contention seems inescapable – it is difficult to understand why anyone would think, or have thought, otherwise, though many have – but it does not, of course, preclude the writing of bad history, bad poetry, or, for that matter, bad music. Indeed, Andrew Bowie's call for philosophy to ask what it might learn from music, rather than simply to enquire into the nature of music – often, alas, in the Anglo-American world, using sadly inadequate analytical tools – seems just as urgent a matter for history.[4] We may justly turn things around, and say that philosophy might aspire to history, or music to philosophy, and so on, but those aspirations, valid though they may be, are perhaps less pressing. Or at least, for this writer, as an historian, they are less immediately pressing. Try as one might, there is a limit to how many balls – or Muses – one may keep in the air at the same time: always a problem *and* an opportunity in the case of a polymath such as Wagner.[5]

Perhaps still more fundamental to our concerns is the question, to borrow from White's introduction, 'The Poetics of History': 'What does it mean to *think historically*, and what are the unique characteristics of a specifically *historical method* of inquiry?'[6] Bearing that in mind, this first part of the book offers a relatively 'conventional' – for want of a better word – historical treatment of musical works, albeit one already relying upon the claim that history's purview extends beyond the alleged security and objectivism of the solely archival. There is, I must stress, absolutely nothing wrong with archival scholarship; indeed, not only is it of great importance, it can also be highly rewarding. Reading, deciphering, interpreting the marginalia in Schoenberg's library, as housed in the Arnold Schoenberg Center, is just as fruitful a task as reading, deciphering, interpreting, a production of *Moses und Aron*. There is no reason why one should exclude the other; there are all manner of reasons why the one should inform the other. The archival, documentary way is not, however, the only path. When treated as if it were, even if not explicitly stated as such, it offers a highly partial view of history, let alone of musical works.

There is also the perennial question, puzzled over often though perhaps

[3]   See, e.g., Roland Barthes, 'Le Discours de l'histoire', in *Information sur les sciences sociales*, 4 (1976), 65–75; Michel de Certeau, *L'Ecriture de l'histoire* (Gallimard: Paris, 1975).
[4]   Andrew Bowie, *Music, Philosophy, and Modernity* (Cambridge University Press: Cambridge, 2009).
[5]   See Mark Berry, 'Introduction', to *Treacherous Bonds and Laughing Fire: Politics and Religion in Wagner's 'Ring'* (Ashgate: Aldershot and Burlington, VT, 2006), pp. 1–15.
[6]   White, *Metahistory*, p. 1.

still not often enough, of what we simply do not know. Donald Rumsfeld's 'known unknowns' and 'unknown unknowns' were far from the nonsense they were somewhat bafflingly claimed to be; Rumsfeld's remarks offered a surprisingly elegant distillation of the problem of how we might allow for the lacunae in our knowledge.[7] His is a question we shall always do well to ask ourselves – and to ask others too. Beyond that question, moreover, there lies the matter of what other 'known' sources, perhaps less amenable than some to more traditional methods of *Quellenkritik*, might have to tell us. And beyond that lies the prospect of considering works in reception and in performance, treated more fully in the final section to this book. Not wishing for that prospect to be considered in isolation, I begin here to broach some issues of performance, especially in the third chapter on Strauss. Many questions are posed by the claim that a 2007 staging of *Capriccio* might suggest a great deal not only about the twenty-first century, but also more than many would expect about Strauss's work 'itself' and the time in which it was written. Even if we find ourselves unable to answer all those questions, that is no reason to shy away from asking them.

[7] 'Reports that say that something hasn't happened are always interesting to me, because as we know, there are known knowns; there are things we know we know. We also know there are known unknowns; that is to say we know there are some things we do not know. But there are also unknown unknowns – the ones we don't know we don't know. And if one looks throughout the history of our country and other free countries, it is the latter category that tend to be the difficult ones.' (Donald Rumsfeld and Richard Myers, 'United States Department of Defense News Briefing,' 12 February 2002.) Quite why one would make that case having so incautiously agitated for the invasion of Iraq remains, of course, another question.

Wagner 'After Wagner': *Parsifal*

I

It may seem quixotic to take a last work as a starting point, but the reasons for this should become clear. With *Parsifal*, Wagner squares up to a challenge he has already presented to himself, and which he continues to pose to his successors. This work may therefore be considered to be Wagner's own attempt at writing 'after Wagner' – and quite straightforwardly is his attempt to write musical drama 'after' the *Ring*.

Parsifal has generally been understood to represent the culmination of an ideological line different from that of his earlier works, perhaps, though only perhaps, with the partial exceptions of *Tristan und Isolde* and the later sections of the *Ring*. The revolutionary of the Dresden barricades in 1849 has finally sold out to the quietism of Schopenhauer and/or to Christianity – or, which amounts to the same thing, he has at last cast off the folly of his radical youthful flirtations. Thus Roger Scruton posits a 'transformation of the *Ring* story, from Young Hegelian beginnings to a quasi-Christian or at any rate Schopenhauerian end', in which 'we witness a process of growing up in Wagner for which there is no equivalent in Marx'. Mention of Marx is far from incidental, since Wagner is thereby achieving an emancipation from Hegel such as Marx never does. The *Ring*, Scruton startlingly claims, is therefore 'not about power or money or even love; it is about original sin'.[1] This nicely sets the scene for the less ambiguously Christian milieu and message of *Parsifal*.[2] Nietzsche was more hostile:

> for what would a seriously intended *Parsifal* mean? Must one really see in it (as somebody has expressed it against me) 'the abortion ... of a hatred of knowledge, spirit, and sensuality'? A curse upon senses and spirit in a single hatred and breath? An apostasy and reversion to sickly-Christian and obscurantist ideals? And in the end even self-abnegation, self-striking-himself-out on the part of an artist who had previously striven with all of his will's might to achieve the opposite, the highest spiritualisation and sensualisation in his art? ... One

[1] Roger Scruton, 'A Quest for Truth,' in *Literary Review*, April 2006, 15.
[2] See, e.g., Lucy Beckett, *Parsifal* (Cambridge University Press: Cambridge, 1981), especially ch. 6.

should remember how enthusiastically Wagner followed in the footsteps of the philosopher Feuerbach. Feuerbach's slogan of 'healthy sensualism' sounded in the '30s and '40s to Wagner as to many other Germans – they called themselves Young Germans – as words of redemption. Did he finally learn otherwise? For it appears that he at least in the end willed to teach differently.[3]

Redemption in later Wagner, then, has become something more profound for Scruton and something reprehensible and perhaps disingenuous for Nietzsche. Either way, its nature is similar and the radical Young Hegelianism of Wagner's more youthful days has been jettisoned. I shall argue, however, that it has not been vanquished; conversion is never completed. That conflict which plays itself out in the *Ring* between Hegel and Hegelianism on the one hand and Schopenhauer on the other continues to do so in *Parsifal*.[4] This can be understood both in terms of its subject matter and in terms of Wagner's understanding of what musical drama might and should be; for, however *Parsifal* is intended, or, for that matter, received, 'entertainment' is rarely the first word to spring to mind. Something more than that is at stake.

II

The work's concern with Christianity is far from incidental, in that it allows exploration of both the cyclical (Schopenhauerian) and the teleological (Hegelian) – or, if you prefer, the archetypal Greek and Jewish strands of the faith. *Parsifal*, like Christianity, is neither merely cyclical nor straightforwardly linear. There is greater progress – and at times regress – than Dieter Borchmeyer allows when he writes of a spiral-like '*restitutio in integrum*', or 'return to the beginning in an intensified form', but the Hegelian characterisation of a spiral remains helpful in considering the ongoing conflict between time and the eternal.[5] Wagner also introduces a crucial Christian agency of mediation, that gift from God commonly and often confusingly known as 'grace', which crucially for us may be

---

[3] Friedrich Nietzsche, 'Nietzsche contra Wagner: Aktenstücke eines Psychologen,' in *Sämtliche Werke: Kritische Studienausgabe*, ed. Giorgio Colli and Mazzino Montinari, 15 vols (De Gruyter: Berlin and New York, 1967–88), vol. 6: 'Wagner als Apostel der Keuschheit,' §3, pp. 430–1.

[4] For a detailed exploration of this theme in the *Ring*, see Mark Berry, *Treacherous Bonds and Laughing Fire: Politics and Religion in Wagner's 'Ring'* (Ashgate: Aldershot and Burlington, VT, 2006).

[5] Dieter Borchmeyer, *Drama and the World of Richard Wagner*, tr. Daphne Ellis (Princeton University Press: Princeton, 2003), p. 239. See Charles Taylor, *Hegel* (Cambridge University Press: Cambridge, 1975), pp. 35, 48, 69.

considered to represent a decisive *act*. In the words of the New Testament scholar James Dunn, 'In Paul . . . χαρις is never merely an attitude or disposition of God (God's character as gracious); consistently it denotes something much more dynamic – the wholly generous *act* of God. Like "Spirit," with which it overlaps in meaning . . ., it denotes effective divine power in the experience of men.'[6] That is not meant in a Young Hegelian, detranscendentalising manner, bringing the divine (back) down to earth in the greatest deeds of man; nor, however, is it quite so inconsistent as one might imagine, especially when dealing with Wagner's associative and agglomerative rather than analytical intellectual method. At any rate, *Parsifal* is far from the 'timeless' work that some commentators have claimed.[7] There is instead a struggle between time and the timeless; for, as so often with the dialectical Wagner, it is not a case of 'either-or'.

This conflict, then, does not merely colour Wagner's works; it is the very stuff of their drama. Wagner's dramas benefit greatly from exploration of their mutual relationships, as Houston Stewart Chamberlain made clear in an essay of 1886. However dubious Chamberlain's later writing turned out to be, this stood at the time as perhaps the most important commentary on *Parsifal*.[8] Chamberlain is unduly eager to deny that *Parsifal* is a Christian work; it is all too easy to say that it is no more Christian than the *Ring* is pagan.[9] Indeed, as Hans Küng suggested upon the occasion of *Parsifal*'s centenary, as the work of a great dialectician, *Parsifal* can be '*both Christian and heathen at once*'.[10] Nevertheless, Chamberlain rightly points to the extent to which *Parsifal* was contemporary with the *Ring* and *Tristan und Isolde* – he might also have added *Die Meistersinger von Nürnberg* – and continues:

> In the *Ring* and in *Tristan* (which the Master considered to be an act of the *Ring*), Wagner had created an image of real life, of the 'world that is only suffering': in

6   James D. G. Dunn, *Romans 1–8* (Thomas Nelson: Dallas, 1988), p. 17.
7   See, e.g., Peter Wapnewski, *Der traurige Gott: Richard Wagner in seinen Helden* (Beck: Munich, 1978), pp. 211–13; and, drawing upon this, Mary A. Cicora, 'Medievalism and Metaphysics: the Literary Background of *Parsifal*', in William Kinderman and Katherine R. Syer (eds), *A Companion to Wagner's Parsifal* (Boydell and Brewer: Woodbridge, 2005), pp. 39–40.
8   On Chamberlain's earlier writings, see Roger Allen, '*Die Weihe des Hauses*: Houston Stewart Chamberlain and the Early Reception of *Parsifal*', in ibid., pp. 245–76. See also Allen's '"All is here music": Houston Stewart Chamberlain and *Der Ring des Nibelungen*', in *wagnerspectrum*, 3 (2006), 155–68.
9   Houston Stewart Chamberlain, 'Notes sur *Parsifal*', in *Revue wagnérienne*, 2 (1886–7), 225.
10   Hans Küng, 'Wagner's *Parsifal*: a Theology for our Time', in *Michigan Quarterly Review*, 23 (1984), 311.

Parsifal – where he intended, specifically, to establish a strict parallelism with the *Ring* – he 'constructed the holy world of a better life'.[11]

Whatever Chamberlain's characterisations of these works, his structural thesis merits consideration. All of Wagner's works tend to raise more questions than they resolve, with the result that he will 'follow on' from the riddles each work poses in its successor or successors. (He cannot do this after *Parsifal*, which may explain commentators' need to view it as a destination or *summa summarum*.)

Intention, then, is matched, indeed surpassed, by outcome. Like many writers, Wagner did not know precisely what he would say when he first put pen to paper; and when he did, he would often change his mind. At the very least, Wagner would make a major contribution, constantly questioned and reformulated, to this new canon in flux. For Wagner's method had never been Socratic; he had never been concerned to correct 'errors' in his earlier work, but rather to explore more profoundly ideas and conflicts already problematised – not, incidentally, a bad cue for producers and other interpreters of his work. Wagner called Beethoven 'the master who was called upon to write the *world history of music* in his works', with all the sense of progression that implies, and such a sense of historical progression is just as marked in Wagner's own œuvre.[12] *Parsifal* has been seen as a 'late' work, even an almost incongruously modern work.[13] For Adorno in 1956, *Parsifal* exhibited both the Wagnerian *Altersstil* and the 'still disconcertingly new'.[14] In many respects, however, it may simply be considered as the work that, owing to Wagner's death, stands at the end of his dramatic explorations, with no more or no less than this entails.

III

Let us begin biographically, in 1845. Wagner completed the score of *Tannhäuser* in April, ready for scheduled performance in Dresden that autumn, departing in July for the Bohemian spa town of Marienbad.

---

[11] Chamberlain, 'Notes sur *Parsifal*', p. 226.

[12] Richard Wagner, 'Das Kunstwerk der Zukunft', in *Sämtliche Schriften und Dichtungen*, ed. Richard Sternfeld and Hans von Wolzogen, 16 vols in 10 (Breitkopf und Härtel: Leipzig, 1912–14), vol. 3, p. 93.

[13] See Anthony Barone, 'Richard Wagner's *Parsifal* and the Theory of Late Style', in *Cambridge Opera Journal*, 7 (1995), 37–54.

[14] Theodor Wiesengrund Adorno, 'Zur Partitur des "Parsifal"', in *Moments musicaux: Neu gedruckte Aufsätze 1928–1962* (Suhrkamp: Frankfurt am Main, 1964), p. 52.

Two decades later, he would recount in his autobiography, *Mein Leben*:

> I intended to abandon myself to a life of the utmost leisure, as is in any case
> essential when undergoing the exhausting regime of a cure. I had therefore
> chosen my summer reading with care: the poems of Wolfram von Eschenbach
> in the versions of Simrock and San Marte, together with the anonymous epic
> of Lohengrin with the great introduction by Görres. With a book under my
> arm I betook myself to the seclusion of the neighbouring woods, where I would
> lie beside a brook communing with Titurel and Parzival in this strange and
> yet so intimately appealing poem of Wolfram. But soon the longing to create
> something of my own from what I found here became so strong that, although
> I had been warned against any stimulus of this kind while taking the waters at
> Marienbad, I had difficulty fighting off the impulse. This soon put me into a
> highly overwrought state of mind: *Lohengrin*, the first conception of which
> dates from the latter part of my time in Paris, stood suddenly revealed before
> me in full armour at the centre of a comprehensive dramatic adaptation of
> the whole material . . . From a few remarks in Gervinius's *History of German
> Literature*, I had formed a particularly vivid picture of Hans Sachs and the
> mastersingers of Nuremberg.[15]

Deconstruction of Wagner's self-mythology has become legion, yet that
account has remained essentially uncontroversial. Indeed, Wagner wrote
the first prose draft for *Die Meistersinger* during that vacation, although
musical composition would not commence until 1862. Wolfram, whom
Wagner had just depicted as an all-too-moral character in *Tannhäuser*, now
furnished as summer reading the legend of Parsifal. However, centre stage
would first be taken by Wagner's first Grail opera, *Lohengrin*, explicitly
connected with the figure of Parsifal. That would later provide cheap
ammunition for Nietzsche: 'Parsifal is the father of Lohengrin! How
did he manage that?'[16] But the dramas themselves are never explicitly
connected, so that *Parsifal*'s Parsifal can be and, so far as we know, shall
remain a chaste hero, whilst being mentioned as Lohengrin's father in
the earlier drama. (In Wolfram, Parzival has a wife early on, a situation
irreconcilable with *Parsifal*.) *Lohengrin* was followed by the ever-expanding
Ring project, its dramas explicitly connected, from which Wagner would
break off to compose *Tristan* and *Die Meistersinger*.

The idea of *Parsifal* was not static; it continued to develop. It
is beyond the scope of this chapter to present a full account of that

[15] Richard Wagner, *My Life*, tr. Andrew Gray, ed. Mary Whittall (Cambridge University Press: Cambridge, 1983), pp. 302–3.
[16] Friedrich Nietzsche, 'Der Fall Wagner,' in *Sämtliche Werke*, vol. 6, §9, pp. 34–5.

development.[17] But there are two instances from the 1850s, both con-nected with the emergent *Tristan* drama, which require attention. (At the same time, we should bear in mind that the *Ring* was the focus of Wagner's attention for much of this period.) The year 1854 was a momentous one. Wagner embarked upon composition of *Die Walküre*. Later in that year, during the autumn, he was introduced to the phi-losophy of Schopenhauer; without exaggeration, this was, as Thomas Mann remarked, 'the great event in Wagner's life'.[18] At the same time, he conceived the idea of an opera on the *Tristan* legend, after Gottfried von Strassburg. One scene sketched, and later (wisely) rejected, intro-duces 'Parzival' as Wagner was still calling him. Visiting Tristan's cas-tle of Kareol during his arduous wandering, Parzival witnesses Tristan in his mortal agony.[19] (The equivalent in *Parsifal* itself would be the extraordinary depiction of time passing and of compassionate wisdom hard-won that is the Prelude to Act III.) Wagner would recollect: 'I identified Tristan, wasting away but unable to die of his wound, with the Amfortas of the Grail romance.'[20]

That does not happen in the completed *Tristan*, yet Wagner retained a subtler connection. At work on the same section of the third act in which he had considered having Parsifal appear, Wagner wrote to Mathilde Wesendonck:

This last act is now a real intermittent fever: – the deepest and most unprece-dented suffering and yearning, and, immediately afterwards, the most unprec-edented triumph and jubilation ... It is this thought that has most recently turned me against Parzival again ... It suddenly became dreadfully clear to me: it is my third-act Tristan inconceivably intensified. With the spear-wound and perhaps another wound, too, – in his [Anfortas's/Amfortas's] heart –, the wretched man knows of no other longing in his terrible pain than the longing to die ... he demands repeatedly to be allowed a glimpse of the Grail in the hope that it might at least close his wounds ... but the Grail can give him one thing only, which is precisely that he *cannot* die; its very sight increases his torments by conferring immortality upon them.

...

And you expect me to carry though something like this? And set it to music,

[17] See, e.g., Beckett, *Parsifal*, pp. 1–23.

[18] Thomas Mann, 'Sufferings and Greatness of Richard Wagner', in *Essays of Three Decades*, tr. H. T. Lowe-Porter (Knopf: New York, 1976), p. 330.

[19] Martin Geck and Egon Voss (eds), 'Dokumente zur Entstehung und ersten Aufführung des Bühnenweihfestspiels "Parsifal"', in Richard Wagner, *Sämtliche Werke*, ed. Carl Dahlhaus, Egon Voss, and others (Schott: Mainz, 1970–), vol. 30, p. 12.

[20] Wagner, *My Life*, p. 511.

into the bargain? – No thank you very much!

...

When my old friend Brünnhilde leaps into the funeral pyre, I shall plunge in after her, and hope to die a Christian! So be it! Amen![21]

During the composition of Tristan's monologue, which pushes mortal agony beyond endurance, Wagner contemplates a drama in which this would be 'inconceivably intensified'. He declines to proceed, though much of this is rhetoric, for *Parsifal* is clearly on his mind. Even the *Ring*'s gods are allowed to die: Wotan's redemption lies in acceptance of his mortality. Amfortas, however, is to be sentenced to immortality. So is Kundry, who therefore must die in redemption. *Parsifal* is thus also to be a drama intimately connected with and yet lying beyond the *Ring*. Moreover, Wagner in his letter connects Christianity with the Immolation Scene from *Götterdämmerung*, whose final version and the meaning thereof would cause him considerable indecision. When facetiously wishing his life to end before composing *Parsifal*, he also points the way towards it, whilst holding back, just as in *Parsifal* itself, from defining the precise nature of his attitude towards Christianity.

IV

An abiding conflict, already starkly dramatised in the *Ring*, is taken further in *Parsifal*. There are various ways, each of them perhaps insufficient in itself, in which it might be characterised, but one lies in considering the conflict between Hegel or Hegelianism and Schopenhauer, or between history and anti-history. Conflict between subject and object lay at the heart of Hegel's ontology, and was expressed in the ensuing drama of history through the alienation (*Entfremdung*) of mind. In Hegel's own words: 'Enquiry as to the *means* whereby freedom produces itself as a [real] world leads us to [consider] the phenomenon [*Erscheinung*] of history itself.'[22] The 'phenomenon' is the actual, realised appearance of what it previously was in purely ideal terms; for *Erscheinung* may also be translated as 'epiphany', which we shall do well to bear in mind when considering what happens in *Parsifal*. History is the progress of the 'Idea'

[21] Letter of 30 May 1859 to Mathilde Wesendonck, in *Selected Letters of Richard Wagner*, tr. Stewart Spencer, ed. Stewart Spencer and Barry Millington (Dent: London, 1987), pp. 456–60.

[22] Georg Friedrich Wilhelm Hegel, 'Vorlesungen über die Philosophie der Geschichte,' in *Werke*, ed. Eva Moldenhauer and Karl Markus Michel, 20 vols (Suhrkamp: Frankfurt am Main, 1969–72), vol. 12, p. 33.

or 'World Spirit', which Hegel sometimes refers to as 'God', as it manifests itself in the phenomenal world. Heinrich von Treitschke would claim in the 1880s, with good reason, that Hegel's 'school' had exercised an influence in German life of a magnitude comparable only to that of the sophists in Athens.[23] When Wagner was at work on *Parsifal* and when, shortly after, Treitschke was writing his history of Germany, that school was not yet dead. Like Christianity, it had been written off several times, not least after the failure of the revolution in 1848–9. Yet obstinately, it continued to fight its corner, every bit as much in the Marx of *Capital* as the Marx of the early, 'humanist' *Paris Manuscripts*. That it did also – in its ambiguity, perhaps still more interestingly – in Wagner.

It is in divergent readings and developments of Kant's philosophy that the conflict between Hegel and Schopenhauer is born, and as for Kant, the categories of time and space 'apply to objects only in so far as objects are viewed as appearances, and do not present things as they are in themselves'.[24] By the same token, the concepts of the understanding are 'mere forms of thought, without objective reality . . . Only *our* sensible and empirical intuition can give to them body and meaning [*Sinn und Bedeutung*].'[25] Kant's forms of space and time are those *a priori* conditions within the subject that render intuition possible. (For the pure concepts of the understanding, there are different categories, such as causality, unity, plurality, and so forth, relating objects to one another.) Schopenhauer disdained history and the philosophy of history as commonly understood, for concerning themselves with '(in Plato's words), what is always *becoming* and never *is*'. Anyone who had studied Herodotus had read enough history from the philosophical standpoint, for humanity was ever the same. Hegelian *Afterphilosophie* numbed the mind by regarding the phenomenon (*Erscheinung*) as the thing-in-itself, therefore concerning itself with the forms and events of the phenomenon.[26]

For Schopenhauer, it is the irrational Will and its consequent principle of individuation, *principium individuationis*, which posits Kant's *a priori* conditions of space and time. Will, in stark contrast to Hegel's Spirit, is resolutely non-developmental, though the two share a crucial priority

---

[23] Heinrich von Treitschke, *History of Germany in the Nineteenth Century*, tr. Eden and Cedar Paul, 7 vols (Jarrold: London, 1915–19), vol. 4, p. 568.

[24] Immanuel Kant, *Critique of Pure Reason*, tr. Norman Kemp Smith (Palgrave Macmillan: Basingstoke and New York, 2003), p. 80.

[25] Ibid., p. 163.

[26] Arthur Schopenhauer, *Die Welt als Wille und Vorstellung*, 2 vols (Deutscher Taschenbuch: Munich, 2002), vol. 1, pp. 516–17, 514.

of one universal principle through which we might comprehend the world. Scorn the self-consciousness of Fichte, Hegel, and their followers as he might, Schopenhauer remains in this respect firmly within the German Idealist tradition. Within Schopenhauer's framework, true reality lies in the noumenal realm of the Will itself, and music is the only art with a direct relationship to that realm. Musical drama becomes for the Schopenhauerian Wagner, and in some sense always had been, the metaphysical vehicle for granting real existence to the categories of the understanding, for penetrating, beyond the 'surface' words of his poem, to the essence of his myth.

Wagner remained in thrall to what Schopenhauer termed, by way of contrast to the categories of time and space, a 'spurious *a priori*, opposed to truth', in the guise of the historical specificity of the Hegelian subject.[27] In an early burst of enthusiasm for Schopenhauer, Wagner exclaimed: 'What charlatans all these *Hegels* etc. are beside him.'[28] His dramatic instinct would always prove more surely dialectical; the imprint of Young Hegelian self-consciousness would mark him and his dramas forever. Yet, from 1854, when the poet Georg Herwegh, himself an erstwhile revolutionary and collaborator with Marx, introduced Wagner to Schopenhauer's writings, Wagner's attitude towards social and political progress became ambivalent.

History is ever-present in *Parsifal*, just as it had been in the *Ring*. At the early stages of the *Ring*-project, Wagner had depicted Beethoven's great orchestral works as 'real poems, in which an attempt is made to represent a real object'.[29] He subsequently extended this analysis to the motivic transformation of Liszt's symphonic poems, portraying them as an intermediary stage between Beethoven and music drama.[30] This sits somewhat uneasily with the chronology but points to the continuing importance for Wagner, even after his acquaintance with Schopenhauer's metaphysics of music, of the musical 'idea' and its manifestation. Preparing for his 1870 Beethoven centenary essay, suffused with Schopenhauerian æsthetics, Wagner noted: 'Sculptors and poets give nation what it would like to seem, – what it really is . . . Beeth. = Schopenhauer: his music,

[27] Arthur Schopenhauer, 'On Philosophy and its Methods,' in *Parerga and Paralipomena*, tr. E. F. J. Payne (Oxford University Press: Oxford, 1974), vol. 2, p. 15

[28] Letter to Liszt of 16 (?) December 1854, in *Selected Letters*, p. 323; Richard Wagner, *Sämtliche Briefe*, ed. Gertrud Strobel, Werner Wolf, Hans-Joachim Bauer, Johannes Forner, *et al.* (VEB Deutscher Verlag für Musik/Breitkopf und Härtel: Leipzig, 1967–), vol. 6, p. 298.

[29] Letter to Uhlig, 13 February 1852, in *Selected Letters*, p. 250; *Sämtliche Briefe*, vol. 4, p. 285.

[30] 'Über Franz Liszt's Symphonische Dichtungen. (Brief an M. W.),' in *Sämtliche Schriften*, vol. 5, pp. 192–4.

translated into concepts, would produce that philosophy.'[31] So Beethoven is still there, a few years before the composition of *Parsifal*, but now allied to Schopenhauer rather than to Hegel and his progeny.

The shift had begun in the *Ring*, an important turning-point both musically and dramatically coming with resumption of work on *Siegfried*. The Prelude to Act III bears all the marks of the intervening composition of *Tristan* and *Die Meistersinger*. The interplay of motifs and their counterpoint is more intense, providing the overwhelming impression of matters being brought to a head, of a world-historical moment, even if, in its apparent rejection or transcendence of world-history, it represents an anti-Hegelian turn. Prior to that, a recurrent and influential theme of Schiller's dramas, namely that man must forge his own destiny, had been steadily acquiring a more marked anti-theological emphasis; indeed Schiller himself had claimed that even the Greeks had 'transferred to Olympus what was meant to be realised on earth'.[32] For man, Wagner had written in notes upon Achilles, 'is God perfected'. The eternal gods were merely the elements of man's creation; man brought Creation to its conclusion. Achilles was therefore 'higher, more complete than the elemental Thetis'.[33]

V

Deeds or acts, *Taten*, had played a crucial role in determining the Volsungs' fate. They should be understood in the context of the Young Hegelian elevation of the historical dynamism in Hegel's dialectic, and into something with relevance not only for the past, not only for the present, but for the future. The teleology of Beethovenian symphonism, so crucial to Wagner's own compositional practice, fused with its philosophical counterpart. Indeed, Wagner had claimed that the content of Beethoven's 'poetic idea', even if this were not the composer's intention, presented to the audience a 'philosophical idea'.[34] As Fichte, principal begetter of much of the Young Hegelian prospectus, had written: 'You act, and your

[31] Richard Wagner, 'Beethoven and the German Nation,' in *The Diary of Richard Wagner 1865–1882: The Brown Book*, ed. Joachim Bergfeld, tr. George Bird (Cambridge University Press: London, 1980), p. 177.

[32] Johann Christoph Friedrich von Schiller, *On the Aesthetic Education of Man*, tr. Elizabeth M. Wilkinson and L. A. Willoughby (Oxford University Press: Oxford, 1967), p. 109.

[33] 'Bruchstücke eines Dramas "Achilleus"', in *Sämtliche Schriften*, XII, 283. It is uncertain whether these notes were intended theoretically or as a sketch for a drama. To ascribe so strong an opposition may in any case mislead.

[34] 'Ein glücklicher Abend,' in ibid., vol. 1, p. 145.

will itself constitutes an act [*Tat*].'[35] There emerged a *Philosophie der Tat*: 'philosophy of the deed' or 'philosophy of action'. '*Tat und Tod*' (deed and death), Siegmund cries, as he prepares to draw the sword from the tree. Siegfried's great act is fearlessly and unconsciously to shatter Wotan's spear of state, enabling the hero to reach Brünnhilde on her rock and apparently to usher in a Feuerbachian revolution of *Liebeskommunismus*. Brünnhilde then ecstatically sends him out into the world, with the words, 'To new deeds [*Taten*], dear hero; how could I love you – if I did not allow you to do so?' Yet, although the deeds seem heroic and just, each of them ultimately fails – as, of course, had the revolutions of 1848–9, in which Wagner had fought on the barricades with the 'real-life' anarchistic hero, Bakunin.

For Wagner had come to believe that the charismatic hero as portrayed in the figures of Siegmund and Siegfried – also Tristan and Walther – could never live up to the revolutionary role designed for them. That was not, however, to say that charismatic heroes as such were to be abjured. Adorno was quite right to remark that the attempt at 'changing the world is unsuccessful, but changing the world remains the point'.[36] Parsifal stands, as Tim Blanning has shown, in a long line of Wagnerian charismatic heroes, whose authority lies not in tradition or in law, but in the authority of a personal gift of grace, in the inspiration of particular, personal, revolutionary devotion.[37] That is a form of authority especially suited to heroes, and which is always likely to be problematical in the modern world, ever wary of and yet constantly hankering after such a potent form of power. Whatever his dark, Schopenhauerian thoughts regarding withdrawal from society, Wagner continued to engage with the external, political world. In Feuerbach's words, 'a man existing absolutely alone would lose himself without any sense of his individuality in the ocean of Nature'.[38]

Like Christ, Siegfried heralds 'freedom', as 'a new religion, the religion of our time', to quote Heine, an important influence upon Wagner.[39] Yet he is possessed of a fatal flaw; he is 'the rebel without consciousness'.[40] Siegmund was conscious, at least in part, of the meaning of his deeds, yet Siegfried never is and therefore falls victim to Hagen's snares. Fafner

[35] Johann Gottlieb Fichte, 'Die Bestimmung des Menschen,' in *Sämtliche Werke*, 10 vols, ed. I. H. Fichte (Viet: Bonn and Berlin, 1834–46), vol. 2, p. 303.
[36] Theodor Wiesengrund Adorno, *Versuch über Wagner* (Suhrkamp: Frankfurt, 1981), p. 110.
[37] Tim Blanning, 'Richard Wagner and Max Weber,' in *wagnerspectrum*, 2 (2005), 96, 107–9.
[38] Ludwig Feuerbach, *The Essence of Christianity*, tr. George Eliot (Prometheus: Buffalo, NY, 1989), p. 82.
[39] Heinrich Heine, 'Englische Fragmente,' in *Sämtliche Werke*, ed. Oscar Walzel, 10 vols (Insel: Leipzig, 1911–15), vol. 3, p. 501.
[40] Wapnewski, *Der traurige Gott*, p. 169.

accurately addresses Siegfried: 'You bright-eyed boy, who do not know yourself'. That is not in itself a problem, for self-knowledge, as in Parsifal's case, can be acquired. However, in Siegfried's case, it never is. If ever there were a community in need of redemption, it is that of the Gibichungs, yet Siegfried goes native and apparently achieves nothing, regaining his nobility only in death.

Parsifal is very different, this difference signifying an attempt to resolve the difficulties raised by Siegfried and Siegmund. What will become of Monsalvat, the Grail castle and community, under his leadership remains unclear, but the drama is that of its rescue or salvation. A letter from 1862 is instructive. Wagner had broken off composition of *Siegfried* and was already thinking about *Parsifal*:

> the myth of a Messiah is the most profoundly characteristic of all myths for all our earthly striving. The Jews expected someone who would liberate them, a Messiah who was supposed to restore the Kingdom of David and bring not only justice but, more especially, greatness, power, and safety from oppression. Well, everything went as predicted, his birth in Bethlehem, of the line of David, the prophecy of the three wise men, etc., his triumphant welcome to Jerusalem, palms strewn before him, etc. – there he stood, everyone listened, and he proclaimed to them: 'My kingdom is not of this world! Renounce your desires, that is the only way to be redeemed and freed!' – Believe me, all our political freedom fighters strike me as being uncannily like the Jews.[41]

Parsifal manages to discover whatever he needs through his own historical experience and the transformative influence this exerts; yet he does not appear to control his historical experience, so this is certainly not the freedom of the Jews or the 'political freedom fighters'. Despite Nietzsche's anti-*Parsifal* venom, it stands very close to his portrayal of Jesus in *The Anti-Christ*:

> One might … name Jesus a 'free spirit' – what is established is nothing to him: the word killeth, whatever is established killeth. The concept, the experience of 'life', as he alone knows it, for him opposes every kind of word, formula, law, belief, dogma … One must not be led into error, however great the temptations lying in Christian, or better Church, prejudices … his 'wisdom' is precisely the pure ignorance [*reine Thorheit*] of all such things. Culture is something he has never heard of; to make war upon it is not necessary for him.[42]

Yet there is a difference, for this Jesus, unlike Parsifal, acts. Indeed, Nietzsche recognises something akin to this distinction a few pages earlier, when he remarks:

---

[41] Letter of 15 June 1862 to Malwida von Meysenbug, in *Selected Letters*, p. 546.
[42] Nietzsche, 'Der Antichrist: Fluch aus Christenthum,' in *Sämtliche Werke*, vol. 6, §32, p. 204.

Herr Renan [whom Wagner had read], this *Hanswurst in psychologicis*, has contributed the two most unseemly concepts to the explanation of the type of Jesus: the concept of the genius and that of the hero ('héros'). But if anything is not of the Gospel, it is the concept of the hero.[43]

If not only the heroism of Siegmund and Siegfried fails, but that of the *Ring* itself does too, then *Parsifal* tells a different story, going beyond what Adorno interpreted as 'bourgeois triumph's drowning out the lie of heroic deeds [*Heldentaten*]'.[44] History may return in a less mendacious guise. Gurnemanz's narrations play an interesting and interconnected dual role here. In the first instance, *Parsifal*'s pre-history is revealed to the audience, both verbally and musically. Were it not for Gurnemanz's account, we should know very little of Titurel's reign, and should hardly be justified in considering it to conform to the proper, or at least original, form of Monsalvat's constitution. At the same time, Gurnemanz's retelling of the story so far plays a crucial contemporary role *within* the drama, imparting a sense of communal history to an increasingly fractured society. The brotherhood would fall apart without its sense of history, which also provides a utopian hope for the future.[45] This is a Young Hegelian understanding of history, as exemplified by August von Cieszkowski, who had asked in 1838 whether the Hegelian philosophy of history might lead to a philosophy of the future, indeed to a political programme of social transformation, which he called 'historiosophy'. Cieszkowski had contended that philosophy in general must 'become a practical philosophy or rather of practical activity, of "praxis", which would exercise a direct influence upon social life and development of the future'.[46] Yet Schopenhauer makes his presence felt, for history is not enough. Gurnemanz's narrations may help prevent the community from collapsing, but they cannot enable it to flourish. That necessitates the noumenal world of the Grail and the *deus ex machina* of the spear's suspension in mid-air at the sign of the Cross, which we might call the (historically necessary?) intervention of grace. Parsifal may have resisted Kundry, but he is not able alone to halt the negative progress of Klingsor.

[43] Ibid., §29, p. 199.

[44] Adorno, *Versuch über Wagner*, p. 47. Adorno refers to Wagner's music but one might also make a dramatic point.

[45] John Bokina gives an interesting account of *Parsifal* as a utopian, not historical, opera: *Opera and Politics from Monteverdi to Henze* (Yale University Press: New Haven and London, 1997), pp. 86–110.

[46] August von Cieszkowski, *Prolegomena zur Historiosophie* (Veit: Berlin, 1838), p. 129.

There is a similar ambiguity in the music. There seems, however, to be less violent tension here and more fulfilment or reconciliation. This would have been anathema to Adorno's relentlessly negative dialectics, if not necessarily to Hegel. Such a reconciliation is doubtless partly a semblance, for the dialectic will not miraculously dissolve, let alone resolve, at the sign of the Cross, but reconciliation perhaps also relates to the nature of the music. Motifs are less object- or idea-bound than those of the epic *Ring*; its tone is more variegated than that of *Tristan*'s noumenal – perhaps even solipsistic – night. Alfred Lorenz claimed that, having 'mastered a [Wagnerian] work in all its detail', the listener could sometimes thereby 'experience moments in which consciousness of time disappears, and the whole work becomes what one might call "spatial", that is, with everything simultaneously and precisely present in the mind'.[47] We may consider that to be the resistance of Schopenhauer to Hegel, a real, noumenal presence in the drama. It does not supplant 'historical' goal orientation; the two forces interact and do battle, Beethoven – and Wagner – claimed for, even captured by, both sides.

VI

In *Parsifal*, then, we deal with a complex interaction between compassion (Schopenhauer), grace (Christianity), and the cunning of historical reason (Hegel). Christian grace, in all its ambiguity, mediates between compassion and history. It leads us to an attempted solution, both Schopenhauerian and Hegelian, to the Kantian problem of divine truth. Theoretical reconciliation of the noumenal and phenomenal words at that level might through grace be knowable to mortals. The more 'dramatic' music of the second act is in some ways an Hegelian foil to the ritualism of the first and third acts. As Arnold Whittall has noted, 'the music of *Parsifal* reflects the greater concern with those more passive states of mind that rituals encourage'.[48] Yet development and ritual co-exist and indeed cohere throughout the work to an extent unique in Wagner's œuvre, perhaps a reflection of the extraordinarily difficult task of dramatising renunciation. Moreover, even Adorno could see that the 'simplicity' (his inverted commas) of *Parsifal*'s orchestration was not merely reactionary, not merely 'fallaciously sacral', but carried out a 'legitimate critique' of the surviving ornamentalism in Wagner's earlier orchestration. This critique

[47] Alfred Lorenz, *Das Geheimnis der Form bei Richard Wagner*, 4 vols (Hesse: Berlin, 1924–33), vol. 1, p. 292.
[48] Arnold Whittall, 'The Music', in *Parsifal*, ed. Beckett, p. 85.

presented itself as much in 'a lugubrious dimming of sound' (*eine düstere Abblendung des Klangs*), foreshadowing late Mahler, as in the 'religiose' brass choirs suggesting Bruckner and the Church.[49] Reconciliation of the dialectic between history and ontology, between time and space, is far from complete, as we shall see upon considering more closely the stage action – and non-action – of *Parsifal*.

Amfortas too is unable to do anything to rectify his plight; he must simply wait. He has acted – with disastrous results – and Klingsor impotently continues to act. The *locus classicus* of the contrast in *Parsifal* comes at the end of the second act, when Klingsor's spear of ambition is stopped in its tracks by the sign of the Cross, making possible the spear's transformation into an agent of healing. Parsifal makes the sign, but the agency comes from beyond.

If Amfortas's suffering and Parsifal's discovery may be understood in some sense as related to the workings of grace, then there is a higher power at work: a higher power which one neglects or disavows at great cost to understanding of the work. For instance, Ruth Berghaus in her 1982 Frankfurt production had Parsifal and Kundry roll back grey canvases in order to reveal the green meadow of Good Friday: a crucial 'deed' on their part.[50] Yet, as she would have been only too aware, this deed that not only desacralises but dechristianises the work stands at odds with Wagner's conception. A good thing, some might say, weary with sanctimony and ritual. However, to downplay, let alone to remove, the role of Christianity actually obscures rather than clarifies; the *telos* of the action becomes less comprehensible, the characters' actions arbitrary. For the moment, we can say that, should there be a higher power, then at least it appears to be the right one: God transcendent, rather than a Feuerbachian projection and inversion of human needs into the all-too-human gods of the *Ring*.

Lorenz, subsequently celebrated and vilified as the author of a vast four-volume study of the Wagner music dramas, the fourth devoted to *Parsifal*, and their allegedly absolute musical forms, wrote in 1901 an article entitled 'Parsifal as *Übermensch*'.[51] He claims that Nietzsche

---

[49] Adorno, *Versuch über Wagner*, p. 75.

[50] See Barry Millington, 'Parsifal: Facing the Contradictions,' in *Musical Times*, 124 (1983), 98; Patrick Carnegy, *Wagner and the Art of the Theatre* (Yale University Press: New Haven and London, 2006), pp. 367–8.

[51] Alfred Lorenz-Gotha, 'Parsifal als Übermensch,' in *Die Musik*, 1 (1901–2), 1876–82; Lorenz, *Das Geheimnis der Form*. Lorenz would subsequently attain notoriety on account of his enthusiastic support for National Socialism, not least in his 1930s articles upon music and race. This does not mean that one should shun insights gleaned from earlier writing. On Lorenz, see Stephen McClatchie, *Analyzing Wagner's Operas: Alfred Lorenz and German*

found the first form (*Gestalt*) of the idea of the *Übermensch* in the figure
of Siegfried, after which Wagner's erstwhile disciple discerned in Parsifal 'Wagner's reversal, a turning away from enthusiasm for the harshness
of heroism'. However, Lorenz argues that the development of the idea
of the *Übermensch* is logically consistent (*folgerichtig*) from Siegfried
to Parsifal.[52] Parsifal begins as a Siegfried-like figure: 'he also unknowingly carries out countless heroic deeds'. Yet he gains the strength, which
according to Nietzsche he lacks, through *Mitleid*, the Schopenhauerian
concept of pity or fellow-suffering, thereby developing into the 'most
glorious victor'.[53] For Schopenhauer and Wagner, *Mitleid* was closely
connected, though not exclusively so, with Christianity, at least as properly understood. Cosima records in 1880: 'R. talks about sainthood
and the withdrawal from life, in Schopenhauer's sense, and in connection with that he plays the Prelude to *Parsifal*.'[54] Again, a year later, she
writes, 'Our conversation concerns Brahmanism, which R. praises as
the religion of intelligence, but then he places Christianity above it as
the religion of suffering.'[55]

Some of Lorenz's analysis is questionable. To speak of the *Übermensch*
clouds the issue. Moreover, it is far from clear that Parsifal initially carries
out countless *Heldentaten*. If his mindless shooting of an innocent swan,
condemned by Gurnemanz as an 'unprecedented act', is heroic, then that
already represents further deconstruction of the heroic idea as commenced
in the *Ring*. The connection between fear (*Bang*), or rather the lack thereof,
which translates into lack of consciousness, and heroic deeds (*Taten*) has
returned, but is presented negatively from the outset. If the *Ring's* boy
without fear has failed, Wagner does not need to show us this again; it
may be assumed that, without development, the same thing would happen
again, and this is not the stuff of a drama that goes further.

> GURNEMANZ:
> You did [*tatest*] this?
> And you are not anxious in the face of the deed? [*Und
> bangt' es dich nicht vor der Tat?*]
> . . .

Nationalist Ideology (University of Rochester Press: Rochester, 1998).
[52] Lorenz, 'Parsifal als Übermensch,' 1876.
[53] Ibid., 1877.
[54] Cosima Wagner, *Cosima Wagner's Diaries*, ed. M. Gregor-Dellin and D. Mack, tr. G. Skelton, 2 vols (Harcourt Brace Jovanovich: NLondon, 1978–80), 24 February 1880, vol. 2, p. 442.
[55] Ibid., 25 March 1881, vol. 2, p. 646.

> Act unheard of!
> You could murder, here in the holy forest,
> whose silent peace surrounded you?

Such is certainly an unknowing act. Lorenz is right to point to the turning-point in Act II of *Parsifal* feeling Amfortas's agony and to the general developmental tendency in Wagner's presentation. He is also right to see Parsifal as a development of what is 'positive' in Siegfried, and not, whatever Nietzsche might say, as 'a weakening'. Lorenz provocatively declares that it is 'incomprehensible' to associate the word *Mitleid* with weakness.[56] Schopenhauer's denigration of the phenomenal world notwithstanding, this Schopenhauerian notion of pity or compassion is perforce social; it entails sympathy with (*mit*) others' sorrow (*Leid*). Parsifal's mother was called Herzeleide ('Heart's Sorrow'). Her tragedy had been her separation from society, to the extent that even Parsifal had forgotten about her and left her to die. There had been no *Mitleid* to leaven the sorrow of her heart.

Absent from Lorenz's article and from many other treatments is consideration of grace as the fount of what Parsifal might accomplish through true strength rather than toy-soldierish deeds. Parsifal's initial 'Whatever flies I hit in flight!' is the equivalent of Siegfried's proclamation, arriving at the court of the Gibichungs: 'Now fight me, or be my friend!' But this is a starting point for Parsifal, whereas it encapsulates Siegfried's fatal flaw. Wagner is exploring Christian as well as Schopenhauerian critiques of Siegfried's heroism. Christianity is not merely a formal shroud cast over Schopenhauerian content, although a distinction between style and idea may in some cases be valid.

VII

The question remains what it is that Parsifal actually does in order to rejuvenate the decaying community rather than fall prey to it. Why the Monsalvat as opposed to the Gibichung route? The answer lies not in shooting a swan, nor even in felling Klingsor's men and defeating their master. We are helped again by recalling the *Ring*. Wagner had most likely taken words of Feuerbach's Young Hegelian confrère, Max Stirner – 'The unique person will work himself forth out of society all right, but society brings forth no unique person' – as an indication that Siegfried must, like the heroes of old, have a birth and upbringing unlike those of other men.[57]

---

[56] Lorenz, 'Parsifal als Übermensch,' 1877–9.
[57] Max Stirner, *The Ego and its Own*, tr. Steven Byington, ed. David Leopold (Cambridge

Some of that remains in Parsifal: his sheltered, fatherless upbringing by Herzeleide and ensuing development through self-defence in the deserts and dales. Following its 1882 performances, Wagner wrote that the work *Parsifal* itself owed much to 'flight from the world', for:

> Who could look all his life long with an open mind and a free heart, at this world of murder and theft, organised and legalised through lying, deception, and hypocrisy, without having to turn away, shuddering in disgust? Whither then would one avert one's gaze? All too often into the vale of death. To him, however, who is otherwise called and singled out by destiny, there appears the truest reflection of the world itself, as the foretold exhortation of redemption, despatched by its [the world's] innermost soul.[58]

Couched in the language of post-Schopenhauerian metaphysics, there nevertheless remains here a Bakunin-like anger at the world of lies, deception, and hypocrisy, tempered by Christian redemptive prophecy.

That, however, is but a prelude to Parsifal's development as witnessed on stage. Wagner realises that if society brings forth no unique person, then some form of external intervention may be necessary. Even the oddest upbringing cannot evade the dialectical relationship between the monad-like bourgeois individual and civil society. The relationship is not that of the vulgar-Hegelian thesis and antithesis; rather the historically developing nature of each is inextricably linked to that of the other. This is why, in *Die Meistersinger*, a 'later' work than is often credited, mediation is required for the proper exercise of æsthetic judgement: Hans Sachs – or Wagner – both returns art to the people and transforms popular art into something far more valuable. Grace, however frustratingly undefined, might act similarly, on a more metaphysical level, providing redemption to the redeemable. This is not a mere return of Erda's Fate under another name; though there may be something of Fate *aufgehoben*, there is also something quite new and spontaneous. It is quickening, to use an appropriately Christian term, or, if one prefers, it appertains to the Spring (*Lenz*) of Wotan's initial hopes for Siegmund and Sieglinde's union. If the Incarnation were the world-historical event, which for Hegel had changed everything, then another divine intervention, perhaps to some extent related to that singular event, might exert a transformative effect for one of Hegel's followers on the Left. Thus Wagner was not being disingenuous, nor was he simply changing his mind, when, having described *Parsifal* in 1879 as 'this most Christian of works', he could then write quite differently,

University Press: Cambridge, 1995), p. 238.
[58] Wagner, 'Das Bühnenweihfestspiel in Bayreuth 1882,' in *Sämtliche Schriften*, vol. 10, p. 307.

or at least more ambiguously, more dialectically, a year later.[59] This is very much a Young Hegelian writing, albeit one who has managed to a certain degree to reconcile the god-man with Schopenhauerian metaphysics:

> I am almost afraid that we shall have difficulty in reaching an understanding with our friends and patrons on the future meaning and significance of the incomparably and sublimely simple and true redeemer who appears to us in the historically intelligible figure of Jesus of Nazareth, but who must first be cleansed and redeemed of the distortion that has been caused by Alexandrine, Judaic and Roman despotism. Nevertheless, although we are merciless in abandoning the Church and the priesthood and, indeed, the whole historical phenomenon of Christianity, our friends must always know that we do so for the sake of that same Christ whom – because of His utter incomparability and recognisability – we wish to preserve in His total purity, so that – like all the other sublime products of man's artistic and scientific spirit – we can take Him with us into those terrible times which may very well follow the necessary destruction of all that at present exists.[60]

Parsifal, it is worth stressing, is not Christ, nor even Jesus of Nazareth. Wagner criticised Hans von Wolzogen, in an essay on *Parsifal* he otherwise admired, for 'calling Parsifal a reflection of the Redeemer: "I didn't give the Redeemer a thought when I wrote it."'[61] The latter claim ought probably to be taken with a large pinch of salt, but the anxiety to avoid identification should be noted, however we may account for it. Indeed, in a letter to Mathilde Wesendonck, Wagner had long before forecast the work's final, enigmatic line, 'Erlösung dem Erlöser!' (Redemption to the Redeemer!) Wagner here makes clear a Feuerbachian, or perhaps better David Straussian, understanding of what this might entail, albeit though *echt*-Schopenhauerian language and understanding of suffering. He wishes somehow to retain the impulse to transcend without its attainment, almost presaging a Nietzschean morality of strenuousness:

> But I am also clear in my own mind why I can even feel greater fellow-suffering for lower natures than for higher ones. A higher nature is what it is precisely because it has been raised by its own suffering to the heights of resignation [think of his Wotan], or else has within it – and cultivates – the capacity for such a development. Such a nature is extremely close to mine, is indeed similar to it, and with it I attain to fellow-joy. That is why, basically, I feel less fellow-suffering for people than for animals. For I can see that the latter are totally denied the capacity to rise above suffering, and to achieve a state of resignation and deep,

---

[59] Letter of 25 August 1879 to Ludwig II, in *Selected Letters*, p. 897.
[60] Letter to Hans von Wolzogen of 17 January 1880, in ibid., pp. 898–9.
[61] *Cosima Wagner's Diaries*, 21 October 1878, vol. 2, p. 177.

divine calm. And so, in the event of their suffering, as happens when they are tormented, all I see – with a sense of my own tormented despair – is their absolute, redemption-less suffering without any higher purpose, their only release being death which confirms my belief that it would have been better for them never to have entered upon life. And so, if this suffering can have a purpose, it is simply to awaken a sense of fellow-suffering in man, who thereby absorbs the animal's defective existence, and becomes the redeemer of the world by recognising the error of all existence. (This meaning will one day become clearer to you from the Good Friday morning scene in the third act of Parzifal.)[62]

That is the moment at which Parsifal is ready to act not as Christ in any divine sense, but is ready, through his increased capacity for compassion, to act in Christ's stead as an earthly redeemer to Kundry and thereafter to the moribund community of the Grail. We can understand in Young Hegelian *and* Schopenhauerian terms such deputising, demystification, or transformation. (The precise characterisation depends on how one interprets the undeniable fact that Christ, unlike God, is never named in the drama.) Those positive attributes man had once denied himself by granting them to the deity are now returned to earth: this is pure Feuerbach. In more metaphysical terms, because, as Ulrike Kienzle points out, 'every individual represents the whole of existence, each individual can become, according to Schopenhauer, either Adam (fallen mankind) or Christ (the Redeemer)'.[63] Beyond naïve supernaturalism and reductive rationalist naturalism lay what David Strauss had called the 'new viewpoint', the 'mythical'.[64] In *Parsifal*, the two views are united and indeed extended, for through Parsifal's redemption of others he himself may be redeemed.

That awakening of fellow-suffering of which Wagner writes to Mathilde Wesendonck has earlier been portrayed on stage, when Gurnemanz chides Parsifal for his wanton slaughter of the swan:

> GURNEMANZ:
> Act unheard of!
>
> . . .
>
> What did that innocent swan do to you?
>
> . . .
>
> Here – look! – here, you struck him;

---

[62] Letter to Mathilde Wesendonck of 1 October 1858, in *Selected Letters*, pp. 423–4.

[63] Ulrike Kienzle, '*Parsifal* and Religion: A Christian Music Drama?' tr. Mary A. Cicora, in *Companion to Wagner's 'Parsifal'*, ed. Kinderman and Syer, p. 93.

[64] David Friedrich Strauss, *Das Leben Jesu, kritisch bearbeitet*, 2 vols (C. F. Osiander: Tübingen, 1835–6), vol. 2, p.iv.

his blood is still congealing, his wings hanging feebly,
his snowy plumage darkly stained –
his eyes are glazed over, can you see his look?
*(Parsifal has heard Gurnemanz with growing emotion:
now he breaks his bow and throws away his arrows.)*
[Now] do you feel your sinful deed [*Sündentat*] from
within?

I described this earlier as an unknowing act, yet it is also the first stage, if only in retrospect, of Parsifal's awakening to suffering and to consciousness. Grace comes to play a greater part in *Parsifal* than those words of Wagner to Mathilde Wesendonck might suggest, yet there remains a battle between transcendence and its opposite. However, even there, that 'capacity to rise above suffering' – and we should note that it is a 'capacity' rather than an attainment of all – does seem to point towards grace. The ability of some, such as Wotan, the saints, or Wagner himself, to rise above is not so very far removed from Christian mysticism. And Wagner, both before and during his writing of *Parsifal*, would evince increasing interest in that tradition, not least in the writings of Meister Eckhart, also greatly admired by Schopenhauer. 'Our conversation leads us to the mystic Meister Eckhart,' Cosima records. 'R. begins to read a sermon by him, which fascinates us to the highest degree. Everything turned inward, the soul silent, so that in it God may speak the highest word!'[65]

Moreover, Wagner, again in conversation with Cosima, contrasted Christ with the founders of other religions and saints in that he was without sin; others 'started as sinners and became saints.'[66] That sets Wagner at odds with Renan. Strauss and other predecessors had not really offered a 'life of Jesus'; theirs had been works of Biblical criticism. Renan, however, had produced a biography, albeit a biography that made it difficult to understand why Jesus might have been considered, let alone might yet be considered, the Son of God. If anything, success appears to have gone to his head, and therefore the hero, like Siegfried, has been corrupted by civilisation, as is most starkly illustrated in the fraudulent 'resurrection' of Lazarus. 'Everything, in fact, seems to lead us to believe that the miracles of Bethany contributed sensibly to hasten the death of Jesus.'[67] We may recall that Siegfried's death had been hastened by recounting his 'miracles' to Hagen and the vassals. However, Parsifal, by the grace of grace, never succumbs to such hubris.

---

[65] *Cosima Wagner's Diaries*, 26 October 1873, vol. 1, p. 690.
[66] Ibid., 12 May 1877, vol. 2, pp. 306–7.
[67] Ernest Renan, *The Life of Jesus*, tr. unknown (Black: London, 1904), pp. 124–5.

Yet the lack of development distinguishes Wagner's Christ from Parsifal too. For Hegel, in this at least an orthodox Christian, the Incarnation had been a unique event, both historical and so utterly transformative that it might just as readily qualify as coming from without history altogether, that which is necessary to enable modern history to commence.[68] That has nothing to do with Parsifal, who is but a man. Like Siegfried, Parsifal must at least commence his journey with Stirnerian 'uniqueness' and only thereafter be enabled, whether by grace or destruction – perhaps the distinction is false – to accept such 'redemption'. And so, Parsifal arrives upon the scene knowing nothing and shoots dead a swan, to music as hapless in its (mock?) heroism as that of Siegfried entering the Gibichung court. Parsifal's deed achieves nothing except first to rouse the ire of those he meets and to expose his ignorance. The latter, it seems, may have fortunate consequences, but that hope is dashed when Gurnemanz realises that Parsifal is not the pure fool required, but just a fool. In any case, none of this was Parsifal's intention, if indeed he had one, when shooting the bird; it seems far more of a Siegfried-like unconscious deed. Parsifal than *re*-acts to Kundry during the second act, and thereby experiences Amfortas's pain; yet once again, he does not really *do* anything himself.

The exception, arguably, is making the sign of the Cross with the spear and thereby annihilating Klingsor and his magic garden. This is worth returning to, but at the moment it should be emphasised that it is not a straightforward exception: Parsifal is only able to do this because of some miraculous, supernatural intervention, which suspends the spear hurled by Klingsor in mid-air. We seem here to be in the realm of symbolism, or at least closer to the realm of symbolism than elsewhere. In fact, Wagner, as Robin Holloway has pointed out, is in practice stubbornly realistic, even when the content is symbolic.[69] There are no instances of Bachian number-play, no Brahmsian ciphers in Wagner: he calls a spear a spear, even if the Hegelian concept (*Begriff*) of the spear is far more complex than its initial representation (*Vorstellung*) might suggest. Those Hegelian words with which Wagner opened his contemporaneous essay, *Religion and Art*, should always be borne in mind:

> One could say that when religion becomes artificial, it is reserved for art to grant salvation to the kernel of religion, by having us believe that mythical

---

[68] Hegel, 'Philosophie der Geschichte,' pp. 385–93.
[69] Robin Holloway, 'Motif, Memory and Meaning in "Twilight of the Gods",' in Nicholas John (ed.) *Twilight of the Gods / Götterdämmerung* (John Calder: London and New York, 1985), pp. 13–38.

symbols, which the former [that is, religion] would have us believe in their real [*eigentlich*] sense, may be comprehended through their symbolical value, in order to discern therein, via an ideal presentation, the concealed profound truth.[70]

At any rate, Boulez is right to say that Kundry's calling of Parsifal's name and the kiss are '*revelations* that help Parsifal first to understand and then to cast himself in his true role'.[71] The mature Parsifal certainly does not lie 'beyond good and evil', however ingenious Lorenz's portrayal of Titurel as 'representative of the customarily-good [*Sittlich-Guten*]' and Klingsor of 'the customarily-evil [*Sittlich-Bösen*]', with a third way all too readily available for the Wagnerian *Übermensch*. Lorenz remarks that Parsifal must symbolically ask in Act I, who is good and who is evil.[72] True enough, yet that is but his point of departure. Parsifal must go beyond his ignorance on this matter, and realises perfectly well after his moment of recognition that Kundry's blandishments are evil and therefore to be resisted. He is no longer a *reine Tor*, nor a *Mann ohne Eignenschaften*, a man without qualities; part of the urgency for resisting Kundry is to reach Amfortas, a goal announcing itself through the transformative epiphany of compassion.

However, Boulez goes a little too far to say that these are 'the *revelations*', implying that these accomplish rather than point the way. What actually accomplishes Parsifal's transformation occurs between acts, or during the Prelude to Act III. Whilst Robert Morgan has rightly pointed to a circularity to this prelude, related to Parsifal's as yet fruitless search for the Grail, there is an equally important dynamism, as noted by William Kinderman.[73] What Parsifal subsequently learns on his travels – which may still in some sense encompass the knowledge gained from the envisaged visit to Tristan – is not to be attributed to his own agency, nor even perhaps that of any other mortal. Whether secular or atheist commentators like it or not, and whether indeed *Parsifal* 'is' a Christian work or not, this is the realm not just of self-realisation, but also and primarily of that divine gift known as grace, which might alleviate the sorry lot of man's sinful existence. Grace supplants or at least permits self-realisation. Michael Tanner argues that there is 'no point in Parsifal's development at which

[70] Wagner, 'Religion und Kunst', in *Sämtliche Schriften*, vol. 10, p. 211.
[71] Pierre Boulez, 'Approaches to *Parsifal*', in *Orientations: Collected Writings*, ed. Jean-Jacques Nattiez, tr. Martin Cooper (Faber: London and Boston, 1986), p. 247.
[72] Lorenz-Gotha, 'Parsifal als Übermensch', p. 1880.
[73] Robert Morgan, 'Dissonant Prolongation: Theoretical and Compositional Precedents', *Journal of Music Theory*, 20 (1976), 62–72, esp. 72; William Kinderman, 'The Third-Act Prelude of Wagner's *Parsifal*: Genesis, Form, and Dramatic Meaning', in *19th-Century Music*, 29 (2005–6), 180.

one could say that without the intervention of divine grace he would have remained powerless to accomplish his mission'.[74] Yet that is to ignore the several, far-from-incidental references to *Gnade* in Wagner's text – its first theological usage in a Wagner drama since *Lohengrin* – and to transform the terms of his drama. That is perfectly permissible as an idea for a production of *Parsifal*, but more questionable for an interpretation of the work itself, a concept to which Tanner certainly holds.[75] It is more difficult to consider the ongoing, developing role in the drama of grace as merely symbolic than it is, say, the Grail or Klingsor's sorcery. Boulez and Wieland Wagner agreed in correspondence on the importance of 'desacralisation' of *Parsifal*, and were probably right to do so; those last gasps of early-twentieth-century 'Bayreuth Idealism', which had somehow survived the 1951 institution of 'New Bayreuth', could hardly have been perpetuated beyond the death of Hans Knappertsbusch.[76] It does not follow, however, that *Parsifal* has no theological message to impart. When, in Act III, the hero returns to Monsalvat in search of the Grail, his search is successful either through chance or through the intervention of something higher, if something higher exists – and it appears that it does. It is that and that alone which enables him finally to carry out his deed, to heal Amfortas's wound, and thereby to put Amfortas out of his eternal agony and, crucially, to rejuvenate the community. Carl Dahlhaus therefore writes that Parsifal 'does not act, nor direct himself towards a goal (except in his search for the Grail, which he finds through grace not effort) . . . he comes to himself through reaction, not resolution'.[77]

There is much truth in that claim, and it sheds interesting light upon the question of the later Wagner's relationship towards Christianity. Wotan's deeds have failed owing to his power-lust and his concomitant desire to perpetuate any achievement beyond its natural life-span; Siegmund's deeds have failed owing to his lack of actual freedom, Wotan still hovering in the background, and Siegfried's deeds have failed owing to his lack of consciousness. Parsifal may yet succeed through the intervention of something transcending that exclusively human agency upon which the Young Hegelian Wagner had insisted in his tale of the gods' downfall.

---

[74] Michael Tanner, *Wagner* (HarperCollins: London, 1996), p. 198.

[75] Nikolaus Lehnhoff's English National Opera production presented a fine if problematical case for a production which entirely dispensed with Christian aspects of the work, taking as its starting point *The Waste Land*. It may be seen in its Baden-Baden incarnation on Opus Arte DVD OA 0915 D.

[76] Boulez, 'Wieland Wagner: "Here Space becomes Time"', in *Orientations*, p. 243.

[77] Carl Dahlhaus, *Richard Wagner's Music Dramas*, tr. Mary Whittall (Cambridge University Press: Cambridge, 1979), p. 147.

Cosima records Wagner, whilst at work on the score in 1878, sounding as atheistic as Schopenhauer or Feuerbach:

> Our final words yesterday had to do with the Godhead; I: 'I must believe in it – my unworthiness and my happiness lead me to believe.' He: 'The first part, your unworthiness, you can cross out; Godhead is Nature, the will which seeks salvation and, to quote Darwin, selects the strongest to bring this salvation about.'[78]

Yet there is something mystical even here, as indeed there is in different ways in Schopenhauer and Feuerbach, about the force at work. Indeed, a few months later, Wagner condemned 'this trivial cult of atheism'.[79] And when it came to his dramatic composition, it seems that he was able and willing to go further along a Christian route than in such comments. To accuse him of disingenuousness places the burden of proof upon the accuser. The dramatic imperative of going beyond the *Ring* wins out over his hostility towards the Church. Almost despite himself – on account, we might say, of the Will's striving towards salvation – he is drawn or driven towards Christianity, or at any rate towards important elements of Christian teaching. In this respect, Wagner resembles Wotan and Kundry: 'R. sees a resemblance between Wotan and Kundry: both long for salvation and both rebel against it, Kundry in the scene with P., Wotan with Siegfried.'[80] Yet both, whether through the urgings of the Will or through the mediating agency of grace, go beyond their respective rebellions and are saved, Kundry less ambiguously so than Wotan. 'I do not believe in God,' Wagner said, 'but in godliness, which is revealed in a Jesus *without sin*.'[81] That is certainly not orthodox Christianity, but it is inconceivable without Christ, or indeed without Christianity.

VIII

This comes close to Wagner's meaning when telling Ludwig II of the 'purity of content and subject-matter of my *Parsifal*'. To that end, he wished to restrict performances to Bayreuth or, better understood, to protect the work from 'a common operatic career'. He would 'not entirely blame our Church authorities if they were to raise an entirely legitimate protest against representations of the most sacred mysteries upon the selfsame

---

[78] *Cosima Wagner's Diaries*, 24 January 1878, vol. 2, p. 22.

[79] Ibid., 6 August 1878, vol. 2, p. 130.

[80] Ibid., 5 June 1878, vol. 2, p. 85.

[81] Ibid., 20 September 1879, vol. 2, p. 367.

boards in which, yesterday and tomorrow, frivolity sprawls in luxuriant ease'.[82] Boulez understood this when he admiringly portrayed Wagner loathing a system in which 'opera houses are . . . like cafés where . . . you can hear waiters calling out their orders: "One *Carmen*! And one *Walküre*! And one *Rigoletto*!"' That was not simply a matter of offended *amour propre*, but of Wagner's works' incompatibility with existing theatrical conventions and norms.[83] Likewise, Cosima writes of Wagner looking 'forward to the better times in which such men as Shakespeare, now prophets in the wilderness, will be brought in to form, as it were, part of a divine service. Thus the world once *was* – first a ceremonial act spoken, then to Holy Communion.'[84] The religious nature of Attic tragedy is to be renewed by, not in spite of, the fruits of (Christian) modernity. Wagner assumes the place Goethe had allotted to Shakespeare, when writing that the Englishman combined old and new to an 'extravagant' degree: whilst each character 'must' (Greek fate, or tragic necessity), he also 'willed' (modern subjectivity).[85] The essential nature of Wagnerian music drama was as much at odds with the apparent trivialities of contemporary 'opera' as was its subject matter. *Parsifal* presents the *ne plus ultra* in both respects.

Wagner, it should be noted, does not claim that *Parsifal* itself *is* a sacred rite, but that it *presents* such a rite, namely Holy Communion, on stage. One no more receives Communion than one becomes initiated into a quasi-Masonic order by watching *Die Zauberflöte*. The rite, however, is not merely staged, but re-presented at a time of profound crisis for the community of Monsalvat. Amfortas, not only king but high priest, has succumbed to the blandishments of Kundry and therefore been caught off guard by Klingsor, wounded, apparently irreparably, by his own spear, captured by Klingsor and yet the only weapon that can heal the wound. Without the spear, moreover, the Grail, which the increasingly frail Amfortas can hardly bear to uncover, stands in danger of capture by the community's adversaries. As Suzanne Stewart points out, crisis is intensified by Wagner's continual diverting of the audience's gaze towards Amfortas's wound.[86] That, in accordance with his musico-dramatic precepts, he accomplishes gesturally, verbally, and musically. The second-act cry of

---

[82] Letter of 28 September 1880, in *Selected Letters*, p. 903.

[83] Boulez, 'Time re-explored', in *Orientations*, p. 262.

[84] *Cosima Wagner's Diaries*, 5 April 1881, vol. 2, p. 651.

[85] Johann Wolfgang von Goethe, 'Shakespeare und kein Ende!', in *Sämtliche Werke, Tagebücher und Gespräche*, 39 vols in 43, ed. Dieter Borchmeyer *et al.* (Deutsche Klassiker: Frankfurt am Main, 1985–99), vol. 19, pp. 641–5.

[86] Suzanne R. Stewart, 'The Theft of the Operatic Voice: Masochistic Seduction in Wagner's *Parsifal*', in *Musical Quarterly*, 80 (1996), 607.

recognition, 'Amfortas! – the wound!' is preceded by Kundry's kiss and its *Tristan*-chord: 'love's first kiss', according to her trivial (Flowermaiden) or warped (Klingsor) understanding of 'love'. The *Tristan*-chord marking the kiss makes the connection with Wagner's earlier drama and its Nietzschean 'voluptuousness of hell' far more profoundly than Parsifal appearing on stage in it could ever have done.[87] Parsifal recoils in terror. 'His demeanour', read Wagner's stage directions, 'expresses a terrible change; he presses his hands forcefully against his heart, as if to overcome a rending pain [*wie um einen zerreißenden Schmerz zu bewältigen*].' Pain is not only verbalised but also sounded in the screams of the orchestral sequences, both harmonically and melodically, of more or less unresolved diminished seventh chords, their dissonance enhanced and their tonal function complicated, though not eliminated, by added notes. In fact, these mixture chords both loosen the bonds of tonality and bind the chords on their own terms more closely together, thereby anticipating Schoenberg and the final crisis, agonising *and* emancipating, of tonality itself. As Adorno noted, in Parsifal's cry Wagner exceeded in power even Tristan's curse upon love, 'so he placed eight bars in the centre of his work, which, in their total structure stand immediately upon the threshold of atonality'.[88] Yet it is only, as Adorno then reminded us, upon the threshold. This is not *Erwartung*, nor even the atonal flirtation of Liszt; it is more akin to late Mahler. Scruton rightly objects to the understandable tendency to view *Tristan* as a 'final jettisoning' of tonality, even though it points the way in retrospect.[89] The same holds for the expanded and at times floating tonality of *Parsifal*. Reconciliation – societal, liturgical, and tonal – is still held out as a hope, however pious, and will be attempted both within this act and within the work as a whole.

The agony of the wound intensifies and symbolises the crisis of Monsalvat; it is worth noting that the intensity of this *Mitleid* is such that it passes, in Arnold Whittall's words, 'beyond relationship into identification. Parsifal's memory of Amfortas's lament and the Grail ceremony is so acute . . . that his own motifs do not appear at all.'[90] Yet the crisis itself has not suddenly presented itself; it lies in the modern, subjectivist decay or degeneration of the ancient community. I therefore dispute Stewart's claim that the principal question concerning *Parsifal*, assuming that such a question should

[87] Nietzsche, 'Ecce homo,' in *Sämtliche Werke*, vol. 6: 'Warum ich bin so klug,' §6, p. 290.
[88] Adorno, *Versuch über Wagner*, p. 62.
[89] Roger Scruton, *Death-Devoted Heart: Sex and the Sacred in Wagner's 'Tristan and Isolde'* (Oxford University Press: Oxford and New York, 2004), p. 79.
[90] Whittall, 'The Music,' p. 77.

exist, is 'not so much … of its thematics (*Parsifal* is clearly *about* religious themes) but rather a question regarding its status as ritual, its performative impact'.[91] The distinction is false, for the 'performative' impact partly relies upon the 'thematics'. It is indeed the crisis of ritual within the drama that provides a starting point for the greater success of ritual, certainly on stage and perhaps as a rite in some ambiguous sense incorporating the audience, in Act III. Parsifal as well as the audience needs the agony of Amfortas's wound, although it will take divine intervention for the fool to feel it, to be enlightened through fellow-suffering: 'durch Mitleid wissend, der reine Tor'. These words and their music are repeated in ritualistic fashion, but at the same time develop in their meaning, owing to the development of the drama. Only after grace imparts to Parsifal the *Mitleid* concerning this impediment to Communion will he gain the understanding necessary to save Monsalvat and its rite, and thus to fulfil and to resolve the 'durch Mitleid …' prophecy, however ambiguously. We might play with the celebrated opening of St John's similarly predestinarian Gospel: In the beginning were Will's sorrow and Heart's sorrow (Herzeleide), and the sorrow *(Leid)* was with *(mit)* the Will, and the sorrow was Will; *Parsifal* was the representation both of that Will and of that *Mitleid*.

The drama and the hero who bears its name may therefore redeem, or at least appear to redeem, the rite on stage and renew, or at least appear to renew, the communal, religious, and indeed political role of Attic tragedy, without sacrificing – and this is unambiguously Hegelian – the introduction of Christian subjectivity into the world. Wagner had attempted this in the *Ring* and makes a further attempt, starting from where he had left off, in *Parsifal*.[92] Æschylus's Herald in *Agamemnon* had been able to ask: 'who, except the gods, can live time through forever without any pain?'[93] For Hegel and his followers, the subjectivity of the modern world rendered such a standpoint untenable; the agony of the god-man upon the Cross was a paradigmatic case in every sense. Amfortas's agony, with which Parsifal through grace may come to sympathise, is not, given the uniqueness of the Incarnation in Hegel's case and of Jesus' perfect example for Wagner, identical to this paradigm. The agonies experienced in *Parsifal* are, however, dependent upon this subjectivist agony of Christ.

[91] Stewart, 'Theft of the Operatic Voice,' p. 598.

[92] Mark Berry, 'Richard Wagner and the Politics of Music Drama,' in *Historical Journal*, 47 (2004), 666–70.

[93] Æschylus, 'Agamemnon,' tr. Richmond Lattimore, in *Greek Tragedies*, ed. David Grene and Richmond Lattimore (Chicago University Press: Chicago and London, 1991–), vol. 1, lines 553–4.

It is no coincidence, moreover, that Kundry's agony of reincarnation dates back to her laughter at the foot of the Cross. This original moment of laughter, in philosophical, historical, and dramatic terms, remains the defining moment of fracture, which she is doomed to relive throughout eternity, that is, beyond history, unless grace should revivify history and its concomitant of death. James Plaskitt observes that Wagner grants death 'a positive value of the sort given to life itself by the Romantics', a thoroughly Hegelian transformation.[94] In fact, similar thoughts are voiced by, or at least pointed to, by some of the Romantics themselves, such as Novalis: 'Life is the beginning of death. Life is for the sake of death. Death is at the same time an ending and a beginning, a parting and closer reunion with the self. Through death purification is completed.'[95] Both Amfortas and Kundry long for death and, before them, Wotan's salvation had lain in acceptance of death, personal and political. Kundry's curse is a negation demanding a reconciliation, whose discovery is modernity's challenge; the curse is visited upon her in every modern (Christian) generation and upon those generations themselves.

IX

For Suzanne Stewart, Wagner's 'entire theological and æsthetic system for *Parsifal* comes together in the Eucharist'.[96] If so, this raises questions rather than answers them, for we must consider the historical state in which the Eucharist now finds itself, in terms of both Monsalvat and the nineteenth century. In 1865, following the birth of his daughter, Isolde von Bülow, Wagner held a number of discussions with a Benedictine priest, Father Petrus (Anton) Hamp, expressly to further his understanding of the Mass, its origins, and the doctrine of transubstantiation.[97] Moreover, Wagner's friendship with the Abbé Liszt would soon be closer than ever, once the breach over Cosima had been mended.

[94] James Plaskitt, '"The Language of Passion": Wagner and Romanticism,' in Stewart Spencer (ed.), *Wagner 1976: A Celebration of the Bayreuth Festival* (Wagner Society: London, 1976), pp. 156–65.

[95] Novalis, 'Pollen,' in Frederick Beiser (ed.), *The Early Political Writings of the German Romantics*, tr. Frederick Beiser (Cambridge University Press: Cambridge, 1996), §§14, p. 11 (translation slightly modified).

[96] Stewart, 'Theft of the Operatic Voice,' p. 603.

[97] Anton Hamp, *Ein Blick in die Geisterwerkstatt Richard Wagners: Von einem alten geistlichen Freunde des Meisters von Bayreuth zur Erinnerung an dessen Schwanengesang – den 'Parzival'* (Berlin, 1904), p. 14; Kurt Küppers, 'Richard Wagner und der christliche Gottesdienst,' in *Forum katholische Theologie*, 8 (1992), 51–2.

However, the Eucharist is not for Wagner an ahistorical given; its status and meaning change, in Young Hegelian style, through history. A Lutheran, however heterodox, Wagner had, through profound study, 'taken the trouble to find out all that he could – in so far as it was possible at the time – about the genetic development and structure of the Roman Mass, but at the same time he penetrated its problems'.[98] He then re-presents the rite, *aufgehoben* through the agency of some intervention equating either to grace or the movement of the world-historical spirit. (For many an Hegelian, the two would be difficult to disentangle.) The Church authorities might justifiably raise 'an entirely legitimate protest' against such heterodoxy, though Wagner does not say so. Nevertheless, Cosima records him stating his belief 'that Christianity can still be rescued for future ages and that up till now it has only experienced its barbarian epochs'. This he remarked whilst reading Renan's *Life of Jesus*. The following day, contrary to Cosima's request, he attended her daughter Blandine's Communion.[99]

It is not only the Eucharist whose *Aufhebung* Wagner attempts, but that of Christianity and even of society itself. Wagner never quite surrenders his Hegelian view of purpose to the essential meaninglessness Schopenhauer saw in the world and its representation, although the latter certainly complicates the quest for the former. Monsalvat (*mons salvatoris*) is more a realm 'in need of salvation' than 'of salvation' – just like the meaning of the final motif in *Götterdämmerung* had been closer to redemption *of*, rather than *through* love.[100] Monsalvat is equivalent to the *Ring*'s decaying Valhalla and Gibichung Hall; Parsifal must renew and transform it. Goethe's 'eternal youth of the Greek gods' could hardly be more distant from this world of late Christian practice.[101] It seems that the conventional Christian understanding of God may have been true for previous historical epochs. Radical renewal will, however, be needed, if indeed it is not too late already. As Heine, one of Wagner's fellow exiles in Paris, had written:

Our hearts are thrilled with compassion, for it is old Jehovah himself who is making ready to die. We have known him so well, from his cradle in Egypt... We saw him bid farewell to those companions of his childhood, the obelisks and sphinxes of the Nile, to become a little god-king in Palestine to a poor

[98] Küng, 'Wagner's *Parsifal*,' p. 322.
[99] *Cosima Wagner's Diaries*, 15 and 16 June 1878, vol. 2, p. 94.
[100] Berry, *Treacherous Bonds*, pp. 260–4.
[101] Johann Wolfgang von Goethe, 'Maximen und Reflektionen,' in *Goethes Werke*, 9th edn, ed. Erich Trunz, 14 vols (Beck: Munich, 1981), vol. 12, §§748, 470.

nation of shepherds ... We saw him move to Rome ... he obtained power and, from the heights of the Capitol, ruled the city and the world, *urbem et orbem* ... We have seen him purify himself, spiritualise himself still more, become paternal, compassionate, the benefactor of the human race, a philanthropist ... But nothing can save him!

Do you not hear the bell? Down on your knees! The sacrament is being administered to a dying God![102]

That seems an apt metaphor for Monsalvat, especially by the time of the third act, when Titurel is dead and the tainted Amfortas can no longer bear to uncover the Grail. It is the world in which the Church, not Jesus, holds sway. Cosima records: 'Renan's book [*L'Eglise chrétienne*] provides him with another opportunity to talk about "the most horrible thing in history", the church, and the victory of Judaism over all else: "I can't read two lines of Goethe without recognising the Jewish Jehovah; for him Jesus was a problematical figure, but God was as clear as crystal." He explains how Plato's Theos paved the way for the Jewish God.'[103] In this, Wagner stands close to Schopenhauer and his denigration, in the light of Kant's critical philosophy, of Judaism on account of its doctrine of creation in time.[104]

X

Standing just as firmly in the tradition of German idealist æsthetics as he had during his Zurich exile, Wagner continued to see the Athenian *polis* as an embodiment of harmony between the individual and society, private and public. Art and its performance were not merely part of this, but the most important part, the supreme manifestation of harmony. Indeed, in terms of modern scholarship, Paul Cartledge has written that Attic tragedy was 'an active ingredient, and a major one, of the political foreground, featuring in the everyday consciousness and even the nocturnal dreams of the Athenian citizen'. That, despite the undeniable cultic tendencies of Bayreuth, the danger of transformation into a gathered congregation of initiates, remained Wagner's dream. The problem was how to do this in modern society, itself the product of the Christian subjectivity that had introduced fragmentation into the world. Could this negation yet

---

[102] Heinrich Heine, 'Of Germany since Luther,' in *Revue des Deux-Mondes*, 4 (1834), 408. Translated in Henri de Lubac, *The Drama of Atheist Humanism*, tr. Edith M. Riley (Sheed & Ward: London, 1949), p. 21 (translation slightly modified).

[103] *Cosima Wagner's Diaries*, 10 February 1880, vol. 2, p. 438.

[104] Schopenhauer, *Welt als Wille und Vorstellung*, vol. 1, pp. 614–15.

be negated? And if tragedy for Wagner were to hold out both the Young Hegelian promise of *political* liberation and the Schopenhauerian promise of *metaphysical* liberation, then if that latter were not to be from the will-to-live, as in the later parts of the *Ring*, then from what would it be, and, as much to the point, what would be liberated?

The Waste Land's 'heap of broken images' is thus for Wagner and for *Parsifal* the starting point, not the end.[105] To choose to dwell on the negativity of Monsalvat's breakdown is to miss what has to modern minds become the more difficult, indeed problematical, half of the story. Christianity would help to rebuild society, and vice versa. The Buddhism of Wagner's projected drama *Die Sieger*, which undoubtedly left its mark upon *Parsifal*, could never have done this by itself. Just as much as when he penned the following words in Zurich, Wagner was involved in creating a 'new religion . . . containing the necessary conditions for the artwork of the future'.[106] But now, unlike in Zurich, Christianity could both be redeemed and act as redeemer: 'Erlösung dem Erlöser' indeed. Such thoughts are strongly related to the Christian incorporation of time into eternity, and/or *vice versa*.

In this connection, there is in Kundry and her previous incarnations an element of the 'surreal simultaneity' that Mary Cicora identifies as a hallmark of the drama. The 'succession of generations' has not, however, 'yielded' to this simultaneity; like leitmotif technique itself, it provides a weight of developmental memory that supports, questions, and conflicts with the present.[107] The partial simultaneity is in fact quite real: the mark of existence and its perpetual conflict between past, present, and future. This is how we experience them all. The Prelude to Act I portrays, like a drama in miniature, this conflict between the near-stasis of ritual and development, both of which will gain the upper hand at various points during the work, but neither of which will vanquish the other. The action of Act II and of the period prior to Act III prepares the way for the transformed circumstances of that act, with its symphonic synthesis and hard-won resolution of the various grail motifs in the opening tonality of A-flat major. Yet that relies upon existing forms, rejuvenated yet far from radically original. Good Friday is detranscendentalised and the Eucharist is more ambiguously rescued from decay, but Good Friday and the Eucharist they remain, just as Feuerbach had wished, in the *Essence of Christianity*, to preserve the essence of that faith and its rituals in a

[105] T. S. Eliot, 'The Waste Land,' in *Collected Poems 1909–1962* (Faber: London, 1963), p. 63.
[106] 'Das Kunstwerk der Zukunft,' p. 123.
[107] Cicora, 'Medievalism and Metaphysics,' p. 40.

fashion appropriate to the dictates of history. *Parsifal* itself benefits from such treatment, though to remain true to the work's developmental spirit, this should not be taken as an excuse for mere reductionism.

Moreover, Wagner intends to use Christian myth and Christian history to correct their errors. Thus Cosima records: 'Much about church and state; he says, "For me Christianity has not yet arrived, and I am like the early Christians, awaiting Christ's return." – But in the search for ideality, he adds, things look different!'[108] Not only religion, not only Christianity, but even theology might be *aufgehoben*. Hegel – the philosophy of history – might yet vanquish Feuerbach, or at least render him less one-sided in his apparent atheism. Wagner, whilst lauding in 1851 the 'ability of Christian myth to enthral our minds' via its depiction of '*transfiguration through death*', had also condemned it for having distorted and denied the anthropomorphism of Germanic myth and having constructed instead a new theology. Rendered incapable of necessary regeneration, myth – like political and artistic unity – had 'fragmented into its individual, self-contained, component parts ... its dramatic nucleus broken down into a plethora of unrelated deeds'.[109] Now Christian myth and Christian theology, even if of questionable orthodoxy, might help renew that initial unity. If the *Ring*, despite its incidental Teutonism, had pointed the way, then *Parsifal* would recognise the necessity of religion in general and of Christianity in particular for any post-Incarnation society. Christ is reintroduced to a community that has abandoned Him. Whilst discussing the issue of Hermann Levi as conductor of *Parsifal*, Cosima told her husband: 'the community into which the Israelite would be accepted has itself abandoned Christ, whereas previously blood was shed and everything sacrificed on his behalf'. Wagner responded that he had certainly remained true to Christ. '"The trouble is," he exclaims, "that all great personalities reveal themselves to us in time and space, and are thus subject to change."'[110] Hegel and history once again intervene, even when the Schopenhauerian language of time and space is invoked.

This conflict is re-dramatised in the dialectical opposition in *Parsifal* between the characteristic, indeed almost normative, chromaticism and diatonicism of *Tristan* and *Die Meistersinger* respectively. It is noteworthy that the most 'advanced' music is given to Klingsor, Amfortas, and Kundry, not to Parsifal, just as it had been to Alberich and Hagen. This

---

[108] *Cosima Wagner's Diaries*, 15 July 1879, vol. 2, p. 339.

[109] Richard Wagner, *Oper und Drama*, ed. Klaus Kropfinger (Reclam: Stuttgart, 1994), pp. 167–74.

[110] *Cosima Wagner's Diaries*, 19 January 1881, vol. 2, pp. 601–2.

diatonic–chromatic opposition takes concrete form in the opposition of the two worlds of Monsalvat and Klingsor's realm. It is heightened by the incursions of the latter into the former, notably the agonising chromaticism of Amfortas's wound and Kundry's kiss, which renders Parsifal able to sympathise with Amfortas's agony. As Kinderman points out, 'Kundry's kiss serves ... as the point of connection between the heavenly, diatonic realm of the Grail and the diabolical, chromatic realm of Klingsor; from her kiss comes the "pollution of the sanctuary," reflected in the chromatic contamination of the third bar of the Communion theme.'[111] Yet this 'pollution' is enabling too, in a very real sense a *felix culpa*, for without it redemption could never occur. Grace needs it, as well as vice versa.

And so, when reconciliation, the ultimate driving force of Hegel's philosophy, comes, it is, despite some appearances, dialectical. Kinderman observes:

> The arrival of this final tonic chord of A-flat major thus provides the simultaneous resolution of the Grail and Communion motives, standing in place of the dissonance that had represented a primary source of musical tension from the very beginning of the work, four hours earlier. In these closing bars, both motives are subsumed into the final subdominant cadence, completing and perfecting the musical form as an audible symbol for the utopia of redemption.[112]

Perhaps, however, it remains but a utopia; it can hardly be the end of the story. We cannot be any more sure of the outcome than at the end of *Götterdämmerung*. Such a plagal cadence was closely associated, especially during the historicising nineteenth century, with the great tradition of sacred music. The music, in a sense, is intoning 'Amen!' to the words' 'Redemption to the Redeemer!' That is not to suggest that Wagner straightforwardly assents to the dogmas upon which Christian tradition is based. He remains for that both too much a Young Hegelian, adamant upon the time-bound nature of supposedly eternal truths, and too much a Schopenhauerian, with a metaphysical though not æsthetic bent of atheism. Rather, Wagner is daring to subsume the truths of that tradition into the world of musical drama; he portrays the 'truest' elements of Christian mythical tradition on stage and in the orchestra, and thereby contributes to their development. He subsumes the truths, partial though nevertheless real, into a greater, post-Hegelian search for systematic truth: a vain attempt perhaps but an impulse to renewal.

---

[111] William Kinderman, 'Wagner's *Parsifal*: Musical Form and the Drama of Redemption,' in *The Journal of Musicology*, 4 (1985), 441.

[112] Ibid., 446.

XI

The struggle delineated above may in turn be seen to be part of the general dialectic of modern music drama, between the objective demands of the material and the subjective demands of the composer's creative voice. Both are of course mediated by history, yet together they remind us, in the celebrated words of Marx, also building upon and battling with Hegel, that: 'Men make their own history, but they do not make it just as they please; they do not make it under circumstances chosen by themselves, but under circumstances directly encountered, given and transmitted from the past.'[113] A few twists of the dialectic later, in Thomas Mann's *Doctor Faustus*, we see:

> Leverkühn's progress in music, contingent on a brilliant pact with a devil who cites from Adorno's musicological writings, goes hand in hand with an alienation from human relations. The specifically non-communicative æsthetics of hermetic art seems to mirror the imperviousness of the dictatorial Nazi regime; yet at the same time, only that same rigorously hermetic art is capable of a mournful expressivity which can articulate suffering in an adequately uncompromising manner... The problem of the subject, diagnosed to be so helpless in [Döblin's] *Berlin Alexanderplatz* or so vulnerable in [Schnitzler's] *Fräulein Else*, finds its ultimate formulation here.[114]

A problem rather than a solution it nevertheless remains. Either one heeds the Frankfurt School and sees that Enlightenment must somehow be deflected in order that it might confront its increasingly violent inadequacies, or one turns with Heidegger – Spengler even – against rationalism altogether, a course turning us back towards a 'timeless' mythical understanding of the world Enlightenment was held to have vanquished. What tends to happen is that the two paths come into conflict. Perhaps this is the only course now open; modern reality cannot fail to be agonistic. To evoke *Doctor Faustus* again, there is something of Adrian Leverkühn and Serenus Zeitblom in all of us – if only because there remains some residue of Zeitblom's world in Leverkühn. Even Boulez, whom many would suspect of strenuous insistence upon the demands of the material, is quite 'Romantic' in this respect. His persuasiveness as a conductor of Wagner and of *Parsifal* in particular is far from incidental here:

[113] Karl Marx, 'The Eighteenth Brumaire of Louis Bonaparte,' in Karl Marx and Friedrich Engels, *Selected Works*, 3 vols (Progress: Moscow, 1969–70), vol. 1, p. 398.
[114] Russell A. Berman, 'The Subjects of Community: Aspiration, Memory, Resistance 1918–1945,' in *Philosophy and German Literature, 1700–1990*, ed. Nicholas Saul (Cambridge University Press: Cambridge, 2002), p. 242.

There is no such thing as historical inevitability. History is what one makes of it. I hold very firmly to this principle. When someone speaks of being compelled by historical necessity it means he is no longer capable of acting for himself; in one sense history is something we enact, not something to be submitted to.[115]

That is not so far removed from Wagner's presentation of the problematics of grace, agency, history, and redemption. Just, then, as in Mann's novel and in *Parsifal*, elements of the past and indeed of the future are not only with us in the present, but are dramatically created both by and in the present. This understanding also informs Boulez's conception of *Die Meistersinger*:

The Romantics rediscovered the Gothic style. At the end of the nineteenth century there were Gothic churches in profusion. This was the most striking example of stylistic reference. On the other hand, although in *The Mastersingers* there are [*sic*] no end of references to the *Minnesänger* and to the forms of sixteenth and – even more so – fifteenth century music, Wagner's music actually has nothing to do with the historical truth about the town of Nuremberg. This is why I feel really ill at ease when people try to depict the historical town on the stage when it is absent from the music.[116]

The case of *Parsifal* is more complex: here there are very real nods to sacred musical tradition from Palestrina onwards. Yet they are undeniably transformed and subsumed into a nineteenth-century dramatic and harmonic reality, holding out the prospect of historical reconciliation. Indeed, as Boulez has written:

The words of Gurnemanz ['You see, my son, here time becomes space'] are of vital significance ... because they bring these two fundamental constituents together to form a unity. This is an idea adumbrated but never really pursued, though it reappears incidentally in the magic transformation of Klingsor's domain, in the evoking of Kundry and in the narrative of Parsifal's wanderings. On each occasion place and time are linked by a kind of osmosis, explained superficially by clairvoyance and magic but implicit, at a deeper level, in the very stuff of the dramatic action.[117]

Boulez errs in saying that the idea is never really pursued, yet the pursuit is, in his words, 'implicit, at a deeper level', and it appears more than 'incidentally' in the instances he presents. The conflict is not merely re-presented, but dramatised, as is always Wagner's tendency; this is in

[115] Pierre Boulez, *Conversations with Célestin Deliège*, tr. Robert Wangermée (Eulenburg: London, 1976), p. 33.
[116] Ibid., p. 32.
[117] Boulez, 'Approaches to *Parsifal*', p. 249.

some sense the dialectic of Enlightenment.

What could still approach at least an illusory reconciliation in *Die Meistersinger* and *Parsifal* had no chance of doing so by the time of Schoenberg and his successors; the antagonism between objectivity and subjectivity has become a necessary part of the modernist artwork, a crucial component of that creative enactment of history of which Boulez speaks. That is not simply an æsthetic but, all the more importantly, a social deed, a deed which must not, moreover, be misunderstood as some kind of archaism (neo-classicism, so far as Boulez is concerned). *Parsifal* would barely be a drama at all if one removed the second act and its *Taten*, although it might stand as a closer model for Messiaen's *St François d'Assise*. The deed is an imperative, a post-Fichtean connection of the alienated self with the world through action: the Young Hegelian *Philosophie der Tat*. In this sense, it is the subject or ego – in both a Fichtean and a modern, Freudian sense – which actually posits its opposite, the world of objects. Young Hegelianism is far from dead, although absolute subjectivity certainly is. Martin Scherzinger writes perceptively regarding post-modernist denial of modernism's social praxis:

> The separation of art from social functions during the first half of the twentieth century was less an absolute denial of a relationship between the two and more a forging of a peculiar linkage between the two that was complex and dialectical ... The *antagonistic* side of æsthetic autonomy, which was tied to notions of critique and negation, has largely been forgotten. ...
>
> ... Modernism sought to heighten the tension between various extreme dialectical tendencies in an effort to arrest critical space in an increasingly administered world. While it insisted on its self-sufficiency and its ability to disclose truths about the world (principally in negative terms), modernism's adversarial impulse also acted as an agent for social change (or resistance to unwanted change).[118]

It hardly matters in this respect whether one understands modernism to be purely æsthetic, or condemns modernism for its failure to be purely æsthetic. Both errors embrace a monistic, emotionalist irrationalism, which does not beg the question but evades it.[119] Subjectivism is not

---

[118] Martin Scherzinger, 'In Memory of a Receding Dialectic: The Political Relevance of Autonomy and Formalism in Modernist Musical Aesthetics,' in *The Pleasure of Modernist Music: Listening, Meaning, Intention, Ideology*, ed. Arved Ashby (University of Rochester Press: Rochester and Woodbridge, 2004), p. 69.

[119] It would be as if the Prussian government's appointment of the ageing Romantic Schelling to the chair of philosophy of Berlin, 'to slay the dragon-seed' of Hegelianism, had succeeded. See, e.g., Warren Breckmann, 'Politics in a Symbolic Key: Pierre Leroux, Romantic Socialism,

enough; its claims to autonomy are severely overstated. History, neither rigidly deterministic nor haplessly arbitrary, will continue to demand recognition. *Parsifal* with all its necessary contradictions stands in this sense as an exemplar and crucible.

Three entries from Cosima's diaries are instructive in this regard, returning us to the legacy of Kant's attempt in the *Critique of Pure Reason* to establish the absolute ideality of time and space. Cosima records in 1880:

> Prof. [Johann Karl Friedrich] Zöllner sends him his book on transcendental physics with a very nice letter, and in this connection R. remarks on how a misunderstanding of Kant and Schopenhauer can lead to such aberrations as the assumption [Zöllner's, which led him to defend the séances of the American psychic, Henry Slade] of a fourth dimension; ideality, he says, is difficult to grasp, and particularly difficult to keep in mind, and people are constantly losing sight of it. 'If Schopenhauer and Kant were really understood, how could new philosophical books possibly keep on emerging?'[120]

New books – and dramas – kept on emerging because there remained many difficulties to be resolved, not least when the writer, even should he refuse to acknowledge this, retained a great influence from Hegel and his school. A couple of months later, we read: 'After breakfast he talks about philosophy and says that Kant found something eternal in his quiet avenue in Königsberg, an ideality of time and space, like Jesus in Galilee: "My Kingdom is not of this world."'[121] The contemporary attempt at reconciliation in *Parsifal* will heighten rather than abjure the countervailing stream in Wagner's thought. Cosima also has Wagner, whilst at work on this drama, announce: 'Today I have set a philosophical precept to music: "Here space becomes time."'[122] It may be on the way to the Castle of the Grail that time becomes space but this is also the arena in which space becomes historical time. Perhaps that offers something for Augustinians and Schopenhauerians alike to ponder.

and the Schelling Affair,' in *Modern Intellectual History*, 2 (2005), 61–86.

[120] *Cosima Wagner's Diaries*, 11 November 1879, vol. 2, p. 392. See Johann Carl Friedrich Zöllner, *Die transcendentale Physik und die sogenannte Philosophie: eine deutsche Antwort auf eine 'sogenannte wissenschaftliche Frage'* (Staackmann: Leipzig, 1879); Tom H. Gibbons, 'Cubism and "The Fourth Dimension" in the Context of the Late Nineteenth-Century and Early Twentieth-Century Revival of Occult Idealism,' in *Journal of the Warburg and Courtauld Institutes*, 44 (1981), 130–47.

[121] *Cosima Wagner's Diaries*, 31 January 1880, vol. 2, p. 434.

[122] Ibid., 21 December 1877, vol. 1, p. 1007. The generally excellent English translation has the inaccurate 'hence space becomes time', for 'hier wird der Raum zur Zeit'. (Cosima Wagner, *Die Tagebücher*, 2 vols (Piper: Munich and Zurich, 1976–7), vol. 1, p. 1098.)

CHAPTER 2

Arnold Schoenberg's 'Biblical Way':
Towards *Moses und Aron*

I

Schoenberg, perhaps even more so than Wagner, conceived of his musical and artistic development as a journey. Perhaps even more so than Wagner, Schoenberg was certain of a goal, if uncertain whether it would or even could be reached. This journey was more a seeking after faith than the following of a trustworthy map. As early as 1909, he wrote to Busoni that interpretation of his recent, atonal compositions demanded 'belief and conviction'. They could only be played by 'someone, who like yourself, takes the side of all who seek'.[1] Such mystical seeking after faith might seem soon to have been outmoded by the more obvious constructivism of his later works, and not only the twelve-note works, but little is ever outmoded in Schoenberg. Instead, the dialectic became more complicated as the search became more intense. Faith and organisation both oppose and necessitate one another, as does their content. Schoenberg's early atonal music has been seen on the one hand as amenable to, indeed dependent on, a set of structural definitions, and on the other as a realm of perhaps unprecedented compositional freedom.[2] In Bryan Simms's words, Schoenberg was keen to experiment 'with ways by which . . . "impressionistic" composing could be folded into a newly "worked out" procedure'.[3] At other stages of Schoenberg's career, 'worked out procedure' might be

[1] Letter of 13 July 1909, in Ferruccio Busoni, *Selected Letters*, tr. and ed. Anthony Beaumont (Columbia University Press: New York, 1987), p. 382. The word 'atonal' is not an unproblematical designation for Schoenberg's works of the period c. 1908–23, yet it is more widely accepted than any other. On these works as a whole, see Bryan A. Simms, *The Atonal Music of Arnold Schoenberg* (Oxford University Press: Oxford, 2000).

[2] See Allen Forte, *The Structure of Atonal Music* (Yale University Press: New Haven, 1973), for an example of the first understanding, and for the latter, George Perle, *Serial Composition and Atonality: An Introduction to the Music of Schoenberg, Berg, and Webern*, 6th edn (University of California Press: Berkeley and Los Angeles, 1991).

[3] Simms, *Atonal Music of Arnold Schoenberg*, p. 162. Simms refers here to Schoenberg's fragmentary Symphony (1914–15), but the same could be said of various works from a similar period, not least *Die Jakobsleiter*.

folded into 'impressionistic' composition, for, as Michael Cherlin has remarked, 'a tendency to think in terms of . . . *dialectical oppositions* is a basic constituent of Schoenberg's creativity'.[4]

This chapter attempts to follow part of Schoenberg's arduous journey. *Moses und Aron* will be our destination, though it certainly does not represent a terminus for the ideas under consideration. Written between 1927 and 1932, *Moses* started life as an oratorio text, which was then transformed into the libretto for an opera.[5] Notwithstanding Schoenberg's continual insistence upon his intention of completion, the work remained unfinished, the only music for the third act amounting to a few sketches. Only the first two acts of the work are usually performed, although the composer sanctioned the possibility of presenting the final act in spoken form. Indeed, there are actually two versions of this final act, the first slightly longer, though Schoenberg seems to have considered the second superior. The work has generally been performed without the third act, although there have been attempts to stage it, either in a spoken presentation, or with other music by Schoenberg. Hermann Scherchen's 1959 performances in Berlin had the third act spoken against a recording of music from Act I. This is not generally considered to have been an experiment worth repeating. The final version of the text and the music were written during the three years 1930–2: that is, just before the Nazi seizure of power and Schoenberg's constructive dismissal from his chair in Berlin. On 1 March 1933, at a meeting of the senate of the Berlin Akademie der Künste, the Akademie's president, Max von Schillings, announced the government's intention to rid the Akademie of Jewish influence. Schoenberg walked out and treated this announcement as his dismissal, although this did not come into effect until October, in breach of his contract which should have guaranteed him employment for two more years. At the time, Schoenberg was still officially Christian. However, after his flight from Germany, he would publicly re-convert to Judaism as a mark of solidarity – and a mark of something more than that too.

The work as we know it dates from the late 1920s, yet its roots extend deep into the previous two decades. Before considering some of the more immanent issues with respect to Schoenberg's drama itself, it would there-

---

[4]   Michael Cherlin, 'Dialectical Opposition in Schoenberg's Music and Thought', in *Music Theory Spectrum*, 22 (2000), 157.

[5]   As Daniel Albright mordantly observes, surveying musico-dramatic appearances of Moses, he 'was always more at home in oratorio than in opera, where his lack of a dramatic sex life was a handicap'. ('Butchering Moses', in *The Opera Quarterly*, 23 (2007), 441).

fore be helpful to say something about his intellectual and spiritual path, with particular reference to two earlier works: the unfinished oratorio *Die Jakobsleiter*, or 'Jacob's Ladder', and the spoken drama *Der biblische Weg*, 'The Biblical Way'. To follow this path is not simply better to understand its outcome, for the path itself is of intrinsic importance. It may be summarised in general terms as leading from religious syncretism via Zionism to negative monotheism, strongly influenced by both Schoenberg's German (Lutheran) inheritance and his Judaism. The interplay between these two influences is both problematical and productive, the latter coming increasingly to the fore though never exclusively so. I therefore seek to examine the fraught path towards negative monotheism as shaped by Schoenberg's Lutheran–Judaic dialectic. Such is Schoenberg's own 'Biblical Way'.

Like Kant's Categorical Imperative, Schoenberg's path may be formulated in more than one fashion, for the technical and the theological are inextricably intertwined. Both formulations of Schoenberg's path, that from religious syncretism towards negative monotheism, and that centred upon the dialectic between freedom and organisation, will be examined, as part of the claim that they are ultimately one and the same. The former lays greater stress upon the goal, the latter upon the journey, but this is somewhat misleading, for the goal is never reached and yet is always present; any difference is perspectival rather than fundamental. For Schoenberg, both formulations lead towards a higher form of spiritual awareness, in which the Idea – that most problematical yet truly fundamental concept in his thought – may be perceived.[6] The 'unrepresentable God' of the opening quotation is, as Schoenberg identifies, also the 'inexpressible Idea of many meanings'. And yet, the attempt to express the unity of that Idea remains Schoenberg's goal throughout the works considered here.

II

Schoenberg wrote the text to *Die Jakobsleiter* between 1915 and 1917, and partially composed the music between 1917 and 1922. He worked further on the score, albeit briefly, in 1944.[7] Here Schoenberg essayed a work which, taking as its starting point Genesis 28 vv. 12–23, refers and alludes to exotic, heterodox religious ideas, including reincarnation, theosophy, and Swedenborgian mysticism. This New Jerusalem does not reject the old Jerusalem, but challenges its claims to exclusivity. A specific

[6] See John Covach, 'The Sources of Schoenberg's Aesthetic Theology,' in *19th-Century Music*, 19 (1996), 252–62.
[7] Winfried Zillig, in his performing version, generally follows Schoenberg's 1944 revisions.

inspiration was the vision of Swedenborg's heaven at the end of Balzac's novella, *Séraphîta*, a tale of illness, redemption, and finally ascension – and an elitist tale at that. 'None but the loftier spirits open to faith can discern Jacob's mystical stair,' writes Balzac.[8] The necessity of faith and the emphasis upon an initiate journey of ascent could hardly have failed to appeal to Schoenberg. His knowledge of Swedenborg apparently came more via Balzac than directly from the mystic; many pages of the single volume of Swedenborg in Schoenberg's library were uncut.[9] Nevertheless, its presence suggests that this was something he considered he *ought* to read, or at least to have to hand.

Schoenberg wrote in 1940 of how the dawn of talking pictures had led him to hope for an artistic renaissance, which needless to say had never occurred:

> I had dreamed of a dramatisation of Balzac's *Seraphita* [to which a few bars were actually composed in 1912], or Strindberg's *To Damascus*, or the second part of Goethe's *Faust*, or even Wagner's *Parsifal*. All of these works, by renouncing the law of 'unity of space and time' would have found the solution to realisation in sound pictures. But the industry continued to satisfy only the needs and demands of the ordinary people who filled their theatres.[10]

Renunciation of the dramatic unities of space and time also suggested to Schoenberg, as we shall see, a sphere outside of space and time, which chimed strongly with his knowledge of Wagner and Schopenhauer. It was not a great step beyond Gurnemanz's invitation to the castle of the Grail, 'You see, my son, time here becomes space,' to Schopenhauer's Will, which lay beyond the Kantian cognitive forms of space, time, and causality; nor was it a great step beyond *that* to transform the Will, the one enduring force in Schopenhauer's philosophy, into the one truly eternal force in Schoenberg's oratorio.

Outlining his intentions in a letter of 1912 to Richard Dehmel, Schoenberg wrote:

> For a long time, I have wanted to write an oratorio with the following content: how the man of today, having passed through materialism, socialism, and anarchy, and having been an atheist, has still retained a tiny remnant of the

---

[8]   Honoré de Balzac, *Séraphîta*, tr. Clara Bell (Dedalus: Sawtry and New York, 1989), p. 123.
[9]   Clara Steuermann, 'From the Archives: Schoenberg's Library Catalogue,' in *Journal of the Arnold Schoenberg Institute*, 3 (1979), 203–18.
[10] Arnold Schoenberg, 'Art and the Moving Pictures,' in *Style and Idea*, ed. Leonard Stein, with translations by Leo Black (Faber: London, 1975), p. 154. Schoenberg omits the accents from *Séraphîta*, as does the German translation he owned.

old belief (in the form of superstition), how this modern man wrestles with God (see also: Strindberg's *Jacob Wrestling*), and finally succeeds in finding God and becoming religious. Learning to pray! *Not* through action, blows of fate, still less a love-story, shall this transformation come about. Or at least these should be at most background hints, providing impetus. And above all: the mode of speech, the mode of thought, the mode of expression, should be that of modern man; the problems addressed should be those besetting us. For those who wrestle with God in the Bible also express themselves as men of their own time, speaking of their own concerns, upon their own social and intellectual level. Therefore, artistically strong though they may be, they do not lend themselves to a modern composer who observes his duty.[11]

Schoenberg claims, then, that an historical impasse has been reached; various solutions have been attempted, for instance socialism and materialism. In connection with the former, Malcolm Macdonald's view that, 'although Schoenberg was genuinely interested n socialist ideas at this period [his youth], it was probably more as an ideal of human conduct than a politically attainable goal', seems judicious.[12] It might be added that the 'religious' and 'ethical' thus already tended to determine the 'political' in his world-view. Moreover, Schoenberg always rejected materialism in terms of the contrast he drew with spiritualism.[13] None, then, of the 'solutions' proposed in the letter has worked, yet a residue of ancient faith, if only in superstitious form, has remained to be built upon. The idea is less reactionary than it might sound when one considers the syncretic nature of the work's message, for newer doctrines appear to contribute to the possibilities of the present, just as in Swedenborg's pretended revelation. For both Swedenborg and Schoenberg, creation remains incomplete without man; one might say the same of the Bible, or indeed of Haydn's oratorio, *The Creation*. Moreover, without man's second or spiritual creation, he is incomplete. And, indeed, the historico-theological situation is similar to the musico-historical situation. Schoenberg detested the negative term 'atonality', preferring if necessary 'pantonality': drawing upon all keys rather than none. His musical language and his music more generally were to advance not by means of a rupture with a past but in a developmental understanding of progress, in which drawing upon the structural organisation principles of Bach and Brahms was as important, indeed as progressive, as moving beyond Wagner's chromaticism.

[11] 13 December 1912, in Arnold Schoenberg, *Briefe*, ed. Erwin Stein (Schott: Mainz, 1958), p. 31.

[12] Malcom Macdonald, *Schoenberg* (Oxford University Press: New York, 2008), p. 32.

[13] See Jean Christensen, 'The Spiritual and Material in Schoenberg's Thinking', in *Music and Letters*, 65 (1984), 337–44.

Nineteenth-century socialism had represented at least as much an attempt to found or to reinvent a religion as to address economic developments. Schoenberg could therefore see it as a creed which fell short and which could yet be reincorporated into a valid modern conception of truth. As he would recall:

> In my early twenties, I had friends who introduced me to Marxian theories. When I therefore had jobs as *Chormeister* – director of men's choruses – they called me 'Genosse' – comrade, and at this time, when the Social Democrats fought for an extension of the right of suffrage, I was strongly in sympathy with some of their aims.
>
> But before I was twenty-five, I had already discovered the difference between me and a labourer; I then found out that I was a *bourgeois* and turned away from all political contacts.

It would not be surprising to find a touch of exaggeration in a declaration from McCarthyite America – he ends, truthfully, 'I was never a communist' – but the progression outlined is accurate in moving away from socialism even if not towards political quietism.[14]

Continuing with the quotation from Schoenberg's letter, we see prayer exalted over 'action, blows of fate, ... a love-story'. One might see various writers rejected or found insufficient here, including Goethe, Wagner, Marx, and Mahler; or at least, they are found insufficient. There is no Eternal Feminine drawing us on upwards, no *Parsifal*-like redemption to the redeemer in whatever guise, no revolution, whether Marxist or Wagnerian. Instead, there is God, a representation not wholly dissimilar from the syncretic vision of Mahler's Eighth Symphony: its first part a setting of the Whitsun hymn, *Veni creator spiritus*, its second a setting of the final scene of Goethe's *Faust* (Part II). The two parts are intimately connected, musically and philosophically. Schoenberg's 1911 tribute to Mahler is instructive:

> everything which will characterise him is already present in the First Symphony ... Here are his devotion to nature and his thoughts of death. He is still struggling with fate here, but in the Sixth he acknowledges it, and this acknowledgement is resignation. But even resignation becomes productive, and rises, in the Eighth, to the glorification of the highest joys, to a glorification only possible to one who already knows that these joys are no longer for him; who has already resigned himself; who already feels that they are merely an allegory for even higher joys, a glorification of the most supreme bliss, as he also expresses it verbally in the letter to his wife where he explains the final scenes of *Faust*:

---

[14] Schoenberg, 'My Attitude towards Politics,' in *Style and Idea*, pp. 505–6.

'... The Eternal Feminine has drawn us upward – we are there – we are at rest – we possess what we on earth could only long for, strive for ...'

That is one way to reach the goal! Not just with the understanding, but with the feeling that one already lives there *oneself*. He who looks on the earth thus no longer lives upon it. He has already been drawn upwards.[15]

Thus, in Mahler's and Schoenberg's presentations, they have already gone beyond Goethe and his Eternal Feminine. Jennifer Shaw therefore writes of the androgyny – albeit sometimes unsuccessful – of Schoenberg's oratorio.[16] But there is a theological point here too. The Eternal Feminine is a staging post towards a state at which we shall need no more representation; the question is whether what remains real and eternal can ever be represented. On the eve of the First World War, Schoenberg had planned a large, post-Mahlerian choral symphony, which would have set Biblical passages, and poems by Dehmel and Rabindranath Tagore (the latter, naturally, in translation). Dehmel's dual-sexed, 'bürgerlich' god, the union of a father-spirit and a mother-soul, is ultimately rejected in favour of Tagore's neutral god of quasi-nothingness.[17] That should be understood in theological as well as sexual terms: Schoenberg already edges away from a representation of divinity, without yet considering this 'failure' tragic or indeed really a 'failure' at all. An interesting precedent is provided for *Die Jakobsleiter*, in which everything, even resignation – for which read Schopenhauer, perhaps Wagner, and certainly the difficulty of representation – feeds into the drawing upwards. To borrow from Nietzsche, this is Schoenberg saying 'yes'.

One final point to be made from Schoenberg's letter to Dehmel: he emphasises the contemporary duty of his enterprise, which will not be lost in subsequent works. The false immediacy of idolatry is a problem ancient and modern. In *Die Jakobsleiter*, each petitioner passing before the Archangel Gabriel considers that he has a special reason for consideration, be it his calling, his rebellion, his struggle, his election, his monastic life, or his death. All of these reasons, whilst setting the petitioners above the materialist multitude, still rely too much upon the 'material' as opposed to the 'spiritual'. Schoenberg's idealist insistence upon an absolute distinction

[15] Schoenberg, 'Gustav Mahler', in *Style and Idea*, pp. 469–70. Cf. letter of June 1909 in Alma Mahler, *Gustav Mahler: Memories and Letters*, tr. Basil Creighton, ed. Donald Mitchell, 3rd edn (John Murray: London, 1973), p. 321.

[16] Jennifer Shaw, 'Androgyny and the Eternal Feminine in *Die Jakobsleiter*', in *Political and Religious Ideas in the Works of Arnold Schoenberg*, ed. Charlotte M. Cross and Russell A. Berman (Garland: New York and London, 2000), pp. 61–76.

[17] Ibid., pp. 64–5

between mind and matter is starkly dramatised here. And so, each petitioner is rejected, requiring transformation and ultimately serial rebirth. (The latter occurs in the second part of Schoenberg's text, never set to music, but he thought highly enough of the libretto to publish it independently, in 1917.) The exchange between Gabriel and the first petitioner, 'One who is Called', contains the only music in the oratorio which could be considered tonal. Steven J. Cahn goes so far as to describe this petitioner as representing the nineteenth-century artist.[18] Bryan Simms connects his *credo* of beauty above all with music imitative of the late-Romantic style, 'a great aria for *Heldentenor*', no less.[19] One who is Called is concomitantly rebuked for favouring beauty over truth: that is, for idolatry: 'You are self-satisfied: your idol [*dein Götze*] grants you fulfilment, before you, *like those who seek* [my emphasis], have tasted the torments of longing... You, heathen, have beheld nothing.' The contrast with Schoenberg's approbation of Busoni, cited at the beginning of this chapter – 'someone, who like yourself, takes the side of all who seek' – is clear. In Schopenhauerian terms, Heaven is Will, not representation. 'When you return,' Gabriel tells One who is Dying, 'leave your lamenting behind you. When you no longer lament, you will be nearer. Then shall your ego be extinguished.' Egoism is another form of idolatry, of substituting something else for truth.

Considered collectively, we might profitably compare the souls in *Die Jakobsleiter* with those of Mahler's Second Symphony, especially its final movement.[20] Both works are concerned with spatial effects, employing off-stage instruments to evoke the apocalyptical. Moreover, they share a sense of a march towards something, Mahler's symphony explicitly evoking the Last Judgement, portraying confusion but not terror. Belief here is operative: 'O believe, my heart,' the contralto urges, 'o believe, nothing of you will be lost!' This is Mahler's not entirely orthodox way to resurrection. Schoenberg's mystical vision is less Christian, more obscure, and incomplete. There is movement towards something, yet that something is far less easily defined, and only in part because the work is unfinished. Whilst there is no resurrection, there is judgement. Yet, whilst each soul fails to pass muster, it will be given another chance, through rebirth.

---

[18] Steven J. Cahn, 'The Artist as Modern Prophet: A Study of Historical Consciousness and its expression in Schoenberg's "Vorgefühl," Op. 22 no. 4,' in *Schoenberg and Words: The Modernist Years*, ed. Charlotte M. Cross and Russell A. Berman (Garland: New York and London, 2000), p. 246.

[19] Simms, *Atonal Music of Arnold Schoenberg*, p. 170.

[20] For an illuminating comparison between the programmes of this Mahler symphony and Schoenberg's projected six-movement symphony, see ibid., pp. 154–6.

Schoenberg was already associating ultimate truth with oneness, even at a stage when religious exploration was more important to him than orthodoxy. This is exemplified not only by the somewhat obscure unity of the souls' final goal, something ineffably divine lying beyond the extinction of ego, but also by his compositional method. The 'cello ostinato – C sharp, D, F, E, G sharp, G – (Ex. 1) with which the work begins is a hexachord from which Schoenberg creates many of the work's motifs.

Ex. 1. *Die Jakobsleiter* hexachord

Looking back in 1948 – there seems no reason to suspect his hind-sight – Schoenberg wrote that he 'had contrived the plan to provide for unity – which was always my main motive: to build all the main themes of the whole oratorio from a row of six' notes. Moreover, the remaining six notes 'entered gradually, one in every measure', until all twelve had been sounded. Schoenberg may have exaggerated when he spoke of this as 'a real twelve-tone composition'.[21] For one thing, the hexachord is not used as an ordered series; the work's musical themes are derived from it by reordering the six notes. Nevertheless, as Ethan Haimo remarks, this is 'a critical conceptual stage in the development of the serial idea. It indicates Schoenberg's interest in forging unity by relating disparate events back to one referential origin'.[22] Indeed, as Haimo has pointed out elsewhere, it was, for Schoenberg, no accident that systematic manipulation of numbers produced musically meaningful relationships, but 'rather confirmation not only that the universe was ordered but, more important, that numbers and music together play an essential role in expressing that order'.[23] Moreover, Schoenberg remains interested in the relationship between space and time, understood here in musical terms by an initial approximation in expansion of the work's horizontal and vertical dimensions. This is not maintained throughout, but may be heard very clearly in bars 6–9, where, to quote Haimo, 'the simultaneities created between the moving voices are vertical statements of the very hexachord that appears as a line in each

[21] Schoenberg, 'Composition with Twelve Tones (2)', in *Style and Idea*, p. 247.
[22] Ethan Haimo, *Schoenberg's Serial Odyssey: The Evolution of his Twelve-Tone Method, 1914–1928* (Oxford University Press: Oxford, 1990), p. 67.
[23] Ethan Haimo, 'Schoenberg, Numerology, and *Moses und Aron*', in *The Opera Quarterly*, 23 (2007), 393.

of the moving voices'.[24] Triplet teeming of life on woodwind instruments and violas puts one in mind of two earlier creative proliferation from initial unity in the 'Representation of Chaos' from Haydn's *Creation* and, closer to home, the Prelude to *Das Rheingold*. However, the initial unity is more readily apparent in those works, in that both begin with unisons, whereas for Schoenberg there is already a difficulty, bordering upon the idolatrous, in such musical representation.

And so, in terms of thematic content both religious and musical, there is very much a sense, and not only in retrospect, of being part of the way on a journey. This path takes us from a putative unified origin that appears to promise a further, dialectical unity ahead. Whether that goal will ever be reached is a moot point, but the journey depends upon the goal. Equivocal optimism has replaced the blazing triumph of Mahler's Second Symphony, yet there remains at least the possibility of redemption, which will contrast with the tragedy of *Moses und Aron*. Before turning to Schoenberg's *magnum opus*, we should profit, however, from considering the intervening years in his development; it is worth reiterating that the path itself is as important as the destination, which remains tantalisingly out of reach.

III

The First World War and its aftermath proved a cultural as well as a political watershed for many Europeans. Dreams of universal brotherhood were not necessarily dead, but they would never be quite the same again. This was brought home to Schoenberg in very clear terms in the summer of 1921. He and his family were forced to leave Mattsee, the town in which they had a holiday retreat, now held by its inhabitants to be restricted to Aryans. Thereafter, Schoenberg's assertion of Jewish identity and his prescient conviction that the Jews would soon be confronted by unprecedented acts of violence intensified. This is witnessed by an angry letter to Kandinsky, provoked by reports of anti-Semitism at the Bauhaus:

> Why do people say that the Jews are like their black-marketeers?
> Do people also say that the Aryans are like their worst elements? Why is an Aryan judged by Goethe, Schopenhauer, and the like? Why do people not say the Jews are like Mahler, Altenberg, Schoenberg and many others?
> ...
> You will call it an unfortunate individual case if I too am affected by the results of the anti-Semitic movement. But why do people not see the bad Jew

---

[24] Haimo, *Schoenberg's Serial Odyssey*, p. 67.

as an unfortunate individual case, but rather as typical?[25]

If the Jews were not part of European civilisation, then there was all the more reason for them to look to themselves and to their own history and culture – and to their own God. *Völkisch* nationalism could work both ways.

Just after having fled Berlin, Schoenberg wrote that *Der biblische Weg* presented a 'contemporary version (written 1926–27) of the Jews becoming a people'.[26] In many respects, Schoenberg and the Freud of *Moses and Monotheism* diverged greatly. Yet here there is common ground. Freud in the 1930s saw the tradition of a 'great past' as having inspired the Jews to reawaken the abandoned monotheistic religion of Moses.[27] Schoenberg saw the necessity for this to happen once again; it was clear to him from quite an early stage that politics, and liberal politics in particular, would not be enough to save the Jews, any more than liberal politics could save Germany from the catastrophe of National Socialism. This might seem closer already to *Moses und Aron* than to the religious syncretism of *Die Jakobsleiter*, but it is worth noting the connection between the role of Moses and the prophetic mission handed to the 'Chosen One' in *Die Jakobsleiter*. 'Here you have eye and ear,' Gabriel tells him, and proceeds to speak of the wonderful gift of being able, like the Most High, to reveal oneself in the smallest things. Moreover, the Chosen One's music displays significant intimations of twelve-note writing.[28] Schoenberg, like Wagner, tended to 'follow on' from previous works and to use their successors as ways of exploring the questions begged by their dramatic and technical presentation. As we read in Schoenberg's Mahler tribute: 'Only on closer study does one perceive in the potentialities of the earlier period the certainties of the later one.'[29]

The play, *Der biblische Weg*, itself deals more explicitly with contemporaneous issues than *Die Jakobsleiter* or *Moses*; it would not be exaggerated to speak of an agitprop drama, dedicated to mobilisation of the Jews. It

[25] 4 May 1923, in Schoenberg, *Briefe*, pp. 91–2.

[26] Letter to Jakob Klatzkin of 26 May 1933, in ibid., p. 197. The text and an English translation by Moshe Lazar may be found in *Journal of the Arnold Schoenberg Institute*, 17 (1994), 162–330; the former is reproduced at: <http://www.usc.edu/isd/archives/schoenberg/bibliweg.htm>.

[27] Sigmund Freud, 'Moses and Monotheism,' in *The Origins of Religion. Totem and Taboo, Moses and Monotheism, and Other Works*, tr. James Strachey *et al.*, ed. Albert Dickson (Penguin: Harmondsworth, 1985), p. 312.

[28] See Fusako Hamao, 'The Origin and Development of Schoenberg's Twelve-Tone Method' (Ph.D. dissertation, Yale University, 1988), pp. 38–75.

[29] Schoenberg, 'Gustav Mahler,' p. 468.

has been aptly termed an '"unhistorical history play," a characteristically modern form which, in examples such as Hofmannsthal's *Der Turm* and Brecht's *Mutter Courage*, employs the conventions drawn from earlier historical drama to simulate a representation of history'.[30] One should not exaggerate the 'unhistorical' aspect, for the history plays of Shakespeare or Schiller would be found wanting as historical accounts. In Schoenberg's play, the great events of Israel's history are all present, albeit at a slight remove. Despite its title and unlike *Moses*, this drama is not given a Biblical setting. Instead, we find ourselves first in 1920s Europe, that is the present day, and subsequently in an African New Palestine, a successful version of Theodor Herzl's Ugandan project, as a prelude to a return to the true Promised Land. The second location presents a corollary to the Jews' forty years in the wilderness (the location of *Moses*, albeit, as we shall see, at a considerable level of abstraction). Prophecy is crucial here, but in this case it focuses upon the concrete goal of a Jewish state in Palestine, which would fulfil 'the strict, unadulterated, relentless Idea, that there is only one, eternal, invisible, and unimaginable God'. These are the words of its hero, Max Aruns, described by his Orthodox antagonist, David Asseino, as wanting to be 'Moses and Aron in the same person'. We saw Schoenberg earlier speak of his plans for *Die Jakobsleiter* in terms of treating with 'modern man, [who] having passed through materialism, socialism, and anarchy, and despite having been an atheist, still having in him some residue of ancient faith'. Here we witness the leader's attempt to unify the diverse Jewish interests: 'orthodox and assimilationist, socialist and capitalist'. The combination of Idea and deed, Moses and Aron, in one man brings about his failure, but also confuses the dramatic distinction, at least when compared with the opera to come. Aruns insists that 'Moses and Aron represent two activities of *one* man – a *statesman*, whose two souls ignore each other's existence. The purity of his Idea is not blurred by his public action; and these actions are not weakened by his thoughtful consideration of yet unsolved problems that the Idea presents.' He is wrong, however – not that Asseino, who believes that the Jews can enter the new promised land without further wandering in the desert wilderness, has right on his side either. Nevertheless, the monotheistic Idea survives. When Aruns lies dying, he recognises his hubris, addressing God:

> Lord, thou hast smitten me. Thus I have brought it upon myself. Thus Asseino was right, when he accused me of being presumptuous, of wanting to be Moses

---

[30] Herbert Lindenberger, 'Arnold Schoenberg's "Der Biblische Weg" and "Moses und Aron": On the Transactions of Aesthetics and Politics,' in *Modern Judaism*, 9 (1989), 58.

and Aron in one person. Thus I have betrayed the Idea... I am dying, but I feel
that thou wilt allow the Idea to survive. And I shall die in peace, for I know that
thou wilt always provide our nation with men ready to offer their lives for this
concept of the one and only, eternal, invisible, and unimaginable God. (*dies*)

Thus politics seem to have brought us back to the necessity of theology.
Indeed, the repetition of Aruns's final words by the Joshua-like Guido
prepares us for Schoenberg's explicit 'following on' in *Moses und Aron*.
These last words are the first words of his opera. What the spoken drama
has not attested to, though Schoenberg's own practice would, is the
necessity of reintroducing music. Partly this is a product of Schoenberg
being first and foremost a composer; he could no more have become a
mere verbal dramatist than Wagner. Yet music also appeared to vouchsafe
the possibility of remaining steadfast to the Idea, of sacrificing one's life
in more than a political sense, to that unimaginable God. The more
'difficult' his music became for the public – or so, at least the public
believed, for often it disdained actually to listen to the music – the more
absolute became the necessity for Schoenberg to express himself musically. This creative dilemma is not only akin to but also in some sense an
historical representation of the original impossibility of Creation. For
God, the Unrepresentable, commands His own representation. Might it
be possible that music and Schoenberg's music in particular – or at least
Schoenberg's music drama – could deal better than mere words with this
ultimate paradox? In its lack of historical specificity, might 'spiritual' or
metaphysical music, like myth, actually become both more specific and
more abstract than the signification of mere words, let alone the easy
seduction of all-too-material images?

IV

The turn from modern play to timeless myth should not be understood
in the sense of Schoenberg turning his back upon the present; rather, the
problem has become more theological and less programmatically political.
Schoenberg heeds Wagner's celebrated claim that what is 'incomparable
about myth is that it is true at all times and its content, by virtue of poetic
compression, is inexhaustible for all times.'[31] As Walter Benjamin would
observe, the sequence of ceremonial images forming the nucleus of tragic
myth is not the stuff of historical drama: 'In tragedy, every simple yet
incalculably profound interpretation of the saga material is capable of

[31] Richard Wagner, *Oper und Drama*, ed. Klaus Kropfinger (Reclam: Stuttgart, 1994), p. 199.

damaging the mythic world order and of undermining it prophetically with unassuming words.' The more ancient a given subject might be, 'and the more it has been worked on, the more it becomes the object of poetry, as opposed to the pretext for it'.[32] Whereas the Enlightenment had tended to attack mythical barbarism, the Romantics had taught Wagner, Nietzsche, and Schoenberg that myth was in fact a necessary route to self-knowledge. The Enlightenment view leads ultimately to the ultra-realist disparagement of all art, which perforce remains mere imitation, if not pathology or phantasmagoria, ever falling short of the 'original' reality. As Schoenberg became ever more wary of representation, his employment of myth strengthened his neo-Romantic defence against such anti-art realism.

Despite the extreme difficulties Schoenberg imposed upon himself, this is definitely an opera, a *Gesamtkunstwerk* even, not the concert-work originally conceived. Concert performances can work very well, as can concert performances of almost any opera, but that is not to posit them as an ideal. Having previously conducted the work in concert for the BBC, Boulez was interviewed after his staged performances in Amsterdam and Salzburg. He commented:

> People always say that it's not an opera but an oratorio, which Schoenberg later turned into an opera. That interested me, because I disagree with it. The chorus, for example, is the most important character in the opera. It's like a chameleon, speaking for or against, sometimes even internally divided or emphatic in its support of one particular party; it is angry, it is docile, it comments on the action.[33]

The chorus might be likened to its counterpart in the Bach Passions, which is often regarded as the most important character, and ultimately to the chorus of Greek tragedy, especially that of Euripides; for there is a limited sense, which Moses fails to appreciate, in which the opera chorus gains some understanding of God's message through reception of its dual interpretations by Moses *and* Aron.

Of course, Bach's Passions are not operas, despite criticism in Bach's day of them as too 'operatic'. Yet, like *Moses*, they are dramas that draw

---

[32] Walter Benjamin, 'Calderón's "El Mayor Monstruo," "Los Celos," and Hebbel's "Herodes und Mariamne". Comments on the Problem of Historical Drama,' tr. Rodney Livingstone, in *Selected Writings*, ed. Michael W. Jennings *et al.*, 4 vols (Harvard University Press: Cambridge, MA, 1996–2003), vol. 1, pp. 365–6.

[33] 'Boulez on Schoenberg's "Moses und Aron". An Interview with Wolfgang Schaufler,' tr. Stewart Spencer, in booklet accompanying Deutsche Grammophon CD 449 174–2, p. 14.

their strength from orthodoxy, rather than rebel against its constraint. By contrast, Mahler's symphonies had represented a humanistic triumph against externally imposed restrictions, whether political, religious, or æsthetic. Likewise, in *Die Jakobsleiter*, the goal had been a never-composed vision of æthereal freedom, in which off-stage orchestras would vouchsafe us a glimpse of eternal peace. Even the torso prepared for performance after Schoenberg's death by his pupil, Winfried Zillig, grants us that impression. The 'Great Symphonic Interlude' with which the performing version comes to an end draws us onwards and upwards via instruments and female voices, but without words, until petering out on the stratospheric verge of vocal impossibility with a soprano high C. When publishing the text, Schoenberg himself described the interlude as expressing 'the tableaux and scenes that follow in place of words', encouraging us to understand the 'incompletion' as part of the work proper. The Eternal-Feminine, should this be it, remains some way from the ultimate, perhaps unreachable goal. Zillig wrote:

> Strangely enough, the conclusion of the 'Jacob's Ladder' fragment is one of the most impressive endings in the whole of Occidental music. Schoenberg's invention of sounds floating in space does in fact lead to new regions. The enchantment is complete despite the fragmentary character. Indeed, one cannot help thinking that this strange and unique enchantment arises directly from the work's unfinished state; for such a work, given its intellectual premise, can provide only an incomplete answer in view of mankind's limitations when facing the eternal.[34]

In June 1922, shortly before he gave up work on the music, Schoenberg opened a new sketchbook by writing on the cover: 'Mit Gott'. He still hoped to reach that stage of unity, just as he would in the third act of *Moses*.

Bach and the later Schoenberg share this uncompromising 'view of mankind's limitations when facing the eternal', but confront this through insistence upon the necessity of constraint; nowhere is this more evident than in the law-giving properties of Schoenberg's twelve-note method of composition. Echoes of the Mosaic law, of Kantian radical autonomy, and of Bach's musical organisation resound. Not for nothing did Schoenberg, pointing to the B minor fugue from the first book of the *Well-Tempered Clavier*, call Bach 'the first composer with twelve tones'. Nor was it for nothing that he insisted that Bach, like Moses, was 'only the mouthpiece of

---

[34] Bayerischer Rundfunk: Konzerte mit Neuer Musik, 14 (1963), p. 20, quoted in Rudolph Stephan, 'Editor's Preface', to Arnold Schoenberg, *Die Jakobsleiter*, ed. Winfried Zillig, revised ed. Rudolph Stephan (Universal Edition: Vienna, 1980).

a power which dictates what to do'. The *Art of Fugue* was a miracle, 'which no human power can produce'.[35] The 'style', and questionable style at that, of the neo-classicists' Bach was for Schoenberg triumphantly refuted by the 'idea' of Schoenberg's Bach in the celebrated B-A-C-H- statement of the finale to the *Variations for Orchestra*, op. 31. As Arnold Whittall has remarked: 'It certainly did not escape Schoenberg's notice that Bach's name was embedded in his own (if his initial "A" is included), and so in a sense op. 31 culminates with a double signature, and a very direct homage to a great tradition.'[36] Perhaps more tellingly still, neo-classicism's idolatrous – indeed, Hindemith notwithstanding, un-German – veneration of pseudo-Baroque style at the expense of the musical Idea could be countered in the construction of a large-scale musico-dramatic work, whose teeming thematic proliferation could all be traced back to a single twelve-note row. If Bach were to be the prophet, Schoenberg, not Stravinsky, would be the anointed successor, ever intent upon expression of the Idea.

Many would now contest the view Schoenberg presents of Bach the pedagogical saint, but it is emphatically Schoenberg's Bach. In a drama concerned with the antinomy between appearance and reality, and yet which places itself so emphatically in – at the end of? – a tradition dependent upon that very distinction, we witness conflict between an unattainable, even undesirable 'Bach as he really was' and the sainted, progressive 'Bach as we re-create him'.[37] Every bar in *Moses*, every note even, is derived from the initial note-row, just as everything ultimately must come from the Eternal One. As Webern put it, 'To develop everything . . . from *one* principal idea! That's the strongest unity . . . But in what form? That's where art comes in!'[38] Law and creation are two sides of the same coin; yet, is it given to man to create? It seems that the astonishing variety of expression, from the hushed tones of the Burning Bush to the depravity of the Golden Calf Orgy, could only come forth from such strict organisation. Such is the Unity of Creation. Only through this increasingly draconian system can autonomy be maintained, as we have seen prefigured in Schoenberg's plan to derive all of the music in *Die Jakobsleiter* from a row of six notes: halfway to Moses, as it were. The

[35] Schoenberg, 'Bach,' in *Style and Idea*, pp. 393, 396.
[36] Arnold Whittall, 'Schoenberg: "Erwartung", etc.,' in booklet accompanying EMI CDC 55212 2: 7.
[37] See Mark Berry, 'Romantic Modernism: Bach, Furtwängler, and Adorno,' in *New German Critique*, 104, vol. 35 no. 2 (Spring/Summer 2008), 71–102.
[38] Anton Webern, *The Path to the New Music*, ed. Willi Reich, tr. Leo Black (Presser: London, 1963), p. 35.

unity is greater in *Moses*. As Haimo points out, the accompaniment in *Die Jakobsleiter* frequently has little or nothing to do with the hexachord, and there are lengthy stretches of music in which no themes or motifs derived from the hexachord appear at all.[39]

However, in *Moses*, the stricter organisation is also accompanied by a mystical remove; here, unlike in *Die Jakobsleiter*, the row (Ex. 2) is not employed thematically. Indeed, like God Himself, it is ever present in its ordering capacity but rarely heard 'whole'. The ability to partition notes between different voices had granted Schoenberg's twelve-note technique not only the requisite initial unity but also creative variety. As the row moved into the compositional – and auditory – background, its grip could be exerted over greater stretches of music: such, again, is the Schoenbergian dialectic between freedom and organisation. In *Moses*, it is not until the second scene that the row is presented in linear fashion in a single voice, and that is upon Aron's appearance (Ex. 3), perhaps suggesting something idolatrous about thematic understanding or employment of a row.

Ex. 2. *Moses und Aron* primary note-row

Ex. 3. Aron's entrance: use of row thematically

That is not Moses' way. For the most part, creation, in both a musical and a theological sense, appears both already to have taken place and to be ongoing; to pin it down would be akin to blasphemy.

[39] Ethan Haimo, 'The Evolution of the Twelve-Note Method,' in *The Schoenberg Companion*, ed. Walter Bailey (Greenwood Press: Westport, CT, and London, 1998), p. 109.

V

The miracle of which Schoenberg spoke with reference to Bach could not be produced by any human power, but rather by the terrifying nameless presence in the Burning Bush with which *Moses* opens. As Franz Werfel wrote in a sixtieth birthday tribute (1934) to Schoenberg:

> In Arnold Schoenberg's personality and art, we revere above all the relentless striving after the absolute ... this master of music perhaps most closely resembles the old masters of the cabbala. As they attempted, through the 'Sanctification of the Name', to draw the Divine into the earthly realm, so Arnold Schoenberg attempts, through the sanctification of the artwork, that is, through the elimination of all impure secondary goals (effect, success, accessibility), to draw the absolute into the world of tones.[40]

There is already a problem of representation, which will only be intensified as the work proceeds. Adorno summarises the problem of using what seem to be autonomous musical structures, which yet remain the product of subjective intention:

> If the text creates the theological scandal of speaking of the One God as the idea [*Gedanken*], then this is a scandal that is duplicated in the texture of the music, though rendered almost unrecognisable by the power of the art. The absolute which this music sets out to make real, without any sleight of hand, it achieves as its own idea of itself: it is itself an image of something about images – the very last thing the story wanted.[41]

Schoenberg at the opening comes perilously close to representing God, at least musically, although the abstract 'Voice' – in fact, a chorus and six solo voices – does not appear on stage. Indeed, for that brief introduction prior to the curtain's rise, we have pure song, set to the vowel 'O' rather than human language. Pamela White remarks: 'The humming energy of the opening wordless chords represents God's own self,' yet 'as soon as interaction with the human world and Moses takes place, the chordal singing sonority of the six-voice choir is combined with a rustling *Sprechstimme* choir not heard before'.[42] Music, it seems, may permit a divine presence that could never be staged, yet we must

---

[40] Franz Werfel, in *Arnold Schönberg zum 60. Geburtstag, 13. September 1934* (Universal Edition: Vienna, 1934), p. 14.

[41] Theodor Wiesengrund Adorno, 'Sacred Fragment: Schoenberg's "Moses und Aron"', in *Quasi una Fantasia: Essays on Modern Music*, tr. R. Livingstone (Verso: London and New York, 1998), p. 229.

[42] Pamela C. White, *Schoenberg and the God-Idea: The Opera 'Moses und Aron'* (University of Michigan Press: Ann Arbor, 1985), p. 153.

always be on our guard against a false divinity. And on what grounds can we judge?

From the moment of human involvement, signalled by Moses' spoken voice, an unbridgeable chasm has opened. With but one exception, Moses only speaks, in what Gary Tomlinson aptly terms a 'Michelangesque *terribilità*'. Tomlinson plays down the contrast between Moses' *Sprechstimme* and Aron's song, in favour of their common individuality when set against the mass.[43] That seems odd, given the extraordinary affective power of the contrast between speech and song, which is fundamental to the listener's experience of the entire work. For the moment, this contrast allows the question to remain open as to whether Aron's song can ever truly function as his brother's mouthpiece. It is, however, perfectly clear that, were Moses somehow to acquire the ability to express himself, he could still never return to this opening realm of spirit, of wordless or uninterpretable divine immediacy. For God to be represented, for the Idea of God to be interpreted, would turn them into a god and idea unworthy of representation or interpretation. Likewise, were God swayed by sacrifice, as Aron considers possible, then that would render Him a particular, tribal god. The orgy around the Golden Calf therefore *must* end in the tragedy of destruction, suicide, and ultimate nihilistic exhaustion. Reto Nickler's 2006 production for the Vienna State Opera thus presented video images of advertising and pornography as the orgy progressed. Such representations of a superficial cult of beauty and easy eroticism, as encouraged or at least indulged by Aron, did not merely reflect Schoenberg's drama, but furthered it. By contrast, God is unimaginable in the very real sense of it being impossible to make Him into an image. Were the Israelites to succeed in seeing Him, He would no longer be their God.

Yet Moses' inability to express his thought is as much a cause for despair as the straying of his people. He does not even appear always to be right. Aron points out to him that the Tables of the Law are 'images also, just part of the whole idea'; to acquiesce to representation is but to 'yield before necessity'. Likewise, Aron is quite right to argue that the pillars of cloud and fire, which Moses, in a startling transformation of the Biblical narrative, condemns as idolatrous images (*Götzenbilder*), are actually sent by God: 'The Eternal One shows not Himself, but the way to Himself.' He shows the way, as opposed to the Christian understanding in which He is the Way. As Adorno points out, the only way in which the Mosaic

---

[43] Gary Tomlinson, *Metaphysical Song: An Essay on Opera* (Princeton University Press: Princeton, 1999), p. 152.

prohibition can be dramatised is through changes in the text. That would not usually matter, but 'where the subject matter dons the authority of a sacred text, it verges on heresy'.[44]

The accusation of heresy reminds us that Schoenberg had a Christian as well as a Jewish heritage. Never one to make life easy for himself, he had converted in the Vienna of 1898 not, like Mahler, to Roman Catholicism, but to Lutheranism. Henceforth the Lutheran Bible would be 'rarely out of his reach . . . in the course of a lifetime that embraced two world wars, various revolutions, and long years of exile'.[45] Many commentators have missed the importance of the image and representation in the tradition in which he had at least partially placed himself. The great Protestant and specifically Lutheran controversy over the Second Commandment, involving Luther's claim that it applied only to pagans, not to Christians, and its subsequent ejection from the list of ten, may be of importance here. The relevant passage from Exodus makes uncomfortable reading for a Christian artist:

> Thou shalt not make unto thee any graven image, or any likeness of any thing that is in heaven above, or that is in the earth beneath, or that is in the water under the earth: Thou shalt not bow down thyself to them, nor serve them: for I the LORD thy God am a jealous God, visiting the iniquity of the fathers upon the children unto the third and fourth generation of them that hate me.[46]

Reformation controversy over iconoclasm fed into the classical German concept of self-cultivation or *Bildung*, the very word incorporating *Bild*, or 'image'. Such was the basis upon which Jewish emancipation had proceeded, connecting individual (Kantian) autonomy and the universality of humanism, just as the political right began to see community as based upon *völkisch* ties of blood rather than cosmopolitan ties of *Bildung*. This latter, eighteenth- and early-nineteenth-century world seemed desperately detached from reality by the time National Socialism prohibited performances of one of its key texts, Lessing's plea for mutual respect and toleration, *Nathan der Weise*. *Der biblische Weg*, and *Moses* both testify to that transformation.

If humanism had run out of steam, that might well seem to Schoenberg, drawing upon his Lutheran and Jewish heritages, that this was connected with the hubris of representation. Music had traditionally been considered

---

[44] Adorno, 'Sacred Fragment,' p. 230.

[45] Alexander Ringer, *Arnold Schoenberg: The Composer as Jew* (Oxford University Press: Oxford, 1990), p. 7.

[46] Exodus 20: 4–5

imageless and therefore exempt from the *Bildverbot*; Romantic and post-Romantic dreams of artistic unity rendered this exemption more problematical. His conception of what was forbidden is expressed in very broad terms in the text (his own) to the first stanza of the chorus, op. 27 no. 2 (1925):

> Thou shalt not fashion thyself an image!
> For an image limits,
> demarcates, grasps,
> what should remain undemarcated and unrepresented.

Schoenberg, with his Jewish and Lutheran heritages, stood in perhaps a unique, if hardly enviable, position to confront the prohibition's implications for modernist art.

On the one hand, the Romantic conception of the autonomous artwork is taken to such an extreme in Schoenberg's opera that it can hardly bear the strain. On the other, the work's status as a work about itself, about the impossibility, even blasphemy, of music drama not only shines through, but deals the very concept of the artwork a savage blow. Moses laments 'O word, thou word that I lack!' but his lament is not sung. It is song rather than words that in one sense at least he lacks. This is the price paid for truth; no one will or even can listen. As for the mellifluous, seductive Aron, to whom the Israelites will listen, he betrays the truth. He represents it and therefore betrays its form. Romantic rebellion and *Heimweh* have been transformed into the full-scale social alienation of music.

If *Die Jakobsleiter* takes us back to Mahler, then *Moses* takes us back to Wagner and to the increasing tension between the democratic and the hieratic in his later works: the *Ring* and even more so *Parsifal*. The Schoenbergian transformation from Romanticism to modernity has taken place via the cultic, sacralising tendencies of *Parsifal*: in place of a truly communal celebration of the *polis*, we have the semi-exclusive rite of a gathered congregation. Adorno described such social alienation as 'that assembly of phenomena for which an overhasty and unenlightened reformism employs derogatory terms such as individualism, charlatanism, and technical esotericism.'[47] It nonetheless was and remains an ongoing social reality of production. *Moses* exhibits its defiance in its fragmentary nature, as Adorno saw only too well:

[47] Theodor Wiesengrund Adorno, 'On the Social Situation of Music,' tr. Wesley Blomster, revised Richard Leppert, in *Essays on Music*, ed. Richard Leppert (University of California Press: Berkeley, Los Angeles, and London, 2002), p. 392.

Important works of art are the ones that aim for an extreme; they are destroyed in the process and their broken outlines survive as the ciphers of a supreme, unnameable truth. It is in this positive sense that *Moses und Aron* is a fragment and it would not be extravagant to explain why it was left incomplete by arguing that it could not be completed.[48]

For, if 'failure' there be in *Moses*, its dramatic form renders it 'successful', such success lying in radicalisation rather than resolution. As Joseph Auner has put it, 'The power of the work is not that it gives us simple answers, but that it poses questions and problems admitting of no solution.'[49] In that, it could hardly be a more Wagnerian work; it might even be considered *plus royaliste que le roi*. The halves of what Adorno would have called integral freedom, the characters of Moses and Aron, are permanently rent asunder; they can never again become a whole. The dying words of Max Aruns spring to mind: 'Asseino was right, when he accused me of being presumptuous, of wanting to be Moses and Aron in one person.' Presumption now becomes idolatry.

Aron's error has lain not so much in the attempt to communicate to a people on the verge of revolt but in communicating through the old gods, who would urge him – and Schoenberg – to complete their work. A little æsthetic, political, or religious compromise seems a price worth paying to avoid absolute rupture; after all, perfection is divine, not mortal. Such old idolatrous gods of demagoguery are also, of course, new idolatrous gods of demagoguery: Adorno's gods of 'individualism, charlatanism, and technical esotericism', which dialectically become the gods of false, even totalitarian, communitarianism. Aron is seduced into seducing; his representation brings him perilously close as Leader to becoming the object of representation. The music surrounding the Golden Calf, rigorously dodecaphonic though it be, seems too seductive, too comprehensible – at least when judged by the stringency of the Schoenbergian Idea. Schoenberg appears to be perpetrating the sin of which George Bernard Shaw accused Wagner in *Götterdämmerung*, of succumbing to grand opera; and yet, to dramatise the opposition between Moses and Aron he could hardly do otherwise.[50] Moses, on the other hand, would be more God-like than God and predictably fails. The state of divinity, lying beyond the Kantian division of noumenon and phenomenon, is unknowable to us, even to Moses – indeed,

---

[48] Adorno, 'Sacred Fragment', p. 226.

[49] Joseph Auner, 'Schoenberg as Moses und Aron', in *The Opera Quarterly*, 23 (2007), 382

[50] George Bernard Shaw, *The Perfect Wagnerite: A Commentary on the Niblung's Ring*, 4th edn (Dover: New York, 1967), pp. 75–6, 83

one might suggest, particularly to Moses with his one-sided rigidity. God knows, should we dare speculate about His Idea, that the communicative strategy of Aron or something similar is necessary. Moses' Idea appears truer than the all-too-easy *bel canto* simplifications of Aron, yet if it cannot be expressed truthfully, how can Moses bear witness, how can he lead his people? It is hardly surprising that they have turned away. As the Chorus laments during the Interlude between the two acts, 'Abandoned are we! Where is his God? Where is the Eternal One? Where is Moses?' The final words of Act II, and therefore the final words set to music, render this antinomy painfully clear:

> Unrepresentable God!
> Inexpressible Idea of many meanings,
> wilt thou permit this explanation?
> Shall Aron, my mouth, fashion this image?
> Thus, I have fashioned an image too, false,
> as an image can only be!
> Thus, I am defeated!
> Thus, everything I believed before was madness,
> and can and must not be voiced!
> O word, thou word that I lack!

Moreover, the rupture is musical as well as verbal. The long F-sharp violin unison builds to a fortissimo and then subsides into silence. Such unity is by now perhaps the only way one might musically represent God; the textural richness of the God heard in the Burning Bush would, paradoxically, seem diffuse and unmediated: negative dialectics indeed. Michel Poizat goes so far as to see this F sharp as the pendant to the E-flat pedal that opens *Das Rheingold*; the former is 'perhaps the most perfect musicalisation of the silence that imposes its absolute presence when all words fail . . . From here on nothing more can be said: opera can go no further.'[51] God cannot be spoken of. Beyond the F sharp does there lie God, nothing, or the unity of God and nothingness? We need to know, yet cannot.

'One who is struggling' in *Die Jakobsleiter* had also resorted to speech when talking of the mystery of divine law: 'Why was no instinct granted us that might sense unspoken laws, no eye to see, no ear to hear?' Both Gabriel and Moses speak rather than sing, which seems to indicate a suspicion of seductive song when it comes to prophecy and truth. Interestingly,

---

[51] Michel Poizat, *The Angel's Cry: Beyond the Pleasure Principle in Opera*, tr. Arthur Denner (Cornell University Press: Ithaca, 1992), p. 109.

Gabriel does sing when he tries to represent 'One far higher', prefiguring the contrast with Aron. Freud, in *Moses and Monotheism*, would speak of 'the most striking fact about Jewish religious history' being the 'yawning gap between the law-giving of Moses and the later Jewish religion'. Schoenberg, by contrast, saw the striking fact of the 'continuity between' the 'contemporary period' of the 'priestly narrative' disavowed by Freud, and the apparently 'remote Mosaic past'.[52] It is less law in general than the ban on graven images that constitutes Schoenberg's drama.

Or at least that is the case with the words. The music suggests that true freedom lies not in licence but in strict organisation, in the authority of the twelve-note-row; this is the musical and the divine Idea. What is most important, divine even, about the Idea of the row is not only its omnipresence, but the very abstraction of that omnipresence. In David Lewin's words, the row 'can only be perceived, or realised, by means of an aggregation' of specific representations. 'Or, more exactly, the *composer*', for whom we might theologically substitute the Creator, 'may perceive it as a sort of resonant abstraction, but it remains unrealised and unfulfilled until it is manifested through performance and communicated to an audience by means of material sounds.'[53] The sphere beyond space and time, at least as conventionally understood, is now embodied musically, as Schoenberg explained in his article, 'Composition with Twelve Tones':

> the validity of this form of thinking is ... demonstrated by the ... law of unity of musical space, best formulated as follows: *the unity of musical space demands an absolute and unitary perception*. In this space, as in Swedenborg's heaven (described in Balzac's *Seraphita*) there is no absolute down, no right or left, forward or backward. Every musical configuration, every movement of tones has to be comprehended primarily as a mutual relation of sounds, of oscillatory vibrations, appearing at different places and times.[54]

An identical phrase is employed at the beginning of *Die Jakobsleiter*: 'Whether to right or left, forward or backward, upwards or downwards, one must go on, without asking what lies ahead or behind.' But in *Moses*, that prophecy is more clearly represented musically. The (artist's) task is, in the following order, to define one's thoughts, to approach the Idea, and to present a coherent argument. In Schoenberg's case, this is a musical

[52] Freud, 'Moses and Monotheism', p. 307.
[53] David Lewin, 'Moses und Aron: Some General Remarks, and Analytic Notes for Act I, Scene I', in *Perspectives of New Music*, 6 (1967), 1.
[54] Schoenberg, 'Composition with Twelve Tones', in *Style and Idea*, p. 223.

argument and, in Moses' case, an argument that is nothing less than a revelation. Yet ever present is the danger, which at times shades into the certainty, of betrayal.

Boulez rightly points to the important question pertaining to the relationship between art and effect: 'Is it conceivable that one could have an artistic language capable of producing some effect? Can I convince anyone without it?'[55] It might well be argued that Schoenberg, or at least Moses, has lost as soon as music begins to be written, or to put it slightly differently, that the composer Schoenberg knew better than the theologian Schoenberg. In Alexander Goehr's words, *Moses* '"works" as an expressionist opera rather than as an exemplification of [Karl] Kraus's ideals [pertaining to purity and clarity of language]; it is a work about ideas, in the traditional sense, rather than a discourse on the nature of Idea itself'.[56] *Moses* is not a work that eschews representation. Abstract it is not.

On the other hand, the lack of music for the third act makes the theologian Schoenberg's point clearly: to stage this act would diminish its impact. Mysterious references to the 'unfinished third act' seem more powerful than the text itself, for the drama does not seem to have advanced. Moses reiterates that God is eternal, unimaginable, invisible, that He is not bound to do anything, but we knew all this before. Without the representational or mediating 'effect' of the music, we do little but walk in circles. An apt metaphor for the Israelites' years in the wilderness, it is nevertheless a dramatic anticlimax to the rupture of Moses' despairing 'O word, thou word that I lack!' It is, moreover, difficult to imagine – an intentionally loaded word – how Schoenberg could have composed music for this act. Schoenberg's music drama has reached such an impasse that there really does seem nowhere to go. He was both the only man who could fulfil the task and the man who above all others could not – just like Moses.

The third act could have added one of two things: more of the same, or the false consciousness of illusory reconciliation. This is a failure that bears important witness to the contradiction of reality. A musico-dramatic antinomy is a different creature from its purely logical, Kantian confrère, not least since it can, if only temporarily – tragically – preserve some representation of what has been lost. If God is not quite there, neither is He quite absent. The error of so many artworks in this view is that they attempt to do more than this, or rather in reality they do less: they

[55] 'Boulez on Schoenberg's "Moses und Aron"', p. 14.
[56] Alexander Goehr, 'Schoenberg and Karl Kraus: The Idea behind the Music,' in *Finding the Key: Selected Writings of Alexander Goehr*, ed. Derrick Puffett (Faber: London, 1998), p. 139.

do not recognise the impossibility of representational reconciliation, and therefore fall back upon a false immediacy. This is the 'desire for reconciliation' the young Boulez found so suspicious in Berg.[57] Boulez was setting up an implicit contrast with Webern, but the contrast is at least as great with Schoenberg. It is also akin to that 'Happy End', which, the destruction of the world notwithstanding, Adorno detected in the Immolation Scene of *Götterdämmerung*. What music really must do was not to present an illusory 'peacefulness above all conflicts', but rather achieve 'the pure, uncompromising representation of absolute conflict'.[58] Music, the 'transcendental' Romantic art *par excellence*, might yet be the most modern, in its resistance to the idolatry of transcendence.

That does not conflict with the empirical fact that Schoenberg always intended to complete the third act – although this might have had to involve revision of the text. Boulez suggests that Schoenberg might have had to write a dialogue between Moses and someone else, perhaps the people or God.[59] Yet, despite the difficulties Schoenberg faced in exile, the terrible struggle he endured simply to survive, a greater, indeed ultimately intractable difficulty, explains why *Moses* remained incomplete – just as *Die Jakobsleiter* had. After all, he wrote a great deal of other music after 1933, whilst considering that six to eight weeks' further work was all that would be needed to finish *Moses*.[60] Moreover, he feared as early as 1933 that it might never be finished, telling Berg: 'It is strange that all my larger works (beginning with *Gurrelieder*) have been in danger of remaining torsos: *Jakobsleiter, Der biblische Weg, Moses und Aron*, the counterpoint book, and the other theoretical works. Will I finish it?'[61]

We might seem to have come a long way from *Die Jakobsleiter*'s world outside time and space, though not so far as might be suspected. The non-specificity of the drama's location challenges, as Bluma Goldstein has remarked, 'crucial ideas of the biblical narrative about nationhood and religion'. Absent is the Bible's 'concern with liberation from Egyptian bondage and with the creation of an exemplary nation through adherence

[57] Pierre Boulez, 'Alban Berg,' in *Relevés d'apprenti*, ed. Paule Thévenin (Seuil: Paris, 1966), p. 323.

[58] Theodor Wiesengrund Adorno, *In Search of Wagner*, tr. Rodney Livingstone (Verso: London and New York, 1981), p. 149; 'Classicism, Romanticism, New Music,' in *Sound Figures*, tr. Rodney Livingstone (Stanford University Press: Stanford, 1999), p. 122.

[59] 'Boulez on Schoenberg's "Moses und Aron"', p. 15.

[60] Letter to Jakob Klatzkin of 26 May 1933, in Schoenberg, *Briefe*, p. 198.

[61] Letter of 17 September 1933, in *The Berg-Schoenberg Correspondence*, ed. Juliane Brand, Christopher Hailey, and Donald Harris (Macmillan: Basingstoke, 1987), p. 445.

to commandments and law for the governance of communal life'.[62] This is very different from the picture Freud would shortly paint, in which an Egyptian, 'perhaps called Tuthmosis, like many other people at the time', threw in his lot with a Semitic tribe in the wake of the demise of the original monotheistic religion of Aten.[63] The argument for Egyptian identity ironically strengthens the Jewish nationalist case. Whilst the factors driving Schoenberg's path back towards Judaism may have been primarily social and political, the drama seems more universal than this might imply – or at least the mission of the Jews seems more universal, just as the Germans had been to many nineteenth-century thinkers, some of them Jews, some of them not. Moses Hess, the founding father of Zionism, had thus declared: 'We Germans are the most universal, the most *European* people in Europe.'[64] One could imagine Wagner in some moods at least having said the same.

In Schoenberg's vision, God's chosen people must bear witness to the strictest monotheism – to be a light to lighten the Gentiles. The Jews, he wrote in 1938, were less a race than a people who 'belong together on account of our religion'. They had been 'chosen to survive, to endure through the centuries, to refute the laws of nature'; they were marked by their 'devotion to an idea, to an ideal', which sprang from their 'deep devotion to our inherited faith'.[65] And so, the final line of Act III presents Moses' unattainable *telos*: 'But in the desert you shall be invincible and shall achieve the goal: unity with God.' Not in Palestine, but in the desert: this is the true Biblical way. Moses' conception, as Goldstein writes, 'of a permanent wilderness existence', is identified with neither a specific location nor culture but 'with universal spiritualised devotion'.[66] Once again, Moses, Schoenberg, and the Jews stand as witnesses to the impossible – to the truth of the wilderness rather than to settlement, even if that wilderness should ultimately incorporate some form of territorial settlement. Unlike Adorno, who seems to have had no interest in a Zionist state, Schoenberg continued to be a fervent supporter, yet it would be as a means rather than an end: a means to a universal witness to the one, eternal truth. The stringency of monotheism leads to the most necessary

[62] Bluma Goldstein, 'Schoenberg's "Moses und Aron": A Vanishing Biblical Nation,' in *Political and Religious Ideas*, ed. Cross and Berman, pp. 167, 159.

[63] Freud, 'Moses and Monotheism,' p. 301.

[64] Moses Hess, 'Die europäische Triarchie,' in *Philosophische und sozialistische Schriften 1837–1850*, ed. August Cornu and Wolfgang Mönke (Akademie-Verlag: Berlin, 1961), p. 118.

[65] Arnold Schoenberg, 'Four-Point Programme for Jewry,' in *Journal of the Arnold Schoenberg Institute*, 3 (1979), 51–2.

[66] Goldstein, 'Schoenberg's "Moses und Aron"', p. 186.

universalism, but in quite the opposite way from Freud's thesis. For Freud, 'the central fact of the development of the Jewish religion was that in the course of time the god Yahweh lost his own characteristics and grew more and more to resemble the old god of Moses, the Aten.'[67] For Schoenberg, the central fact of the development of the Jewish religion was that the Jewish God and His Idea retained their own characteristics, the religion thereby remaining true to the only God of Moses. And yet, Freud and Schoenberg do come together at the next level, in seeing the Mosaic prohibition as having 'elevated God' to what Freud calls 'a higher degree of intellectuality', and thereby enabling Moses, whether at the time or in the present, to convey to the Jews 'an exalted sense of being a chosen people.'[68] Rather like Moses and Aron, Schoenberg and Freud cannot help pointing the way towards the same object, perhaps because monotheism, at least in its pre-Trinitarian form, cannot logically suffer different interpretations – even if Schoenberg would most likely have rebuffed Freud's claims as angrily as Moses rejects Aron's. That might help us to understand what Schoenberg meant when claiming that not only could there be no art without ethical inspiration, but also that there 'could be no human ethics not inspired by the spirit of Judaism.'[69]

VI

Let us finally consider Schoenberg's modernism more explicitly. In an apologia for Richard Strauss, Leon Botstein writes that the music dramas of Wagner, Busoni, Debussy, Berg, and Schoenberg constitute, 'in narrative and style, part of a different [from Strauss] and seemingly more ambitious tradition crucial to twentieth-century modernism'. In those works, characterised by what he somewhat oddly terms 'surface modernist originality', our experience of art 'becomes explicitly didactic ... The intent of art becomes confrontational and therefore ultimately redemptive.' Strauss, however, is content to abandon 'these modernist conceits and ambitions', and to employ irony, ornament, and detachment, not to 'undercut wisdom', but rather as its instruments.[70] Schoenberg would have accepted and contested these claims in almost equal measure. For him, art

[67] Freud, 'Moses and Monotheism', p. 305.
[68] Ibid., p. 362.
[69] Quoted in Edward Latham, 'The Prophet and the Pitchman: Dramatic Structure and its Musical Elucidation in "Moses und Aron," Act 1, Scene 2', in *Political and Religious Ideas*, ed. Cross and Berman, p. 131.
[70] Leon Botstein, 'The Enigmas of Richard Strauss: A Revisionist View', in *Richard Strauss and his World*, ed. Bryan Gilliam (Princeton University Press: Princeton, 1992), pp. 22–3.

was distinguished from entertainment by its presentation (*Darstellung*) as a form of knowledge.[71] He would not have contested the placing of his dramas in Botstein's tradition; nor would he have questioned the claim of redemptive intent and, more importantly, arguing for the redemptive *result*, of a great work of art.

However, Schoenberg would certainly have contested the claim that there was anything of the surface about his true originality and he would never have accepted that ornament, detachment, and most likely irony, could ever really have proved instruments of wisdom, let alone those foundations of 'belief and conviction', which we saw him tell Busoni were requirements of even his earliest atonal compositions. Thus Schoenberg could write in response to Strauss's remark that 'in each of my works, there must be a melody which can be understood by the most stupid fellow in the hall':

> Problems arise for him and are solved by him in the same way: he misunderstands them. But it cannot be disputed that he has dealt with them: he has hidden them under a coating of sugar icing, so that the public sees only the . . . world of a *Marzipanmeister*. This is not the way of thinking of a man whom God has given a mission.[72]

Strauss, then, was enslaved; he was not free, but heteronomously enslaved to the material requirements of the lowest class of listener, as was reflected in both his technique and his musical language. Through prophetic calling, however, a composer might be radically free. For whatever the rigours of Schoenberg's musical organisation, we should never forget the liberating tendency of the break with tonality, the extension of chromaticism, the state of being in no key or all keys at once – however one wishes to characterise what had happened in the 1908 Second String Quartet. That was why Ernst Krenek claimed that atonality had 'given speech to the individual, liberating him from delusive chains and seductive illusions'.[73] Had not dissonance itself been emancipated?[74] Krenek spoke of the world of *Die Jakobsleiter*.

---

[71] See Arnold Schoenberg, *Zusammenhang, Kontrapunkt, Instrumentation, Formenlehre*, ed. Severine Neff, tr. Charlotte M. Cross and Severine Neff (University of Nebraska Press: Lincoln, 1994).

[72] Fragment quoted in Christensen, 'The Spiritual and the Material', p. 344

[73] Ernst Krenek, 'Atonality', in *Music Here and Now* trans. Barthold Fles (Norton: New York, 1939), p. 165.

[74] The term 'emancipation of the dissonance' seems first to have been used by Rudolf Louis in his 1893 dissertation, 'Die Widerspruch in der Musik', in which the author associates it with the idea that modern music has progressed beyond the 'absolute sovereignty of the beautiful'. (Robert Falck, 'Emancipation of the Dissonance', *Journal of the Arnold*

Such liberation inexorably pointed to a destination beyond, to the hope for a Promised Land, even if it were of the metaphysical variety; for, again in Krenek's words, atonality 'had not hesitated to raise the issue of a new type of musical order'.[75] Such a stance required faith in and despite tradition.

Abhorrence of ornament is crucial here; the *taste* of façadism should be banished by the *truth* and *conviction* of modernism. Generalisations about modernism are as elusive – as useless? – as generalisations about Romanticism, but the belief that a work's æsthetic should be derived from its structural integrity, rather than from its surface characteristics and ornamentation, is a sound claimant to the title of a fundamental principle at least. Always the Idea, one might say. It is no coincidence that Schoenberg had belonged to the Vienna Circle of Karl Kraus and Adolf Loos, for whom rejection of ornament was as much an ethical as an æsthetic principle – or, rather, the two forms of principle were identical.[76] Loos had branded ornament a crime in 1908, the year of Schoenberg's break with tonality; Schoenberg was still lauding Loos in a letter dating from 1930, the first year of composition on *Moses*.[77] The composer praised the architect for his 'nigh forty years of ... activity as a reformer and an artist', in which he had nevertheless failed to receive any public honour.[78] Prophets rarely do in their own time, as Schoenberg knew very well – biographically and dramatically.

The surface of Schoenberg's music might repel many conservative listeners, but Schoenberg would retort that they hear only the surface of any music, or indeed retreat into a world of images they fancifully believe the music has evoked. They would feel at home with Brahms whilst lacking the slightest understanding of his structural integrity, of the true richness or the true 'idea' of his work.[79] These listeners' ornamental crime against modern music is identical to their crime against the classics. Lazy Aronic substitution of images for the Mosaic truth of the Idea must be rejected. Schoenberg had made this quite clear writing in Kandinsky's

Schoenberg Institute, 6 (1982), pp. 106–7.) It would soon, however, be employed by and associated with Schoenberg, not least in his *Harmonielehre*.

[75] Krenek, 'Atonality', p. 165.

[76] On Schoenberg and Kraus, see Goehr, 'Schoenberg and Karl Kraus', pp. 124–41.

[77] Adolf Loos, 'Ornament und Verbrechen', in *Sämtliche Schriften*, ed. Franz Glück, 2 vols (Herold: Vienna and Munich, 1962), vol. 1, pp. 276–88. For an interesting discussion of Schoenberg and Loos, including consideration of Schoenberg's relationship to specifically urban modernity, see Holly Watkins, 'Schoenberg's Interior Designs', in *Journal of the American Musicological Society*, 61 (2008), 123–206.

[78] Letter of 6 November 1930 to Alexander Amersdorfer, in Schoenberg, *Briefe*, p. 156.

[79] See Schoenberg, 'Brahms the Progressive', in *Style and Idea*, pp. 398–441.

1912 *Blaue Reiter*: 'The assumption that a piece of music must summon up images of one sort or another, and that if these are absent the piece of music has not been understood or is worthless, is as widespread as only the false and banal can be.'[80] Such modernism evinces no fear of elitism. Schoenberg's refusal to separate style and idea evinces a stand against idolatry, a Platonic stand against the illusory retreat into a world of appearances, a stand even against the ornamental superficiality that would damn him on account of his race. The political, the religious, and the æsthetic are at one here. There is no realm in which God's writ does not run, no refuge for *l'art pour l'art*.[81] In a 1947 declaration of what he considered to be true 'human rights', number thirteen read as follows: 'Surely the Ten Commandments represent one of the first *déclarations des droits humaines* set forth in word and script. They assure the right to live and to have possessions; they protect marriage, vows, and work, but deny from the very beginning freedom of faith, because there is only ONE God.'[82] To return to Botstein's contrast between 'modernists' and Strauss, it is difficult to see that Schoenberg's stance could ever be anything other than confrontational, at least in a bourgeois society. That is not to say that intention must be confrontational in the straightforward sense of *épater les bourgeois*, but that a true understanding of Schoenberg or even a true approach thereto must be so; the same must follow for Brahms or Bach, 'because there is only ONE God'.

The fundamental problem for Schoenberg was theological rather than socio-political. Unity with God, Schoenberg's goal in Act III of *Moses*, was impossible, but the necessary prophecy of that unity compelled him to adopt an uncompromising æsthetic position. To quote Oliver Neighbour:

> Schoenberg once suggested that Beethoven, Bruckner and Mahler had not been permitted to compose tenth symphonies because they might have revealed something that we are not permitted to know; a ninth seemed to represent a limit beyond which the composer must pass into the hereafter. To have composed music adequate to the idea of unity with God would have been to write a tenth symphony.[83]

[80] Arnold Schoenberg, 'Das Verhältnis zum Text', in Vasily Kandinsky and Franz Marc (eds), *Der blaue Reiter* (Piper: Munich, 1912), p. 60.

[81] Cf. Murray Dineen, who argues that for Schoenberg, 'the composer's sole purpose is musical: art for art's sake.' ('Modernism and Words: Schoenberg, Adorno, Moses', in *Schoenberg and Words*, ed. Cross and Berman, p. 361.)

[82] Schoenberg, 'Human Rights', in *Style and Idea*, p. 510.

[83] O. W. Neighbour, 'Schoenberg, Arnold', *Grove Music Online. Oxford Music Online.* 8 December 2009 <http://www.oxfordmusiconline.com/subscriber/article/grove/music/25024>.

Adorno was right to point to the work's 'absolute metaphysical content', which 'would prevent it from becoming an æsthetic totality', and to argue that Schoenberg must have been aware of this.[84] It has clear implications in terms of musical development. Whatever the example of certain occasional works, there is no reason to think that Schoenberg's break with tonality was ever something to be reversed; there might be a few good tunes still to be written in C major, but not by Moses. The Darmstadt School's total serialism did not really emerge from Schoenberg's music, for it was Webern who showed the way to the Promised Land. Boulez had every reason, shortly after the first performance of the Dance round the Golden Calf, to declare Schoenberg dead.[85] Nevertheless, part of Darmstadt's teleological ideology did emerge from Schoenberg's uncompromising vision, albeit in the guise of a secularised, quasi-scientific version of Schoenbergian historical necessity. Music conveyed for Schoenberg 'a prophetic message revealing a higher form of life towards which mankind evolves'.[86] If Boulez would always have shunned such overtly religious language, Stockhausen's latter-day mysticism ventured far beyond that of Schoenberg's relative orthodoxy. More importantly, they shared an obligation of prophetic witness.

But the 'absolute metaphysical content' and the concomitant failure to which Adorno refers also have implications for the art of the past and how it should be viewed. One should not simply rummage around and take what one fancied from the historical museum; this was to adopt what Adorno termed the '"as if" attitude . . . [of Schoenberg's] antipode Stravinsky'.[87] Stravinsky, 'little Modernsky', therefore came in for some coruscating, if heavy-handed, criticism in Schoenberg's *Three Satires*, op. 28 (1925). Indeed, some works, too much of their time, would simply have passed their sell-by dates, and needed to be discarded or at least stood in need of drastic surgery, as witnessed by Schoenberg's reworking of a Handel concerto grosso into a 'Concerto for String Quartet and Orchestra'. Schoenberg made his position quite clear in a postcard to Berg: 'in the end it will be a very good piece and that won't be Handel's doing, if I do say so.'[88] Adorno was thinking along similar, albeit more theoretical lines when he wrote in 1951, following the bicentenary of Bach's death:

[84] Adorno, 'Sacred Fragment', p. 226.
[85] Boulez, 'Schönberg est mort', in *Relevés d'apprenti*, pp. 265–72.
[86] Schoenberg, 'Criteria for the Evaluation of Music', in *Style and Idea*, p. 136.
[87] Adorno, 'Sacred Fragment', p. 228.
[88] August 1933, in *Berg-Schoenberg Correspondence*, p. 444.

Justice is done Bach not through musicological usurpation [that is, through attempts at quasi-archaeological reconstruction] but solely through the most advanced composition which in turn converges with the level of Bach's continually unfolding work. The few instrumentations contributed by Schoenberg and Anton von Webern, especially those of the great triple fugue in E flat major and of the six-part *Ricercata*,... are models of an attitude to Bach which corresponds to the stage of his truth. Perhaps the traditional Bach can indeed no longer be interpreted. If this is true, his heritage has passed on to composition, which is loyal to him in being disloyal; it calls his music by name in producing it anew.[89]

Is it yet time to take this attitude towards Schoenberg? Such creative disloyalty would not necessarily entail completion of *Moses*; it is almost certainly best left as it is. However, the ban on graven images was relaxed by the Incarnation. Images of God the Son trouble us less. Moses' last words, excluding the third act, are 'O word, thou word that I lack!' In a world transformed by the Word made flesh, a new form of subjectivity was born, albeit a subjectivity with strong roots in the Jewish faith. This is not to say that *Moses* and Schoenberg have somehow been superseded, but that it might be worth returning to Boulez's question as to whether an artistic language is capable of producing some effect. The dramatic success of Schoenberg's music drama presents us with a resounding yes and a need to question the direction in which Schoenberg and Moses want to take us but yet cannot quite do so. It also, rather startlingly, may be seen to link the theology of the Incarnation upon which its æsthetic depends with that of the apophatic, which forms the crux of the drama on stage.

For the Moses in Schoenberg's drama is a mystic, possessed of a 'truly "illuminated" faith [which] grasps the essence of the invisible God in all his profundity', or at least in much of His profundity.[90] Schoenberg's interest in mysticism had not died with the suspension of work on *Die Jakobsleiter*; it continues with the illuminated refusal actively to form concepts about God. This represents generally a denial of the humanistic image-making drive towards *Bildung*, and specifically a creative rupture with Schiller and the Romantics and their conception of man as essentially creative. The apophatic need not necessarily end in failure, whether for Moses or for Schoenberg; knowledge of God obtained only through negation was hardly an incredible concept for Adorno, the negative dialectician *par excellence*.[91] Neo-Platonism dies hard, for it had been several

---

[89]   Theodor Wiesengrund Adorno, 'Bach Defended against his Devotees,' in *Prisms*, tr. Samuel and Sherry Weber (MIT Press: Cambridge, MA, 1981), p. 146.
[90]   Willi Reich, *Schoenberg: A Critical Biography*, tr. Leo Black (Praeger: London, 1971), p. 179.
[91]   See, e.g., Hent de Vries, *Minimal Theologies: Critiques of Secular Religion in Adorno and*

centuries earlier that Thomas Aquinas had presented a *via negativa*, which removed from our statements concerning God everything that He is not. Notwithstanding the Lutheran ejection of the Second Commandment, Kant had described it as 'perhaps the most sublime passage in the Jewish Law'. We need not worry, he had claimed, that the feeling of the sublime would lose something, were it exhibited in a wholly abstract, even negative fashion. 'For though the imagination', he wrote, 'finds nothing beyond the sensible that could support it, this very removal of its barriers also makes it feel unbounded, so that its separation [from the sensible] is an exhibition of the infinite can as such never be more than merely negative, it still expands the soul.'[92] This, moreover, does not stand so very far from the final Chorus Mysticus of Goethe's *Faust* (and Mahler's Eighth Symphony), in which the realm of the beyond can only be described in terms of what it is not. Whatever one thinks of the 'Eternal Feminine' panacea, one can still accept:

> All things transitory
> are but a parable;
> here the *in*sufficient
> captures our attention,
> here the *in*describable
> is accomplished[93]

To turn that form of negativity back upon Schoenberg, to begin to understand him in terms of what he is not – Strauss or Stravinsky, for instance – is one way in which we might call his works by name, and in particular those under consideration here, in producing them anew. We might thereby salvage something of the tradition of *Bildung* whilst remaining aware of its shortcomings. This tradition both fashioned and repelled Schoenberg, a Jew and a Lutheran. To consider how he rejects it helps us to understand how he remains part of it. For Schoenberg's imperative is not only negative. Op. 27 no. 2 ends not with the first stanza's *Bildverbot* but with a positive commandment, its necessity or 'must' twice reiterated: 'Thou must believe in the Spirit! . . . Thou must, Chosen one, must, to remain so [chosen]!' This thought, which

Levinas, tr. Geoffrey Hale (Johns Hopkins University Press: Baltimore, MD, and London, 2005); Josh Cohen, *Interrupting Auschwitz: Art, Religion, Philosophy* (Continuum: New York and London, 2003).
[92] Immanuel Kant, *Critique of Judgment*, tr. Werner S. Pluhar (Hackett: Indianapolis, 1987), 'On the Modality of a Judgment about the Sublime in Nature,' §29, p. 135.
[93] My italics. Johann Wolfgang von Goethe, *Faust: eine Tragödie*, ed. Erich Trunz (Beck: Munich, 1999), p. 364.

harks back to *Die Jakobsleiter* and beyond that to Mahler's Second Symphony, suggests that Jewish mystical belief might yet salvage the German tradition, with its punishing yet creative dialectic between freedom and organisation, whose burden and privilege Schoenberg felt so keenly.

CHAPTER 3

Richard Strauss: Paths to (and from) *Capriccio*

I

Richard Strauss may well be the most difficult 'case' in this book; indeed, there is perhaps no more difficult case in all opera. There are numerous 'political' ways in which his work may be considered. A strong argument exists for consideration of his œuvre as a running commentary, perhaps disreputable, for some even repellent, upon the course of that German history in which it was written, created, and experienced. 'Consumed', one might be tempted to add, by way of Adornian reference to the Culture Industry. There is also good reason to consider the position of Strauss's work with respect to the past glories of German culture, to which it might appear to mark if not a climax, then an ambivalently modernist/anti-modernist coda, Schoenberg notwithstanding. Those wedded or at least disposed to organic models of cultural rise, climax, and decline will hardly fail to see the potential for decadence here. Should one not follow Nietzsche, employing the French word, *décadence*, for the Wilde opera, *Salome*, and for a good deal else besides? Is it a coincidence that, relatively early in his operatic career, he was drawn to the court of Herod Antipas? Does not Strauss in decadent and, some would say, uncomprehending, fashion, parody and perhaps even travesty Wagner there and in *Elektra*, Mozart in *Der Rosenkavalier*, and both in *Die Frau ohne Schatten*? Even longevity presents its own problems, especially when combined with the claim that Strauss turned his back on 'modernism' after *Elektra*. Indeed, it might seem perverse to have him follow rather than precede Schoenberg, who was influenced more by Strauss than he latterly wished, but since the history in this chapter finds its culmination in *Capriccio* and the Third Reich, that seemed more fitting: Aron 'after' Moses.

Moreover, even when biographical issues – as in Wagner's case, both more complicated and more interesting than the tired formulations served up by their accusers – are put on one side, one often encounters a sense of moral outrage, or at least distaste, that a composer of such gifts is, for more or less reprehensible reasons, letting them go to waste, frittering them away, acting dishonestly. One senses a school-report-like suspicion that Strauss could easily have done so much 'better', 'ease' suggesting the composer's dangerous facility: a Mendelssohn without Protestant probity. Carl Dahlhaus, far from an outright anti-Straussian, opines: 'The break between self-satisfied cantabile and orchestral sophistication in Strauss ... is impossible to ignore,' the 'relationship between technique and expression' being 'precarious'.[1] That implies a squandering of fabulous technique, an easy way out, almost *because he could*. Elgar, Rachmaninov, and Hans Pfitzner are, for instance – and irrespective of one's gauging of their music's musical worth – generally seen as 'honest' or 'honourable' conservatives. There is integrity to what they are attempting, even for those who doubt the quality of the outcome. Strauss is, in a word, *irresponsible*, whereas an authentic modern artist must, in post-Romantic style, shoulder *responsibility*, for the development of his art, and even for the moral health, instruction, and progress of the world around him. For Strauss, poets or artists should not be the legislators of the world, not because they are unimportant, but because being an artist is so much more important than being a legislator. His creed is æstheticism through and through.

This is a composer who notoriously could not understand the pre-occupation with redemption evinced by Mahler, who has latterly come to be seen as the prophet of twentieth-century music. With candid honesty, Strauss told Otto Klemperer: 'I do not know from what I am to be redeemed. When I sit down at my desk in the morning and I get an idea, I do not stand in need of redemption. What did Mahler mean by it?'[2] Nevertheless, a Mahlerian ascendancy has been achieved, whether in musicological, compositional, or performing circles, and the qualities for which Mahler is admired, be they moral, modernist, or both, tend to be viewed as lacking in Strauss. Indeed, Schoenberg, declining a request for an appreciation on Strauss's fiftieth birthday, would claim: 'since I have understood Mahler (and I cannot grasp how anyone can do otherwise) I have inwardly rejected Strauss'.[3]

In that respect, Michael Steinberg makes an interesting claim. Speaking specifically of *Metamorphosen*, Strauss's great string requiem for

[1] Carl Dahlhaus, 'Structure and Expression in Scriabin,' in *Schoenberg and the New Music*, tr. Derrick Puffett and Alfred Clayton (Cambridge University Press: Cambridge, 1987), p. 202.

[2] Otto Klemperer, *Meine Erinnerungen an Gustav Mahler* (Atlantis: Zurich, 1960), p. 21.

[3] Letter to an unknown correspondent of 22 April 1914, in Arnold Schoenberg, *Letters*, tr. Eithne Wilkins and Ernst Kaiser, ed. Erwin Stein (Faber: London and Boston, 1964) p. 51. (This was in response to Strauss's notorious claims, also quoted in the letter (p. 50): 'The only person who can help poor Schönberg now is a psychiatrist,' and 'I think he'd do better to shovel snow instead of scribbling on music-paper.')

German humanism, he posits a contrast with the subjective struggles of consciousness in a generic Mahler *Adagio* – though, interestingly, the formulation might work just as well for a Bruckner slow movement. There are, Steinberg writes:

> almost no pauses in the music, no moments of Mahlerian silence in which the composing subject stands back, takes stock, ponders the legitimacy of his own mode of expression, questions the possibility of music – and decides whether and how to continue. Strauss does not ask, in music, *the* question that musical modernism asks, and that is whether a musical subject can engage in dialogue with the world legitimately. What remains is not a soul or a subject but a mode of movement and interaction with the world.[4]

That latter claim is not quite true of *Metamorphosen*, in a sense *the* work in which Strauss's mask(s) most obviously slip(s), allowing not only the subject's but the composer-subject's own lament and its genealogy to be heard. There are, moreover, other instances of such self-revelation, such as the Composer's – here, surely Strauss's – hymn to the power of music at the end of the Prologue to *Ariadne auf Naxos*, though in *Metamorphosen* this is not just an instance; it is an entire work and the very idea, maybe even Idea, of that work. It is true that Strauss is not here problematising the question in modernist terms; he probably never does, or at least such is not his intention, insofar as that matters. Nevertheless, for once – or as a rare example – his work appears to answer Steinberg's modernist question. Yet if we consider Steinberg's claim more generally with respect to Strauss, there seems to be something well worth considering here. There may be a sense in which, irrespective of ultimately fruitless arguments about musical language – honourably Romantic or pusillanimously reactionary? – Strauss may pose a disturbing post-modernist challenge to the modernist canon, a challenge more worthy of consideration than the descent into populism that has characterised self-proclaimed neo-Romantics or anti-modernists.

There remains, then, an abiding moral question, itself unavoidably political: what is this music *for*? Are we straightforwardly – or better, cynically – being manipulated? If so, to what end? Or, is this evidence of something more radically Nietzschean to Strauss, in this sense more so than Schoenberg and arguably more than Nietzsche himself, namely a refusal – or should that be an inability? – to transcend? Certainly, if we consider, for instance, the music of John the Baptist in *Salome*, especially when Jokaanan speaks of one to come far greater than he, there is little

[4] Michael P. Steinberg, 'Richard Strauss and the Question,' in *Richard Strauss and his World*, ed. Bryan Gilliam (Princeton University Press: Princeton, 1992), pp. 185–6.

more than a mild gravity that one can hardly take seriously. Strauss would not have denied the cultural accomplishments of Christianity, but otherwise he seems less to have opposed than merely disregarded it; he was less a conscious child of the Enlightenment or Young Hegelianism or even a Goethian pagan than a nihilist by apparent default. Why? It is certainly not the product of ignorance; Strauss's level of cultural accomplishment seems almost the ideal advertisement for a *Gymnasium* education. Is the composer, in his portrayal of Jokaanan and elsewhere, failing to communicate the reality of metaphysics? Can he simply not be bothered? Or is his an almost Voltairean realism, exhausted by the weight of idealist claims imposed upon music and resulting from both Hegelian and Schopenhauerian schools (in Wagner, both in one person)? Perhaps Strauss is actually saying, *il faut cultiver notre jardin*. What are the implications, including the political implications, of such a standpoint? And how do the answers to those various questions fit together?

Take the following words from Adorno, which could never be applied to Strauss, who would apparently therefore stand as Schoenberg's retrograde antipode:

> [Schoenberg's] music denies the very thing we have been accustomed, since Shakespeare's days, to expect from music as the magical art: consolation. In the era of music's emancipation it claims to be nothing more than the voice of truth, without the crutches of the familiar, but also without the deception of praise and false positivity. The strength to do this, not illusion, is what is consoling about it. One could say that Schoenberg translated the Old Testament ban on images into music.[5]

If Schoenberg stands for truth, does not Strauss stand for something false, for consolation, for 'the deception of praise and false positivity', for illusory images? Thomas Mann's Adrian Leverkühn contracts venereal disease from his visit to the prostitute Esmerelda after the first Austrian performance of *Salome* in Graz, in 1906. (Mahler, Puccini, Berg, Schoenberg, Zemlinsky, and Hitler were in attendance.) The book's narrator, Serenus Zeitblom, had 'never been able to think of that encounter without a religious shudder – for in that embrace, one party forfeited his salvation'.[6] Straining to become Schoenberg was to be Leverkühn's impossible penance.

[5] Theodor W. Adorno, 'Toward an Understanding of Schoenberg,' tr. Susan H. Gillespie, in *Essays on Music*, ed. Richard Leppert (University of California Press: Berkeley, Los Angeles, and London, 2002), p. 638.

[6] Thomas Mann, *Doctor Faustus: The Life of the German Composer Adrian Leverkühn as Told by a Friend*, tr. John E. Woods (Vintage: New York, 1999), p. 165.

Julius Korngold, the all-too-influential music critic and father of the composer Erich, wrote a sceptical but not entirely unappreciative review of *Der Rosenkavalier* in the *Neue Freie Presse*. The opening words of the review, regarding Strauss, his role, and the Germans, are perceptive:

> Although his pre-eminent talents call him to the role of leading musician, no one is less suited to it than Richard Strauss. The Germans want a priest, someone who will champion an art with deep intentions. Strauss is driven by the ego sensibility of the modern artist, who wants above all to serve himself and his sensations.[7]

Less Richard III, then, as Hans von Bülow had once dubbed the young Strauss, than Richard II, of whom Bülow had said there was no musical equivalent, or perhaps even Richard Cromwell.[8] The language of the ego points clearly to Freud's Vienna and the language of sensations most likely refers to Ernst Mach and Hermann Bahr's 'sensations, nothing but sensations': an anti-Romantic alternative modernity – or modernism – that fits Strauss, especially at this time in his career, rather well.[9] A priestly, Romantic or post-Romantic, calling is not for Strauss, though that does not in itself support Karl Kraus's biting description – does he ever fail to draw blood? – of the composer as 'certainly more of a stock company [*Aktiengesellschaft*] than a genius'.[10]

Stravinsky, perhaps anxious concerning Strauss's claims to the human-istic fatherhood of neo-Classicism – *Pulcinella*, not only before the letter, but with a heart, at least of sorts? – delivered a typically *de haut en bas* judgement: 'I would like to admit all Strauss's operas to whichever purgatory punishes triumphant vulgarity. Their musical substance is cheap and poor; it cannot interest a musician today. That now so ascendant *Ariadne* [*auf Naxos*]?...[it] makes me want to scream.'[11] Strauss was also guilty, Stravinsky declared after a 1963 performance of *Der Rosenkavalier*,

---

[7] Julius Korngold, review in *Neue Freie Presse*, 9 April 1911 (16750), p. 1.

[8] Richard Strauss, 'Reminiscences of the First Performances of my Operas', in *Recollections and Reflections*, ed. Willi Schuh, tr. L. J. Lawrence (Boosey and Hawkes: London, 1953), p. 149

[9] Ernst Mach, *The Analysis of Sensations and the Relation of the Physical to the Psychical*, tr. Sydney Waterlow (London: Routledge/Thoemmes, 1996); Bahr is quoted in Erich Ruprecht and Dieter Bänsch, *Literarische Manifeste der Jahrhundertwende, 1890–1910* (J. B. Metzler: Stuttgart, 1970), p. 169; Bertha Zuckerkandl, 'Hermann Bahr, Ernst Mach und Emil Zuckerkandl im Gespräch', in Gotthard Wunberg (ed.), *Die Wiener Moderne: Literatur, Kunst und Musick zwischen 1890 und 1910* (Reclam: Stuttgart, 2000), pp. 171–7.

[10] Karl Kraus, 'Kulturpleite', in *Die Fackel*, 649–56 (June 1924), 53.

[11] Igor Stravinsky and Robert Craft, *Conversations with Igor Stravinsky* (Faber: London, 1959), p. 75.

of a lack of commitment; he could charm and delight, but never move. 'He didn't give a damn.'[12] Stravinsky certainly knew what it was like to be accused of a lack of sincerity, of not being 'genuine', so his words seem of particular force.

Alex Ross, summing up the case for the defence, employs words upon which Strauss's detractors would readily seize:

> If, as Leonard Bernstein once said, Mahler is the prophet of a century of death, Strauss shows how a weakened, wounded, obdurately human art can survive the catastrophe. Music, he suggests, cannot mirror all the terrors of the age. It cannot even do them justice. Instead, it should do what it has always done – play upon the emotions and conjure emotions from notes.[13]

The claim that music has 'always done' something is debatable and is certainly anti-historical. But it is the identification of *what* it has 'always done' – playing and conjuring – which arouses the most suspicion in (our) modernist hearts and minds. Is Strauss perpetrating all of the time what Wagner, advised by Cosima, might have been doing at the end of *Die Meistersinger*, deflecting attention from devastation by engaging us in a paean to holy German art? Worse still, does he even care? Far from the most unambiguous of modernists, Henze would nevertheless voice this accusation with particular force:

> Beethoven regarded his whole enterprise as a contribution to human progress. As with Marxism, his goal is not God but Man, whereas there are other artists who have never given a thought to the moral function of their work; for instance Richard Strauss, who is for me – perhaps I'm going too far – something like a court composer to Kaiser Wilhelm II.[14]

II

Let us begin, then, in 1892, in the early years of Wilhelmine Germany and perhaps a little earlier than might be expected, with what in the traditional sense might qualify as Strauss's most overtly political opera: his first, *Guntram*. There is nothing of the Kaiser's court to be found in this work, although there is plenty of its era in the influence of Max Stirner, whose anarchistic manifesto, *The Ego and its Own*, appears frequently in

[12] Robert Craft, *Stravinsky: Chronicle of a Friendship* (Knopf: New York, 1973), p. 215.
[13] Alex Ross, 'The Last Emperor: Richard Strauss,' in *The New Yorker*, 20 December 1999, 93–4.
[14] Hans Werner Henze, 'Does Music have to be Political?' in *Music and Politics: Collected Writings 1953–81*, tr. Peter Labanyi (Faber: London, 1982), p. 171.

Strauss's *braunes Tagebuch*.[15] Ross writes that Strauss read Stirner 'seeking an alternative to Wagnerism', which might seem an odd claim given the powerful influence Stirner had exerted upon Wagner and in particular upon the *Ring*.[16] However, Strauss forgets, does not realise, or perhaps dissents from, the later *Ring*'s developing critique of Wagner's earlier, less sceptical individualism.[17] In one sense at least, *Guntram* is not so very 'political', since Strauss is more interested in using Stirner or at least Stirner-like ideas – the rejection of all oppressive forces: moral, legal, religious, political – to write himself out of politics, in order to concentrate on playing and conjuring. There is a selfish æstheticism here that perhaps has a rather more apposite Wagnerian precedent. Like Lohengrin, though unlike the still more problematical Tannhäuser, Strauss's hero renounces not only his love, Freihild, not only God, but the *Parsifal*-Bayreuth-like community of a mediæval Christian brotherhood. In breaking his lyre, Guntram breaks with the brotherhood's teaching that art, and music in particular, might bring redemption. Romantic art-religion is eschewed. But so, in one very important sense, is Schopenhauer, at least according to Strauss's Nietzschean reading of the philosopher. Adrian Daub has argued that 'any Schopenhauerian storyline would have to be dramatised without drama – a Schopenhauerian opera is, at least at first blush, a *contradiction in adiectum*'.[18] The Will that must be renounced would remain as music. Wagner had, after all, 'corrected' Schopenhauer in *Tristan*, albeit in terms of elevating at least as much as renouncing sexual love. Strauss may be understood to be continuing Wagner's post-Schopenhauerian work in a sense that goes beyond the stylistic and beyond the similarity, even affinity, of gathered congregation.

Wagner had attempted artistic redemption of religion in the celebrated opening words to his *Religion and Art* essay:

> One could say that when religion becomes artificial, it is reserved for art to grant salvation to the kernel of religion, by having us believe that mythical symbols, which the former [that is, religion] would have us believe in their real

[15] Charles Youmans, *Richard Strauss's Orchestral Music and the German Intellectual Tradition: The Philosophical Roots of Musical Modernism* (Indiana University Press: Bloomington and Indianopolis, 2005), p. 23.

[16] Alex Ross, *The Rest is Noise: Listening to the Twentieth Century* (Fourth Estate: London, 2008), p. 15; Mark Berry, *Treacherous Bonds and Laughing Fire: Politics and Religion in Wagner's 'Ring'* (Ashgate: Aldershot and Burlington, VT, 2006), esp. chs 6 and 8; and chapter 1 of this book.

[17] Ibid., pp. 230–3, 270–1.

[18] Adrian Daub, '"Taceat Muller in Theatro": Guntram, Schopenhauer, and the Female Voice,' in *Opera Quarterly*, 25 (2009), 241.

[*eigentlich*] sense, may be comprehended through their symbolical value, in order to discern therein, via an ideal presentation, the concealed profound truth.[19]

In place of what was ultimately a late-Romantic redemptive strategy, Strauss considered the knot of art and religion already to have been cut by his other great nineteenth-century heroes: Goethe, Schopenhauer, and Nietzsche (though not really by Beethoven). Indeed, following Nietzsche, it appeared that truth would no longer be a question for art – or perhaps even at all. Both Nietzsche and Strauss may be considered as perspectivists. Schoenberg – arguably Berg and Webern too – would arrive at the fragmentary whilst straining towards the absolute, or should that be the Absolute? Strauss was not looking for it in the first place, or at least he soon reckoned to have learned the error of his juvenile idealist ways. Guntram ostracises himself with the lack of humility that entails, arguably both for himself and for his composer-librettist. Strauss's original ending, in which, echoing *Tannhäuser*, Guntram embarks upon a pilgrimage of penitence to the Holy Land, is jettisoned in favour of rejection: rejection almost but not quite as an existential principle. One might even characterise this rejection of the world's strictures but also of its struggles as a mere excuse; unlike Wagner, Strauss is no Bakunin. The solitude for which Guntram opts is not glorious but it might be desirable for one who wants more time in which to compose. Guntram in Garmisch: material, perhaps, for an operetta?

Strauss did not want to transform society, disdain its collective impulses as he might; he, like Stirner, simply wanted to be free of it. For all of his Classicism – and few, if any composers, can have been so well versed in that respect – it was the literature of the ancient world, not its art-religion, that inspired Strauss. How very different from Wagner, of whom Cosima recorded, 'Herr [Heinrich] v. Stein reads to us the translation he has made of Æschylus's Chorus, and it seems very good. "That is religion," R. exclaims.'[20] What is most telling about the disagreement between Strauss and his more conventionally Wagnerian, that is epigonal, friend, the composer and violinist Alexander Ritter, is that Strauss simply could not or would not understand why Ritter saw Guntram's act – and thus that of Strauss, Ritter's protégé – as immoral. Ritter had suggested the

[19] Richard Wagner, 'Religion und Kunst,' in *Sämtliche Schriften und Dichtungen*, ed. Richard Sternfeld and Hans von Wolzogen, 16 vols in 10 (Breitkopf und Härtel: Leipzig, 1912–14), vol. 10, p. 211.

[20] Cosima Wagner, *Cosima Wagner's Diaries*, ed. Martin Gregor-Dellin and Dietrich Mack, tr. Geoffrey Skelton, 2 vols (Harcourt Brace Jovanovich: London, 1978–80), 24 November 1879, vol. 2, p. 400.

subject to Strauss in the first instance and had, through a reading of late Wagner and Schopenhauer especially influenced by Wagner's *Religion and Art*, wanted Guntram to remain an heroic agent of reconciliation between art and religion.[21] That was not so much objectionable to Strauss as incomprehensible. As Stirner had put it, 'Every higher essence above me, be it God, be it man, weakens the feeling of my uniqueness, and pales only before the sun of this consciousness.'[22] In that, Strauss was a truer disciple of Stirner than the more self-critical – yes, whatever his detractors might claim – Wagner. It is difficult to discern why Ritter had not understood that in an earlier and more recognisably Straussian work, the 1888 *Don Juan*, its protagonist no more despatched to Hell than Guntram would be to Heaven; nevertheless, he did now. For all of Strauss's Nietzscheanism, there is something of the nihilist in him, but then one might say the same of Nietzsche. Strauss was, in Charles Youmans's splendid phrase, 'a musical atheist … – a composer utterly without interest in or patience with romantic (and non-romantic) beliefs concerning music's extramusical capabilities'.[23] Strauss became, one might say, more atheist than Nietzsche himself. Again, perhaps Stravinsky ought to have recognised a kindred spirit – that is, were Stravinsky the composer to be identified with Stravinsky the æsthetician.

Music and art more generally, then, were and would always be the thing for Strauss. The orchestra of *Elektra*, as Lawrence Kramer notes, is 'to a degree extreme even for Strauss, dependent on the narrative action, obsessed with illustrating every detail, emotional and physical, remembered or imagined. The result, since the action is wholly dominated by Elektra – by her voice, her presence, her desire – is that the orchestra comes to seem as obsessed with her as she is with her family tragedy.'[24] The result is also, crucially for us, that the drama, in a sense, becomes obsessed with Wagner. Indeed, it becomes embroiled in a kind of hyper-Wagnerism. Gesture, to which Wagner had ascribed such importance in *Opera and Drama* – a high watermark from which he had spent much of his dramatic

[21] Norman Del Mar, *Richard Strauss: A Commentary on his Life and Works*, 3 vols (Barrie and Rockliff: London, 1962–72), vol. 1, pp. 112–13. Wagner, 'Religion und Kunst,' pp. 211–53. For an example of Ritter's own views, see *Verfall und Reform. Eine Schilderung deutscher Theater-Zustände nebst einem Vorschlag zur Reorganisation der Provinzial-Bühnen* (Stuber: Würzburg, 1864).

[22] Max Stirner, *The Ego and its Own*, tr. Steven Byington, ed. David Leopold (Cambridge University Press: Cambridge, 1995), p. 324.

[23] Youmans, *Richard Strauss's Orchestral Music*, p. 46.

[24] Lawrence Kramer, *Opera and Modern Culture: Wagner and Strauss* (University of California Press: Berkeley, Los Angeles, and London, 2004), p. 194.

life from retreating – is treated hyper-realistically.[25] The more it is, the more the music threatens to run out of control. It is a startling dialectic, though it should be familiar to students of musical drama from Monteverdi onwards – think of the Torquato Tasso-derived *Il combattimento di Tancredi e Clorinda* – given that there is a very real sense in which the music is serving as handmaiden to the written text. And so, liberation seems to reside in the liberation of music itself, an idea whose possibility runs throughout Strauss's œuvre, and not just in materialist fashion. *Wort oder Ton*, as *Capriccio* asks?

III

Walter Benjamin suggested in 1936 that resistance towards fascism's æstheticisation of politics could be achieved by the politicisation of art.[26] Strauss's record in this respect might well be seen as lamentable by those who wish to 'judge'; theirs is a curious yet widespread understanding of history. Yet some aspects of his later work and in particular *Capriccio*, his final opera, may be understood to tell a different story, more akin to the following words from Norman Del Mar:

> Strauss's position during the last years before the second World War was more doubtful and delicate than he had ever experienced. Tolerated for the sake of his world-wide eminence, yet frowned upon by the German authorities whom he made no efforts to placate, although he had learnt to fear them, he was driven almost to become a recluse.[27]

Del Mar's judicious words are all too rare in a world that apparently wishes not so much constantly to denazify, as constantly to nazify. However, even they do not quite prepare us for what we find in *Capriccio*, should we permit ourselves to look. This is not to portray Strauss as a hero, his life as *Ein Heldenleben*, but to claim that in so overtly unpolitical a work, we perhaps find the composer at his most political, sometimes in spite of himself, sometimes not.

Strauss had all along been considered dubious by Goebbels. However, the 1935 interception by the Dresden Gestapo of an unguarded letter, carelessly posted in a hotel letter-box, put paid to any official status

---

[25]   Richard Wagner, *Oper und Drama*, ed. Klaus Kropfinger, 2nd edn (Reclam: Stuttgart, 1994), p. 250.

[26]   Walter Benjamin, 'The Work of Art in the Age of its Technical Reproducibility,' in *Illuminations*, tr. Harry Zohn, ed. Hannah Arendt (Harcourt: New York, 1969), p. 242.

[27]   Del Mar, *Richard Strauss*, vol. 3, p. 179.

the composer had enjoyed. The Saxon Gauleiter, Martin Mutschmann, forwarded the letter to Hitler. Goebbels, seizing the opportunity, had Strauss resign his presidency of the *Reichsmusikkammer* on grounds of ill health. *Die schweigsame Frau* ran for just four performances. 'Your letter of the 15th is driving me to distraction!' Strauss had written in that letter to Stefan Zweig. (Unfortunately, Zweig's letter of that date has been lost or destroyed.) 'This Jewish obstinacy! Enough to make an anti-Semite of a man! This pride of race, this feeling of solidarity!' One can only imagine what Schoenberg would have made of such words, however 'casual' their formulation, given the letter we saw him write to Kandinsky. But Strauss continued in a somewhat different vein:

> Do you believe that I am ever, in any of my actions, guided by the thought that I am 'a German' (perhaps, *qui le sait*)? Do you believe that Mozart composed as an 'Aryan'? I know only two types of people: those with and those without talent. The people [*das Volk*] exist for me only at the moment they become audience. Whether they are Chinese, Bavarians, New Zealanders, or Berliners leaves me cold. What matters is that they pay the full price for admission ... Who told you that I have exposed myself politically? Because I have conducted a concert in place of [the Jewish] Bruno Walter? That I did for the orchestra's sake. Because I substituted for Toscanini [who, vehemently anti-fascist, had withdrawn from his Bayreuth engagement following the NSDAP's seizure of power]? That I did for the sake of Bayreuth ... Because I am the President of the Reich Music Chamber? That I do only for good purposes and to prevent greater disasters! I should have accepted this troublesome honorary office under any government. But neither Kaiser Wilhelm nor Herr Rathenau [the former Jewish foreign minister] offered it to me.[28]

Those words, it is worth reiterating, are in no sense those of a hero. The financial aspect should be taken with a pinch of salt, though not disregarded. Strauss, to the frustration of his admirers, was keen to play the Philistine in such matters, but that was often an act or at least exaggerated. More important is his devotion, admirable or misguided, to art – Michael Kater calls him an 'aesthetocrat' – and above all to German art, which devotion shone through even in his letter of apology to the Führer, to which no response materialised.[29] Thereafter began a cat-and-mouse game with the authorities in which Strauss and, he feared, his family

[28] Letter of 17 June 1935, in Willi Schuh (ed.), *A Confidential Matter: The Letters of Richard Strauss and Stefan Zweig, 1931–1935*, tr. Max Knight (University of California Press: Berkeley and Los Angeles, 1977), pp. 99–100 (translation slightly modified).
[29] Michael H. Kater, *Composers of the Nazi Era: Eight Portraits* (Oxford University Press: Oxford, 1999), p. 218

could only lose – at least in the 'real' world. Del Mar again comes close to the mark when he speaks of 'Strauss's pathetic encounter with the Nazis. He was constitutionally unable to grasp that there *was* no logic in their arguments.'[30] That does not mean that there was none in his.

It is of course maddeningly inconvenient for Strauss's apologists that he was appointed president of the *Reichsmusikkammer* in 1933, upon Hitler's rise to power, even though Strauss's aim was to protect 'serious' music against the depredations of popular culture. One can scarcely begin to imagine the apoplexy that would have been provoked in Adorno by the idea of attempting to employ the organs of the National Socialist state to battle the Culture Industry; but then, Strauss was almost as suspect for Adorno as he was for Goebbels. However, it remains just as inconvenient for Strauss's accusers that he defended Zweig, librettist for *Die schweigsame Frau*. It was with Zweig's discovery in the British Museum of Antonio Salieri's (and the Abbé Giovanni Battista Casti's) little work of 1782 for the Schönbrunn Orangery, *Prima la musica e poi le parole*, that the idea of *Capriccio* may justly be said to have begun. If we at least try to stop judging and begin to listen, we may progress a little further.

IV

Capriccio itself probably also requires a brief introduction. The opera originated in that idea from Zweig, taking his cue from Casti, a rival of Lorenzo da Ponte. Zweig had wished to create a new work exploring one of the fundamental issues in operatic creation, namely the relationship between words and music. Upon his flight from Austria, Zweig had hoped that Joseph Gregor would take up the plan for a libretto, but Strauss, ever the productively difficult taskmaster, found Gregor's proposals wanting, eventually proposing to the conductor Clemens Krauss that he take on the task. Krauss and Strauss ended up writing the text in collaboration, though the music was of course entirely Strauss's own. What arose was a metatheatrical conversation piece, very much in the line of the Strauss-Hofmannsthal *Ariadne auf Naxos*. Set in the salon of Countess Madeleine outside Paris 'around 1775', that is at the time of controversy over Gluck's operatic reforms, we witness disputes between the Countess, her brother, the composer Flamand, the poet Olivier, and the theatrical impresario La Roche, over the nature of music, drama, and opera; the Count hits upon the idea that the events arising should themselves be turned into an opera, a

---

[30] Del Mar, *Richard Strauss*, vol. 3, p. 51.

collaboration between the artists present. The Countess proves as incapable, at least on the surface, of choosing æsthetically between words and music as she is romantically between poet and composer. Unlike Strauss's preceding opera, *Die Liebe der Danae*, *Capriccio* received wartime performances, being premiered at the Nationaltheater in Munich on 28 October 1942, not long before it went up in flames, its obsequies to be celebrated in Strauss's outpouring of cultural grief, the Goethian *Metamorphosen*.

The opening string sextet – the conceit being that it is itself a new work by Flamand – had already been performed at the villa of Baldur von Schirach, the Vienna Gauleiter who helped Strauss secure his Viennese Belvedere home and who concluded an agreement that would, the letter to Hitler having gone unanswered, have had Strauss to play a role in furthering Viennese musical life in return for protection for his Jewish daughter-in-law, Alice, and his grandsons. (They would not have to wear the Star of David in public and would enjoy the privilege of an 'Aryan' education.[31]) Schirach had acted as patron to the 1941 Mozart Week of the German Reich, held in Vienna, during which Goebbels had given a speech at the State Opera, declaring that Mozart's 'music rings out every evening over homeland and front. It is part of what our soldiers are defending against the wild assault of Eastern barbarism.'[32] One might, if so inclined, draw a parallel or indeed a contrast with the reference to Eastern hordes, nowadays often disingenuously excised, in the third act of *Lohengrin*, but equally one might draw a parallel or contrast between the Nazis' fear, as Goebbels spoke, about the halting of the German advance upon Moscow and 'Eastern barbarism' and the fears of musicians such as Strauss and Furtwängler about the onslaught of barbarism closer to home.[33] As one of the two defendants, the other being Albert Speer, who spoke against Hitler at Nuremberg, Schirach would serve twenty years in Spandau Prison.

In negotiating with him, Strauss was simply – or not so simply – acting as he had long done so with other patrons, royal, noble, political, or otherwise.

[31] Bryan Gilliam, *The Life of Richard Strauss* (Cambridge University Press: Cambridge, 1999), p. 168.

[32] Quoted in Erik Levi, *Mozart and the Nazis: How the Third Reich Abused a Cultural Icon* (Yale University Press: New Haven and London, 2010), p. 178.

[33] In 1876, Wagner had felt compelled to accede to a request from the director of the Vienna Court Opera to cut the passage, so as not to offend the easily-offended sensitivities of the newly-founded Dual Monarchy's Magyar 'half'. (John Deathridge and Klaus Döge, 'Dokumente und Texte zu "Lohengrin"', in Wagner, *Sämtliche Werke*, ed. Carl Dahlhaus, Egon Voss, and others (Schott: Mainz, 1970–), vol. 26, p. 197.) That seems no reason to continue the practice, as many performances still do today.

Ariadne had shown that, though the patron called the tune, the artist might yet retain integrity. Whether that were the case in such a radically different situation is another matter; now, as Bryan Gilliam has pointed out, the arch-manipulator – and here, let us include his music as well as his dealing with patrons – 'was in the end the one who was manipulated'.[34] And so, as the Prelude begins, we enter musically and historically into a mordent-ornamented – decidedly anti-Schoenbergian – and mordantly ironic conversation, both playful and with higher stakes than one might ever have thought, a conversation which, it seems, might have been in progress for a little time prior to our eavesdropping. What might we have heard had we been listening earlier? We both want and do not want to know, like the Countess Madeleine herself in the opera.

What, then, do we make of an opera conceived and first performed in such circumstances? It is hardly a work of overt protest, though how could it be? In its 'aristocratic' refinement, both verbally and musically, it stands at one level about as distant from the catastrophe enveloping Europe as one could imagine. Yet when one begins to consider it a little more deeply, all sorts of difficulties, intentional or otherwise, emerge. This might seem facile, but the very setting in France has resonances. Moreover, to have the Countess comparing the musical merits of Rameau vis-à-vis Couperin at this time in Nazi Germany is perhaps more telling than one might think. Brahms might have edited Couperin, but one will struggle to find his name or his music in Third Reich performances and musicology. Moreover, Lully and Rameau had found their contributions to musical history minimised to make way for still greater emphasis upon German composers, in texts such as the 1934 revision of Emil Naumann's *Illustrierte Musikgeschichte*.[35] Even leaving aside matters of nationality, however, such composers were not part of the musical mainstream; indeed, many *composers*, let alone others, would not necessarily have been well acquainted with their music. Strauss certainly was – and showed through his composition that he was: sometimes through direct quotation, for instance the 'Air italien' from Rameau's *Les Indes galantes*, when the composer is mentioned, at other times through allusion. There seems, then, to be an assertion of humanist, perhaps aristocratic, values: lightly done, as it had to be, but which connects very well with Strauss's increasing re-immersion

[34] Gilliam, *Life of Richard Strauss*, p. 148.

[35] Erik Levi, *Music in the Third Reich* (Macmillan: Basingstoke, 1994), p. 225; Eugen Schmitz, *Emil Naumanns Illustrierte Musikgeschichte von den Anfängen der Tonkunst bis zur Gegenwart, neu gestaltet* (Union Deutsche Verlagsgesellschaft: Stuttgart, 1934).

in the work of Goethe. The apolitical, especially at times such as this, may actually be read as highly political, whatever the straightforward intention.

Arguably true, perhaps, but the Rococo – or should that be neo-Rococo? – setting cannot help but seem like a refuge, a retreat. We have, perhaps, returned to the *Rosenkavalier* problem – albeit intensified, for retreating from harmonic experiment after *Elektra* is one thing, withdrawing from a world of war and genocide quite another. Even in eighteenth-century terms, the aristocratic salon with exquisite manners and rarefied æsthetic debate contrasts sharply with what we know was to come after 1789: the alleged 'truth' of revolutionary art, exemplified by the studio of Jacques-Louis David, let alone the Paris of the *sans-culottes*, seems distant indeed.

There is also the fact that, perhaps surprisingly, this is just the sort of setting that was favoured by Nazi cultural policy. Goebbels wanted entertainment, *Unterhaltung*, rather than Wagnerian challenge. (*Parsifal*, we may recall, was not performed at Bayreuth during the Second World War.) *Capriccio* is certainly not unusual in offering an eighteenth-century setting. What is more unusual, though not unique, is the combination of that setting with such reflection, explicit and implicit, upon the nature of art and its relationship with its historical context. Once again, masks and games both gratify and haunt us: Straussian detachment and irony works its wonders through its posing of questions without evident response (at least from the composer). In context, this was a reinstatement of the artistic criticism that so troubled Goebbels, who had requested that journals comment only upon the content of a piece rather than attempting assessment of its aesthetic quality.[36]

Krauss, a skilled careerist, secured the 1942 Munich premiere, which he conducted, his wife Viorica Ursuleac as the Countess, by persuading Goebbels, with whom Strauss had once again fallen out of favour, to assume its patronage as part of a Strauss festival mounted in the *Hauptstadt der Bewegung*. The director Rudolf Hartmann, present on that evening, would recall, doubtless not without a dose of sugary romanticism, although that tells its own contemporary as well as subsequent story:

Who among the younger generation can really imagine a great city like Munich in total darkness, or theatre-goers picking their way through the blacked-out street with the aid of small torches giving off a dim blue light through a narrow slit? All this for the experience of the *Capriccio* première. They risked being caught in a heavy air raid, yet their yearning to hear

[36] Levi, *Music in the Third Reich*, p. 188.

Strauss's music, their desire to be part of a festive occasion and to experience a world of beauty beyond the dangers of war led them to overcome all these material problems ... Afterwards it was difficult to relinquish the liberating and uniting atmosphere created by the artistic quality of the new work. But outside the blackened city waited, and one's way homewards was fraught with potential danger.[37]

Strauss's æstheticism almost seemed confirmed, then, in such an experience. What might once have seemed anti-political now offered an alternative, complementary, or even utopian community to that of the 'real' world. Aerial bombing would soon send the Munich Nationaltheater up in flames. Wartime performances would nevertheless be heard subsequently in Darmstadt, in Dresden, whose destruction lay close, and almost inevitably, given Schirach's patronage and predilections, in Vienna.[38]

And yet, since so much of the drama concerns itself with artistic patronage, we almost seem invited, by the material if not the composer, to consider the patronage of Schirach and Goebbels. How do we read in such a context a work in which it is the patroness, the Countess, who insofar as anyone can, resolves or, perhaps better, suspends dramatic conflicts? On the other hand, it seems clear that the representation of La Roche takes an affectionate cue from the Jewish impresario Max Reinhardt, an old and valued collaborator of Strauss from before even their foundation of the Salzburg Festival, indeed from the premiere of *Der Rosenkavalier*. In that context, it becomes crucially important, even a case of dissent, that La Roche/Reinhardt, riled by the impudence of callow poet and composer, should have his say, above all in his dignified panegyric to the theatre:

Hola, you ignorant fools! You deride and abuse my magnificent theatre! What grants you the right to speak with such arrogance and to revile me, the knowledgeable expert?...Sharpen your wits; offer the theatre new laws – new content!! If you cannot, then leave me in peace with your criticism...Without my kind, where would the theatre be? Without my heroic daring and finally – without my [financially] helping hand?...Respect the worth of my stage! My goals are honourable; my contributions indelible! I fight for beauty and the noble manners of the theatre...and I shall live on in the annals of its history! 'Sic itur ad astra!' On my tombstone, you shall read this inscription: 'Here

[37] Rudolf Hartmann, *Richard Strauss: The Staging of his Operas and Ballets* (Phaidon: Oxford, 1982), p. 261.

[38] The status of Vienna during the Third Reich is interesting. No reader will need reminding that Hitler's experience there had been less than happy. Whilst there was no attempt actively to destroy its cultural riches, and Schirach enjoyed considerable leeway in furthering his agenda, the Führer wished to establish Linz not only as the centre of artistic life in Austria, or Ostmark, but of the entire Reich.

lies La Roche, the unforgettable, the immortal theatre director. The friend of the cheerful muse, the patron of serious art. To the stage a father, to artists a protective spirit. The gods loved him; men admire him.' – Amen.

The monologue is boastful. Yet what La Roche says of himself, we might also take to be Krauss and Strauss speaking about theatre and art more generally. It is not so very different from the age-old allegorical devices of the operatic Prologue; artistic precedent might not come close to redemption from, let alone of, the political present, yet it can chip away at its totality. Subject matter that might, in *Ariadne* – dedicated to Reinhardt, its first director – have concerned itself more exclusively with the business of putting together and putting on an opera, takes on a different light in different times.

Consciously or otherwise, there may also be an echo of Pfitzner's *Palestrina*, itself a defence of aristocratic culture, albeit during the First World War rather than the Second, the first performance having taken place in Munich in 1917. Pfitzner's increasingly virulent nationalism and anti-modernism make him another fascinating, if difficult, case. In a stroke of irony – perhaps someone should write an opera about this – Pfitzner would be interned opposite Strauss's villa in Garmisch in 1945. A parallel, or perhaps presentiment, closer to home might be Kunrad's attack, in Strauss's 1901 second opera, *Feuersnot*, on the *Wagnerphilister* of Munich. If only Strauss had not joined the party he had once excoriated by signing, alongside Pfitzner, Hans Knappertsbusch, and several others, the 1933 protest by the 'Richard Wagner City Munich' against 'Mr Thomas Mann'. Mann, having delivered his celebrated address, *Sufferings and Greatness of Richard Wagner*, at the University of Munich on 10 February, the protest had appeared in the *Münchner Neueste Nachrichten* of 16/17 April, subsequent to the 'national restoration of Germany . . . [having] taken on definite form'.[39] Strauss was compromised, indubitably; that renders *Capriccio* all the more interesting.

V

Christian von Götz's production for the Cologne Opera, which I saw at the 2007 Edinburgh International Festival, heightened the contrast between political reality and work, and made a powerful case for political

---

[39] Reprinted and translated in Sven Friedrich, 'Ambivalenz der Leidenschaft – Thomas Mann und Richard Wagner. Zum 125. Geburtstag Thomas Manns,' in *Programmhefte der Bayreuther Festspiele*, 2000, 142, 150.

reality as part of both the work and our inevitable response to it. In one of the archetypal operas about the making of an opera, it seemed more than usually appropriate to add another narrative layer, in which the era of the making of *Capriccio* itself featured on stage. Our first sight, disturbingly set against the aristocratic finery of what we might be tempted now to call the Schirach sextet, was of the Wehrmacht marching down the Champs-Elysées. The opera therefore remained in France, in 'a château near Paris' (*ein Schloß in der Nähe von Paris*). The bulk of the action, *Capriccio*'s creation of an opera as opposed to the production's creation of *Capriccio*, took place in eighteenth-century costume: a final house party, in which the coming of the Gestapo might – vainly, in more than one sense – be put out of mind for a couple of hours. Was that perhaps what Strauss himself was doing?

There were from time to time reminders of approaching fate, growing more numerous as time went on, a crucially important concept as attempts at self-distraction became more numerous and more desperate. Every aspect of the production, be it 'political' or 'aesthetic', showed that very dichotomy to be false and worked inexorably towards the Count's preparation of a cyanide capsule, the final vain attempt to answer or perhaps to evade not only the vexed question of words or music, but also to answer or to evade other questions too, and most chillingly of all, to the yellow-star-clad prompter, Monsieur Taupe, being left behind by the departure of the main party and offered his own carriage 'home'. In this context, the actress Clairon's constant refrains that she must depart for Paris sounded differently indeed. The final scene then depicted the Countess bidding farewell, though to whom or to what, exactly? Who knew when or indeed whether she would ever return after being escorted to the railway station? Railways attain quite a different meaning when we, in the shadow of Auschwitz, deal with the Third Reich. And yet, there was another, equally important side to what was going on. Strauss's music arguably offered some sense of hope, 'utopian' in a sense Ernst Bloch would have understood, against this terrible backdrop.[40] Whether the hope were in vain or even irresponsible remained unanswered, at least explicitly. Yet just as surely as music always wins out against the words, the apparently insoluble argument answered by Strauss in the delicate autumnal glory of the closing music set against the banality of the Major-Domo's announcement of supper, so perhaps does art against its surrounding evil. The former certainly does not prevent the other; nor, however, does it necessarily submit entirely. For the music

---

[40] Ernst Bloch, *Geist der Utopie*, 2nd edn (Suhrkamp: Frankfurt am Main, 1980).

to the final scene – self-consciously 'beautiful' perhaps, but even in that respect offering yet another rebellious tribute to Strauss's craftsmanship and taste – becomes all the more moving when it confronts rather than retreats from evil. Or at least when, Strauss donning tactical masks or otherwise, it is made to do so.

The identity of Monsieur Taupe was from the outset concealed until his wry epiphany on stage in the opera's twelfth, penultimate scene. At Krauss's suggestion, he is simply listed in the *dramatis personae* and, should this intention be respected, in theatre programmes, as 'Monsieur Taupe, Tenor'.[41] Appearing on stage, he announces himself as the *souffleur*, that is, the prompter. He, however, has failed in the single yet singular task assigned to him, by falling asleep on the job – shades, perhaps of the steersman in Wagner's first canonical opera, *Der fliegende Holländer* – thereby finding himself 'forgotten' and therefore *im Stich*: abandoned or left in the lurch, just as he might have left the players. Is there a hint of Wagner's Nibelungs – 'I spend my life underground. Unseen –' – and perhaps even of their overlord, Alberich, 'I am the unseen lord of a magical world'? If comedy this be, and I think it probably is, then it is comedy of the curious. But there is more going on here. The Major-Domo welcomes his curious guest to 'unserer wirklichen Welt' (our world of reality). Answers might be invited upon a postcard for how we should read reality and the real world in this context. Perhaps the words should simply be taken at face value; perhaps not. The interpretative choice thereby becomes self-dramatised, likewise the prompter's confession that to him the essence of all reality (*Wirklichkeit*) is *unheimlich-schattenhaft* (uncanny-shadowlike). Such is typical of the world of mirrors, of mediated elegance, in *Capriccio*. Yet M. Taupe knows, or at least he thinks, that he is controlling, almost Sachs-like, this Schopenhauerian world of illusion. As he 'portentously' announces, 'If I sleep, I become an event! The actors can no longer speak – the public awakes!' Oddly, this does not seem to have happened here; we all have our illusions, and perhaps never more so than in wartime – not on stage but of course in 'reality'. In another sense, we – if we are *das Publikum* – do awaken here. The illusion of performance and the nature of stagecraft are brought to our minds, less overtly perhaps than in *Ariadne*, but with the same caution that moments of supreme beauty, maybe even of great art, depend upon artifice, in work as in performance. And yet above, beyond, even through, such artifice, we recalled in Edinburgh –

---

[41] Del Mar, *Richard Strauss*, vol. 3, p. 232.

and presumably also in Cologne – that M. Taupe had his own carriage home. So, very nearly, did Strauss's family.

The use of music associated with La Roche as impresario (Ex. 4) suggests to us that 'art' might depend upon the theatre more than vice versa. It also, bearing in mind the likeness we have observed with Alberich, has a scurrying quality that may put us in mind of him, at least in his relatively innocent opening scene of *Das Rheingold* self.

Ex. 4. La Roche motif

What, then, of the 'real' world 'outside'? What of Strauss's compromises with Schirach in order to safeguard his villa – irredeemably *reichsdeutsch*, Henze might have said – near the Belvedere? That outside world, real or unreal, will not stop intruding. Schirach was not the most favoured member of the Nazi establishment by this time, partly on account of his criticism of the conditions attending deportation of the Jews. And the high command – Hitler, Goebbels, and Himmler – would find occasion, even at this point, when they might have had more pressing concerns, to visit petty humiliations upon the composer, ensuring that he receive no public honour.[42] One would certainly not claim Strauss's conduct as that of a moral beacon, still less so that of one who would be convicted at Nuremberg, although released in 1966. Yet that does not mean that we should make no distinctions between them and the aforementioned trio. Strauss's accommodation with Schirach was, as we have seen, owed partly to his need to safeguard his grandsons, Richard and Christian – somehow it all sounds very much more 'real' when one names them – from the very 'real' danger they faced on account of their Jewish descent.

None of that is necessarily to imply that such thoughts were in the minds of Strauss, Krauss, or even their audience. Yet the sentiments afflicting those of us as the Major-Domo assured M. Taupe of safe passage to Paris, whence the Count, having taken his suicide pill, had already returned, are indicative of the variety of resonances provoked by even an allegedly 'apolitical' work, especially – a theme to which the third part of this book will return in greater detail – in performance. They are indicative of a small measure of resistance, perhaps all the more so when measured

[42] Ibid., p. 243.

against the objectives of totalitarian *Gleichschaltung*; such resonances are not merely imposed from outside but bore a dialectical relationship with the *unheimlich-schattenlich* existence of character and work. It had all, of course, been hinted at in that mysterious, Schopenhauerian volume with whose reading Hans Sachs had opened the third act of *Die Meistersinger* – and with whose reading, or at least of something similar, Strauss had begun his materialist journey.

VI

As an opera about opera, *Capriccio* will always offer an unusual number of resonances, some of them quite personal. I have often found myself, perhaps unsurprisingly, being led to think in oppositional terms of *Moses und Aron*. However, I am also reminded of Alexander Goehr's first opera, *Arden Must Die* (*Arden muss sterben*), above all its murder scene's twin parody setting of Leonardo's *Last Supper* and the music of a Nazi song. The newly introduced character – that is, she does not appear in the original tragedy, *Arden of Faversham* – of Mrs Bradshaw speaks especially clearly to a post-war audience. She stresses that she was never part of the murder plot; she was always against it. (We shall hear such claims amongst the society in which Henze came of age too, the same *Reich*, if not quite the same milieu, from which Goehr and his father, a Schoenberg pupil in Berlin, had to flee.) But society as a whole must take responsibility, as the spoken epilogue makes clear to the audience. The use of speech echoes *Moses*, of course, yet that Brechtian move also performs, despite Brecht's own lack of real interest in music, a similar function to that which an intelligent staging such as Götz's can accomplish in and with *Capriccio*.

At work on the *Ring* in Bayreuth, Boulez observed, in a *Performer's Notebook*:

> There have been endless discussions as to whether this conclusion is pessimistic or optimistic; but is that really the question? Or at any rate can the question be put in such simple terms? Chéreau has called it 'oracular', and it is a good description. In the ancient world, oracles were always ambiguously phrased so that their deeper meaning could be understood only after the event, which, as it were, provided a semantic analysis of the oracle's statement. Wagner refuses any conclusion as such, simply leaving us with the premises for a conclusion that remains shifting and indeterminate in meaning.[43]

---

[43] Pierre Boulez, 'A Performer's Notebook,' in *Orientations: Collected Writings*, ed. Jean-Jacques Nattiez, tr. Martin Cooper (Faber: London, 1986), p. 279.

Chéreau himself wished:

> that the orchestra pit be, like Delphi's smoking pit, a crevice uttering oracles – the Funeral March and the concluding redemption motif. The redemption motif is a message delivered to the entire world, but like all pythonesses, the orchestra is unclear, and there are several ways in which one might interpret its message … Should one not hear it with mistrust and anxiety?[44]

Might we not say that those words apply just as much to *Capriccio* as to *Götterdämmerung*? Not in identical fashion, but nevertheless to a similar degree? If so, it might reasonably be responded that, especially to a cynical age, one can hear anything like that; it is certainly difficult not to regard the final scene of *Così fan tutte* – to whose ensemble writing *Capriccio*'s octet stands as a loving tribute – similarly. Yet *Così* is, even by Mozart's standards, a strikingly modern work, more clear-eyed in its devastating indictment of romantic – and Romantic – love than, say, the Novalis-infused *Tristan*; it is no coincidence that Beethoven found it shockingly immoral. For us, it is perhaps more a successor, if unknowingly so, to the Monteverdi of *L'incoronazione di Poppea* than to the moral dignity and Enlightenment didacticism of Gluck. The questioning of *Così* and its downright nihilism are quite intentional – at least on the composer's part, if not necessarily on his librettist's. Mozart's score, exquisitely sado-masochistic horns of cuckoldry and all, throughout speaks of something lying far beyond the comedic intentions of Da Ponte and, at the end, implying their wholesale negation. Strauss, needless to say, adored it, proving a key figure, arguably *the* key figure, in its modern, anti-Romantic revival.

What we are considering here, however, is somewhat different, neither Wagner nor Strauss being able to escape the attentions of Romanticism. In Wagner's case, we experience the attempt to transcend in; in Strauss's, the attempt is made to evade even the question of transcendence, by positing a more 'aristocratic', classicising evasion of the Countess's choice. Schoenberg, in *Moses und Aron* and elsewhere too, had attempted consistency, an undoubtedly 'honest' attempt to follow the demands of material and epoch wherever they would take him. All three attempts have, *in those terms*, 'failed'; or rather, Wagner and Strauss unquestionably have, whereas Schoenberg may be understood to have succeeded, albeit at the cost of his work remaining 'incomplete', an Adornian fragment.

The oracular or at least indeterminate quality to Wagner's and Strauss's conclusions is not necessarily intentional. It is almost certainly not so in

[44] Pierre Boulez and Patrice Chéreau, 'Commentaires sur "Mythologie et idéologie"', in *Programmhefte der Bayreuther Festspiele*, 1977, no. 6, 87.

Wagner's case. Should it be so in Strauss's, outcome and intention differ to at least a certain extent in quality. Much of what he wished to exclude – all those nasty political and metaphysical questions – have defiantly reinstated themselves alongside, beneath, even above, dramatised surface salon playmaking between words and music. Most important for our case, however: whilst neither Moses nor Aron, Arnold nor Richard (III), may lay claim to the answers, both have presented and continue to present crucial questions.

Part II

Composition after the Second World War: From Germany to Italy, and Back Again?

Prelude

G iven that the three composers, Luigi Dallapiccola, Luigi Nono, and Hans Werner Henze, examined in this second part are likely to be less familiar to many readers than Wagner, Schoenberg, and Strauss, I have tried to offer here a greater sense of contextualisation. That has arguably involved treating with our second-part trio more as composers, less exclusively as musical dramatists, hence the titular inclusion of 'composition', but there is no harm in that. Again, different standpoints afford different problems *and* opportunities.

Dallapiccola's *Il prigioniero* contributes to what again proves to be a slight complication of chronological boundaries. Although Dallapiccola began work upon this opera only the year after Strauss completed *Capriccio*, and although both may be considered to be 'war works', the composer is undeniably of a different generation from Strauss and indeed from Schoenberg. Indeed, as we shall see, Dallapiccola most definitely places himself 'after' Schoenberg and Wagner. The avowed political commitment of all three of this section's composers, that of Nono and Henze still more so than Dallapiccola's, was a dramatic concern at least as emphatically as it had been for Wagner, arguably more so, and certainly more than it had been for Schoenberg, let alone Strauss. That does not preclude us from asking similar questions, nor indeed from understanding post-war composers as having asked similar or even some of the same questions, but it also suggests that there might be different questions and, at the very least, different standpoints worthy of exploration.

After all, the meaning of texts – of words, of harmonies, of performances, of stagings, of exegeses – changes over time. In his classic article, 'Meaning and Understanding in the History of Ideas', Quentin Skinner argues, amongst other things, that 'any attempt to justify the study of . . . [the history of ideas] in terms of the "perennial problems" and "universal truths" to be learned from the classic texts must amount to the purchase of justification at the expense of making the subject itself foolishly and needlessly naive'. That does not necessarily deny 'apparently perennial *questions*, if these are sufficiently abstractly framed'.[1] However, such abstraction will not only militate against meaningful interpretation; it will likely also prove to be the case, as Skinner continues, that:

> whenever it is claimed that the point of historical study of such questions is that we may learn directly from the *answers*, it will be found that what *counts* as an answer will usually look, in a different culture or period, so different in itself that it can hardly be in the least useful even to go on thinking of the relevant question as being 'the same' in the required sense at all.[2]

Skinner's claim perhaps downplays the role, conservative yet not necessarily reactionary, that is played by tradition: something a Roman Catholic such as Dallapiccola would never have underestimated. The point nevertheless retains a great deal of validity. Performance, as we shall see, especially in the third and final part to this book, complicates the transformation of questions further. Yet Skinner's argument holds in quite a strong sense for a musico-dramatic work by Wagner or Dallapiccola and for a production by Wagner or Stefan Herheim, perhaps as much as it does for a treatise by Hobbes or Marsilius of Padua.

The chapter on Nono deals less with contemporary national and political context than do those on Dallapiccola and Henze – or, for that matter, that on Strauss. That is not because I think the context less important; it would have been highly illuminating to consider works by Nono, perhaps especially those written between *Intolleranza 1960* and *Prometeo*, more closely in the light of the fortunes of the Italian Communist Party and the Years of Lead. The atmosphere was tense for artists and politicians alike, and perhaps especially for artists such as Nono who made little distinction in terms of their interventions. Maurizio Pollini, speaking in a film on Nono made after his death, recalled one particular incident:

[1] Quentin Skinner, 'Meaning and Understanding in the History of Ideas,' in *History and Theory*, 8 (1969), 50, 52.
[2] Ibid., p. 52.

There was a lot of tension in the air. We have to remember the situation in Italy back then. People were even talking about a possible Fascist coup. There was the example of the colonels in Greece. The fear of a turn towards authoritarianism was serious. After the massacre on the Piazza Fontana in Milan and the bombs, we took it all the more seriously. I think it was the reaction of the whole country that kept it from happening. Back then, I once read, or rather tried to read, a declaration against a hideous atrocity in the Vietnam War when the United States bombed Hanoi and Hai Phong. Several Italian musicians had signed the declaration: Claudio Abbado, Luigi Nono, [Giacomo] Manzoni and the Quartetto Italiano, as well as Goffredo Petrassi, Luigi Dallapiccola. Contrary to all my expectations, at the mere sound of the word 'Vietnam', the audience exploded in a kind of collective delirium, which made it impossible to continue my recital. I made several attempts to read this short statement. This was interrupted by the arrival of the police. Eventually the piano was closed and that was that.[3]

Though certainly not ignored here, that context is an aspect of Nono's career to which closer attention ought to be accorded in another context. The reasons I have not done so here are: first, that it is probably more important still to the period after *Intolleranza*, whereas my concerns lie more with background and the work itself; second, because one cannot do everything at once; and third, because I thought it more important in terms of this particular work to look more closely at what Nono thought he was trying to achieve and how that informed the work itself. In a sense, then, the approach adopted for *Intolleranza*, if it does not quite return to that characterising the first part of the book, nevertheless stands closer to it.

I should similarly like to have said more about Henze's *Der Prinz von Homburg* and *Der langwierige Weg in die Wohnung der Natascha Ungeheuer*, more in particular about their scores; however, in the present case, that desire fell victim to a broader, more biographical, sweep, in which those two works were located in a more general discussion of post-war German musical and political history and of Henze's place within them. In another history, things would have been different. I also thought it important to attempt somewhat different approaches in different cases: suggesting what might also have been done, yet permitting, at least to a certain extent, the material to shape its own progress. Romanticism endures; at the very least, it engenders deep-seated suspicion of formalism. It is not, then, a mere cliché to say that we are

---

[3] *A Trail on the Water*, dir. Bettina Ehrhardt (TDK DVD DVWW-DOCNONO). I have used the translation of Pollini's Italian given in the film's subtitles.

all Romantics, just as we are all modernists, even all post-modernists. It would be in good part unhistorical, as will be suggested by what follows, to claim otherwise.

CHAPTER 4

Luigi Dallapiccola, *Il prigioniero*: Imprisonment, Liberty, and the Word

I

I have so far concentrated upon the Austro-German compositional 'mainstream' – doubtless in part an ideological construct, yet one that it would be perverse to discard in dealing with history, philosophy, music, and politics 'after Wagner'. It is now time to turn south to Italy, as, throughout history, so many Germans have done, not least Wagner and Henze. No one will need reminding that Italy has its own rich operatic tradition, though the extent to which it should be considered 'Italian' prior to unification is debatable; nor will anyone need reminding that its values often differed from those north of the Alps.

Indeed, Italian musical tradition, at least from the early nineteenth century onwards, differed greatly from its German counterpart. In the popular imagination, it was operatic rather than symphonic; but that led to something of a reaction during the earlier twentieth century. Busoni, always a figure of interest for Dallapiccola, provided an especially interesting example of cultural ambivalence: living in exile, much of it in Germany, Busoni had explicitly associated himself with the great German tradition. His four operas, all to his own libretti – shades of Wagner here, however post- or even anti-Wagnerian Busoni's æsthetics – were even written in German. The point is not here to enter into a full-blown comparison, but to broaden our scope and also to bear in mind interaction between the two traditions, especially during the age of Italian composition after Puccini.

It would be perverse to consider Dallapiccola as not in an emphatic sense being an 'Italian composer'. Nevertheless, his birth and early years remind us that nationality in central Europe – for that is what it is – is generally a far more complex matter, involving varying degrees of partial association, than the bright primary colours of the popular imagination might have one believe. The Istrian town of Pisino in which Dallapiccola was born in 1904 was then part of Austria-Hungary and now lies in Croatia. The composer would point out, many years later: 'One should

127

not forget that the little Istrian peninsula where I was born lies at the crossing of three borders. When the train stopped at the station in my hometown, the conductor called out: "Mitterburg, Pisino, Pazin".' How, he mused, might the resulting frontier 'mentality be defined? Perhaps as "restless".[1] Whatever the truth of that construction of his childhood and adolescence, such restlessness might define a journey quite different from that taken by Schoenberg. Nevertheless, Dallapiccola's path was not entirely dissimilar in quality, being once more defined, or at least delimited, by travelling rather than arriving. (Luigi Nono, as we shall see, would also relate explicitly to that idea.) It also involved a greater emphasis upon, inspiration from, foundation in religion than many secular-minded commentators would care to admit.

Moreover, just as Schoenberg would be forced by historical circumstances to move far from Vienna, Dallapiccola's geographical travels would not always be voluntary:

> On 21 November 1916, Franz Joseph died. Charles I, his successor, a man doubtlessly aware of many urgent problems – among them, the necessity for a united Europe – was crowned too late at least to attempt a solution. One of his first steps was to abolish the concentration camps which had aroused such profound indignation throughout civilised Europe at the time. The Irridentists, the political suspects – or rather the '*P.U.*', *politisch unverlässlich* ('politically unreliable') were to be expelled from the border zones and sent to the interior of Austria. The school my father had directed with such love, where he had taught for so many years, was closed overnight . . . And so my family, escorted by a policeman, was obliged to arrive at Graz on 27 March 1917.[2]

This is not the place to recount the story of Dallapiccola's life, even up to the writing of *Il prigioniero*, but it is worth noting that during this brief sojourn in Graz – he would return home in November 1918 – he would encounter much Wagner: 'Standing in the gallery, a boy of thirteen could listen effortlessly to such operas as *Die Meistersinger* or those of *The Ring*.' He would recall, furthermore, when his father took him to a performance of *The Flying Dutchman*, that it was 'the first time I heard an opera of Wagner. Previously I had heard operas by Rossini, Verdi, Puccini, etc. It is certain that even before Wagner's overture came to an end, I had decided to become a musician.'[3]

---

[1]   Luigi Dallapiccola, 'The Genesis of *Canti di prigionia* and *Il prigioniero*,' in *Dallapiccola on Opera – Selected Writings of Luigi Dallapiccola: Volume One*, ed. and tr. Rudy Schackleford (Toccata Press: London, 1987), p. 38.

[2]   Ibid., pp. 40–1.

[3]   Ibid., p. 42; quoted in ibid., p. 42, n. 11.

Tristan would be one of Dallapiccola's first musical experiences upon moving in 1922 to Florence to study and he would encounter Schoenberg's music, hearing the composer conduct *Pierrot lunaire* at the Palazzo Pitti in 1924.[4] It would be a while before Schoenberg's influence would truly be felt, however, twelve-note tendencies only emerging in the late 1930s, when Dallapiccola announced himself as the first Italian composer to adopt dodecaphonic methods. Falling under Wagner's spell was hardly unusual, of course; Puccini's Wagnerisms are legion. Moreover, Puccini famously travelled to Florence especially to hear that very same performance of *Pierrot*, organised by Alfredo Casella's *Corporazione delle Nuove Musiche*. In 1949, Dallapiccola would write to Schoenberg:

> I had seen you in Florence at the time of the first Italian tour of *Pierrot lunaire*, but how could I, a Conservatory student, find the courage on that evening to come and shake your hand? In any case, I have never forgotten the attitude of Puccini with regard to you on that 1 April 1924 [Puccini listened intently and had Casella introduce him to Schoenberg], and since that evening I have considered the popular Italian composer to be of an intelligence and a humanity that I had not suspected.[5]

What perhaps strikes one most immediately from those words is that Puccini is presented not only admiringly but also as somehow more 'other' than Schoenberg. Dallapiccola positioned himself, and not without reason, after Wagner.

II

What of politics? They also require contextualisation. Dallapiccola was initially an enthusiast for Mussolini, a far from unusual stance for an interwar artist. Italian Fascism after all had a good number of roots – often violent – in the Futurist movement; in its way, it was as much an æsthetic phenomenon as Nazism. Moreover, Fascism was popular at all levels of Italian society. Amongst Italian Communists, however, it was only really Antonio Gramsci and Palmiro Togliatti who recognised that Fascism was not simply, to quote Stanley Payne, 'a natural result of "bourgeois" parliamentary democracy', that it 'was a genuine mass movement, in some ways more a consequence than a cause of the defeat of the revolutionary

---

[4] Raymond Fearn, *The Music of Luigi Dallapiccola* (University of Rochester Press: Rochester and Woodbridge, 2003), pp. 5–6.
[5] Letter of 9 September 1949, quoted in ibid., p. 6.

left'.[6] That is not to dishonour the memory of those who resisted, but to recognise how things were. And of course, as Togliatti observed when delineating the contradictions of the regime, the social basis of the movement – just, we might add, as in the case of National Socialism or indeed almost any other political movement of whatever complexion – might have interests and ideological imperatives very different from those of the governing regime.[7]

The elitist strands of Fascism could appeal to artists too. These words from the æsthetically and politically authoritarian Stravinsky, spoken in an interview with the music critic of Rome's *La Tribuna*, are difficult to explain away, however many lashings of historical empathy we might smotheringly apply: 'I do not believe that anyone venerates Mussolini more than I. To me, he is the *one man who counts* nowadays in the entire world . . . I have an overwhelming urge to render homage to your *Duce*. He is the saviour of Italy and, let us hope, of Europe.'[8] Perhaps Mussolini's neo-Classical artistic tastes, wishing to emulate Imperial Rome rather than to abet his Futurist allies, appealed too. Indeed, as Richard Taruskin has noted, by permitting 'himself to be described in print by Arthur Lourié . . . as . . . the "dictator of the reaction against the anarchy into which modernism degenerated," Stravinsky . . . consciously cast himself as the Mussolini of music'.[9] But then Churchill too, on the twenty-fifth anniversary of the Anti-Socialist and Anti-Communist Union in 1933, hailed Mussolini as 'the greatest living legislator' and Freud, that same year, sent him a copy of one of his books, with the dedication, 'To Benito Mussolini, from an old man who greets in the Ruler the Hero of Culture.'[10] After all, neither Mussolini nor Hitler could justly be excused of indifference to culture, and Mussolini's attitude towards modernism was more ambivalent – perhaps more trivial – than that of the Führer. The 1932–4 *Mostra della revoluzione fascista*, described by one historian as having a 'spiritualised character . . . a fascist *Gesamtkunstwerk*', was

[6] Stanley G. Payne, *A History of Fascism 1914–45* (Routledge: London, 1995), p. 125; Renzo De Felice, *Il fascismo: Le interpretazioni dei contemporanei e degli storici* (Laterza: Rome, 1970), pp. 106–35.
[7] Palmera Togliatti, *Sul fascismo*, ed. Giuseppe Vacca (Laterza: Rome, 2004).
[8] Alberto Gasca, *Da Cimarosa a Stravinsky* (De Santis: Rome, 1939), p. 452.
[9] Arthur Lourié, *Sergei Koussevitsky and his Epoch* (Knopf: New York, 1931), p. 196; Richard Taruskin, 'Stravinsky and the Subhuman,' in *Defining Russia Musically: Historical and Hermeneutical Essays* (Princeton University Press: Princeton, 1997), p. 452.
[10] Quoted in Piero Melograni, 'The Cult of the Duce in Mussolini's Italy,' in *Journal of Contemporary History*, 11 (1976), 233; Ernest Jones, *Sigmund Freud Life and Work, Volume Three: The Last Phase 1919–1939* (Hogarth Press: London, 1957), pp. 192–3.

a genuine celebration of modernism and rationalism; it was certainly no forerunner of the reactionary yet also hugely popular 1937 Munich exhibition intended to mock *Entartete Kunst*.[11]

For Dallapiccola, adoption of dodecaphony offered an opportunity to expand, certainly not to restrict, expressive possibilities, a view with impeccable warrant in the heritage of all three Second Viennese School composers. 'It is not (as has been too hastily stated and then repeated without verification)', he protested, when writing about Webern, 'an insidious force that would reduce music in all countries to a lowest common denominator; it is, rather, a language which contains within itself exceedingly varied possibilities, whose total realisation we shall not perhaps live to see.'[12] (When 'total' serialism did come to pass, it would certainly not prove to be Dallapiccola's thing, but that is not really his meaning here.[13]) Yet his imperative seems to have been more melodic – dare one say more Italianate? – in nature: 'it seemed to me that twelve notes would enable me to articulate a melody better than seven – to write a richer and … more expressive melody'. Interestingly adoption of the Schoenbergian method seems explicitly to have held the connotation, in Dallapiccola's own words, of 'opposition to neo-Classicism'.[14]

Moreover, that rejection of neo-Classicism went hand in hand with disillusionment and subsequently outright opposition towards fascism. Laura Dallapiccola recalled her husband having said that his eyes had been opened by the invasion of Abyssinia in 1935, when they saw on film the aerial bombardment of the 'poor African huts', and subsequently by 'the Spanish Civil War, the alliance with Germany, etc.'.[15] The 1936–7

---

[11] Marla Stone, 'Staging Fascism: The Exhibition of the Fascist Revolution', in *Journal of Contemporary History*, 28 (1993), 218.

[12] Luigi Dallapiccola, 'Meeting with Webern (Pages from a Diary)', tr. John C. G. Waterhouse, in *Tempo*, New Series, 99 (1972), 3.

[13] An isolated example to the contrary might be certain sections of the 1956–7 *Dialoghi*. (See, e.g., Sandro Perotti, *Iri de Iri: Analisi della musica strumentale di Dallapiccola* (Guerini: Milan, 1988), pp. 163–81; Dietrich Kämper, *Gefangenschaft und Freiheit: Leben und Werk des Komponisten Luigi Dallapiccola* (Gitarre und Laute: Cologne, 1984), p. 142.) However, even here, as Raymond Fearn points out, it is most likely born of a desire for symmetry rather than indicating more general attraction towards the organisation characteristic of Boulez and Stockhausen (*Music of Luigi Dallapiccola*, p. 214). The ideological impetus towards 'Darmstadt' total serialism, insofar as one may speak of that in any form of singular, was at any rate as foreign to Dallapiccola as to Henze.

[14] Letter of 7 July 1957, quoted in Hans Nathan, 'The Twelve-note Compositions of Luigi Dallapiccola', in *The Musical Quarterly*, 44 (1958), 303–4.

[15] Letter of 10 September 1993 from Laura Dallapiccola to Pierre Michel, quoted in Pierre Michel, *Luigi Dallapiccola* (Contrechamps: Geneva, 1996), p. 30.

Tre laudi was the first work in which Dallapiccola seems consciously to have employed a twelve-note theme; not only was it conceived of as a protest against the invasion of Abyssinia, it was intended as a 'protest in the form of religious belief'.[16] Dallapiccola was not the first artist or indeed person to have felt political enthusiasm for a cause he, let alone posterity, would later find questionable. So, after all, had the writer of one *Sinfonia eroica composta per festeggiare il sovvenire di un grand' uomo*, and we do not tend to suspect his Ninth Symphony, *Fidelio* (one of the operas Dallapiccola heard as a teenager in Graz), or indeed even the *Eroica* itself, on account of naïve Bonapartism from which Beethoven would subsequently recoil. (Maybe we should, but that is a question for another day.)

The suffering of the individual, as opposed to the requirements of the collective, was emphasised in the opera of 1937–8, *Volo di notte*, premiered in 1940, although the regime also seems to have sought and found affirmation of its own ideology here.[17] After all, the work won the composer his chair in Florence. The Italian alliance with Nazi Germany proved the final straw, if not for Stravinsky, then for Dallapiccola, not least given the Jewish identity of Laura. The 1938 race laws, imported, as it were, from Nuremberg, coincided with and indeed helped to provoke the *Canti di prigionia*, in which we hear songs of Mary, Queen of Scots, Boethius, and Savonarola: all prisoners on account of their words, their beliefs, even simply their identity. The concentration camps of Dallapiccola's Austrian youth were springing up once again, though he could hardly yet imagine what they were to become. In these songs the early stirrings of twelve-note writing already heard in *Volo di notte* become more fundamental, more generative. Dodecaphony, as for Schoenberg, seems to have evoked for Dallapiccola a strenuous dialectic between freedom and its foes. It is certainly striking to imagine those prison songs being premiered in Rome on the day, 11 December 1941, on which Italy declared war upon the United States, 'the streets ... swarming with police and Fascist militia', the first of the three, 'Preghiera di Maria Stuarda', having been performed on the Belgian Radio of Brussels, just weeks before the German invasion: 'the last broadcast from that courageous radio station I was to hear before its

[16] Everett Helm, 'Luigi Dallapiccola in einem unveröffentlichten Gespräch,' in *Melos/Neue Zeitschrift für Musik*, 6 (1976), 471.
[17] On *Volo di notte*, see Ben Earle, 'The Avant-Garde Artist as Superman: Aesthetics and Politics in Dallapiccola's *Volo di notte*,' in Roberto Illiano (ed.), *Italian Music During the Fascist Period* (Brepols: Turnhout, 2004), pp. 657–716.

five-year silence'.[18] Material from them makes its way into *Il prigioniero*. For instance, Dallapiccola's setting of the words 'Languendo, gemendo et genu flectendo', from Mary Stuart's Prayer, is sung by the off-stage Chamber Choir in the final scene after the Grand Inquisitor has cruelly bade the Prisoner have courage.

In 1943, following the German occupation of Italy, the neo-Fascist Salò regime set up with Mussolini 'virtually a prisoner of the SS', the Dallapiccolas fled Florence and work began upon *Il prigioniero*.[19] Dallapiccola did not conceal his horror. Here the subject matter is anti-fascist for all to see, and to hear. (I use the lower case 'fascist' on purpose, since the occupiers and their regime probably represented a greater, certainly more horrific, foe than the home-grown variety with all the equivocations, personal and national, that entailed.) It often takes a conversion to realise the horrific error of one's former ways.

III

Dallapiccola prepared his own libretto, after Villiers De l'Isle-Adam's *La Torture par l'espérance*, which he had encountered in Paris shortly before the outbreak of war in 1939, and Charles De Coster's *La Légende d'Ulenspiegel et de Lamme Goedzak*. A story from the former, 'La torture par l'espérance' ('Torture by hope'), was, on the journey back from Paris, suggested by Laura as an operatic source. Composition took place between 1943 and 1947: during and after the war in which the Dallapiccolas had been compelled to go into hiding, prisoners of a kind themselves. Having immersed himself in the sixteenth-century Wars of Religion, he saw:

> the necessity of writing an opera that could be at once moving and contemporary despite its historical setting, an opera that would depict the tragedy of our time – the tragedy of the persecution felt and suffered by the millions and tens of millions. Entitled simply *Il prigioniero*, the opera would not adopt as its protagonist Rabbi Aser Abarbanel, whom we meet in the story by Villiers de l'Isle-Adam and whose presence would only limit the scope of the now universal problem.[20]

The exigencies of wartime and Dallapiccola's difficulties in coming to terms with what had happened – 'In 1946 I suddenly became blocked.

---

[18] Dallapiccola, 'Genesis,' p. 49.
[19] Payne, *History of Fascism*, p. 412.
[20] Dallapiccola, 'Genesis,' pp. 51–2. Moreover, Adorno's claim that Wagner stood in need of such rescue should not necessarily be taken as read.

Weariness, exhaustion.' – help explain the relatively long time it took to write a one-act opera (with Prologue).[21]

Ben Earle has offered a provocative re-evaluation of the opera: briefly, an attempt at a post-Adornian rescue (*Rettung*), Slavoj Žižek looming large, of 'a work even (or especially) at the expense of Dallapiccola's own thoughts on contemporary music and its relation to history and society'. In his essay, Earle questions the deletion of the specifically Jewish name of the protagonist.[22] Yet, sometimes a desire for greater universality is simply that; if it were, Dallapiccola would be following in the footsteps of Wagner, amongst many others. Moreover, at the risk of stating the obvious, Dallapiccola's 'tragedy of our time' would still be set in the Spain of Philip II whether the prisoner were a rabbi, a Gentile, or anyone else. It is not clear to me that there is so pressing a need for a *Rettung* as Earle thinks. More to the point, we are simply doing different things, the concerns of this chapter standing closer to and in some senses being that which he wishes to discard.

Dialectics pervade the opera: darkness and light, torture and hope, captivity and liberty (the latter pair forming the German title for a book on Dallapiccola).[23] And they are dialectical, not mere binary, opposites; they are shown to entail, even to contain, one another, although unsurprisingly the negative side always emerges stronger. (Adorno probably ought to have been more generous to the opera than he was in his claims of 'musical events of drastic simplicity' – though occasions on which one might accuse him of undue generosity are admittedly few and far between.[24]) Thus the stage instructions for the opening of the Prologue request a black stage, relieved only by the white face of the Mother, about to visit her imprisoned son for what she is convinced – rightly so – will be the last time. Hope is shown to be the ultimate torture in the false dawn of the final scene, in a downright inversion of *Fidelio*. As for liberty: the opera, as we shall see, ends with a question, an almost Schoenbergian (*Moses*) recognition of impossibility.

[21] Ibid., p. 59.

[22] Ben Earle, 'Dallapiccola and the Politics of Commitment: Re-Reading *Il prigioniero*,' in *Radical Musicology*, 2 (2007), paragraphs 6–9.

[23] Kämper, *Gefangenschaft und Freiheit*.

[24] Theodor Adorno, 'On the Contemporary Relationship of Philosophy and Music,' tr. Susan H. Gillespie, in *Essays on Music*, ed. Richard Leppert (University of California Press: Berkeley, Los Angeles, and London, 2002), p. 158.

IV

The opening orchestral chords – three tetrachords – of terror, repeated almost like a Monteverdi *ritornello,* have a sense of twelve-note Puccini to them. *Tosca,* another tale of officially sponsored, wartime sadism masquerading as religious righteousness, comes to mind and to ear. If the melodrama of Puccini's first three bars is not quite available to Dallapiccola (Ex. 6), does he nevertheless echo the fortissimo accented syncopations of the following bars (Ex. 5)?

Ex. 5. *Tosca,* bb. 4–7

Ex. 6. *Il prigioniero*: opening bars

They even share the opening high G and the D beneath, that interval of a perfect fourth, with its tonal implications, reproducing itself on several occasions – the first as soon as the following chord. Beneath that perfect fourth lies a perfect fifth, its tonal associations if anything stronger still. Indeed, for all Dallapiccola's adoration of Webern, Berg was often just as important. There is perhaps here, notwithstanding the undoubted agitation, more than a little of the 'desire for reconciliation' the young Boulez would soon disdain in Berg's later music: *Der Wein,* the Violin Concerto, and *Lulu* (whose first performance Dallapiccola had heard via radio broadcast from Zurich in 1937).[25] We may also recall the Schoenberg of the First Chamber Symphony, so bold in its superimposed harmonies of fourths that have been outlined melodically at its opening.

---

[25] Pierre Boulez, 'Alban Berg,' in *Relevés d'apprenti,* ed. Paule Thévenin (Seuil: Paris, 1966), p. 323.

At any rate there can be little doubt that Scarpia would have relished the role of Gaoler/Grand Inquisitor. Puccini looking forwards – and there is nothing wrong with such teleology, in its place – and Dallapiccola looking backwards meet somewhere halfway, a fuller encounter than that at the Palazzo Pitti, though perhaps it had in some sense been set up then. Austrian and Habsburg connections – historical, autobiographical, musical, and dramatic, for this is, we should remember, the Spain of Philip II, son of Charles V – remain very much in the air; the complexities of *Mitteleuropa* are far from dead, however much nationalist conquering forces, including those commanded by a dictator born in Braunau am Inn, might wish their troops to simplify, even to quell, them.

But talk of the Gaoler is to move a little ahead of ourselves. In the Prologue, the Mother tells of her recurring dream as she waits in front of a black curtain to visit her son. The nightmare involves a tyrant, Philip the Owl, around whose neck hangs the Order of the Golden Fleece: 'He advances. His cold lips of iron have never so much as known what a smile is, and, like a death knell, his heavy step resounds. In his eyes lurid fires of torture are reflected, now and then fanned with his own breath.' His face, already terrifying enough, is transformed into the head of Death itself, waking her screaming, 'My beloved son, my s. . .'. That Hitler is referred to, though by no means exclusively, seems every bit as clear as in Viktor Ullmann's 1943 Theresienstadt opera, *Der Kaiser von Atlantis, oder Die Tod-Verweigerung* ('The Emperor of Atlantis, or Death's Denial'). The anguished lyricism with which the Mother tells of her dream (Ex. 7) can hardly fail to be considered 'Italianate', however much that term may then stand in need of deconstruction, albeit Italianate with Austro-German predecessors, even Webern and Wagner, let alone Mozart, whose national protestations need also to be leavened – and are – with the evidence of their actual compositional styles.

Ti ri-ve-drò,   mio fi - glio!   Ti ri__ ve drò...
cresc. sf

Ex. 7. The Mother tells of her dream

Sweetly seductive in its intensity, the orchestral writing that accompanies her description of Philip/Death has strong harmonic echoes of the abyss into which the madness of *Wozzeck* descends; the Mother tells of Philip's 'insane imaginings'. This descending chromatic musical material will prove generative, pervasive, insidious even, throughout the score, a powerful dramatic point composed of and from political as well as musical insanity. The fourth and fifth intervals between the three violin parts, the seconds being divided, will again be noted (Ex. 8). The first of a series of choral liturgical interventions is made, it never being clear whether they be signs of hope or claustrophobic fate; the chorus here is perhaps just as important, albeit in a different way, as that in *Moses und Aron* – or, as we shall see, that in Nono's *Intolleranza 1960* and *Al gran sole carico d'amore*.

Ex. 8. 'Insane imaginings'

It is in darkness that the first scene of the opera begins, in a 'horrible cell' in the dungeon of the Saragossa Inquisition. Yet there seems to be hope, the Prisoner ('as if continuing a narrative') telling his Mother that there had been darkness, but then the Gaoler had broken his silence to utter the sweet word of friendship, 'Fratello' (brother). For modern man, the fraternity of the holy French Revolutionary trinity will never lie far behind such a word, especially when dealing with an imprisoned successor to Florestan. One of the three rows upon which the opera is based (Ex. 9), that associated with hope – in Raymond Fearn's words, 'gradually expanding from its first hesitant, close intervals, to the full confidence of the octave' – will arise from the (illusory) comfort of this drooping three-note motif (Ex. 10).[26] That motif is marked both

[26] Fearn, *Music of Luigi Dallapiccola*, p. 120.

cantata and *soave*, palliative at least for the moment. If the resuscitation, apparently opening out into freedom and light, of a neo-Bachian wedge theme as twelve-note row sounds too good to be true, it will be shown to be just that. The Mother has already given a clue to the unreality of this promise, offering a Prologue presentiment – to employ an aptly Wagnerian term – of the 'Fratello' motif on the word 'sogno' (dream); its reiteration, both in the Prisoner's reported speech and soon from the Gaoler himself, will encapsulate the dialectic of torture between hope and its ultimate denial. As Brian Alegant has observed, the sprinkling of 'Fratello' motifs throughout the opera, the preparation of the '"Fratello" idea', helps make 'the betrayal such a powerful event'.[27]

Ex. 9. 'Hope' row

'Fra - tel - lo.'

Ex. 10. 'Fratello'

For once the Mother has left – as she knows, for the last time – the Gaoler continues to offer his (false) words of fraternal comfort, broadening his message to the political situation outside: the uprising against Spanish tyranny in Flanders has begun. Soon Roelandt, the bell Charles V had removed, will once again sing of liberty. Schiller's, and by extension Verdi's, *Don Carlos* would have been likely to come to many listeners' minds with an operatic portrayal of the Inquisition. However, in Schiller, even Philip himself is revealed to be helpless in its face, as witnessed by the Grand Inquisitor's 'Better [bodily] corruption than [Carlos's] freedom', to which judgement the King assents.[28] Whatever the political realities of the world depicted in *Il prigioniero*, there remains a preference for corruption, in more than one sense, over freedom, whose status should be considered enigmatic.

The scene, however, has already been lit by the Gaoler's lamp – and will soon be lit further, both physically and metaphysically, politically

27   Brian Alegant, *The Twelve-Note Music of Luigi Dallapiccola* (University of Rochester Press: Rochester, NY, 2010), p. 138.
28   Friedrich Schiller, *Don Carlos: Infant von Spanien* (Göschen: Leipzig, 1804), p. 395.

and spiritually. And yet, when we listen to the Prisoner's response, as well as to the Gaoler's words themselves, our suspicions are roused. Sinuous chromaticism – 'That voice, that word of friendship in the silence and in the darkness' – suggests the delusion of the Prisoner's condition: *Wahn*, in Schopenhauer's and Wagner's terms, or the presence of Aron's representational magic in Schoenberg's. Klingsor, however, will seem positively benign when contrasted with the evil at work here; hope will be dashed just as it would be – or had been – in the case of the 1944 July Plot against Hitler, successor to the 'murderer', Philip II, and the 'vile' Duke of Alba. Even human speech – the recitative-like phrase uttered by the Prisoner when he hears the voice that will break the unbearable silence perhaps makes reference to early 'Italian' opera and the expressive hopes it had engendered – must *and* must not be trusted. For the reconciliation offered by the 'Fratello' motif, whether vocally or when sweetly sung, *molto espressivo*, by the violas, truly sounds cause for alarm, sounding to us not unlike late Berg appears to have sounded to Boulez, or the positive philosophy of Hegel had to his Young Hegelian and Marxist successors. Wagner too would have attested to the dashing of false revolutionary hopes in 1848–9, when, in A. J. P. Taylor's phrase, 'German history reached its turning-point and failed to turn'.[29] Now the failure to turn, if one dare partially resurrect the *Sonderweg* thesis, receives its punishment. Germany, Italy, Europe, the Left, the Prisoner: all are trapped, even if they do not know it. In that context, the ecstatic duet on the words 'della libertà!' between Prisoner and Gaoler chills all the more – rather as Siegfried and Brünnhilde had unknowingly yet truthfully hymned 'radiant love, laughing death', at the end of *Siegfried*, ushering in *Götterdämmerung*. Yet if one can share the joy of their moment, even whilst feeling foreboding, the hallucinatory quality of Dallapiccola's writing and the overwhelming weight of Fate – which Wagner believed Wotan had banished, along with Erda – tells another story.

The Gaoler has indeed left the door open; that, despite the Prisoner's initial fear, does not represent one of his 'hallucinations'. Yet Dallapiccola's (quasi-)tonal writing always sounds secondary, predicated upon its negation, rather akin to Dahlhaus's description of the diatonicism in *Die Meistersinger*, which bears in itself the chromaticism of *Tristan*. 'Nowhere, not even in *Parsifal*, is Wagner's music so artificial as in the appearance of simplicity with which it clothes itself in *Die Meistersinger*.'

---

[29] A. J. P. Taylor, *The Course of German History: A Survey of the Development of German History since 1815* (Hamish Hamilton: London, 1961), p. 68.

The harmony is 'somehow dreamlike, not quite real in the 1860s: not so much restoration as reconstruction.'[30] Likewise: hope in the 1940s. The greater crisis is musically dramatised by the new reality that even Bergian chromaticism sounds suspect, unreal, incapable of assent. Take, say, a lovingly moulded *espressivo e dolcissimo* clarinet phrase, which might almost have come from Berg's Violin Concerto, heard against cloyingly chromatic celesta harps, and strings (Ex. 11), opening out in hope, as the Prisoner prays for safe passage upon emerging tentatively from his cell. The listener wants to believe; he is almost seduced into doing so. Yet most likely, he nevertheless cannot. In any case, has not beauty itself been thoroughly deconstructed by events?

Ex. 11. Prayer for safe passage

Further tragic irony is afforded by the ricercari that follow, the first upon the Prisoner's prayer and its associated row, the second upon 'Fratello' (Hope), the third on 'Roelandt', the bell of Ghent (*not*, tellingly, upon the Liberty row, thereby alerting us to the failure to recast a bell which, in reality, remains shattered). The form, style, or whatever one wants to call it, has resonances old (Italian Renaissance) and new (Webern's Bach transcription and more generally the labyrinthine writing of Berg and perhaps Schoenberg too). There is a sense of escape, the very word *ricercare* being the Italian 'to search', though searching suggests also that the object has not been found; there is also a sense of working out in the contrapuntal manner, certainly apt to Dallapiccola's writing here, though tragically, that working out will in dramatic terms be thwarted in blind alleys.

What ought to be the *Fidelio* moment comes when, once past two priests – knowingly or unknowingly? – engaged in what might be casuistic

---

[30] Carl Dahlhaus, *Richard Wagner's Music Dramas*, tr. Mary Whittall (Cambridge University Press: Cambridge, 1979), p. 75.

discussion of transubstantiation and heresy, the Prisoner believes that he has heard the bell. 'Roelandt is pealing! O Philip! O Philip! The days of your reign are numbered!' With that, the black curtain falls and the second choral intermezzo is heard, *organo pleno* and all: *Domine, labia mea aperies: et os meum annuntiabit laudem tuam.* Even though those words from the *Miserere* ('Thou shalt open my lips, O Lord: and my mouth shall shew Thy praise') have led, like Dallapiccola's setting, to no liturgical consummation – the lack of comfort should be indicative – the final scene still seems to offer hope. The black curtain rises to reveal a starry sky, a cedar tree, mountains in the distance, and the air of spring. Yet, following the Prisoner's final Alleluia, 'in the highest ecstasy, he spreads out his arms in a gesture of love for all humanity', the embrace is returned. The Grand Inquisitor reveals himself with the inevitable word, 'Fratello'. Salvation will come via the stake.

As the off-stage choir continues its soulful yet soulless intoning, the final words, spoken – inevitably recalling Schoenberg's Moses – or rather whispered are the Prisoner's, almost unconscious: 'La libertà?' The question mark answers its own question; the curtain's darkness once again falls. Dallapiccola signed off his score, 'Fine. DEO GRATIAS. Luigi Dallapiccola. 3 maggio 1948'. Perhaps there is a riposte here not so much to Mozart and to *Don Giovanni* as to a time when libertinism or revolution might have offered an answer. If calls of 'Viva la libertà!' are both the most thrilling and the most terrifying glimpse of a world on the edge of outright dislocation – still more so for some of us than the Stone Guest Scene – then Dallapiccola bears witness as a shell-shocked survivor, reporting back from the Hell to which Giovanni had heroically but perhaps too readily assented. And yet, Dallapiccola, writing between completion of his score and its first performance, saw Mozart's *dramma giocoso* rather differently: Giovanni is 'not the leading character of the opera ... [because] he is subject to the will of the Commendatore – the one who, as Kierkegaard wrote, represents conscience. Don Giovanni is damned at the very instant he slays the Commendatore.'[31] He is not free, then; he is, like the Prisoner, a tool of Fate, in a work that 'offers the first example of expressionism in opera.'[32] The God whom Dallapiccola thanks at the end of *Il prigioniero* remains as inscrutable as that of *Moses*, or the *Missa Solemnis*; yet once again, modern antinomies seem somehow to have led him – and Him – there.

---

[31] Dallapiccola, 'Notes on the Statue Scene in *Don Giovanni*', in *Dallapiccola on Opera*, p. 200.
[32] Ibid., p. 210.

Why no hope? After all, however difficult the peace, the war had been won. One might argue that when Dallapiccola wrote the text, victory for those opposing fascism was anything but sure. That is certainly true, but it would not have been impossible to alter the libretto whilst at work on the score; there must be more to it than that. In a sense, this must remain speculative and is perhaps a more fruitful pursuit for stage directors than anyone else. What we probably can say is that it would be difficult for a reflective person to feel unalloyed jubilation at the end of the Second World War, given the lives lost, the revelation of the true horrors of the Holocaust, the devastation in which much of the continent now found itself, and of course the continued subjugation of its peoples, whether by Western capitalism or its Soviet cousin – more state-sponsored, more overt in its brutality, yet utterly different from anything Marx might have envisaged, let alone hoped for. The very notion of emancipation increasingly stood under or even beyond question for many on the Western Marxist Left, perhaps most famously by Adorno and Horkheimer in *Dialectic of Enlightenment*.[33] In Earle's words, the Prisoner's '"La libertà" brings with it not an affirmation of autonomy, but silence. At the moment when, beyond hope, the subject is existentially "free", the notion of its lonely, truth-telling interior is revealed as a sham.'[34] That seems a *Rettung* worth lauding – and it is in good measure Dallapiccola's own.

V

The opera was first performed in concert, conducted by Hermann Scherchen, broadcast by RAI on 1 December 1949; it received its first theatrical performance at Florence's Teatro Comunale on 20 May 1950. Needless to say, the work and Dallapiccola's intentions proved eminently capable of being misunderstood. In 1967, Dallapiccola would recall a meeting with Francesco Siciliani, the artistic director of the Teatro Comunale:

> Without beating around the bush, he said that he regretted my allowing the world premiere of *Il prigioniero* to be given as a radio broadcast. And he added: 'We could have worked together in secret, without telling anyone...'. I replied that, while I wasn't conversant with the operations of subsidised institutions, I was astonished all the same that we should have had to work surreptitiously, as if the performance of one of my works were at least something to be ashamed of. And there the conversation abruptly ended.

[33] Theodor Adorno and Max Horkheimer, *Dialectic of Enlightenment*, tr. John Cumming (Verso: London and New York, 1997).

[34] Earle, 'Dallapiccola and the Politics of Commitment', p. 77.

Evidently the artistic director knew more about it than I . . . But could he have suspected even then what would happen between January 1950 and the date of the performance? Letters to the government, one of which said: 'It is a disgrace that an opera which casts a dim light on the Holy Spanish Inquisition should be performed in Italy during the Holy Year'. In other words, *Il prigionero* was essentially an attack on the Catholic Church.[35]

That should be understood within the context of Pope Pius XII having named one of the 1950 Jubilee objectives to be defence of the Church against constant attacks by her enemies, although Dallapiccola might reasonably have objected that the Spanish Inquisition distinguished itself from its mediæval predecessors by being a state rather than a Papal body, the Pope no more responsible for its actions than he was for those of Philip II. (At the time of composition, there were hopes that Franco might actually reintroduce it.)

Not dissimilarly, the Italian Communist Party, many years before its Eurocommunist disavowals, expressed its judgement that the work represented an attack upon Stalin. 'So in the Spring of 1950, I had the honour of being "displeasing to God and to his enemies" – displeasing, that is, to the Catholics and the Communists alike.'[36] Seven years later, he wrote to his publisher concerning the possibility of a performance in Moscow, to which he had no objection, 'on condition that the sponsor promise to include a note in the programme' explaining that the portrayal of the Inquisition ought to be understood symbolically, not literally. 'As a believer, I wish to emphasise that there is nothing against the Catholic Church in *Il prigioniero*, only a protest against tyranny and oppression.'[37]

Earle would find in this confirmation for his view that 'the confidence of Hans Werner Henze, that "[a]s a good Italian intellectual, [Dallapiccola] belonged of course to the Italian left", is difficult to sustain.'[38] Much here, as so often, hangs on definition. If one considers the Left and Catholicism to be mutually exclusive, harking back perhaps to the days when the Enlightenment and Catholicism were similarly considered, then one would have to assent.[39] Liberation theologians and many others would,

[35] Dallapiccola, '*Job*: A Mystery Play,' in *Dallapiccola on Opera*, pp. 61–2.

[36] Luigi Dallapiccola, 'The Birth-Pangs of *Job*,' in *Musical Events*, 15/5 (May 1960), 26, quoted in ibid., p. 62, n. 4.

[37] Luigi Dallapiccola, *Saggi, Testimonianze, Carteggio, Biografia e Bibliografia*, ed. Fiamma Nicolodi (Suvini Zerboni: Milan, 1975), pp. 91–2.

[38] Earle, 'Dallapiccola and the Politics of Commitment,' para. 9. Henze's words are quoted from Elisabeth Lutyens, Hans Werner Henze, and Hugh Wood, 'Tributes to Dallapiccola,' in *Tempo*, 108 (March 1974), 16.

[39] See, e.g., Tim Blanning, 'The Enlightenment in Catholic Germany,' in *The Enlightenment*

however, beg to differ – and whatever anyone thinks of modern Catholic social teaching, it is anything but a cheerleader for capitalism, let alone for neo-liberalism. Earle is surely right to emphasise Dallapiccola's closeness to Sartre: 'in so far as Dallapiccola's work is "committed", it aspires to the quality of the dialectic'.[40] Again, however, the one need not exclude the other – or others. Just as Wagner brought Hegel and Schopenhauer together, sometimes more harmoniously than others, so could Dallapiccola, who was clearly upset by accusations of bad faith from *both* the Church and the Italian Left, create and explore a different synthesis, far from unusual, which, irrespective of whether we might happen to assent to it, had its own imperatives.

VI

Such has the stature of *Il prigioniero* in reception turned out to be that it was chosen by Esa-Pekka Salonen to partner Beethoven's Fifth Symphony, the archetypal Romantic journey from darkness to light, in a January 2012 concert with the Philharmonia Orchestra to mark the fiftieth anniversary of Amnesty International. (The concert also inaugurated a cycle of Beethoven symphonies, marked by such imaginative pairings.) '*La libertà?*' was clearly posed as an answer to Beethoven. And indeed, the horrors of the twentieth century indicative of why our age finds it almost impossible to reckon with his music, especially his great symphonic statements, however much it may be routinely – in every sense – programmed. Performance, whatever its intentions, seemed to acknowledge that, for it was in *Il prigioniero* that Salonen and the Philharmonia shone; the price for a performance of blazing conviction seemed to be an indifferent first half, a sad but telling reflection that the world in which that orchestra had once played this music for Otto Klemperer was no more. The transition to the finale entirely lacked mystery; that moment when, harmonic tension having been screwed up so as finally to become unbearable, its forcible culmination opening the very portals of Heaven, sounded in its manicured present more akin to the opening of a private health club. At any rate, metaphysics seemingly having been banished more finally than even Strauss had ever accomplished, it was not at all clear that a

---

in National Context (Cambridge University Press: Cambridge, 1981), ed. Roy Porter and Mikulás Teich, pp. 118–26; Derek Beales, *Prosperity and Plunder: European Catholic Monasteries in the Age of Revolution, 1650–1815* (Cambridge University Press: Cambridge, 2003).

[40] Earle, 'Dallapiccola and the Politics of Commitment,' para. 3.

materialist Beethoven made sense, especially in this context. Without Fate, Hope could not be born either. By contrast, Fate, such as we should have hoped to have heard in the Fifth Symphony, proved the sole victor in Dallapiccola, Hope the final torture. The answer to that final, faltering, ironic '*La libertà?*' was clear; in a world of prisons such as Guantánamo and Gaza, we know it too well.

Victory, or at least redemption of sorts, might, however, be found in Dallapiccola's legacy to his fellow composers. Roger Sessions, contributing to a selection of *in memoriam* reminiscences for *Perspectives of New Music*, lamented that 'even the powerful *Il prigioniero*, though it has been performed more often in Europe than any Italian opera since Puccini, has had few and sporadic performances here', that is, in the United States.[41] Yet Sessions went on to say that Dallapiccola had always been 'devoted to the cause of human liberty, both on the individual and the political level ... unfettered by limitations of a sectarian, narrowly partisan, or doctrinaire kind. This too, is reflected, richly and eloquently, in the music he has left us.'[42] A few years later, Luciano Berio would recall, 'Dallapiccola was a point of reference that was not just musical, but also spiritual, moral and cultural in the broadest sense of the word. It was perhaps he, more than anyone else, who deliberately and unremittingly forged relationships with broader [i.e., beyond Italy] European musical culture.'[43] Berio had already paid tribute to *Il prigioniero* in his *Cinque variazioni* (1952–3, revised 1966), the piano variations based upon the 'Fratello' motif – or perhaps better, in Berio's case, three-note cell: an act of compositional fraternity belying the bitter, somehow heart-rending, irony of its use in the opera.

The American composer and pianist Frederic Rzewski studied with Dallapiccola in Florence in 1960–1 on a Fulbright Scholarship. Rzewski's most celebrated piece, though not an opera, is a defiant example of political commitment, a lengthy 1975 set of variations on Sergio Ortega's song, *¡El pueblo unido, jamás será vencido!* ('The People United will never be defeated'), which had been initially intended as an anthem for Salvador Allende's Popular Unity coalition and had gained further revolutionary currency following the overthrow and death of Allende as a symbol of resistance both within Chile and without. It is difficult to understand

[41] Goffredo Petrassi, Donald Martino, John Perkins, and Roger Sessions, 'In Memoriam,' in *Perspectives of New Music*, 13/1 (Autumn–Winter, 1974), 244.

[42] Ibid., p. 245.

[43] Luciano Berio, *Two Interviews*, with Rossana Dalmonte and Bálint András Varga, ed. and tr. David Osmond-Smith (Marion Boyars: New York and London, 1985), p. 53.

the climactic passages of Rzewski's variations in a sense that does not encompass revolutionary triumph: Siegfried and Notung shattering Wotan's spear, we might say, though both Rzewski and Wagner were aware that *Götterdämmerung* was yet to come.

Musica Elettronica Viva was founded in Rome in 1966 by Rzewski, Alvin Curran, and Richard Teitelbaum; Rzewski's work there explored explicitly socialist concepts of collective improvisation.[44] Indeed, the following words from 1968, whilst given something of a contemporary twist – redolent, like the ideas of Cornelius Cardew, of Stockhausen's 'intuitive music' as well as the very different concerns of the American avant-garde – could also be understood, whether intentionally or otherwise, to evoke the Schiller-Marx conception of artistic creation as a paradigm for human endeavour lying beyond bourgeois, enforced division of labour:

> We are all 'musicians'. We are all 'creators'. Music is a creative process in which we can all share, and the closer we can come to each other in this process, abandoning esoteric categories and professional elitism, the closer we can all come to the ancient idea of music as a universal language . . . we are trying to catalyse and sustain a musical process, moving in the direction of unity, towards a sense of communion and closeness among all the individuals present . . . The musician takes on a new function: he is no longer the mythical star, elevated to a sham glory and authority, but rather an unseen worker, using his skill to help others less prepared than he to experience the miracle, to become great artists in a few minutes . . . His role is that of organiser and redistributor of energies; he draws upon the raw human resources at hand and reshapes them.[45]

That was not in any obvious sense the vision of the far from 'experimentalist' Dallapiccola; neither the death of the composer nor that of the work was on his agenda. Indeed, the lessons Rzewski took with him did not go particularly well, much to Rzewski's subsequent regret, voiced in a 1984 interview:

> With Dallapiccola I made a serious mistake . . . I missed a lesson because I had gone to visit some friends in London, and when I came back from London I found a letter saying that Maestro Dallapiccola felt that I was not the kind of student that he wanted, needed to work with, and would I please go somewhere else. And I realised that I had made a serious mistake . . . I must have given the impression of arrogance . . . And now, it's one thing I've always regretted,

[44] On Rzewski, see, e.g., Ken Terry, 'Frederic Rzewski and the Improvising Avant Garde,' in *Down Beat*, 46 (1979), 20–1.

[45] Quoted in Michael Nyman, *Experimental Music: Cage and Beyond*, 2nd edn (Cambridge University Press: Cambridge, 1999) p. 130.

because I certainly could have gotten a lot from that man if I had approached him correctly.[46]

Yet that Rzewski felt such regret would be a mark of the respect Dallapiccola continued to enjoy and the perceived importance of his work and ideas even amongst composers not necessarily directly 'influenced' by him. His was and remains a revered example.

VII

Having looked forward in terms of performance and composition, it seems fitting to conclude this chapter by returning to Dallapiccola as composer. *Ulisse*, his final opera, written during the 1960s and premiered at Berlin's Deutsche Oper in September 1968, was conceived of very much as Dallapiccola's *summa*. Not unlike *Parsifal*, it both incorporates and attempts to go beyond, even perhaps to transcend, the composer's earlier works. In similar fashion to Busoni in *Doktor Faust*, and very much with Joyce on his mind too, Dallapiccola incorporates passages from his earlier works as testimony to ongoing intellectual preoccupation. Just as *Parsifal* had addressed questions posed in the *Ring* and elsewhere, the attempt being far more important than the 'solution', *Ulisse* turned to the final question prior to the curtain fall of *Il prigioniero*: 'La libertà?' If *Parsifal* is not a Christian work, more a work that is partly concerned with Christianity, *Ulisse* edges closer, in a humanist-tinged Catholicism, or should that be a Catholic-tinged humanism? Nono, unsurprisingly, noted that both Dallapiccola's Catholic texts and Schoenberg's 'tragedy of the Jewish people' tended towards heresy.[47] Hedged between and beyond Monteverdi and Joyce, Homer and Dante, Antonio Machado and Thomas Mann (the latter two both victims and critics of fascism, both cited and transformed in Dallapiccola's own libretto), *Ulisse* reasserts or rejuvenates Wagnerian motivic writing and a thematic method of composition that would have been recognisable to Schoenberg. Liberty is to be found in tradition as well as innovation. Indeed, it seems that there may yet tentatively remain some hope, some reality to 'freedom', the theological, just as in *Moses und Aron*, informing the political. It is not now the Furies

---

[46] Interview with Vivian Perlis, 2 December 1984, in Frederic Rzewski, *Nonsequiturs: Writings and Lectures on Improvisation, Composition, and Interpretation*, ed. Gisela Gronemeyer and Reinhard Oehlschlagel (Edition MusikTexte: Cologne, 2007), p. 70.

[47] Luigi Nono, 'Gespräch mit Martine Cadieu [II]', in *Texte: Studien zu seiner Musik*, ed. Jürg Stenzl (Atlantis: Zurich, 1975), p. 188.

who pursue Ulisse, nor Circe's monsters; the search, that of the hero for himself, becomes existential and yet social:

> Infinite punishments have I suffered,
> . . .
> searching for that which I lack: the Word, the Name.
> Would that I might discover that name, pronounce that
>   name,
> which might render clear the meaning of my quest,
> my long wanderings
> . . .
> Again: I torment myself to understand the truth.
> If a voice might break the silence, the mystery . . .
> Lord (*Signore*)!
> No longer are my heart and the sea alone.

If Schoenberg's quest had been unfulfilled, modernist antinomy brazenly dramatising its necessity and impossibility, here perhaps was the Jewish and Christian 'still small voice of hope' rendered immanent, as in Wagner, not only through the Greek Chorus of the orchestra, but through words – the Word, *la Parola*? – too. Dallapiccola, introducing the 1970 Italian premiere at La Scala, said that he had not pursued 'a subject susceptible to being interpreted in terms of "current events". I wrote this opera because I had carried it inside me for long years. And now that it is finished, I have the impression that its theme is *also* contemporary.'[48]

---

[48] Dallapiccola, '*Ulisse* at La Scala: Notes for the Italian Premiere, 13 January 1970,' in *Dallapiccola on Opera*, p. 266.

CHAPTER 5

Luigi Nono, *Intolleranza 1960*

I

Foremost amongst the politically engaged Italian composers of the generation after Dallapiccola was Luigi Nono. A Venetian by birth (1924)
and death (1990), he also, like Dallapiccola and many others, evinced
considerable interest in early 'Italian', often Venetian, music; Nono's final
music drama, *Prometeo*, often conjures up the impression of a marriage
between Marx and Palestrina, mediated by Walter Benjamin and Nono's
librettist, Massimo Cacciari. For, as Nono's friend and colleague, Claudio
Abbado, attested, Nono 'never lost the deep-rooted ties to the long
tradition of Venetian music, as demonstrated by his unerring feeling for
the relation of sound and space, recalling the music Gabrieli wrote for
the church of San Marco. Gigi's sense of an *espressivo* or *cantabile* line
also stems from this tradition.'[1] We might also remind ourselves that the
lineage of German musical tradition might be traced via Heinrich Schütz
to that very same source.

Nono's studies at the Venice Conservatory with Gian Francesco Malipiero, himself a crucial figure in the rediscovery of Monteverdi, encompassed
study of earlier traditions, for instance the golden ages of polyphony and
the madrigal. (Pieces such as *Sarà dolce tacere*, to a text by a favourite
poet, Cesare Pavese, and *Ha venido*, text by Antonio Machado, are, if not
madrigals, then certainly madrigalian.[2]) Sheer delight in vocal writing
and the potential of the human voice, whether coloured by electronics
or not, would inform Nono's work throughout his life. Nono and his
fellow pupil, Bruno Maderna, owed a good deal of their first knowledge
of twentieth-century music from Malipiero too, although, Mahler's
witness looming large in both their cases, they certainly did not inherit
his nationalistic hostility towards Austro-German symphonism. As Nono
would recall, in a 1973 tribute to Maderna, Malipiero had been:

---

[1] Claudio Abbado, 'My Silent Friend: Remembering Luigi Nono,' in *Contemporary Music Review*, 18 (1999), 3.
[2] On Nono and Pavese, see Jürg Stenzl, 'Luigi Nono und Cesare Pavese,' in Luigi Nono, *Texte: Studien zu seiner Musik*, ed. Jürg Stenzl (Atlantis: Zurich, 1975), pp. 409–33.

a lovingly concerned master, as I learned when he took me as a pupil during the bestial rule of Fascism (from 1943–45) and in his courses and seminars opened the door to study and knowledge of music which at that time lay prohibited in Italy: Schoenberg, Webern, also Dallapiccola, and naturally Monteverdi and the music of the Italian Renaissance.[3]

Like Dallapiccola, with whom a fruitful personal and musical friendship developed after their meeting in 1947, but in contrast to Malipiero, Nono inherited a musical world-view at least as 'German' as it was 'Italian' – arguably more so, as symbolised by his 1955 marriage to Schoenberg's daughter, Nuria. 'Who were the musicians that most influenced you during your earliest years?' Nono was asked in a 1961 interview. He named but one, Wagner, though he did not elaborate and went on to say that childhood memories were not precise.[4] Likewise, Nono's first acknowledged work, the orchestral *Variazoni canoniche sulla serie dell'op. 41 di Arnold Schönberg*, could hardly be more explicit in its title's tribute, the Schoenberg work in question being the furiously anti-Hitler *Ode to Napoleon Buonaparte*. Much of Nono's early success – and, indeed, much of his later success – came courtesy of German musical life. Almost all of Nono's early works were premiered in Germany, seven at the Darmstadt International Summer School for New Music. Italy made him wait until 1961, for the Venice Biennale premiere of *Intolleranza 1960*. Furthermore, that premiere notwithstanding, it is noteworthy that the only recording of *Intolleranza* vaguely available at the time of writing, albeit a recording deleted from the catalogue, comes from a Stuttgart production – in German.[5]

That said, to quote Gramsci, an important influence upon both Nono and Henze, 'The line of development is towards internationalism, but the point of departure is "national" – and it is from this point of departure that one must begin.'[6] Whether one must is a moot point, but I shall – at least in terms of biography and historical context, crucial to understanding the situation of both composers.

[3]   Nono, 'Erinnerung an zwei Musiker,' in ibid., p. 175.
[4]   Nono, 'Gespräch mit Martine Cadieu [I],' in ibid., p. 180.
[5]   Teldec 4509–97304–2, conducted by Bernhard Kontarsky.
[6]   Antonio Gramsci, 'Internationalism and National Policy,' in *Selections from the Prison Notebooks*, ed. and tr. Quintin Hoare and Geoffrey Nowell Smith (Lawrence and Wishart: London, 1971), p. 240. 'After 1945,' Nono would recall, 'there began in Italy the discovery and the discussion of the works of Antonio Gramsci.' ('Gespräch mit Jean Villain,' in *Texte*, p. 300.)

II

Nono came from a family of artists, his grandfather a sculptor and his uncle a painter; his parents were keen amateur musicians with an appreciable record collection. His, then, was an impeccably *haut bourgeois* artistic background. Growing up in the Fascist Italy portrayed in the previous chapter, Nono's experience could have been worse – although there is no doubt that he was nevertheless affected deeply. The Nazi occupation was formative of Nono's relentlessly anti-fascist and soon communist stance, not least in his contacts with the Resistance, but personal experience was less harrowing than for many. Indeed, a hallmark of his life and œuvre would be strength of feeling and advocacy for a number of causes that were not a consequence of direct personal involvement, not least in the 'Third World'. After joining the Italian Communist Party (PCI) in 1952, Nono would recount that his 'further political development' lay in 'debates concerning wars of liberation in Algeria, in Cuba and in Vietnam. Thereby, I have much for which to thank my Latin American comrades in particular.' They helped him avoid what he saw as the easy pitfall of the 'European Leftist intellectual', namely a 'Romantic flight into political wishful thinking'.[7]

Under Dallapiccola's leadership, young composers such as Nono and Maderna took advantage of the end of war to immerse themselves in the music of the Second Viennese School – not that that had been so difficult or impossible a task as it had been in Nazi Germany. Fascist Italy had, as we have seen, tended to be far less hostile to musical modernism and had, until a surprisingly late time, proved less willing actually to proscribe certain works or composers than Nazi Germany. Indeed, despite Nono's words quoted above on Schoenberg and Webern, *Wozzeck* had actually received its Italian stage premiere in Rome in 1942. The Venice Festival of Contemporary Music, at which Nono's *Intolleranza* would be premiered, had been founded in 1930 by Casella, whom we last encountered giving the Italian premiere of *Pierrot lunaire*.

Hermann Scherchen, a good friend of Malipiero, was another key figure in Nono's post-war study of the Second Viennese School. Upon Malipiero's advice, Nono took Scherchen's conducting course in Venice in 1948, then followed Scherchen to Zurich. Listening to his rehearsals, and partaking in analysis of Schoenberg and Webern, he 'came to know and to love the German [musical] tradition'. Since then, Nono had 'particularly admired Schoenberg, for he included everything, achieved everything he wanted

---

[7] Ibid., p. 301.

to achieve, in all directions'.[8] Scherchen conducted the first performance of the *Variazioni canoniche* in 1950 at Darmstadt. Equally importantly, he offered Nono the example of a politically committed, anti-fascist, even communist artist, who was equally committed to new music, and who indeed saw the two to be connected rather than coincidental:

> When I got to know him, he had already been for many years a communist, and he counted amongst those who knew how to combine seamlessly their work as artists with their ideological position. Furthermore, Scherchen brought me closer to German history. Through him, I had entrusted in me the historical, cultural, and political relevance of Berlin in the years before 1933: a world centre for the movement and for exchanges between the new Soviet culture and progressive intelligence from the West. Also, however, he gave me access to the Munich of the Spartacus Rising, with its great political and cultural charisma. And not least, I discovered through Hermann Scherchen the Soviet Union, which he knew very well.[9]

It is also worth noting the significant amount of state support Italian musicians received at this time, not least through the RAI (Radio Audizioni Italia) broadcasting organisation, supporting symphony orchestras on an Italian soil which had traditionally been far less symphonically fertile than its German counterpart. RAI's Terzo Programmo had originally been created in direct imitation of the BBC's Third Programme, but by the early 1960s was broadcasting throughout the day – that is, before the BBC decided to do so.[10] German electronic studios, Cologne perhaps the most famous, had their counterparts in, for example, the Milan Studio di Fonologia, attached to the Milan branch of RAI, founded in 1954 by Berio and Maderna, who joined the PCI at the same time as Nono. There were less fertile soils than post-war Italy for left-wing avant-gardists, notwithstanding Christian Democratic ascendancy in national politics.

For a while at least, the experience of war led to the desire to start afresh, to rid musical and political life alike, however unrealistic the prospect, of the contamination of the past. 'It was not', wrote Reginald Smith Brindle of the 1950s, 'that the Schoenbergian language was already exhausted, nor that attempts to fuse the serial and tonal worlds did not bear good fruit. The truth is that the intellectual climate of the atomic age demanded to be

---

[8] Nono, 'Gespräch mit Martine Cadieu [I],' p. 180.
[9] Nono, 'Gespräch mit Jean Villain,' pp. 300–1.
[10] John C. G. Waterhouse, 'Since Verdi: Italian Serious Music 1860–1995,' in *The Cambridge Companion to Modern Italian Culture*, ed. Zygmunt G. Baranski and Rebecca G. West (Cambridge University Press: Cambridge, 2001), p. 321.

expressed through sounds completely different in nature.'[11] Whatever the 'truth' of that view, it was certainly not unusual to hold it, nor energetically to advance it. Italian post-war composers, not just Nono, but also Maderna and Franco Donatoni, stated more or less explicitly, at least on occasion, that a principal reason 'for the use of predetermined principles was to obliterate memory'.[12] A paradox emerged, then, that serialism – be it of the Schoenberg or the Webern variety, an historical conception through and through – appeared to offer composers the possibility of an escape from history, especially when transplanted to a foreign soil. Webern's Goethian conception of metamorphosis, as applicable to art as to Nature, was traduced or simply ignored – in this sense, Boulez might as well have written, 'Webern est mort' – though with fruitful results.[13]

There is a sense in which the post-war 'extremism' of demands for a *tabula rasa*, or something close to it, had already been voiced – *not* by Schoenberg and his school, wont to stress the evolutionary, even traditionalist nature of their historical position, but by Italian Futurists such as Francesco Balilla Pratella, in his 1911 *Manifesto of Futurist Musicians*, and Luigi Russolo, himself a painter rather than a musician, in his 1913 response to Pratella, *Art of Noises*.[14] Citing Strauss as a precedent for his experiments, Russolo's idea had been to use 'noise' not for what it might explicitly represent – a train whistle, for example – but instead as compositional material. Whether through the complicated nature of Futurism's relationship with Fascism, through the suppression of such ideas, not least in their Russian variety, or simply because the relatively little music they engendered tended not to be very good, it was only really after the Second World War that they were picked up more generally – if, in Nono's case more likely from Varèse, whose Darmstadt classes Nono attended.

For Germans, Italians, and of course French heirs of Messiaen such as Boulez, the strictness of Webern's apparently hermetic compositional method, somehow divorced from his utterly German, post-Brahmsian context, provided a denationalised precedent – or at least so did a 'productive misreading' of his music – for a new beginning, spurning Stravinskian neo-Classicism and the Romantic nostalgia of Schoenberg and Berg

---

[11] Reginald Smith Brindle, *The New Music: The Avant-garde Since 1945*, 2nd edn (Oxford University Press: Oxford, 1987), p. 5.

[12] Ibid., p. 23.

[13] See Julian Johnson, *Webern and the Transformation of Nature* (Cambridge University Press: Cambridge, 1999).

[14] Francesco Balilla Pratella, *Manifesto futurist* (Spes-Salimbeni: Florence, 1980); Luigi Russolo, *L'arte dei rumori* (Carucci: Rome, 1975).

alike. Even the fact of Webern's shooting in 1945 somehow seemed to 'fit' the requirements of post-war 'new music'. *Die Reihe*, or 'The Row', the Darmstadt house journal, published an article in 1958 on Nono's compatriot, Berio. The following passage summarises rather well – and surprisingly reflectively for the time – the imperatives of most of those involved in the avant-garde, even if by 1958 it had fallen a little behind the times:

> Everybody's purpose is authentic organisation of the world of sound, which is finally to be freed from . . . external compulsion . . . Thus, in the years after World War II, new Italian music, too, [note 'too', allocating a leading role to Germany] had a role marked out. Naturally, it profited from study of hitherto unavailable works, and from insights gained elsewhere, but the natural reaction was against our most recent past. To put it more bluntly: there was a reaction against 'expression at all costs', against rhetoric (veiled to a greater or lesser degree), against sentimentality which no longer dared to express itself melodramatically, unreservedly.[15]

Whereas Henze's dissociation from the paths taken by Boulez and Stockhausen – what we might tentatively call the 'mainstream' avant-garde – was more definitive and more focused upon musical language, Nono's political commitment at least offered him a different focus from that of his Darmstadt peers. However, the occasion for his departure from Darmstadt – later than Henze's – was annoyance at the arrival of John Cage, though still more at misunderstanding of Cage and thus what Nono saw as the substitution of reactionary licence in favour of revolutionary liberty. There was also within the avant-garde an increasing sense that, to quote Helmut Lachenmann, 'in terms of compositional technique – as a West German composer put it in 1960, after my return from Germany – Nono had "ground to a halt".[16] The disfavour was returned, for Nono announced himself to his pupil none too keen on Stockhausen, whom he likened to Bismarck, and perhaps still more so to the latter's followers: the 'Cologne clan'. Boulez, Nono lamented, was likewise concerning himself with bourgeois fripperies.[17]

A 1959 lecture witnessed the beginning of Nono's Darmstadt farewell, though he would nevertheless speak there the following year. As transcribed by his student, Lachenmann, Nono's rallying cry would be that his

[15] Piero Santi, 'Luciano Berio,' in *Die Reihe*, 4 (1958), 98.

[16] Helmut Lachenmann, 'Touched by Nono,' in *Contemporary Music Review*, 18 (1999), 19.

[17] Correspondence in Angela Ida de Benedictis and Ulrich Mosch (eds), *Alla ricerca di luce e chiarezza: L'epistolario Helmut Lachenmann – Luigi Nono (1957–1990)*, cited in Ben Earle, 'The Politics of the New Music,' in *Music and Letters*, 94 (2013), 665.

opponents understood 'by "freedom" the oppression of the mind [*Geist*] by instinct. Their freedom is intellectual suicide [*geistige Selbstmord*]'. Theirs, in an ancient formulation, was licence, not liberty. It failed to engage with the present and was profoundly unhistorical. Their fiction of a *tabula rasa*, the very idea of which Nono now utterly abhorred, bore the hallmarks of a reactionary anarchism. Freedom could not, must not, be understood in merely personal terms. 'Music as historical present' must remain a 'witness' to humanity as a whole.[18] It was not that history had even truly disappeared; its temporary denial, however, attested all the more strongly to its ongoing presence. Moreover, its reinstatement was accomplished with contemporary vengeance. Nono's conception of freedom, thoroughly comprehensible within an idealist, even a Rousseauvian, context, was, for Lachenmann, highly attractive upon his first visit to Venice in 1958. Lachenmann saw it as superior:

> to the sense of new departure . . . which – largely constructivist in its motivation – had been generated at the time by young composers keen to shake off the rigidity of traditional academicism. It was superior because it was a quasi idealistic freedom compared with the largely pluralistic, open concept of freedom prevailing in western Europe after the war.[19]

That latter conception was one to which, reacting against all manner of alleged authoritarianisms, Henze, as we shall see, very much subscribed. Such rebellion, however, was, for Lachenmann and Nono, 'hypnotised by prevailing conditions . . . liberation from constraints which are only dimly perceived' required something more.[20] In other words, it required a radical conception of freedom, which, in Kantian tradition, was anything but heteronomous, and yet which, in Hegelian and, still more Marxist, fashion, went beyond Kant, to direct historical and political engagement. It was, moreover, an avowedly modernist conception of freedom, as distant from the consumerism of much post-modernist cultural criticism as from that of its liberal and neo-liberal cousins.

Opera would seem an obvious means of bearing such witness to humanity, yet the semi-detached case of Henze excepted, the post-war avant-garde had remained suspicious of so apparently tainted a form – tainted, that is, by social, political, and æsthetic associations. If all along it were suspected by the avant-garde that the 'last opera' had been *Lulu* – itself, significantly an unfinished work – then the avant-garde took Stravinsky's and

[18] Nono, 'Geschichte und Gegenwart der Musik von heute', in *Texte*, p. 40.
[19] Lachenmann, 'Touched by Nono,' p. 18.
[20] Ibid.

Henze's, let alone Britten's, post-war attempts at rejuvenation as explicit confirmation of the form's death. It had been as strange a death as that of 'liberal England', holding little apparent justification beyond pointing to the absence of 'viable' new works and the moribund production values in reviving those works from the repertoire that might otherwise retain some viability.[21] Yet the claim seemed as self-evident to its proponents as the symphony's demise had to Wagner. Boulez would change his mind, principally through his collaboration with Wieland Wagner on *Wozzeck* and *Parsifal*; but what he saw as the absurdity of Kirsten Flagstad's 'acting' in Wagner seems to have helped persuade him that music drama was dead, a 'museum art' – and even that Wagner's music itself should be viewed with suspicion.[22] Stockhausen would come round to operatic composition in typically spectacular style, but that development lay some years hence. It was left instead to Nono to break the *de facto* prohibition on graven operatic images, and thus, in a sense, as Lachenmann put it, to provoke the 'irritation' experienced by erstwhile colleagues such as Stockhausen at Nono's taking up and preserving 'the traditional "big" expressive tone, the gesture full of pathos, lyricism, drama and emotion such as has been handed down from Monteverdi, Beethoven or Schoenberg'.[23]

III

The latter name is crucial with respect to *Intolleranza 1960*. Nono had never assented to the Boulezian 'Schoenberg est mort' elevation of Webern over his teacher.[24] Indeed, despite the acknowledged debt Nono owed to Webern, he described him as 'certainly restricted' compared with Schoenberg. That might, Nono thought, have been the ground of Webern's greater influence.[25] Perhaps Schoenberg's time was yet fully to come? At any rate, Nono dedicated the score of his *azione scenica* to his posthumous father-in-law. Moreover, a few months before embarking upon composition (an extraordinary short burst between December 1960 and March 1961), Nono made clear once again his overwhelming admiration for the composer he clearly saw, whatever Schoenberg's politics in a narrow understanding,

[21] George Dangerfield, *The Strange Death of Liberal England* (Harrison Smith and Robert Haas: New York, 1935).
[22] Interview with Rupert Christiansen, 'Boulez and the Blight of Opera,' in *The Daily Telegraph*, 7 September 1996, A3.
[23] Lachenmann, 'Touched by Nono,' p. 20.
[24] Pierre Boulez, 'Schönberg est mort,' in *Relevés d'apprenti*, ed. Paule Thévenin (Seuil: Paris, 1966), pp. 265–74.
[25] Nono, 'Gespräch mit Martine Cardieu [I],' pp. 180–1.

as his predecessor in an almost prophetic (Old Testament?) manner. Schoenberg's *A Survivor from Warsaw* was, in Lachenmann's transcription of a lecture Nono delivered on the work:

> the musical-æsthetic manifesto of our era. What Jean-Paul Sartre says in his essay, *What is Literature?*, about the problem 'why write?', is witnessed in utterly authentic fashion in Schoenberg's creative necessity:
>
> 'And if I am presented with this world and its injustices, then I should not look at it coldly, but ... with indignation, that I might expose it and create it in its nature as injustice and abuse ...'
>
> ...
>
> And further, should someone refuse to recognise Schoenberg's [here Nono makes reference to a previous quotation from Arnold Schmitz on Bach] *docere* and *movere*, above all in his *A Survivor from Warsaw*, he should know that the words which the nineteen-year-old student, Giacomo Levi, wrote in his last letter before execution by the Fascists in Modena in 1942, are also addressed to him: 'Do not say that you no longer wish to know anything about it. Consider this, that all that has happened is because you no longer wished to know anything more about it.'[26]

Such was the kind of 'provocation' Nono believed necessary for an artwork, 'The genesis of any of my works is always to be found in a human "provocation": an event, an experience, a test in our lives, which provokes my instinct and my consciousness, as man and musician, to bear witness.'[27] Moreover, that witness was best served in a fashion not only verging upon the traditional, its roots in the Schiller-Marx-Wagner idea of art as the paradigm of labour, but also avowedly technological. Interest in new technical possibilities was of its post-war time yet also claimed good warrant in Marx. Not for nothing had the *Communist Manifesto* hymned the achievements of the bourgeoisie in ecstatic terms: 'It has been the first to show what man's activity can bring about. It has accomplished miracles surpassing Egyptian pyramids, Roman aqueducts, and Gothic cathedrals; it has conducted expeditions that put in the shade all former Exoduses of nations and crusades.'[28]

Nono's socialist humanism, in this respect not unlike that of Wagner, owed much to his avid interest in the other arts, old and new: in theatrical developments, not least Josef Svoboda's 'magic lantern' and

---

[26] Nono, 'Text-Musik-Gesang,' in *Texte*, pp. 47–8. The Sartre quotation comes from *Was ist Literatur?: ein Essay*, tr. Hans Georg Brenner (Rohwolt: Hamburg, 1958), p. 40.

[27] Nono, 'Einige genauere Hinweise zu *Intolleranza 1960*,' in *Texte*, p. 70.

[28] Karl Marx, 'Manifest der kommunistischen Partei,' in *Die Frühschriften*, ed. Siegfried Landshut (Kröner: Stuttgart, 1971), p. 528.

its technical possibilities, but also in literature, the visual arts, and the cinema. For him, creation was paramount, both in a Romantic sense of constituting in itself something essential to human existence and flourishing, and, arguably more importantly still, in its crucial communicative role. Technical developments, especially the use and advancement of electronics, were always crucial in this respect. Gianmario Borio has written that the composer's entire body of work from the mid-1950s onwards 'can be seen as an attempt to provide a satisfactory answer to Sartre's question, "Why write?"; the Sartre-like reply, while varied in its musical expression over the course of time, was "in order to fulfil our duty to produce the world". It was not for Nono – unlike, as we shall see, Henze – a matter 'of reproducing in music the emotions of suffering, scorn, anger, rebellion, desire and love of which the texts speak, or to which the titles of instrumental compositions refer; rather, it was the idea of formulating on a musical level, in the unshakable unity of sound, issues for which humanity demands urgent resolution.'[29]

For, however much Nono might salute Schoenberg, his concept of expression was very different. If anything, we stand closer to an updated Busoni – teacher not only to Weill but also to Varèse. In his *Sketch for a New Aesthetic of Music*, Busoni had declared that 'the greater part of modern theatre music suffers from the mistake of seeking to repeat the scenes passing on the stage'. Its 'proper mission', rather, was to interpret 'the soul-states of the persons represented', which might actually stand in opposition to the action.[30] More than three decades on, this claim still seems to have provoked Schoenberg's ire:

> when I had asked not to add external expression and illustration, . . . [other composers] understood that expression and illustration were out, and that there should be no relation whatsoever to the text. There were now composed songs, ballets, operas, and oratorios in which the achievement of the composer consisted in a strict aversion against all that his text presented.
>
> What nonsense!
>
> . . .
>
> I remember how Busoni was the first to claim that music in opera must not express what is expressed by the action.
>
> The opera is principally the product of four factors: the text, the music, the stage, and the singer. If one of these constituents is allowed to disregard what

29 Gianmario Borio, 'Nono, Luigi,' *Grove Music Online. Oxford Music Online.* Oxford University Press. Web. 15 March 2012. <http://www.oxfordmusiconline.com/subscriber/ article/grove/music/20044>.

30 Ferrucio Busoni, 'Sketch of a New Esthetic of Music,' in *Three Classics in the Aesthetic of Music* (Dover: New York, 1962), tr. Theodore Baker, p. 83.

the others do, why should they not also enjoy the same privilege? For instance, the singer?

Could not Monastasos ask Sarastro to dance a 'pas de deux' with Pamina? Or could not Lohengrin immediately after his arrival sell the swan to a butcher and start auctioning his gondola?[31]

That seems quite a misunderstanding, most likely a wilful one, of what Busoni had said. Nevertheless, the fact that Schoenberg could have interpreted it thus is indicative of how important a problem this seems to have been, how determined composers were either to break free from Wagner – for Busoni, 'incapable of greater intensification' – or to continue to execute Wagner's legacy.[32] Nono would not have used such Romantic language as Busoni's, but nevertheless creation and dramatisation here mean something very different from what they do in the work of the other composers we have considered. He did not want, as Schoenberg believed some composers to desire and as Stravinsky was widely understood to have declared, to ensure 'that music does not express something – or more: that it does not express something provoked by the text'.[33] But nor was such expression straightforwardly the purpose of Nono's nevertheless gestural conception of musical composition.

IV

In the case of *Intolleranza 1960*, Nono's necessary 'provocations' were manifold: negligence leading to a mining accident in Marcinelle in Belgium, Italian popular demonstrations in July 1960 resisting the purported return of Fascism, events in colonial Algeria, and the catastrophe ensuing in Polesine from flooding by the River Po. They were transformed by Nono into scenes from the life of an emigrant – or, depending on one's point of view, immigrant – worker, his experience witnessed and commented upon in different situations, indeed different geographical locations. However, the Emigrant is not, according to Nono, in himself the true protagonist. Rather there are two conceptual 'principal elements' (*Hauptelemente*), viewed in those different situations: intolerance and opposition thereto, hence the work's title. Thus on the one side are ranged 'capitalist exploitation, fascism, and colonialism', on the other, 'an emigrant miner who rebels, the people in

[31] Schoenberg, 'This is my Fault,' tr. Leo Black, in *Style and Idea: Selected Writings*, ed. Leonard Stein (Faber: London, 1975), p. 146.
[32] Busoni, 'Sketch of a New Esthetic,' p. 80.
[33] Schoenberg, 'This is my Fault,' p. 146.

opposition, and the struggle against colonialism'.[34]

Though avowedly, then, a contemporary, even ultra-contemporary, work, the roots of *Intolleranza*, especially in terms of Nono's æsthetic, lay deeper. While there is little evidence of direct 'influence' from the Wagnerian *Gesamtkunstwerk*, some of Nono's influences conspired to create something not entirely dissimilar – and certainly just as provocative. Nono's desire to create a musico-theatrical piece had not suddenly arisen. Indeed, many of his works written during the 1950s, especially those for voices, as well as his analyses of opera, *Moses und Aron* included, may be understood to have led up to *Intolleranza*, though its immediate occasion was the commission from Mario Labroca, in October 1960, for a piece for the following year's Venice Biennale. Reading of writers such as Alfred Andersch – who would make the German translation of the work – and Italo Calvino, still more the technical possibilities of the Prague 'laterna magika' and pre-Stalinist Russian experimental theatre – itself of course soaked in Wagner's influence – had made their way into Nono's evolving vision. Having learned from the writings of Angelo Mario Ripellino of Vsevolod Meyerhold's theatre, Nono initially approached Ripellino for a libretto. He found that difficult to set, but incorporated some of Ripellino's material, as well as his *Vivere è stare svegli*, into the work. Meyerhold's idea of multiple areas of action and Erwin Piscator's political vision of a mobile theatre were likewise attractive and suggestive. From the techniques of the 'laterna magika', developed by Svoboda, Alfred Radok, and Vaclav Kašlik, and viewed by Nono during a visit to Prague in 1958, arose the idea of a 'multilayered presentation in the conception and setting of the text'. There was even originally an idea that Svoboda might contribute more directly; he came to Venice, but his architectural and other slides were not in keeping with Nono's conception. Instead, Nono's friend, the painter Emilio Vedova – himself a Venetian participant in the Italian Resistance – designed the scenes, both abstract and more specific, which were then projected on to Svoboda's screens. (Vedova would also provide the lighting for *Prometeo* in 1984.)

In addition to Ripellino, Nono made use of a good number of sources for his 'Textmontage'. Verse came from Paul Eluard's *La Liberté*, Mayakovsky's *Our March*, and Brecht's '*An die Nachgeborenen*'. 'Direct documentation' came from popular slogans – the German anti-war *Nie wieder!*, the anti-Franco *No pasaran!*, the communist partisan *Morte al fascismo e libertà ai populi!*, the anti-racist *Down with discrimination!*, and the Indo-Chinese

---

[34] Nono, 'Genauere Hinweise,' pp. 68–9.

accusation of *La sale guerre!* It also came from the Nazi interrogation of the Czech communist journalist and literary critic Julius Fučik, from Henri Alleg's *La Question*, from Sartre's introduction to Alleg's revelation of French torture methods in Algeria, from recorded comments by Paris policemen, and from testimony of an Algerian torture victim recorded in the 1959 book *La Gangrène*.[35] Nono's *Composizione per Orchestra no. 1* from 1951 had already offered an as-yet-secret memorial – programme music hardly the thing for Darmstadt – to Fučik, hanged following captivity in Berlin in 1943 and an official hero for socialist Czechoslovakia.

V

Nono never allotted any role to pessimism, not so much out of 'optimism' – though he never lost faith in the class struggle and its necessary outcome – but because the question never arose. That is neither socialist realism, which he explicitly rejected, nor Frankfurt School-criticism.[36] It is, rather, a Gramscian philosophy of praxis in which theory and practice are not only as one, but energetically so. The Gramscian project of Communism – and the Communist Party – acquiring cultural and political ascendancy was of course important here. But, ideological claims apart, for Nono, 'provocation' and sonic response were vital in themselves, just as they would be for Abbado in performing and recording *Il canto sospeso* in 1992, two years after Nono's death, when 'Germany ... three years after the fall of the Berlin Wall, is once again in the grip of an increasing hatred of "foreigners"', when, across Europe, 'nationalism, xenophobia, racism, and anti-Semitism are once more on the increase'.[37] In conversation in

[35] Nono, 'Genauer Hinweise,' pp. 70–1; Paul Eluard, 'La liberté,' in *Œuvres complètes*, ed. Marcelle Dumas and Lucien Scheller (Gallimard: Paris, 1968), pp. 1105–7; Wladimir Majakowski, 'Unser Marsch,' in *Werke*, ed. Leonhard Kossuth, 10 vols (Insel: Frankfurt, 1966–73), vol. 1, pp. 34–5; Bertolt Brecht, 'An die Nachgeborenen,' in *Gesammelte Werke*, 20 vols (Suhrkamp: Frankfurt, 1967), pp. 722–5; Julius Fučik, *Reportage unter dem Strang geschrieben*, tr. Felix Rausch (Pahl-Rugenstein: Cologne, 2000); Henri Alleg, *La Question*, with introduction by Jean-Paul Sartre (La Cité: Lausanne, 1958); Henri Alleg, *La Gangrène* (Minuit: Lausanne, 1959).

[36] Nono, 'Genauere Hinweise,' p. 68.

[37] Concert programme declaration from Abbado and the Berlin Philharmonic Orchestra, 9/10 December 1992, printed in the accompanying booklet to the CD release of Abbado's live Berlin recording, Sony CD SK 53360, p. 8. Signatories are Abbado, Bernd Gellerman, Hansjörg Schellenberger, Ulrich Meyer-Schoellkopf, Helmut Stern, and Rudolf Watzel. The recording was (p. 12) 'intended as a message on the part of the Berlin Philharmonic Orchestra and Claudio Abbado that we condemn all brutality and resurgent violence against people who think differently and that we do so from the

1972 – though it could readily have been a dozen years earlier – Nono declared that resignation was the stock-in-trade of bourgeois passivity; it had nothing to do with his art. Whilst one could learn much from Adorno and Marcuse, 'they have nothing to do with us Marxists'. (Adorno for his part seems to have shown little interest in Nono.) Nono continued: 'There are composers, who ... [believe] that music can change nothing. But the truth is otherwise. Music can intervene in a social situation ... For me, music and politics are a unity.'[38] Richard Taruskin's brief, typically partisan sketch in his *Oxford History of Western Music* could not be further from the truth, then, in its claim that 'Nono defended his musical idiom in terms borrowed from Adorno, another Marxist who turned a blind eye to the actual historical consequences of Marxist philosophy.' Indeed, Taruskin achieves 'balance' only by equal misunderstanding or misrepresentation of both Nono and Adorno.[39]

Nono's very conception of serial technique is quite different from that expressed – an operative word – in musical drama haunted or nurtured by the ghost of Expressionism. Athematic and concerned principally with expression of the intervallic relations of the various parameters, it attempts to express not so much that which perhaps cannot be expressed – the heroic attempt of Schoenberg's *Moses* – but that which would never have been considered 'expressive'. It goes beyond the Romantic, in an entirely different fashion from the Stravinskian path of appropriating the past. For instance, writing on the orchestral opening, Nono tells of a 'perspectival "continuum" of tensions, structured in the unity of a band of sound (*Klangfläche*)' (bars 40–79).[40] That band takes the form of a major seventh from C sharp to C natural (Ex. 12), played by all but the bass instruments.

Ex. 12. Band of sound, bb.40–79

The twelve notes of the chromatic scale, all lying within that band of sound, are continuously combined and varied in terms of single or multiple

very bottom of our hearts', *Il canto sospeso* being 'music born of deep dismay, painful and accusing'.
[38] Nono, 'Gespräch mit Wolfgang Becker-Carsten,' in *Texte*, pp. 278–9
[39] Richard Taruskin, *The Oxford History of Western Music*, 5 vols (Oxford University Press: New York, 2010), vol. 5, p. 89.
[40] Nono, 'Genauere Hinweise,' p. 78.

timbres, dynamics, sound production, and so on. Tensions within that band constitute 'a specific form of musical expression both as such and in relation to the dramatic action that will follow'.[41] Thus what might conceivably be considered 'dramatic' content in a conventional sense, what the Emigrant experiences, is not really sequential at all, but instead appears to be presented in a fashion analogous to the serial conception of the music. The band of sound has its dramatic counterpart in what I shall term a band of action; dramatic 'intervals' are brought together continuously and varied through multi-layered declamation. Nono's point here is not, as Stockhausen believed with respect to *Il canto sospeso*, to divest the text of meaning; it was not 'to withdraw it from the public eye where it has no place'.[42] Instead, the text seems rather to denote, even to express, the compressed, non-linear form dramatic events take on in our consciousness. Such is the role allotted to the subject in Nono's musical conception of the class struggle.

And yet, even before that orchestral section of the introduction, before the curtain begins to rise, a different form of tension has manifested itself to the visual accompaniment of projections. In the preceding *a cappella* choral music, we first hear an intricate mass of female voices, later joined by tenors and basses, whose humanity seems very much to be the point. The expressive capability – very much in a more 'traditional' sense – of the human voice brings to mind both the music of the Renaissance, which Abbado suspected might explain why Nono's 'most moving and most beautiful music has the human voice at its centre, be it for solo voice or for chorus', and the Burning Bush of *Moses und Aron*.[43] That still small voice of calm, even if not intended in anything approaching a conventionally 'religious' sense, retains a quality we might consider to be noumenal. If it would be an exaggeration to say that it counsels against all-too-easy subsequent identification of the chorus with the political slogans it might be voicing, then at least it reminds us, like the chorus in Bach's Passions, that the drama is more multivalent than one might otherwise believe. One might indeed make much the same comparison at the other end of the 'dynamic' scale, when Nono unleashes his chorus through loudspeakers, challenging 'traditional' distinctions between chorus and audience. Shocking? Neo-Brechtian agitprop? Perhaps, but also in a sense drawing upon, or at least capable of being readily assimilated to, communal tradition, for instance that of the congregation singing chorales, whether in the

[41] Ibid.
[42] Karlheinz Stockhausen, 'Music and Speech,' in *Die Reihe*, 6 (1964), 48–9.
[43] Abbado, 'My Silent Friend,' p. 3.

St Matthew Passion or, on stage, in *Die Meistersinger*. History reasserts itself, invited or otherwise, especially given the insistence and persistence of opera as a genre, however often it might also find that status attacked, subdivided, even dissolved. Nono's conception of expression is both modified by a more Romantic conception and modifies that conception – and that dialectic plays itself out throughout the drama.

VI

Part of that playing out is the story, or perhaps better scenic representation, of the Emigrant, an angry successor to Dallapiccola's resigned, betrayed Prisoner. The first two scenes set him in a mining community – he is an immigrant there too – from which he must now take his leave. Other miners would like to follow him, but poverty's necessity (*bisogno*) is stronger than dreams. Though the libretto tells us that the Emigrant starts his journey, it is more a resumption – and, in terms of Nono's insistence upon non-linear form, the journey is in any case ongoing. We might think of Schoenberg's Israelites, lost in the desert, the Prisoner's captivity, or even Parsifal's wanderings, but with a decidedly post-war serial twist to the action as well as to the music.

When scorned by the Emigrant's imminent departure, the woman with whom he has been staying turns racist, her nasty accusations concerning one who seems only to be from the south of her country – though in many senses, southern Italy is indeed another country – presenting a turn to the language of parasitism, first medical and then bestial:

> Cursed emigrant!
> No longer shall my body serve you!
> Black catarrh!
> Unstick yourself from my throat!
> Black worm (*verme*)!
> Stop your suckling at my breast!
> Implacably shall I chase you!

It is almost the melodramatic language, updated, of nineteenth-century Italian opera, an impression heightened by her exit following a curse – but of course she is not really the protagonist; intolerance is.

The third scene offers, in Nono's words, an 'ideological and physical clash between the two principal elements: the attempt at fascist restoration is portrayed on stage, first indirectly – in the demonstration that necessarily arise against it, with unambiguous slogans – and then also directly – the intervention of the police, *sua longa manu* –, the demonstrators, the chorus, the shouting, the banners'.[44] Babel-like choral combination of languages in the popular slogans listed above imparts a true sense of internationalism, of peoples resisting intolerance, and yet perhaps 'Babel' offers a clue to the protestors' downfall. It is easier for their foes to organise than for them; casualties and arrests ensue.

And so, in the fourth scene, we find ourselves at a police station, for interrogation. The Emigrant is one of those who have been arrested, though he claims simply to have been passing through, but denial of the charges is not an option the gendarmes will permit. Torture, 'instrument [of intolerance] since time immemorial', is the guise here adopted by one of Nono's two *Hauptelemente*, in what may well be an allusion to *Il prigioniero*. The 'neo-Nazi torture-methods employed by the French paras, carried out in an attempt to crush the movement' for Algerian liberation are the provocation here.[45] Much of what we hear falls under the rubric of 'documentary material', since it is based on a report in Alleg's *La Gangrène* and ends with a quotation from 'reality', as it were, in the guise of Alleg's 'Voice', from *La Question*, the autobiographical work that had exposed the brutal methods employed by French forces. It had suffered severe censorship in France, although an American publisher, George Braziller, had made available an English version, and it was also available in French via Switzerland.

This is clearly highly political material, then, yet Nono cautions us against understanding this as imposing 'musico-theatrical validity *as such*'. For the 'ideological themes' in his material could only 'inform artistic consciousness in the present engagement with the material; the engagement is fulfilled in their elaboration and in the technical-expressive outcome'.[46] Indeed, the *Hauptelement* here represented in torture is all the more powerfully conveyed in the pain and the almost unbearable Webern-like beauty of the instrumental postlude, itself as shocking in context as the torture itself. Of course, *Intolleranza* employs a great deal of singing, vocal and choral, but there is much speech heard too: although the Emigrant here is heard in *Sprechstimme*, the gendarmes employ everyday speech. Again, whether intentionally or otherwise, a parallel with *Moses* is clear: representation is no easy task, especially when interrogated. However, the orchestra seems to sing more freely when less tied to the words – and here it sings with music from the fourth movement of the Resistance-inspired 1956 work for soloists, choir, and orchestra, *Il canto sospeso*. Interestingly,

---

[44] Nono, 'Genauere Hinweise', p. 69.
[45] Ibid., pp. 69–70.
[46] Ibid., p. 71.

the row employed by the latter, heard in linear fashion for the first time during the same fourth movement, is of a wedge variety that may recall that we saw Dallapiccola allot to Hope in *Il prigioniero*. The false hope of 'Fratello' continues to captivate, even as it should repel. And indeed, writing in 1963 on the possibility and necessity of 'a new musical theatre', Nono would laud 'Alban Berg's masterly *Lulu* and Luigi Dallapiccola's principal work, *Il prigioniero*', as twin steps along the path to a 'modern conception of the theatre'.[47]

Lest we find ourselves too captivated – in more than one sense – by the siren beauty of torture, the fifth scene, 'La tortura', confronts us directly, in a 'Chorus of the Tortured':

> The paras in this section
> torture, torture,
> day and night, night and day.
> *Turning to the public:*
> And you?
> Are you deaf?
> Following the herd
> in its ugly shame?
> Are you not roused by the laments of our brothers
>   [*fratelli*]?
> Megaphones! Amplify this cry!
> Before slander deforms it
> and indifference throttles it!

Sartre's 'Voice' heightens the dialectic of struggle, pointing out that at no time has the wish for liberation been stronger and yet at no time has state oppression been more violent and better armed. And so it continues, through a concentration camp and an escape therefrom, the tolling of bells perhaps calling upon a spatial Venetian past to inform the specific fate of prisoners' present. Fučik's 'Voice' signals Nono's refusal to bend to pessimism: sadness, he insists, should never be conjured by his name. The important thing is not to forget. Whether or no we believe in the 'libertà' hymned by the Emigrant and an Algerian who has also escaped, Nono, unlike Dallapiccola, clearly wishes us to do so. Hope does not seem so forlorn, so impossible. The centrality of the chorus, now in outright revolt as 'Algerians and Emigrants' – though we should not of course forget its more ambiguous role at the opening – brings us as close to an agitprop marching song as Nono ever came, providing as triumphant a close to the first part as anyone might reasonably have expected, arguably more so.

[47] Nono, 'Möglichkeit und Notwendigkeit eines neuen Musiktheaters', in *Texte*, p. 94.

The second part opens with a purely spoken scene, courtesy of tape. 'Some absurdities of contemporary life' are presented, as the Emigrant moves around the stage, confused by its assemblage of voices, mimes, and projections. 'Voices' offer the bureaucratic oppression of the modern state: 'Identify yourself!'; 'Papers are the soul of the state'; 'Proibito – défendu – verboten – forbidden'; and so forth. Newspaper items, the stuff of the Culture Industry and thus the enemy, assail us as much as the Emigrant: 'Mother of thirteen was in fact a man'; 'Elephants in revolt attack Luang-Prabang!'; 'An atomic weapon explodes by mistake on the naval base of Dummyland!' Finally, we are asked: 'Ultimatum to Dummyland or by Dummyland?'

What follows has very much the sense of taking place during after-shock, however 'absurd' that scene may have been. (What, after all, could be more absurd than mutually assured destruction?) The crowd is on stage, but, cowed by the explosion, remains silent, allowing us to hear an encounter between the Emigrant and his female Companion. She laments that, whilst they could have been peacefully discovering the wonders of Nature, 'the fumes of Hiroshima spread through a thousand delirious nervous systems', cormorants of death swarming above. 'Laments' doubtless is the word, for there is something of the ancient operatic lament to her music, 'expressive' in a sense Nono had supposedly disavowed. What might have seemed undesirable, even in a Schoenbergian sense impossible, no longer does. This is not Puccini, nor even Dallapiccola, yet it elicits sympathy nonetheless – and irrespective of intention. Moreover, the instrumental writing sounds less angry, even less overtly committed, unusually delicate for this work; the timbres of vibraphones, glockenspiels, woodwind, strings, sounding closer to the world of Boulez, the sensuous world of *Le Marteau sans maître*, than we have previously heard, or indeed than we shall hear again. Is there a message of hope there for Darmstadt too? Certainly the Emigrant retains 'a decisive voice of hope in my solitude'. Again, one might think of the Burning Bush. And if it would be a stretch to speak of a love duet between the two companions, it would be a stretch rather than an absurdity.

The return of the woman who had warned she would pursue the Emigrant is accompanied by a group of fanatics and projections of violence, intolerance reasserting itself, culminating in a synagogue wall daubed with the slogan 'Juden heraus!' Upon the Emigrant's cry of 'Never again!' and his and his Companion's hurling themselves against the projected symbols of fanaticism, they disappear, answered once again by a choral tattoo of revolt. The PCI might come to believe that its day would come peacefully, but neither Nono nor indeed Gramsci, always convinced that capital must be broken by force, would have agreed. Doing what one could to further class consciousness was one thing; revisionism was another entirely.

Crucially, through the interaction between the two *Hauptelemente*, a third has emerged, the awakening of the Emigrant's awareness. The resulting dialectic, for Nono, has its own musical and scenic reality, belonging moreover to 'a part of the public', though certainly not the bourgeoisie, which, invoking Sartre, wished only to see an image of itself, not in any sense to undergo investigation of the world around it, to see its dominion challenged.[48] Though in the flight the Emigrant witnesses from a disaster zone, the flood itself seemingly a result of governmental negligence, he sees in his own past – and indeed he would, given the non-linear nature of the drama – that advance in consciousness cannot be reversed, even as, *Götterdämmerung*-like, the Po bursts its banks and envelops those who remain. However, whereas Wagner had famously granted the orchestra the last word, Nono opts for voices, again *a cappella*, the audience once more addressed directly:

> You who emerge from the waters
> that overwhelmed us,
> think
> also of the dark times
> you have escaped.
> We moved around, changing countries more often than
>   shoes,
> through class wars, despairing
> when there was only injustice.
> You, when the time comes
> for man to help another man,
> think of us
> kindly.

VII

Where Nono's conception of the *Gesamtkunstwerk* differs from Wagner's is perhaps not so much in its nature or even effect as in ideological intent. (It would be perfectly possible for audiences to wallow in its sound, still more so in a later work such as *Prometeo*, for the Nono-equivalent of Nietzsche's accursed 'Wagnerians' to emerge.) Even here it is a matter

---

[48] Nono, 'Genauere Hinweise', p. 69; Jean-Paul Sartre, 'Théâtre épique et théâtre dramatique', in *Un Théâtre de situations*, ed. Michel Contat and Michel Rybalka (Gallimard: Paris, 1972), p. 120.

of degree, but the critical (self-)consciousness engendered by communal experience is more explicitly Nono's aim than it had ever been Wagner's, whether in the envisaged revolutionary memorial of the *Ring* or the still more complex, more elusive observance of *Parsifal*. One might well argue that the experience of *Parsifal* is very different, and for many of us it is, the more reactionary elements of Wagner's dramaturgy being vanquished by the overwhelming dynamism of the work as a whole, but the distinction remains worth making, if not exaggerating.

Although it would take more than a decade until Nono wrote another music drama, the distinction between his works written for the opera house and others does not necessarily amount to a great deal. The need for 'provocations', or rather the need to respond to them, remained, as did a keen sense of drama, whether in vocal, instrumental, or electronic works. So too did a hostility towards bourgeois institutions, leading to more serious attempts than many at least to circumvent them at times. Part of the attraction, both for Nono and for us, of a work such as the furiously anti-capitalist *La fabbrica illuminata* (1964) was not only the use of sounds of both men and machines, from a Genoese factory, but dissociation from the bourgeois concert world, the specification of a factory itself as the location for performance. One may argue over whether recorded listening at home betrays that intention – even if one considers it must be honoured – more or less than listening to *Parsifal* at home, but in both cases, and indeed in many others, it is doubtless something to bear in mind, to add some grit should the oyster become unduly æstheticised.

Composition is not the only issue here; reception and indeed patronage played an important role, just as they had in music of the past. For instance, in 1970, the PCI organised twenty-five lecture-concerts in different locations across Tuscany and Umbria, faithfully attended by workers. Nono had been involved in such lecture-concerts throughout Italy since 1964. And his contemporary and compatriot Sylvano Bussotti's opera *Lorenzaccio*, dedicated to the Party, was even before its premiere guaranteed performances at several Italian opera houses, located in provinces of predictable political persuasion.[49] Advocacy of Nono's music by performers such as Abbado and Maurizio Pollini took place in the concert hall, the opera house, and beyond, in the car factories of northern Italy. Both musicians collaborated, for instance, on the 1972 first performance of *Como un ola de fuerza y luz*, also at La Scala. The importance of Abbado as a music director in Milan committed to Nono and to new music in general can

---

[49] Smith Brindle, *The New Music*, p. 183.

hardly be exaggerated.

In 1987, looking back over his career, Nono would claim with specific though not exclusive reference to a piece for tape, *Non Consumiamo Marx*: 'Technical innovation moves, excites, disrupts the reality of the emotions, and *vice versa*: "thoughts are born with language".'[50] However, as Michael Gorodecki points out, though Nono 'may have … wished this in the 60s, the radical modernity which Nono insisted on in his music probably did not help comprehension of his "thoughts" by an audience which increasingly came from factories, workers clubs and unions, as well as left-wing organisations and universities'.[51] Yet, if that incomprehension were to a certain extent a bind, it was also a spur to further creativity, to attempts at new methods and languages of communication, which did not eschew 'radical modernity' but rather challenged and in that process extended it. There was to be no retreat, but there would come, as we shall see in the final chapter's treatment of *Al gran sole carico d'amore* and its aftermath, a recognition that travelling was necessary even when there was no longer any path along which to travel. In a tribute to Nono, his student and 'latterly … close friend', Lachenmann opened with a quotation from George Steiner's *Antigones*:

> 'Greek tragedy honoured human freedom by letting its heroes fight against an overpowering fate'. The 'limits of art' require Man to be defeated in this struggle, even when the error or guilt which cause such a defeat are, in the strict sense of the word 'fatal' (even for the crime committed through fate). Fatum in Greek tragedy is an 'invisible force which cannot be achieved by any natural force and which even the immortal Gods have no power over'. But out of the downfall of Man his freedom is crystalline – that clear necessity to act, and to act polemically, which constitutes the substance of the ego.[52]

That, as we have seen, and as we shall continue to see, could be understood as a hallmark, often in very different ways, of the various dramas, composers, and later productions, examined 'after Wagner'. Given Wagner's vision of a renewal of Greek tragedy, at least as much in its social, religious, and political senses as in terms of dramatic content, there are worse tributes to pay his, as well as Nono's, legacy.[53]

---

[50] Luigi Nono, 'Un autobiografia dell'autore raccantata da Enzo Restagno,' in *Autori Vari*, ed. Enzo Restagno (EDT musica: Turin, 1987), p. 43.

[51] Michael Gorodecki, 'Strands in 20th-Century Italian Music: 1 – Luigi Nono: A History of Belief,' in *The Musical Times*, 1787 (1992), 14

[52] Lachenmann, 'Touched by Nono,' p. 17.

[53] See Mark Berry, 'Richard Wagner and the Politics of Music-Drama,' in *The Historical Journal*, 47 (2004), 666–8.

Henze was more than usually ambivalent about Wagner's legacy; in part that came with the German territory. In a 1967 interview for *Melos*, Henze spoke generously, if not without equivocation, about *Intolleranza*:

> Do I think that the search for new forms of music theatre as undertaken by Nono and Ligeti will be significant for the future of opera? The only work of Ligeti's that seems to have anything to do with theatre is *Aventures & Nouvelles Aventures*, and in all innocence he says something about it that is quite alien to me: 'When aspects of "society" are ironised by being assembled in a new way, indeed caricatured and demonised, this takes place without any political slant. It is precisely a dread of deep significance and ideology that makes any kind of engaged art out of the question for me.' I think that if this dread continues to prevail, we have little hope of drama from him. On the other hand Nono has hitherto undertaken only one experiment that embodies a strong tendency towards 'engaged' drama, without one's being able to speak of a new form of music drama. It is therefore difficult to answer this question. But every striving, even for the future of opera, has a meaning if it is accompanied by humanistic motives, and adopts an unmistakable libertarian anti-fascist stance.[54]

It is to Henze's own anti-fascist stance, its roots and some of its outcomes, that I shall now turn.

---

[54] Hans Werner Henze, 'Experiments and the Avant-garde,' in *Music and Politics: Collected Writings 1953–81*, tr. Peter Labanyi (Faber: London, 1982), pp. 164–5.

CHAPTER 6

Hans Werner Henze:
Paths to (and from) *Natascha Ungeheuer*

I

Henze's way proved very different from but at least as involving as the paths of the composers looked at so far. It was certainly not Schoenberg's Biblical way; nor, despite the title of its most equivocal of (non-)destinations, *Der langwierige Weg in die Wohnung der Natascha Ungeheuer* ('The Tedious Way to Natascha Ungeheuer's Apartment'), could it in any sense be described as tedious. Dallapiccola and Nono have already signalled the complexity of the relationship between Italian and German experience, which should never be viewed a simple opposition. Henze's attraction towards Italy offers further evidence of that complexity. He left Germany in disgust in 1953, escaping in his car, driving south until reaching Italy, where he would spend much of the rest of his life. However, many of his political and compositional imperatives would remain indelibly marked by his nationality and by the inescapable weight of German tradition and history.

Henze was born in 1926, in Gütersloh, Westphalia, growing up in a village thirty kilometres from Bielefeld, which city he occasionally visited for musical events. He saw himself as having been triply cursed. Not only was he a German, but a German cut off from the preferable 'south German, Bohemian, and Austrian world of sun and pleasure', and also – important for his experience both during and after the war – a German homosexual in what was, to put it mildly, an unfriendly climate.[1] He felt scarred by having seen his father, an apparently liberal village schoolmaster, be transformed into not just a party member, but an enthusiastic, truly-believing Nazi. In his autobiography, Henze recalls his father, having been alerted to some undisclosed incident by Henze's mother, summoning the teenage boy into his presence and telling him that '"people like me" belonged in concentration camps. I shall never forget his words. I was

---

[1] Hans Werner Henze, *Bohemian Fifths: An Autobiography*, tr. Stewart Spencer (Faber: London, 1999), p. 22.

forbidden to write any music and for three weeks had to spend two hours every afternoon chopping wood instead of practising the piano.'[2] Though admitted to the Brunswick State Music School, Henze was conscripted during total war, eventually spending several months as a prisoner of war in Schleswig-Holstein. During that time he met Willy Meyer, an oboist from the Staatskapelle Dresden – Wagner's old orchestra, with a lengthy Strauss association too – from whom he first heard the phrase 'dictatorship of the proletariat'.[3]

And so, whilst Nono was studying composition at the Venice Conservatory, Henze was rather haplessly serving in Magdeburg, Prague, and Berlin. Once the war was over – though in a sense for him, and not only for him, it would never be over – he came to feel, as a German, responsible for the sufferings of the entire continent and sickened by the attitude of many of his countrymen. He wrote, concerning his return to Bielefeld:

> The crimes committed in the concentration camps were now being talked about more or less openly, resulting in a growing sense of shame and horror. No one had known a thing. Everyone had been against it. The men and women of the occupying armies looked disbelievingly at us Germans, or their eyes were filled with loathing. Ever since then I have felt ashamed of our country and of my fellow Germans and our people. Wherever my travels have taken me, my origins – my nationality – have always caused me problems, even in Italy. Nor is it any wonder, since the devils who dragged us into this war did such unforgivable and unforgettable things to our neighbours, especially in Rome, not only in their persecution of the Jews but also following Mussolini's fall from power and during the subsequent partisan struggles.[4]

With respect to specifically cultural life, this being far from an atypical reaction, 'German art – especially the middle-class, nationalistic art of the nineteenth and early twentieth centuries – became insufferable and suspect. For a time I was unable and unwilling to take any interest in it.'[5] What remained was the German art that had been proscribed by the Nazis, art that therefore remained untainted by association.

II

A little background, however cursory, to the importance of music in German cultural history may be helpful here. Without straying into

[2]   Ibid., pp. 26–7.
[3]   Ibid., p. 50.
[4]   Ibid., p. 53.
[5]   Ibid.

denigration of other traditions, it can safely be said that there is something qualitatively and quantitatively different in this case, partly as a consequence of German territorial fragmentation, which had resulted in every major city and court boasting its own opera house and orchestra. The weight of tradition had grown steadily after Beethoven, notoriously making Brahms so loath, even for a lengthy period unable, to complete a first symphony. Johann Nikolaus Forkel, in his celebrated 1802 biography of Bach, had portrayed the composer as the musical equivalent of the classical texts upon which German humanist curricula were founded. Bach, the 'first classic that ever was, or perhaps ever will be', was 'an invaluable national patrimony, with which no other nation has anything else to be compared'.[6] The posthumous role played thereafter by Bach, Beethoven, and, more controversially, Wagner as German national heroes is well known. Even Handel, adoptive Englishman and staple of English choral societies, had been repatriated during the nineteenth century as Händel, a process which would continue during the early twentieth century and the Third Reich, and, after a fashion, into East Germany's secularised but also nationalised promotion of the oratorios.[7] The Mayor of Halle, in his opening statement to the first GDR Handel festival in 1952, lauded Handel's 'defiant humanism' and 'democratic patriotism'.[8] Interestingly, the more gradual renaissance in staging of Handel's operas left its mark in Henze's allocation of the effete Emperor to a counter-tenor in his 1970s anti-imperialist collaboration with Edward Bond, *We Come to the River*, quite a different form of political inspiration from that intended by the Mayor of Halle, let alone the bizarre, though far from uncontested, Aryanisation of Handel's oratorio texts during Henze's childhood and adolescence.[9] But talk of the 1970s is to get a little ahead of ourselves; the important point here is that the nationalism of East Germany was not necessarily reciprocated, and certainly not in the same fashion, in the West. Indeed, various overtures from the East for cultural co-operation would find themselves curtly rejected.

National Socialism had prevented German musicians, composers

---

[6]   Johann Nikolaus Forkel, *Über Johann Sebastian Bachs Leben, Kunst und Kunstwerke*, ed. Claudia Maria Knipsel (Henschel: Berlin, 2000), pp. 21–2.

[7]   See Martin Zenck, 'Zur Aneignung Händels in der nationalen Literaturgeschichtsschreibung des 19. Jahrhunderts,' in *Bericht über den internationalen musikwissenschaftlichen Kongreß Stuttgart 1985* (Bärenreiter: Kassel, 1987), pp. 273–80.

[8]   Pamela M. Potter, 'The Politicization of Handel and his Oratorios in the Weimar Republic, the Third Reich, and the Early Years of the German Democratic Republic,' in *The Musical Quarterly*, 85 (2001), 329

[9]   See Erik Levi, *Music in the Third Reich* (Macmillan: Basingstoke, 1994), pp. 77–81.

included, for the first time in centuries from keeping in touch with the latest developments. Thus for composers such as Henze and the young Stockhausen, the International Summer School for New Music in Darmstadt, founded in 1946 by Wolfgang Steinecke, offered the opportunity to catch up. As early as that very first year, 1946, Henze's Chamber Concerto, his opus one, received its first performance there. After initial attention paid to composers such as Bartók, Stravinsky, and Hindemith, emphasis was swiftly transferred, from 1948 onwards, under the influence of René Leibowitz, to twelve-note music. What had previously been condemned as abstract, degenerate, un-German, and of course Jewish, now offered the opportunity for redemption of German music: a message for 'outsiders' that would never leave Henze and would inform the construction, conscious or otherwise, of his image.[10]

Henze had grown up in 'the bourgeois world of Bielefeld, to which I had been admitted thanks to my being musical. Here the Nazis were considered unseemly; people tacitly rejected them, and found that Hitler fellow more and more of a nuisance, especially now that he was losing us the war and had landed us with air-raids.' What he called 'this "I was always against the Nazis" represents', he would claim 'a banal and frivolous stance (created on the stage by Auden in the last scene of *The Bassarids*)'.[11] And also, of course, by Henze himself. Even, then, when proscribed composers, at first Hindemith, only later the Second Viennese School, were once again performed, there was to him – at least in retrospect – something suspect about the enterprise. When, in its first post-war concert, the Bielefeld orchestra played Hindemith's *Mathis der Maler* Symphony, 'it went down with a discreet cultural *frisson* of "We're permitted to, we're able to, we have the freedom to play Hindemith . . . even if we hadn't actually missed this music."' However, there was also, more ominously, 'an undertone of "Now that Hindemith can be played again, our guilt is removed, everything is right with the world again, isn't it?"' Fascism, it could be claimed, 'had been no more than a bad dream'. Perhaps he is a little harsh, since he admits that he was simply 'thrilled to have survived'.[12] However, as time went on, and more of what he saw to be the old Germany

---

[10] Barrie Gavin's excellent 1994 film, *Hans Werner Henze: Memoirs of an Outsider* (Arthaus Musik DVD 100360), presents a view close to Henze's own with contributions from a host of distinguished musicians, including Oliver Knussen, Sir Simon Rattle, Ingo Metzmacher, Markus Stenz, and Henze himself.

[11] Henze, 'German Music in the 1940s and 1950s', in *Music and Politics: Collected Writings 1953–81*, tr. Peter Labanyi (Faber: London, 1982), p. 35.

[12] Henze, *Bohemian Fifths*, p. 36.

was restored – or shown never to have gone away – Henze could readily reinterpret, or perhaps just interpret, what had passed before.

The alleged 'abstraction' of twelve-note music – however absurd a conception of *Moses und Aron* or *Lulu* – was, however, often considered to offer some degree of safeguard against political misuse. That conception was paralleled in a similar renewal of interest in Italy, for instance in Milan's 1949 first International Congress of Twelve-note Music and, indeed, across the continent. Participants in the Milan congress included Leibowitz, Maderna, Scherchen, Cage, Dallapiccola, and Karl Amadeus Hartmann. A principal question at the Milan conference had been to what extent twelve-note technique was bound to the person and practice of Schoenberg and his direct pupils.[13] Schoenberg was of course still alive, in American exile, but he would die in 1951, whilst Berg and Webern were already dead; soon the present would seem more than typically free of the past. The idea of a *tabula rasa* in Germany was just as much an illusion as in Italy, if anything more so. Figures such as Hartmann and Scherchen – who, for its 1956 Berlin premiere, would cut Henze's opera, *König Hirsch*, a Straussian act of *Ariadne* Music Master to Composer, never to be forgiven by the latter – remained, as we saw Nono acknowledge, a crucial link to the historical roots of a compositional method many of whose sternest advocates seemed determined to deny them. Henze would recall with fondness at least the earlier years of Darmstadt precisely because of that re-establishment of historical connections the Third Reich had done its utmost to sever:

> The second summer school [1947] was attended by the conductor Hermann Scherchen and the composer Karl Amadeus Hartmann and proposed a completely different sort of aesthetic agenda from the one with which I had been familiar until now: in their world, music was regarded as a specifically human means of expression that posited moral and political commitment. This encounter was to have a profound influence on my own philosophy of music.[14]

III

In Edgar Reitz's *Heimat*, the opening of a scene set in 1947 lays bare the illusion or delusion of the *Stunde Null* or 'zero hour'. Just before her death, the matriarch Katharina, who has always warned against the temptations

[13] Jürg Stenzl, *Von Giacomo Puccini zu Luigi Nono. Italienische Musik 1922–1952: Faschismus–Resistenza–Republik* (Fritz Knuf: Buren, 1990), p. 188.
[14] Henze, *Bohemian Fifths*, p. 64.

of buying 'on tick', the Third Reich included, scoffs at the very idea, pointing out how many 'new ages' had been proclaimed before, from the outbreak of two world wars to the coming of the new motor highway in 1938. Why should this time be any different? Occupiers and occupied had in many ways, we might add, equal motive to pretend that it might be, but a shared imperative towards reconstruction would not do for anyone capable of and inclined towards critical thought and art. Of course the very term *Heimatfilm*, to which Reitz's series refers ironically, denotes just the sort of German evasive sentimentalism to which Henze also reacted, and the concept of a German *Heimat*, or homeland, could hardly fail to be problematical to all but the most blinkered or disingenuous of the political Right by this stage.

The occupying powers and subsequently West Germany's allies were generally happy to encourage and indeed to subsidise the 'break' with the country's past, although reconstruction, as in other areas of German cultural life, was encouraged too.[15] 'Despite calls for political neutrality,' it has been observed, 'government support for the musical experiments of these [avant-garde] young composers was by no means spurned once the officials showed an interest in it.' Indeed, cultivation of serial music 'came to depend entirely', or at least in large part, 'on the official support of politicians that its composers had initially set out to avoid'.[16] Peter Heyworth, writing in 1964 in *Encounter*, that august Cold Warrior (CIA-funded) journal, observed that the very fact that the Nazis had banned what he called, in true English style, 'modern' rather than new music, was 'sufficient to make post-war Germany cultivate it'.[17] Moreover, increasing 'anti-formalist' hostility towards twelve-note and serialist works from the East German authorities and approved 'socialist realism' gave an opportunity for the 'free' West to distinguish itself from 'totalitarianism'

[15] See Mark Berry, 'Romantic Modernism: Bach, Furtwängler, and Adorno,' in *New German Critique*, 104, vol. 35, no. 2 (Spring/Summer 2008), 71–102.
[16] Gesa Kordes, 'Darmstadt, Postwar Experimentation, and the West German Search for a New Musical Identity,' in *Music and German National Identity*, ed. Celia Applegate and Pamela Potter (University of Chicago Press: Chicago, 2002), pp. 212–13.
[17] Peter Heyworth, 'The Gilded Cage,' in *Encounter*, 22 (1964), 75–6. The tenor of Heyworth's article may be ascertained by the following: 'But neither the splendours of Bayreuth under Goering's patronage, nor a series of grand Richard Strauss premières, nor continuing high standards of performance, could hide the fact that within a few months Germany, once the hub of European music, had been reduced to a creative desert. An ice age had descended and it was to persist until those terrible days in the spring of 1945, when to an incessant barrage of Wagner on the radio, Hitler pulled down the pillars of the Hall of the Gibichungs on his own head. For the first time history had had the bad taste to imitate opera.' (Ibid., p. 74.)

not only past but present. Such factors give a number of clues as to why more politically committed composers such as Henze and Nono might eventually find themselves out on something of a limb. How might they reconcile membership of the avant-garde – Henze would later dispute that he had ever really been a member, but we shall let that pass for the moment – with their political commitments, given that the avant-garde seemed increasingly apolitical or, worse, reactionary?

The problem with the 'official' Darmstadt world-view, at least in Henze's sometimes simplistic portrayal, was that it had begun to veer towards a doctrinaire, almost totalitarian, attitude on the part of the high priests of the avant-garde. Henze connected this with a revisiting of the catastrophic German past and contrasted it with the freedom of his immersion in Italian life. The tragic irony was that the attempt to nullify the past, or perhaps in some cases to ignore it, led to its return. His recounting of the first performance of his *Nachtstücke und Arien* in 1957 – even though other accounts read differently – is instructive concerning the chasm he believed to have opened, whether then or in retrospect:

> at its first performance at Donaueschingen, on 20 October 1957 . . . three representatives of the other wing – Boulez, my friend Gigi Nono and Stockhausen – leapt to their feet after only the first few bars and pointedly left the hall, eschewing the beauties of my latest endeavours. Throughout the evening, heads continued to be shaken at my cultural *faux pas* . . . I suddenly found ourselves cold-shouldered by people who actually knew us, foremost among whom was Herr Dr Heinrich Strobel. There was a sense of indignation throughout the building, no doubt made worse by the fact that the audience had acclaimed our piece in the liveliest manner . . . The impression arose that the whole of the world of music had turned against me, a situation that was really quite comical, but also somewhat disturbing from an ethical point of view: for what had become of artistic freedom? Who had the right to confuse moral and æsthetic criteria? Teddy Adorno?[18]

The language is highly politicised: for example, 'representatives of the other wing'. Elsewhere, Henze wrote that what he called the Darmstadt School's 'attempt to make music non-communicative had something to do with the ruling class's belief that art is a thing apart from life, better kept that way, and without any social dimension'.[19] There is also a real sense of outrage: why could his composer-colleagues not at least have stayed to hear the rest of the piece? What right did they have to make split-second

[18] Henze, *Bohemian Fifths*, p. 146.
[19] Henze, 'German Music,' p. 49.

judgements on a fellow artist's work on the basis of its deviation from a highly questionable derivation from Webern? Why was there an 'official line' at all, such as was decried in the visual arts by the painter Werner Gilles, whom Henze would visit both in Munich and in Italy?[20] This particular Donaueschingen event, this recollection of its own rather operatic quality, would continue to rankle. In a 1999 interview with Peter Ruzicka, Henze claimed once again that 'when that trio of my illustrious colleagues marched out of the concert, the result was that no one, or almost no one, would continue to speak to me, at least not that night, even Dr Heinrich Strobel, the director of the festival'. Such behaviour contrasted with the reaction to the second-half premiere of Nono's *Varianti*: 'There were doubts even about the quality of the performance, and there was a strong reaction against it in the audience, there was even laughter – terrible. But, when it was over, Herr Strobel came and openly shook Nono's hand.' In this construction – which is not to impute bad faith, but to recognise the necessarily selective and interpretative nature of such histories – Strobel should 'have shaken my hand. Then at least the gesture of the supreme command would probably have remained ineffective.'[21] Politicised, then, and militarised – like the Federal Republic itself.

For the truest contempt was reserved not even for Boulez but for the camp followers, the *arrière garde*, if you like – or as Henze described them, 'the new arbiters of German music ... no more than jumped-up officials and civil servants'. The 'grotesque' Strobel, who appears several times – always negatively – in Henze's autobiography, was from 1956 to 1969 chairman of the International Society for New Music and had also founded the Donaueschingen Festival. Before that, he, personification of 'Fashion', had been controller of music for the newly founded Südwestfunk in Baden-Baden, where 'frigid unhumanity' had become the 'flavour of the month, a vogue directed not only against the emotionally charged music of Beethoven and the Romantics but also against conductors like Furtwängler and their metaphysical learnings – as if *they* were to blame for the German dilemma'. His reign came to an end when, in Henze's provocative formulation, 'representatives of the smaller countries rebelled against the new German dictator': a cross, then, between a small-time Hitler and a sporting impresario.[22] Those bureaucrats symbolised for Henze

---

[20] Ibid., p. 50.

[21] Hans Werner Henze and Peter Ruzicka, 'Conversation between Hans Werner Henze and Peter Ruzicka', 20 October 1999, tr. Steven Lindberg, in booklet note to Wergo CD WER 6637 2, p. 23.

[22] Henze, *Bohemian Fifths*, pp. 113–14, 67.

something more serious, though: reconstruction of the socio-political order of his youth. In a 1963 lecture entitled *Musik als Resistenverhalten*, delivered at West Berlin's Technische Universität, he would declare:

> In our world, which leans towards self-destruction, a tendency seems to grow up within music to deny its own time, to work from within against its manifestations and objectives ... In the sixteenth and seventeenth centuries music could realise and glorify itself, and its own time, because it was supported by it. Later, increasingly detached from society, it became more and more an individualistic pursuit; today music that truly wishes to speak, to be open, virtually resembles an esoteric cult: under attack, sometimes even persecuted, in flight from the dangers of mass society and standardisation under dictatorships, and elsewhere from the platitudes of æsthetic slogans.[23]

Music thus stood under threat not only from totalitarianism as politically understood (the Eastern Bloc or the Third Reich), not only from the levelling tendencies and pressures of the Culture Industry, but also from the 'platitudes' of Darmstadt and specifically its reception by those whose creative abilities were limited or non-existent. Such *petit bourgeois* attitudes, ostensibly reacting against the excesses of the nineteenth century, served only through 'mechanisation and depersonalisation to restrict the impact of music on provincial "consumers"'. Meanwhile, 'bourgeois-reactionary fans' lauded the reification of manifestos, judgements, and technological pseudo-innovation.[24] 'Small-time Diaghilevs reprimanded grown composers for writing too dissonantly, or too consonantly, issued decrees about what was "in" and what was "out" and knew exactly what one couldn't write.'[25] This was neo-feudal patronage.

Indeed, such people, Henze wrote, became 'prelates, who greeted you with a ceremoniously raised hand that was then lowered in benediction'.[26] Schoenberg, or at least the more acceptable parts of his output, survived longer in Darmstadt than in Donaueschingen, where programming was Strobel's domain.[27] Spirits of 'intolerance', variously manifested, made Henze 'swim even more consciously against the stream than hitherto, and with, in and through my work plead the cause of a life in which brutality, neglect of charity, and the withholding of intellectual and social freedom

---

[23] Henze, 'Music as a Means of Resistance,' in *Music and Politics*, p. 123.
[24] Ibid., pp. 124–6.
[25] Henze, 'German Music,' p. 41.
[26] Ibid., p. 44.
[27] On performances at Donaueschingen, see Josef Häusler, *Spiegel der neuen Musik, Donaueschingen: Chronik, Tendenzen, Werkbesprechungen* (Bärenreiter: Kassel, 1996).

are unknown'.[28] There was, Henze lamented, institutionalisation of 'official musical thinking'. It was, moreover, based not upon Webern, but upon a 'misuse and misinterpretation of his æsthetic and, indeed, of his technique and its motivation and significance'. Those who had known Webern – one assumes Henze had in mind here Leibowitz, a student of both Schoenberg and Webern – were 'out' and the 'technocrats of Darmstadt', willing to offer 'slavish obedience' to the diktats of Boulez and Stockhausen, were 'in'. Worst of all, 'the whole thing was run according to rules and principles, without a trace of humour or humanity'.[29] *Plus ça change . . .?* Iannis Xenakis said something similar concerning 'repulsive firms such as Schott's', ironically Henze's long-time publisher:

> Because Scherchen suggested it, I signed a contract in which they didn't under-take to publish my scores within a certain period of time. After two or three years I wrote to them and asked how much longer I had to wait. They replied that my music was outside the mainstream of the avant-garde and couldn't receive the same treatment as Luigi Nono, who was the central figure of new music. Of course, he was also a serial composer, a member of the Darmstadt group. You see how those people were thinking? I left them and went over to Boosey & Hawkes.[30]

Some such complaints may of course have been merely personal, even inaccurate; the terms in which they are couched remain indicative.

Although Henze's relationship with Adorno would be anything but harmonious, and their targets would often differ, they certainly had something in common here. Adorno warned in 1959 that 'the continued existence of National Socialism *within* democracy was potentially more threatening than the continued existence of fascist tendencies *against* democracy . . . dubious figures make their comeback into positions of power . . . because present conditions favour them'.[31] This was not a matter

---

[28] Henze, 'Music as a Means of Resistance,' p. 124.
[29] Henze, 'German Music,' p. 43.
[30] Bálint András Varga, *Conversations with Iannis Xenakis* (Faber: London, 1996), pp. 38–9.
[31] Theodor W. Adorno, 'What does Coming to Terms with the Past Mean?' in *Bitburg in Moral and Political Perspective*, ed. Geoffrey Hartman (Indiana University Press: Bloomington, 1986), p. 115. Henze amusingly caricatures Adorno's position: 'The existing audience of music-lovers was to be ignored. Their demand for "plain-language" music was to be dismissed as improper . . . On top of this we had to visualise the public as illiterate, and perhaps even hostile. If it was our fate that we, the elite, were exposed to these philistines, we were to arm ourselves with contempt and the smug feelings of martyrs. Any encounter with the listeners that was not catastrophic and scandalous would defile the artist . . . At best one could approach the public with enigmas, without providing solutions. As Adorno decreed, the job of a composer was to write music that would repel, shock, and be the vehicle for

of different preferences concerning the course of coming to terms with history, or *Vergangenheitsbewältigung*; some, it seemed, had not even begun to do so, and some even wished to turn the clock back, though they might use the language of technocracy and technology rather than blood and soil.

Whatever one thinks of his characterisation of 'Darmstadt' – and it is worth noting that, after Henze's departure from Germany, German commissions continued to pour in, just as they did after his dissociation from Darmstadt – Henze had a good deal of historical justification on his side more generally. That despite the fact that for someone lacking the stature of Adorno to voice such fears during the 1950s would often lead to ostracism. Recent writing on the early years of the Federal Republic has tended to stress what Adam Tooze has called 'Bonn's persistent and active efforts to ward off accusations of guilt and to achieve internal integration at the expense of openness about the crimes of the past'. Whereas the Social Democrats under Kurt Schumacher were at least more open to admission and certainly to discussion of guilt and responsibility, Chancellor Adenauer 'was able to leverage West Germany's new centrality in the Cold War to secure rehabilitation for Germany'.[32] The 1952 West German agreement to rearm was extracted at the price of an amnesty for *Wehrmacht* soldiers convicted of war crimes.[33] Moreover, as Henze noted, not only was 'the period of reconstruction around and after 1950 ... also that leading up to the banning of the KPD (German Communist Party); old comrades, who had been imprisoned by the Nazis', imprisoned once again.[34] Protests from a few artists, such as Hans Magnus Enzenberger – who would later provide Henze with texts and inspirations for a number of works, including adaptation of a novel about an escaped slave, Estaban Montejo, for *El Cimarrón*, written during Henze's 1969–70 sojourn in Cuba – went for nothing. It was also, Henze recalled, a time when the newspapers began 'to resurrect the idea of the "German soldier"'.[35] (The

"unmitigated cruelty" ... Thus spake Adorno; this was supposed to be the point of departure for the new international generation of composers.' ('German Music,' pp. 40–1.)

[32] Adam Tooze, 'Reassessing the Moral Economy of Post-war Reconstruction: The Terms of the West German Settlement in 1952,' in *Past and Present*, 210 (2011), 50.

[33] See, e.g., David Clay Large, *Germans to the Front: West German Rearmament in the Adenauer Era* (University of North Carolina Press: Chapel Hill, 1996); Norbert Frei, *Adenauer's Germany and the Nazi Past: The Politics of Amnesty and Integration* (Columbia University Press: New York, 2002); Bert-Oliver Manig, *Die Politik der Ehre. Die Rehabilitierung der Berufssoldaten in der fruehen Bundesrepublik* (Wallstein: Göttingen, 2004).

[34] Henze, 'German Music,' p. 50.

[35] Ibid.

ongoing popularity of Ernst Jünger would surely have attested that it had never gone away.[36]) Henze went on:

> I remember effusive articles that appeared – it may have been in the magazine *Stern* – proclaiming: 'It was wonderful to be a German soldier' . . . The result was a rehabilitation of German militarism. All this was extremely skilfully engineered, and one day there it was: this new army for peacetime and defence, the Bundeswehr – something which in 1945 no one would have thought possible.[37]

Even foreign claims for compensation came up against a powerful (West) German sense of victimhood.[38] That was a status that Henze could never accept – save, perhaps, in his own case, though that of course was as a victim of his nation rather than as a member of a victim-nation. Such then is part of the background to the writing of the first of the two Henze musical dramas on which discussion will focus.

IV

Conflicts between freedom and authority, and the question of what freedom might really entail, politically and æsthetically, are dramatised in Henze's 1960 opera, *Der Prinz von Homburg* ('The Prince of Homburg'). It has its origins in Heinrich von Kleist's *Prinz Friedrich von Homburg*, a surprisingly militaristic, indeed Prussian, text for either Henze or his librettist, Ingeborg Bachmann. Henze and Bachmann had met in 1952, their artistic collaboration having begun in 1955 with Henze's provision of incidental music for Bachmann's radio drama, *Die Zikaden*, its anonymous German narrator having fled to an Italian island.[39] The partnership had also taken in Henze's setting of two Bachmann poems in *Nachtstücke und Arien*, and would continue after *Der Prinz von Homburg*, encompassing Bachmann's provision of a new libretto for Henze's Dostoevsky ballet-pantomime, *Der Idiot*, the opera *Der junge Lord*, and Henze's setting of *Lieder von einer Insel*.

Kleist's play had achieved, or suffered, great popularity during both the Second Reich and the Third, and thus stood potentially as tainted for

---

[36] Ernst Jünger, *In Stahlgewittern* (Klett-Cotta: Stuttgart, 2007).

[37] Henze, 'German Music,' p. 50.

[38] Robert G. Moeller, *War Stories: The Search for a Useable Past in the Federal Republic* (University of California Press: Berkeley and Los Angeles, 2001); Frank Biess, *Homecomings: Returning POWs and the Legacies of Defeat in Postwar Germany* (Princeton University Press: Princeton, 2006).

[39] Ingeborg Bachmann, *Zwei Hörspiele: Die Zikaden, Der gute Gott von Manhattan* (Oldenbourg: Munich, 1969).

Henze and Bachmann as German Romantic music, especially when dealing with a German stage and audience. That held, almost irrespective of the æsthetic admiration its re-creators felt, Bachmann saying that she 'admired' and even 'loved' Kleist.[40] Needless to say, many modifications are made; the Prince's battle-cry, 'In Staub mit allen Feinden Brandenburgs', bidding Brandenburg's foes return to dust, no longer plays a role of jubilation. Quite otherwise: Bachmann's and Henze's conception may be understood to echo Brecht's earlier (1939) rewriting, a sonnet upon the play, the prince lying not dead but 'on his back with all the foes of Brandenburg in the dust'.[41] As Fredric Jameson remarked in that very context, 'where American pop psychology would evoke adaptation, Brecht overtly specifies learning'.[42] So do Bachmann and Henze, knowing, or at least believing, not unlike Wagner with his mediæval sources, that their audience will be aware of the 'original', though without going to the extreme of making appreciation dependent upon that knowledge, without tending to the world, as it were, of meta-art. To present march rhythms on the harp, for instance, rather than trumpets and drums, seems a statement, an inversion, in itself, both of pacification and of passive aggression against the political (and æsthetic) authorities that had brought the world to war and might do so again.

Der Prinz von Homburg was first performed in 1960, Henze provocatively claiming his model to be nineteenth-century Italian opera. 'Every bar', he would write, 'reveals Verdi's influence as a music dramatist.'[43] Up until now, Stravinsky had been one of relatively few modernists wholeheartedly to acknowledge the Italian composer, recalling that, on speaking well of Verdi to Rimsky-Korsakov, 'he would look at me as Boulez might if I had suggested playing my *Scènes de ballet* at

---

[40] Ingeborg Bachmann, 'Entstehung eines Librettos', in *Werke*, 4 vols, ed. Christine Koschel, Clemens Münster, and Inge von Weidenbaum (Piper: Munich and Zurich, 1993), vol. 1, p. 369.

[41] Heinrich von Kleist, *Prinz Friedrich von Homburg* (Echo Library: Teddington, 2007), p. 75; Bertolt Brecht, 'Sonnet über Kleists Stück "Prinz von Homburg"', reprinted with commentary by Walter Benjamin, in 'Commentary on Poems by Brecht', tr. Edmund Jephcott, in Walter Benjamin, *Selected Writings*, ed. Howard Eiland and Michael W. Jennings, 4 vols (Harvard University Press: Cambridge, MA, 1996–2003), vol. 4, pp. 237–8.

[42] Fredric Jameson, *Brecht and Method* (Verso: New York and London, 1998), p. 90. The cry has remained so celebrated that it could, for instance, be used as the headline for a review of Christopher Clark's outstanding history of Prussia (*Iron Kingdom: The Rise and Downfall of Prussia, 1600–1947* (Allen Lane: London, 2006)) without further reference: Review by Harry Nutt, Frankfurter Rundschau, 21 March 2007, <http://www.fr-online.de/literatur/in-staub-mit-allen-feinden-brandenburgs,1472266,2721822.html>, accessed 26 September 2012. (Nutt's review is of the 2007 German translation.)

[43] Henze, *Bohemian Fifths*, p. 161.

Darmstadt'.[44] Such remarks, such intentional implicit criticism of Wagner, could certainly never have emanated from Schoenberg, his circle, nor from anyone seeking to position himself in the role of successor to the Second Viennese School. But Henze's and Stravinsky's words position their writers in a tradition of what Richard Taruskin, in the midst of an often highly contentious, typically partisan comparison of Wagner and Verdi, characterises – and endorses – as the conception of Wagner as '"spook" – a crisis point, a phenomenon that nobody could ignore, and even more than that, a polarising force, a phenomenon about which one had to take sides'.[45] Henze is more interested, whether as polemicist or as composer, in Verdi as anti-Wagner than as Verdi.

Reviewing the premiere of *Der Prinz*, John Warrack doubted Henze's claim – and with good reason. Henze's 'avowed debt to Italian opera' was 'in fact almost as chimerical as Strauss's to Mozart, for there is here a musical-dramatic logic and a lyricism that are at root purely Germanic'.[46] One might well feel alienated during the post-war period from German musical tradition, but it did not follow that one could so simply disavow parentage and nurture. Stravinsky was never really part of it; Henze could not help but be. Indeed, as he admitted:

> In Italy you are repeatedly confronted with German history. Around 1950 I felt this in a concrete way, ... for instance ... when buying my rolls in the little piazza where I lived in Naples. During the last days of the occupation – the famous *tre giornate di Napoli* – Wehrmacht soldiers shot six young men, sons of the tradesmen from whom I, recognisably a German, was now buying my food. But the people were friendly, and I felt ashamed and bewildered.[47]

There were also, however, as we shall see, more fundamental respects – at least in artistic terms – in which Henze would be repeatedly confronted with the German history he could not and indeed would not escape.

Henze tells us, immediately reinstating the tradition he claims to wish to leave behind, that the work 'very much cried out for this contrast between dodecaphony and what – with a pinch of salt – might be termed traditional harmony: the dialectics of the law and its violation, of dreams and reality, of mendaciousness and truth'. This dualism 'was now to become

[44] Igor Stravinsky and Robert Craft, *Expositions and Developments* (Faber: London, 1962), p. 62.
[45] Richard Taruskin, *The Oxford History of Western Music*, 5 vols (Oxford University Press: New York, 2010), vol. 4, p. 567.
[46] John Warrack, 'Henze's "Der Prinz von Homburg" at Hamburg,' in *Opera*, 11 (1960), 460. The claim concerning Strauss is highly questionable, but that is another matter
[47] Henze, 'German Music,' p. 54.

a part of my life as both man and artist', but 'it was only now, at the end of 1958, that I hit upon the idea of seriously examining the phenomena of contradictions through the medium of my music'.[48] Hegel, consciously or otherwise, is reborn; or rather he has never died. One can also point to a Nietzschean dialectic – actually Wagnerian in origin – between Apollo and Dionysus. That is all thoroughly Germanic, not Italian at all, but so of course is the desire to escape from Germany to the warm Mediterranean south. As Andrew Porter, reviewing *Der junge Lord*, would observe: 'The Mediterranean Idyll is an obligatory chapter in the life of a Great German artist,' just as, we might add, Parisian exile had been an obligatory chapter in the life of a Great German radical during the nineteenth century.[49]

Adorno's contrast and contest between righteous Schoenberg and suspect Stravinsky – the cool, opening chords of Henze's seventh scene could almost have been extracted from the *Symphonies of Wind Instruments* – are also re-dramatised; indeed, the score is dedicated to Stravinsky, just as Nono had dedicated his *Intolleranza* to Schoenberg. Writing for a 'Young Composers' edition of *Die Reihe*, Rudolph Stephan had already noted approvingly that Henze shared with Stravinsky a 'preference for "natural" note relationships', treating fifth- and third-relationships 'as a reality, without immediately falling back (like many others) into the major-minor system as a result'. Alarm bells were sounded, however, by the composers' shared 'weakness for parody'.[50] It has often been said that Henze in many of his works attempts a synthesis between Schoenberg and Stravinsky. That can be a misleading claim even in general, but it does little justice to *Der Prinz von Homburg*, in which radical opposition between two sound worlds and two compositional principles is far more important.

The first two scenes of the second act are punctuated by the repetition of distorted brass fanfares, as Friedrich realises that he is hemmed in: 'I am lost.' Nothing changes; what can he do? He has broken the law in order to attain victory for the Elector of Brandenburg, and death will be his reward. The contrast between twelve-note technique and Henze's 'traditional harmony' evokes not only musical but also dramatic crisis – and, in a broader sense, the dialectic of crisis between the modern subject and the objective world. Meanwhile, the Stravinsky-like 'modern' quality of the fanfares suggests the powerlessness of the subject in relation to the fatal

---

[48] Henze, *Bohemian Fifths*, p. 156.

[49] Andrew Porter, 'Henze's "Young Lord"', in *The Musical Times*, 110 (1969), 1028.

[50] Rudolph Stephan, 'Hans Werner Henze', in *Die Reihe*, 4 (1960), 29, 32. The original German version of this issue is dated 1958; the article itself appears to have been written in September 1956.

power of the state and its laws. Friedrich is in prison and, for his love, awaits death; his torture is the vision in his dreams of his grave. Pleading with the Elector to show mercy to Friedrich, Natalie claims that she does not want the prince for herself, but only so that he can be free and independent, that she can take pleasure in him as in a flower. If that be the variety of freedom on offer, is it freedom at all? Independence and even the aspiration thereto have collapsed into heteronomy. Natalie reports that, confronted by the sight of his grave, 'Every wish but to live has gone.' Now Friedrich must settle for mercy from the Elector and æsthetic contemplation – probably rather more than that – from his imploring niece, whilst all the time the music appears to move in circles, never more so than in the interludes linking the scenes of this act. Progress appears unattainable as various forces, the two musical 'languages' included, do battle.

Always we seem to return to the opening scene of this act, to Friedrich's powerless plight. Brandenburg, we hardly need to be reminded, is the forerunner of the Prussian barracks-state, whose rise owed so much to military power and its concomitant, the very 'real' devastation of war which hangs over the 'dream' of Henze's opera. Henze considered the Prussianism of the play to be incidental; he preferred to see it as Greek, pointing to the classicist 'spirit [that] still lingers'. Yet even if the action, as he claimed, could be transposed to today or two thousand years ago, the very tension to which he pointed, 'between the existence of the individual and "reasons of state"', might have been strengthened by establishment of the conflict in more equal terms.[51] When the Elector resolves to offer freedom, it is at the price of consistency, of accepting the rule of law. Friedrich must declare that he believes the verdict of death to be unjust; the Elector will not move towards what he considers to be 'despotism' by abrogating the law. Here, Kleist in his original text and Bachmann in her adaptation echo Romantic criticisms of the Enlightenment machine-state, and the mercy sought by Natalie proves to be a mercy that negates itself: an all-too-typical twist of the dialectic of Enlightenment. As Henze himself observed:

> *Der Prinz von Homburg* ... sets itself against the blind unimaginative application of laws, in favour of an exaltation of human kindness, an understanding of which reaches into deeper and more complex realms than would be 'normal' and which seeks to find a place for a man in this world even though he is a *Schwärmer* and a dreamer, or perhaps because of that.[52]

---

[51] Henze, 'Der Prinz von Homburg,' in *Music and Politics*, pp. 100–1.
[52] Ibid., p. 102.

Henze seems here to be referring to Kleist, but the words hold for Bachmann and Henze too. Are the laws of Brandenburg as impervious as
those of Schoenberg and, after him and deadlier still, Darmstadt, let alone
those of the Third Reich, being reconstructed before their eyes? Could
things actually be otherwise, without a radical transformation of society
as a whole? That brings us to the question of intention. Henze claimed:

> I have striven for greater freedom, or at least what I understand by it: certainly
> not improvisation, but independence, and a preparedness for decisions outside
> established categories. Music is not musicology, and the logic of a work rests
> on a unique constellation of incident, encounter, experience, agreement; it
> transcends inherited rules, construction, calculation. It seems that the vegetative
> element of music surpasses its other, lesser, musicological dimension, and that,
> as in the life of the Prince of Homburg, illuminations and discoveries take place
> in dreams, not in the laboratory. Not, however, in a state of haziness, but in the
> wakefulness of sleepwalkers, where facts are perceived with abnormal clarity.[53]

There is something Romantic about this; we might imagine ourselves
returned to Wagner's Nuremberg. Walther's Prize Song is conceived in
a dream, although it then has to be refined by the Master, Hans Sachs.
Moreover, Walther's songs also transcended inherited rules and calculation,
outstepped established categories. Henze's drama throws up another
Meistersinger problem. Where is the social world; where is the public
nature of art? A dream is all very well, but without transmission and
reception it remains but a dream. There is a trap, which is not in itself
to say that Wagner and Henze – or Strauss, for that matter – fall into it.
Lachenmann, in a 1983 open letter to Henze, delineates the snare:

> that outbreak of the muzzled subject into a new emotional immediacy will be
> untrue, and degenerate into self-deception, wherever the fat and comfortable
> composer, perhaps slightly scarred structurally and therefore the more likely to
> complain, sets up house once again in the old junk-room of available emotions.
> ... Those who believe that expressive spontaneity, and innocent drawing
> from the venerable reservoir of affect, make that struggle of the fractured subject
> with itself superfluous, and spare it an engagement with the traditional concepts
> of material, have disabled their own voice. They are gladly allowed to sit in
> the lap of a society which encourages those who support its repressive game.[54]

It should go without saying that at best – or should that be, at worst? – from
those three named composers, only Strauss could ever have conceived

[53] Ibid., p. 104.
[54] Helmut Lachenmann, 'Open Letter to Hans Werner Henze,' tr. Jeffrey Stadelmann, in
Perspectives of New Music, 35 (1997), 191.

such assimilation as his *intention*; nor, despite the sometimes ugly nature of the polemic between Henze and Lachenmann, would the latter ever have claimed otherwise.

At the end of Kleist's play, Friedrich asks, 'No, tell me, is it a dream?', to which Kottwitz responds 'A dream, what else?' That exchange is submerged by renewed battle-cries, absent from the opera, which returns instead to an earlier line: 'Only feeling can redeem us.' The nationalistic militarism so important to Kleist's play is understandably played down, yet it arguably provides a necessary aspect of that social world which the opera lacks. It is as if the people were exiled from *Die Meistersinger* with the problematical final scene omitted. There would doubtless be some pseudo-radical approval voiced for ending with the Quintet – far better, if only as a one-off, to subject the final scene to Peter Konwitschny's staged 'debate' in his 2002 Hamburg production – but to say that as many questions would be begged as answered is to understate the case. Whilst it would be exaggerated to claim Bachmann's and Henze's path as anything so drastic, there is an undeniable attempt at deflective reconciliation by steering away from the most problematic aspect of the drama. Warrack noted: 'Already *Der Prinz von Homburg* finds . . . [Henze] reconciling his powers. His personal reconciliation with his origins is still so bitterly unresolved that, unlike Kleist, he cannot even bear to establish both sides of the conflict in equal terms.'[55] That despite Henze's avowed 'striving for unity in which my thoughts on theatre and music, music and language, our relationship to history, and our current situation with its problems, questions and counter-questions, all find a place and form a whole'.[56] Whereas part of the battle for subjectivity in the Romantic Kleist lies in the internal conflict between the dreamer and the military man, here it almost seems as though the military man is a dream-figure himself – or maybe that we need to ensure that he becomes so.

Warrack considered this an important work from a 'wonderfully gifted composer'.[57] Such appreciation did not apply, of course, to the 'official' avant-garde of Darmstadt, who viewed Warrack's appeal to German tradition, let alone Henze's alleged homage to Verdi, with downright hostility. (It is questionable to what extent one can speak of 'Darmstadt' in such monolithic terms and I should generally be wary of doing so, but here attempt to present Henze's standpoint.) As Lachenmann would point out in his open letter to Henze, there was something rather unpleasant

---

[55] Warrack, 'Henze's "Der Prinz von Homburg"', p. 461.
[56] Henze, 'Der Prinz von Homburg,' p. 104.
[57] Warrack, 'Henze's "Der Prinz von Homburg"', p. 460.

and indeed disingenuous about the caricatured 'popular mug shots of the typical Darmstadt composers who, closed off from emotional participation, with arrogant gaze towards the future which they have created, do not *want* to be understood by the present'.[58]

That said, Boulez spoke harshly indeed of Henze. For instance, in a 1967 interview with *Der Spiegel*, he is likened to a 'lacquered hairdresser, who pays homage to an utterly superficial modernism'. His *'Prinz von Homburg*, for example, is an unfortunate rehashing of Verdi's *Don Carlos* ... Henze is like De Gaulle; he can bring up any old rubbish [*Mist*] and think that he remains king.'[59] Perhaps as important, however, for our purposes is that Boulez, who scathingly continued – and this was not intended as a compliment to The Beatles – that a Beatles record was 'certainly cleverer than a Henze opera, and shorter as well', was voicing a dissatisfaction with bourgeois opera that was not so very different from that which Henze, at least for a while, would come to feel, though Boulez's accusations might be considered more 'æsthetic' in tone, Henze's more 'political'.[60] In their different ways, both considered the other's concerns to be irredeemably bourgeois, yet both came to a point at which they considered performance and even composition of 'repertory' works could, or at least should, not go on. Whether either composer ever truly recanted remains an interesting question, ideology and practice often remaining difficult to reconcile – but then 'false' reconciliation is from such standpoints a problem in itself, seemingly requiring in response an Adornian call to resistance.

'Darmstadt' in general and Boulez in particular remained a running sore for Henze. *Der junge Lord* received similar brickbats, which clearly wounded and angered its composer just as much as did abusive treatment by West Berlin Senate secretaries of his friends Ruth Berghaus and Paul Dessau, who had come over from the East for the 1965 premiere:

> Where, it was asked, were the outbursts of primeval angst and despair? [Hans Heinz] Stuckenschmidt's review was headed: 'Henze turns the clock back.' ... Which clock did Stuckenschmidt mean? And how late was it anyway? ... Who set the standards? Pierre? Or the frightful Heinrich Strobel? A kangaroo court? A central committee, a shady academy somewhere, in Darmstadt perhaps?[61]

Whether he liked it or not – and he certainly did not – Henze found

---

[58] Lachenmann, 'Open Letter to Hans Werner Henze,' p. 192.

[59] Felix Schmidt and Jürgen Hohmeyer, Interview with Pierre Boulez, 'Sprengt die Opernhäuser in die Luft!', in *Der Spiegel*, 40 (25 September 1967), 172, 166.

[60] Ibid., p. 174.

[61] Henze, *Bohemian Fifths*, pp. 193–4.

himself cast as a latter-day Strauss or Aron. Nevertheless, he increasingly concerned himself with more immediate priorities than doing battle with his musical colleagues or foes, looking instead to the broader political world.

V

Henze's path during the 1960s may be summarised as moving further to the political Left and futher away from the 'official' avant-garde, although it should be added that, insofar as it had ever existed, it was beginning to break down already. In spite of the difficulties, both political and æsthetic, he faced, for the greater part of this decade his career appeared to be going from strength to strength, arguably culminating in the triumphant premiere of *The Bassarids* at the 1966 Salzburg Festival – by now, Herbert von Karajan's citadel, though Christoph von Dohnányi conducted.[62] Yet (relative) adulation from the *haute bourgeoisie* also made him feel uncomfortable: was this really for whom he should be writing, or being taken to write? Moreover, as Webern's pre-eminence, or rather that of Darmstadt's Webern, waned, it became increasing clear that Schoenberg and, behind him, Mahler and Wagner were not dead at all. (Boulez's conducting activities might be taken as parallel, implicit recognition.) Perhaps even Strauss might offer a model, though Henze did not take kindly to a suggestion that Strauss had found his successor in *The Bassarids*. 'Strauss turned sour,' he would, however, accept.[63]

Henze nursed a long-standing antipathy towards much of Wagner, although he had always recognised the greatness of *Tristan*.[64] As preparation for composition of *The Bassarids*, his librettists, W. H. Auden and Chester Kallman, had insisted that Henze attend a performance of *Götterdämmerung*, in order that he should 'learn to overcome' his 'aversions to Wagner's music, aversions bound up in no small measure

---

[62] Karajan, despite their obvious political differences, was well disposed to Henze, conducting the *Sonata per archi* and *Antifone*, inviting Henze to conduct the Berlin Philharmonic (*Bohemian Fifths*, p. 183), attending performances with him, for instance Walter Felsenstein's production of *Othello* (ibid., p. 169), and even granting Henze the use of his private box at the Vienna State Opera for a performance of *Götterdämmerung* for which the conductor – at that time also music director – acted as stage director too (ibid., p. 206). Richard Osborne's Karajan biography quite misunderstands Henze's attitude towards Karajan, confusing genuine admiration for 'ill-disguised disdain' (*Herbert von Karajan: A Life in Music* (Chatto & Windus: London, 1998), pp. 441–2).

[63] Henze, *Bohemian Fifths*, pp. 207–8.

[64] On Henze's own *Tristan*, see Stephen Downes, *Hans Werner Henze: Tristan (1973)* (Ashgate: Aldershot and Burlington, 2011).

with my many unfortunate experiences in the past'. And, of course, with Germany's many unfortunate experiences in the all-too-recent past. Success was at best mixed:

> I was perfectly capable of judging the wider significance of Wagner's music: as any fool can tell you, it is a summation of all Romantic experience ... But I simply cannot abide this silly and self-regarding emotionalism, behind which it is impossible not to detect a neo-German mentality and ideology. There is the sense of an imperialist threat, of something militantly nationalistic, something disagreeably heterosexual and Aryan in all these rampant horn calls, this pseudo-Germanic *Stabreim*, these incessant chords of a seventh and all the insecure heroes and villains that people Wagner's librettos.[65]

Such insecurity might be taken as evidence of a dramatist's gift, of course, but Henze was not yet ready to grant Wagner that order of charity in criticism; nor, perhaps, would he ever be. Nevertheless, he was willing to consider that the musical path from *Tristan*, at least, might be of some importance in his work. In an interview for *Die Welt*, to mark the first performance of *The Bassarids*, he proclaimed his belief 'that the road from *Tristan* to Mahler and Schoenberg is far from finished, and with *The Bassarids* I have tried to go further along it.'[66]

For to bear witness to one's time was, according to Henze, ultimately more important than to extend the grammar of music or to 'invent new systems'. That was why he found Mahler more important than Webern. Recall that phrase, 'weakness for parody', from the review in the 'Young Composer's Edition' of *Die Reihe*: Strauss and Stravinsky had no monopoly on such 'weakness'; Mahler and Henze were equally 'guilty'. At any rate, that conception of bearing witness was shared with and arguably inherited from predecessors such as Wagner and Schoenberg, notwithstanding what Henze termed the 'aristocratic element' – the fashionable term would now be 'elitism' – in the latter's artistic practice.[67] Gramsci, whom Henze had been reading since 1954, had similarly characterised Wagner's æsthetics, as opposed to Verdi's, as 'aristocratic': a judgement likely to baffle the Wagner scholar, yet which is not without interest and which stood close to, maybe even influenced, Henze's view. For such 'aristocratic' æsthetics, Gramsci notes, 'Verdi occupies the same place in the history of music as [Eugène] Sue in the history of literature,' another potentially attractive

---

[65] Henze, *Bohemian Fifths*, p. 207.
[66] Henze, 'The Bassarids: (1) Tradition and Cultural Heritage,' in *Music and Politics*, p. 145.
[67] Henze, 'Does Music have to be Political?' in ibid., p. 170.

point for Henze.[68]

At any rate, Henze could claim impeccable musical and German warrant for what some would decry as his score's eclecticism:

> It may be unfashionable to continue musical traditions in this way [he is specifically referring to the use of symphonic forms in the opera's four 'movements'], but with Goethe under my pillow, I'm not going to lose any sleep about the possibility of being accused of eclecticism. Goethe's definition ran: 'An eclectic . . . is anyone who, from that which surrounds him, takes what corresponds to his nature.' If you wanted to do so, you could count Bach, Mozart, Verdi, Wagner, Mahler, and Stravinsky as eclectics.[69]

The composer could not, should not, 'spend all his time destroying language instead of developing it dialectically'.[70] That dramatised eclecticism we have seen inform *Der Prinz von Homburg* – Schoenberg versus Stravinsky – and shall see again in *Natascha Ungeheuer* was not simply a matter of style, then, but also of idea.

VI

What of Henze's turn further to the Left during this period? It had much in common with paths taken by other artists, intellectuals, and concerned citizens. Stifling denials of the past and the obscenity of a reconstructed present, which had done so much to engineer Henze's departure from Germany, increasingly came under attack. Henze might certainly have done well to reflect, or at least we should, that, whatever his thoughts concerning the alleged authoritarianism of 'Darmstadt' – and the conception seems in some senses to be more metaphysical than actual – that authoritarianism of the Nazi variety would never have permitted his or Boulez's music to be heard in the first place. A counter-argument, though not necessarily Henze's, would have been that post-war capitalism permitted, even to a certain extent encouraged, such music, not only so that it could present an image of freedom to the 'totalitarian' Eastern Bloc – and the GDR in particular – but because ultimately the art was so harmless or at least so powerless. Were it to present any real revolutionary threat, its creators and performers might find themselves treated like the participants in Munich's

---

[68] Henze, *Bohemian Fifths*, p. 126; Antonio Gramsci, 'Popular Literature: [Opera],' in *Selections from Cultural Writings*, tr. William Boelhower, ed. David Forgacs and Geoffrey Nowell-Smith (Lawrence and Wishart: London, 1985), p. 379.

[69] Henze, 'The Bassarids: (1),' p. 145.

[70] Hans Werner Henze, 'The Bassarids: (3) Symphony in One Act,' in *Music and Politics*, p. 153.

1962 'Schwabinger Krawalle', the young Andreas Baader amongst them, or those in the 1967 West Berlin protests against the Shah of Iran, the state's Weberian monopoly of 'legitimate force' reasserted brutally, indeed cynically. The *Social Democrat* mayor of Munich had even gone so far in justifying the savage police response in the Schwabing 'riots' – what one calls such events says much about oneself and one's standpoint – as to say that 'the police cannot allow destruction of the peace and law-breaking on the streets of a democratic state in homage to a mistaken concept of freedom'.[71] Spectres of Nazism and Communism, often contradictory on their own terms, let alone on others', were evoked on both sides.

Moreover, the Christian Democrat Chancellor from 1966 to 1969. Kurt Georg Kiesinger, had actually been a Nazi Party member from 1933 and had worked in the wartime foreign ministry's radio propaganda department. Astonishing though that may now seem, his past proved no impediment to becoming Chancellor – and it attested to growing conviction on the Left, and especially amongst those of Henze's generation, of renazification. Beate Klarsfeld, whose husband, Serge, was a French Nazi-hunter, and who had already caused uproar by shouting 'Nazi' in the Bundestag at Kiesinger, was sentenced to one year's imprisonment for slapping him in the face at the 1968 CDU conference, whilst old SS men walked free. Little wonder that, faced with such bourgeois intransigence, more creative members of the Left would both question their own social and cultural acquiescence and feel the need to move beyond parliamentary means.

At the end of the last chapter, we saw Henze speaking in 1967 about 'engaged' drama. The stronger note of political commitment on Henze's part just seven years after *Der Prinz von Homburg* will have been noted. Henze's move from what in 1971 he called 'generalised anti-fascism', which he had previously thought 'commitment enough', had been, he said, inspired by the example of Italian Marxist friends such as Nono.[72] For a long time, he had thought that their deeper, more radical, more committed approach pertained only to Italy. It is interesting to note Henze's use, even in autobiographical retrospect, of the phrase, 'the Italian Left, especially those to the left of the Italian Communist Party'.[73] Any veteran of the Spanish Civil War would have understood what he meant; so would Adorno; so for that matter would the Red Army Faction.

---

[71] Letter of 16 July 1962 to Anneliese Friedmann, quoted in Nick Thomas, *Protest Movements in 1960s West Germany: A Social History of Dissent and Democracy* (Berg: Oxford and New York, 2003), p. 42.

[72] Hans Werner Henze, 'Art and the Revolution,' in ibid., p. 179.

[73] Henze, *Bohemian Fifths*, p. 240.

Political organisation, Stalinist or otherwise, would never be tolerable to a good number of the most interesting figures on the Left, especially the artistic Left. For there remained the opportunity outlined by Marcuse, whom Henze was now reading: 'Art cannot change the world, but it can contribute to changing the consciousness and drives of the men and women who could change the world.'[74]

Henze had intervened directly in West German political life, not least in 1965 during Willy Brandt's election campaign, though 'with a feeling of impotence and uselessness'. However, from friends such as Rudi Dutschke and his comrades he 'now learned to see contexts, and to see myself within those contexts'. That was why he took the decision that no longer would he write for himself and his friends, but 'to help socialism', that he would embody in his work 'all the problems of contemporary bourgeois music', and yet 'transform these into something that the masses can understand'. That certainly did not involve submitting to commercial considerations, but nor was there any 'place for worry about losing elite notions of value'.[75] In the 1960s, he had begun:

> to read systematically... I started with Marcuse, and read some Adorno; Marx and Lenin were to come later. This marked the start of a period of theoretical study... During this time I went often to Berlin to meet and talk with the radical student group, the SDS [*Sozialistischer Deutscher Studentenbund*, or 'Socialist German Student League'], and Rudi Dutschke in particular... the experiences of the late 1960s – my involvement with the young left in the Federal Republic and West Berlin – were significant for my subsequent political development. As things turned out, that was to take place not in Germany but in Cuba and in Italy, where I had settled. There, with ever-increasing confidence, I began to learn how my music and my political beliefs could support and strengthen each other.[76]

And yet, if not necessarily taking place in Germany geographically – not that Henze absented himself entirely – much of that development took place mentally as a German in self-imposed exile.

The experience of 1968 itself of course also made a huge difference. So did a stay in Cuba, which brought forth works such as the Sixth Symphony and the aforementioned *El Cimarrón*, though the realities of Fidel Castro's regime, not least concerning homosexuality, ultimately proved no more to his liking than those of the GDR. In September 1968, a new arts centre

[74] Herbert Marcuse, *The Aesthetic Dimension: Toward a Critique of Marxist Aesthetics*, tr. Herbert Marcuse and Erica. Sherover (Macmillan: Basingstoke and London, 1979), pp. 32–3.
[75] Henze, 'Art and the Revolution', pp. 179–80.
[76] Henze, 'German Music', pp. 55–6.

in Bielefeld was to be opened; the erstwhile local boy's Second Piano Concerto would receive its premiere at that opening. A custard-powder manufacturer named Rudolf-August Oetker had provided the funds for both work and arts centre, a storm suddenly erupting when 'the appalling news' reached Henze that the sponsors 'wanted their museum to be named after one of the members of their own family, Richard Kaselowsky, an active and influential member of the SS, who had died in 1944'. Upon arriving in Bielefeld, Henze was 'asked by both the old and the new Left to say and write something on the subject of this embarrassing affair'.[77] The result, published in the *Bielefelder Presse* on 28 September 1968, was a declaration, 'Mein Standpunkt', which climaxed:

> Unnecessary are new museums, opera houses, and world premieres. Necessary, to set about the realisation of dreams. Necessary, to abolish the dominion of men over men. Necessary, to change mankind, which is to say: necessary, the creation of mankind's greatest work of art: the World Revolution.[78]

Such words could almost have come straight from an earlier German revolutionary-composer's pen, from Wagner's 1849 *Die Revolution*.[79] There is, moreover, common ground again with Boulez in opposition to the 'museum', though Boulez, even in his *Spiegel* interview, was more pessimistic about cultural transformation, pointing not unreasonably to the 'bourgeois' nature of musical life in the Eastern Bloc – in the Soviet Union, *Eugene Onegin* and *The Queen of Spades* were, he noted, held in the highest esteem – and demurring on the question of Cuba, saying that he did not know enough about it.[80] The difference is nevertheless more striking, as it is with Henze's earlier self.

Henze was now reaching the high watermark of his artistic political engagement. By now he had lent his support to the APO ('Extra-Parliamentary Opposition', which had by now given up on social and political change through constitutional means) as well as to the SDS. The scene was set for the notorious non-premiere in Hamburg of *Das Floss der Medusa*, disrupted as it was by right-wing opposition, with the APO in heavy attendance, and Henze's two collaborations with Gastón Salvatore, the angry violent *Versuch über Schweine* ('Essay on Pigs'), and *Natascha*

[77] Henze, *Bohemian Fifths*, p. 241.
[78] Quoted in Porter, 'Henze's "Young Lord"', 1028.
[79] Richard Wagner, 'Die Revolution', in *Sämtliche Schriften und Dichtungen*, ed. Richard Sternfeld and Hans von Wolzogen, 16 vols in 10 (Breitkopf und Härtel: Leipzig, 1912–14), vol. 12, pp. 245–51.
[80] Schmidt and Hohmeyer, 'Sprengt die Opernhäuser in die Luft!', p. 174.

Ungeheuer, as (self-)critical of the artist and his ilk as the political and socio-economic system.

VII

Natascha Ungeheuer was premiered in Rome on 17 May 1971, Henze's friend and patron Sir William Walton in attendance.[81] Whatever a Roman audience or indeed Walton might have made of it, there was a strong sense in which the German premiere, in September of that year, marked its homecoming, not least since it took place at Berlin's Deutsche Oper, where the 2 June 1967 demonstration had taken place against the Shah. Benno Ohnesorg, a poetry-writing student, had been shot dead by a policeman, Karl-Heinz Kurras, a key moment in the radicalisation of the German student movement.[82] It was then, recalled Joschka Fischer, later to lead the Green Party and to assume office as Foreign Minister, that he had become a 'professional revolutionary'.[83] To a broader segment of the Left than previously, that had been the moment when rebellion became just, even necessary; to a broader section of the Right, repression of revolt had become considered likewise. Henze would never have endorsed, nor indeed failed to oppose, the violence of the Red Army Faction-to-be. However, much of what he had to say and write concurred with Gudrun Ensslin's widely reported declaration at a meeting of the SDS held that night, that the killing was the work of 'the Auschwitz generation', though not with her claim that violence must therefore be met with violence.

Natascha Ungeheuer was, then, a child of 1968, when Henze and Nono had both marched in West Berlin against the Vietnam War, and a child of West Berlin too.[84] Its peculiar status, not only as an enclave within the GDR – the 'besonderes politisches Gebiet Westberlin' as East German maps often had it – but also on account of its remaining under the administration of the occupying powers, meant that it attracted a great number of left-leaning young German men, wishing to avoid conscription in the re-established armed forces. This was, Henze wrote, 'a kind of latter-day *Berliner Requiem*', the mention of Weill's work a reminder of a Berlin

[81] Henze, *Bohemian Fifths*, p. 216.
[82] The revelation in 2009 that Kurras had been a Stasi agent led to speculation that the shooting may have been the act of an *agent provocateur*, but so far no firm evidence has been presented to support that claim.
[83] Paul Hockenos, *Joschka Fischer and the Making of the Berlin Republic: An Alternative History of Postwar Germany* (Oxford University Press: Oxford, 2008), p. 62
[84] Henze, *Bohemian Fifths*, p. 236.

not only before the Nazi seizure of power, before the division of city and country, but also of the (renascent) danger of fascism, of violence on the streets. 'It flatters me', Henze would recall:

> to think that the West Berlin of 1970/1 is easy to recognise in my gaudy colours and montages. There is the same coldness and harshness, the same implacability and cheerlessness that can overcome and overwhelm one in this great, sad city, a 'grey city by the sea', as the artist Werner Heldt used to call it.[85]

Entitled a 'show with seventeen [performers]', the work seems determined to provoke. Many listeners, doubtless unfairly yet understandably, discerned in it little beyond provocation. Work began in January 1971. Henze and friends recorded street sounds from near the Zoo Station in West Berlin – those environs still look as if they stand with half a foot in the 1970s – along with newspaper extracts read onto tape at varying tempi and pitches. The determinedly anti-bourgeois nature of the enterprise is underlined by the composer's account, in which he claims that the 'inadequacy of the results did not worry us too much; the finished product was to have a touch of *arte povera*'.[86] The text's author – 'librettist' seems rather inappropriate here – was the Chilean poet Gastón Salvatore, introduced to Henze by Enzenberger. Salvatore had been an active participant in the events of 1968 as a member of the SDS and was – another good radical box ticked here – a nephew of Salvador Allende, as yet still the President of Chile, though not for long. It is worth quoting at some length from Salvatore's account, which introduces the printed score:

> Natascha Ungeheuer is the siren of a false utopia. She promises the leftist bourgeois a new kind of security, which will permit him to preserve his revolutionary 'class conscience' without taking an active part in class warfare. This false Utopia should be regarded as an all-denying immobility, as a kind of cowardice, which permits itself to appear identified with the 'Revolution' and believe that such an identity could equal the consummation of revolution.
>
> Such an existentialistic, non-historical form of political self-reflection places the leftist bourgeois in the position of exploiting the proletarian struggle, as an occasion for a merely self-indulgent moralising. He 'muddles through' between the temptation either to surrender consciousness and return to the bourgeoisie or to choose one of the two possible forms of helplessness: either that of the lonely Avant-garde in their homes or that of Social Democracy.
>
> Natascha Ungeheuer promises both possibilities. The leftist bourgeois sets out for her apartment, plagued by all the anxieties and insecurities which

[85] Ibid., p. 303.
[86] Henze, 'Natascha Ungeheuer,' in *Music and Politics*, p. 184.

characterise his social position ... Natascha Ungeheuer knows ... [them] only too well. She torments him, she provokes him, yet at the same time she lures him into her apartment ...

The leftist bourgeois . . . refuses to go the full way to the apartment of Natascha Ungeheuer. He has not yet discovered his way to the revolution. He knows that he must turn back on the way he has gone so far, and begin again.

It is also worth adding that Natascha Ungeheuer – the surname translates as 'Monster', and who knows, may in the 'show' also echo Herod's accusation against Salome? – was and is a real person, an artist then living in Kreuzberg, born Ursula Rosa Ungeheuer, although neither Henze nor Salvatore knew her at the time. Involved in street theatre as well as illustration and painting, her work has continued to be exhibited.[87] Henze and Salvatore simply knew, in Henze's words, that an invitation to visit her 'was somehow "in" among left-wing students of the time'.[88] Everything about the work – its ideological intention, its music, and its staging – not only provoked, but was clearly intended to do so, and it was roundly booed when performed in Berlin; this was bourgeois Charlottenburg after all, not (self-consciously) radical Kreuzberg.[89] Gerald Larner's *Musical Times* review spoke of 'a work of self-criticism, in which any conventional audience can find little it understands and less which is relevant to it'.[90] That was clearly not intended as a compliment, but perhaps it should have been, for why should Henze have been writing for a 'conventional audience' at all? And what, in any case, is wrong with a work of self-criticism?

The protagonist's predicament was clearly Henze's own: stuck somewhere between Natascha's flat in Kreuzberg and the German bourgeoisie which, even during his self-exile, had funded so many of his activities to date – and would continue to do so. However, most of his audience had not even begun its journey. In Henze's words, 'our hero does not reach his destination: but ... he hears in his head the sirenlike voice of Comrade Natascha, who, far from welcoming and accommodating, reels off a list of objections to him'. Has Fricka been resurrected, to assail our artist-Wotan, who wills something new yet is perhaps neither able nor resolved to bring it about? 'Attempts to renew his bourgeois connections prove a failure.

---

[87] See, e.g., Natascha Ungeheuer, *Ölbilder* (Ararat: Berlin, 1985).

[88] Henze, *Bohemian Fifths*, p. 303.

[89] See Dieter Krämer, *Kreuzberg 1968–2013: Abbruch, Aufbruch, Umbruch* (Nicolai: Berlin, 2013).

[90] *The Musical Times*, 112 (1971), 1096.

It is a lonely show that our hero stages.'[91] Having turned back from the alleged destination, he does not return to the bourgeoisie, although it remains unclear what will happen next. Such would be the besetting yet fruitful problematic of Henze's career and œuvre.

The musical forces required are: a vocalist in shades (a baritone of sorts), a brass quintet, a Hammond organ, percussion, a jazz ensemble (supposedly evoking the Berlin Underground, though one might think that a few decades too late), and, perhaps most notably, denoting the bourgeois origins of the protagonist, an instrumental quintet identical to that used in *Pierrot lunaire*. Here is sickly, decadent, bourgeois expressionism. (Here, I might add, is perhaps the most compelling music; maybe Henze spoke more truly than he realised.) To underline the already heavy symbolism, Henze, who directed the performances, had the *Pierrot* quintet – Peter Maxwell Davies's Fires of London – dress in blood-soaked white coats, each member sporting a different physical injury: 'one with eye bandaged', presumably a coincidental homage to Wotan, 'another his leg and yet another his arm in plaster of Paris, etc., etc.'. In a 1972 interview, Henze also made an interesting connection with his experience of Italian opera, and the physicality of the human voice he experienced in that and implicitly not in German tradition:

> When I wrote my first opera, *Boulevard Solitude* in 1951 – it had its premiere the following year – 50 per cent of it was dance. The singers were treated in rather a statuesque manner because I didn't believe in the traditional move-ments for them. I overcame that view when I saw Italian opera and I realised that the physical presence of music in a human body is much stronger in a singer because of his voice. This process of making music physically present is still concerning me today. In *Cimarrón* and *Natascha Ungeheuer*, I make even the musicians visible and they more or less become actors. I think I will pursue this line.[92]

The score tells us that 'the work can be performed in gymnasiums, in the open air or on concert platforms'. Yet, the opera house, or at least the theatre, retains a certain primacy; this is not Henze's response to *La fabbrica illuminata*. 'When performed on the stage, dance elements and lighting effects can be increased. It is conceivable to blend in films and to add to the scenic actions.' Shorn of the optionality and translated into Hegelian, Henze's notes might come from Wagner's *Opera and Drama*. This is a *Gesamtkunstwerk* of the early 1970s.

---

[91] Henze, *Bohemian Fifths*, p. 303.
[92] Interview with Alan Blyth, in *Gramophone*, 49 (1972), 1690.

Reaching a musical assessment of the work almost seems to be missing the point – or, which is not necessarily the same thing, the creators seem to wish us to think so. As Paul Griffiths wrote when reviewing the recording Henze made for Deutsche Grammophon, shortly before the West German company rid itself of this turbulent artist: 'It would be irrelevant to complain about the work's messiness, since this is essential to it. But is the work essential? It may be of interest to those wanting to understand Henze's problem – it certainly cannot be listened to as "pure" music.'[93] Is that, then, what politically committed music drama had come to? An updated, semi-staged version of Strauss's *Ein Heldenleben* – with added bombast? Was this not an impossibility similar to that which both Schoenberg and Dallapiccola had run up against? *We Come to the River* would suggest otherwise, yet did retreat to the opera house contradict such suggestion? Was Henze's foundation of the Cantiere Internazionale d'Arte, a festival for and to a certain extent by the inhabitants of Montepulciano, a better path? Questions would remain, never to be answered, but continually to provoke.

VIII

'It is the portrayal of the *eroico furore*, the evil St Vitus' dance, the unending conflict between the creative individual and his environment set against the background of a culture of guilt that permeates Christian and modern European thought.'[94] Henze wrote those words on *Elegy for Young Lovers* for its 1964 production in Munich; they might readily be applied to many of his works. In an introduction he wrote for a performance in 1975, that is, after many of his more obviously 'political' works had been written, and with their experience fresh in his mind, he explained:

> The theme of *Elegy for Young Lovers* is summed up in two lines by Yeats:
>> The intellect of man is forced to choose
>> *Perfection of the life or of the work.*
>
> Aesthetically speaking, the personal existence of the artist is accidental; the essential thing is his production. The artist-genius, as the nineteenth century conceived him, made this aesthetic presupposition an ethical absolute; that is to say, he claimed to represent the highest, most authentic, mode of human existence.
>
> Accept this claim, and it follows that the artist-genius is morally bound by a sacred duty to exploit others whenever such exploitation will benefit

---

[93] Paul Griffiths, Review in *The Musical Times*, 114 (1973), 803.

[94] Henze, '"Elegy for Young Lovers": (1) Birth of the Opera,' in *Music and Politics*, p. 108.

his work, and to sacrifice them whenever their existence is a hindrance to his production.[95]

The claim is clearly, then, to be questioned, as Henze himself questions it. The *Jugendstil* reminiscences that colour much of the *Elegy*'s soundworld may be perceived – through the refraction of Natascha Ungeheuer's call, perhaps more strongly still than at the time of composition – as snares of beauty, or false beauty, of the domination that the bourgeois artist, Gregor Mittenhofer, exerts over the other characters, their purpose being to serve him. Those characters from the Alpine Schwarze Adler of 1910 are, Henze writes, 'actors of our pain, frivolous messengers of games and rituals that would one day be taken to their brutalised conclusion under fascism; incapable of thinking beyond the boundaries of their class'.[96] They seem all-too-familiar reminders of Richard Strauss, Stefan George, and Thomas Mann. (With typical ambivalence, this Auden and Kallman opera, first performed in 1961, is dedicated to the memory of Hofmannsthal. The librettists considered it their equivalent to *Arabella*; Henze certainly did not.) The story is on one level a tale of embourgeoisement. Hilda Mack's music, with its instrumentation perhaps redolent of Darmstadt (obbligato flute, accompanied by harp, celesta, and tuned percussion (a backhanded tribute to *Le Marteau sans maître*?)), becomes, in Henze's words, 'a climate'. 'A whole universe of bourgeois notions', he writes, 'is supported by artificial music.' Just as Dionysus's music expands in *The Bassarids* so that it stifles the 'rational music of Pentheus', Hilda's music encroaches upon both the emergent poem and the music of the remaining characters.[97]

And yet, hope, as for Nono, always remained, even if Henze were more likely to locate it in Italy than in Germany. In a 1971 interview, he could aver:

> The proletariat is, fortunately, far less crippled than we are. It is deliberately kept ill-informed, certainly, and bombarded with miserable mass-produced products of the mass media. But in Italy, for example, the workers react in a lively and inquisitive fashion when one takes the trouble to show them things to which they otherwise have no access. They have a great deal of unused receptivity; Luigi Nono would confirm that. We must not fall into the trap of seeing our path towards solidarity with the working class as an act of self-mutilation.[98]

Moreover, in 1975, municipal elections brought the PCI to power in Tuscany and Umbria, presaging his vision for the Montepulciano Festival

---

[95] Henze, '"Elegy for Young Lovers": (2) The Artist as Bourgeois Hero', in ibid., p. 110.

[96] Ibid., p. 112.

[97] Ibid., pp. 112–13.

[98] Henze, 'Art and the Revolution', in *Music and Politics*, p. 182.

the following year:

> On 17 May, Fausto [Moroni, Henze's partner] and I had joined a quarter of a million other people in the Piazza San Giovanni in Rome for a great celebration at which Enrico Berlinguer [the leader of the PCI] spoke and Severino Gazzeloni played Bach on his flute. For me, it was like a second coming, the birth of modern Italy, the holy land of *resistenza* and *neorealismo*, the land of the anti-Fascist intelligentsia, the land of Gramsci, of sound common sense, of intellectual openness and cultural wisdom.[99]

Evidently, Henze stood nowhere near to relinquishing his political hopes; equally evidently, he continued to regard Italy with the love of a foreigner. However much he might have wished it otherwise, he remained a German through and through, and his later career would mix continued horror at the course of German history, for instance in his avowedly post-Holocaust Ninth Symphony, with something of a *rapprochement* with the German Romanticism that had always been an integral part of his life and œuvre.

L'Upupa und der Triumph der Sohnesliebe, another Salzburg commission (2003), would be in character, if not quite in form, his *Singspiel*, a loving tribute to the composer of *Die Zauberflöte* – a performance of which the Shah had attended that murderous night in 1967.[100] Despite its debts to Wagner and to Berg, Henze still did not feel comfortable with an unalloyed tribute to the former; Mozart was for many reasons more palatable. Verdi, even 'Henze's Verdi', is nowhere to be heard. And yet, in an unguarded moment during a 2010 interview, shortly before the British premiere of his penultimate opera, *Phaedra*, Henze would even admit, 'German music, it's difficult to match isn't it? It's so rich and so deep and has inspired so many adventures – and still can, I believe.'[101] If he had not yet made peace with German politics – why should he have done so during the age of Merkel any more than in that of Adenauer? – then the richness of his engagement with German music, and more broadly German history and culture, would never be in doubt.

That engagement I shall now take forward to the Bayreuth production of *Parsifal* by the Norwegian director Stefan Herheim, who, having elected to settle in Berlin, has taken if not the opposite, then an opposing, path to that of Henze. And yet, an ultimate message of redemption – by and

---

[99] Henze, *Bohemian Fifths*, p. 338.
[100] On *L'Upupa*, see Hans Werner Henze, *L'Upupa. Nachtstücke aus dem Morgenland: Autobiographische Mitteilungen* (Propyläen: Berlin, 2003). Henze's diary includes the libretto (his own).
[101] Interview with Ivan Hewett, *Daily Telegraph*, 7 January 2010.

of *Parsifal* – from Herheim's staging stands close both to Henze's quest and to Wagner's.

Part III

Performance and the Fruitful Instability
of the Work: From *Parsifal* to Nono

Prelude

The first two parts of this book having been organised broadly chronologically, the third part will look more to after-lives, to performative reception, to some of the process of writing history and histories. Such matters have not of course been absent earlier; they may now, however, move centre-stage. 'Working' is shown in the treatment of Stefan Herheim's Bayreuth production of *Parsifal*, opportunities to see that staging in three different seasons having afforded a further opportunity to look back at the progression of my thoughts on work and staging, and also to bring that cumulative experience together through further reflection. That chapter might therefore seem something of an exception, but insofar as it is, exceptionality pertains to style rather than idea. Discussion of Herheim's *Parsifal* remains and indeed participates in a context of what we might learn about musical dramas and their status as artworks, both in and through history.

Parsifal, as already discussed, is in many respects an unusual or, perhaps more accurately, an extreme work. That characteristic of extremity certainly holds for issues of performance, since, as William Kinderman has pointed out, the work's 'special position . . . is closely bound up with the renewal of the Bayreuth Festival in 1882'. What Kinderman unassumingly calls an 'unusual performance restriction' had the consequence of confining the work to Bayreuth.[1] That restriction pertained until its flouting in the so-called theft of the Grail by New York in 1903 – the United States

---

[1] William Kinderman, *Wagner's 'Parsifal'* (Oxford University Press: New York, 2013), p. 8.

not being a signatory to the Berne Convention – and the expiry of copyright shortly before the outbreak of war: the terminus, as we shall see, for Herheim's first act. Though unsuccessful, Cosima's bizarre, if far from financially disinterested, attempt to have the Reichstag pass a 'Lex Parsifal', restricting the work to the temple of Bayreuth in perpetuity, gained support not only from Strauss, who as a conductor had obvious reason to remain in favour with Wahnfried and who spent eight days lobbying the Reichstag, but from farther afield too; petition signatories included Gustave Charpentier and Puccini.[2] Not until 1934 would Bayreuth itself mount a new production, though some changes had been made to the 'original' in the meantime. 'The notion of *Urtext*' could therefore, in this almost unprecedented situation for a repertoire work, be understood as applying to the staging too.[3] Wieland Wagner's post-war staging elicited cries of outrage, though also of admiration; so did Herheim's. Both, however, have come to be recognised as milestones not only in reception and understanding of *Parsifal*, but also in the history of operatic staging more generally. Indeed, Wagner stagings, from those of the Master onwards, have long proved extreme in both their controversy and their influence. Some of that history is interrogated in the rest of this section.

Conclusion, if not resolution, comes with a relatively brief discussion of Nono's *Al gran sole carico d'amore*, in terms of both work and performance: in some ways, a tying together of strands, though really more an attempt further to open up possibilities broached throughout the book. Whilst not, I hope, unduly desultory, it is intended to be suggestive rather than exhaustive; another set of histories could readily follow on, 'after Nono', yet doubtless still 'after Wagner'. In writing history as in staging, as in the very creation of artworks, it is often more fruitful to open doors rather than to close them, just as the tendency of much musico-dramatic composition and performance after Wagner has been to provoke further questioning rather than to offer conclusions, almost irrespective of intention. Wagner and his successors may well have intended to offer answers; however, as we have seen and shall continue to see, the questions have continually proved more provocative. (That word is, I know, a red rag to a certain, ultra-reactionary variety of bull, pining for a *Werktreue* that never was, pining indeed for a *Werk* that never was, but such concerns need not detain us.)

What falls in between *Parsifal* and *Al gran sole*? (The question is not intended as a riddle, though perhaps it should be.) First: a discussion of

[2]   Frederic Spotts, *Bayreuth: A History of the Wagner Festival* (Yale University Press: New Haven and London, 1996), p. 133.
[3]   Kinderman, *Wagner's 'Parsifal'*, p. 8.

some recent stagings and one non-staging of *Lohengrin*. That, however, is a somewhat misleading summary of the eighth chapter, for it is a little while until those performances are actually discussed. Having looked in some detail at Herheim's *Parsifal*, it seemed also necessary to discuss some more general issues concerning not only staging and performance, but also the environment of modern opera houses: the arena in which works are received, questioned, even contested. Such matters deserve a whole book to themselves, but just because they could not be treated more fully, that was no reason not at least to raise a few questions, in the light of which performances of *Lohengrin* and other works might then be considered. I chose *Lohengrin* partly on account of the stagings I happened recently to have seen and the proximity of some of their concerns to those of this book, but also specifically on account of its earlier position in Wagner's œuvre: coming before the 'music dramas', the last 'German Romantic opera', at least so far as he was concerned. The difference between those operas Wagner did and did not term 'music dramas' may equally be under- and overestimated. If we posit a qualitative leap, then we should be wary of considering it the only one; if we assimilate, along the lines of Cosima's Bayreuth 'canon', *Der fliegende Holländer*, *Tannhäuser*, and *Lohengrin* to the ranks of the later works, we stand in danger of losing some of their particularity. (One might say the same of the earlier, non-Bayreuth operas, too, but the baffling neglect of Wagner's first opera, *Die Feen*, must remain a subject for another day.[4]) At any rate, without becoming bogged down in the question of a rupture between *Lohengrin* and *Das Rheingold*, it seemed interesting to explore an 'earlier' work in the light of Wagner's subsequent ideas, not so as to eliminate difference, but so as to explore a little, if only implicitly, the complex workings of reception and canon within an ongoing performative tradition.

A further step is taken in the final chapter, prior to reaching *Al gran sole*. A few cases of attempts to break down the 'work concept' in its strongest sense, some more successful than others, are explored. Performances of *Don Giovanni*, an earlier work in which Wagner took a particular interest, and of which he offered both 'production' and 'version', are thus considered 'after' him; so are very different stagings and versions of Berg's *Lulu*, an obviously problematical work, given its lack of completion. We are thus

---

[4]   For a review of Oper Leipzig's Wagner-bicentenary (2013) staging of *Die Feen* and some more general observations concerning the work, see Mark Berry, 'Where it all Began: Fairies in Leipzig,' in *The Wagner Journal*, 7/3 (2013), 57–60. See also Katherine Syer, '"It left me no Peace": From Carlo Gozzi's *La donna serpente* to Wagner's *Parsifal*,' in *The Musical Quarterly*, 94 (2011), 325–80.

reminded that it is not only in pre- or non-Wagnerian operas that 'even coming up with a text demands a set of complex interpretative judgements'.[5] Thereby prepared, Nono's *Al gran sole*, a work that demands of both performers and audience that they reassemble, reconstruct, redramatise historical experiences, is itself considered in the light of two contrasted stagings: one more metatheatrical, even abstract, the other in a sense more traditionally 'operatic', more successfully engaging with historical and dramatic possibilities present in the invitation to rewriting.

For, whether dealing more overtly with history or the present – and most thoughtful attempts to do the one are likely to involve some elements at least of the other – a driving force of our explorations is, to quote John Dunn, 'an activity which we would recognise, in common sense terms, as "thinking"'. Such might sound like a statement of the blindingly obvious, but it is the word 'activity' that is crucial here. 'The history of thought', Dunn continues, 'as it is characteristically written is not a history of men battling to achieve a coherent ordering of their experience. It is, rather a history of fictions – of rationalist constructs out of the thought processes of individuals, not of plausible abridgements of these thought processes.'[6] Those fictions are probably more necessary than Dunn may have allowed; indeed, there are necessarily elements of the fictive and dramatic within any history. But we should indeed do well to guard against excessive rationalism. That 'battling to achieve a coherent ordering of . . . experience' is in many ways the most interesting idea. A classic example of such in allegedly 'absolute' music would be the overwhelming integrative tendencies of Beethovenian symphonism – overwhelming not least on account of the force of countervailing disintegrative processes. Such battling is also the stuff of writing histories, of writing music dramas – and of their staging and understanding. Even if this remains a dim and distant goal, historical writing and rewriting can do worse than to aspire to the dynamism of Beethoven and Hegel, perhaps better still to the fractured dynamism of late Beethoven, which might thus in its modernity be considered 'truer' than Hegel's system. And that includes the dynamism of Beethoven – for that matter, that of Mozart, Wagner, Schoenberg, or Nono – in performance, on the stage, as well as in the score.

[5]   Nicholas Till, 'The Operatic Work: Texts, Performances, Repetitions, and Repertories,' in *The Cambridge Companion to Opera Studies*, ed. Till (Cambridge University Press: Cambridge, 2012), p. 249

[6]   John Dunn, 'The Identity of the History of Ideas,' in *Political Obligation in Its Historical Context: Essays in Political Theory* (Cambridge University Press: Cambridge, 1980), p. 15

That which applies to what, for the sake of argument, I shall term a more 'traditional' form of history, with respect to both subject matter and narrative form, applies equally to the work concept. Both have a great deal to tell us, and doubtless always will. However, their claims to hegemony, even if less rawly expressed than once they would have been, remain problematical. Subtler persistence of certain intellectual tendencies within a more 'open' intellectual field, one in which history's cultural turn and musicology's performative turn are both readily acknowledged, might yet arouse suspicions of its own, for the ghosts of positivism are far from vanquished. What does it mean to say that objectivity is a goal, even if an unattainable goal, in historical writing or in the staging of a century-old musical work? At the very least, that is a question we should continue to ask, even if we continue to be unsure of our answer. It is creative as well as challenging, returning us to the idea that history has a great deal to learn from poetry, music, philosophy, theology, and so on – just as they do from history and from each other.

The Hegelian impulse towards totality, still present in Wagner, tragically so in Schoenberg, in some senses knowingly reassembled in Nono and Herheim, endures, even strengthens itself; it endures partly on account of its incorporation of and by the fragmentary, by deconstruction. History has not entirely given way to reflection upon history, nor will it ever do so. Nor has the writing of music drama given way to reflection thereupon, be that in criticism or in performance. There nevertheless remains a grain of truth to the claiming of such a tendency for what, in Schiller's terms, we should certainly consider our 'sentimental' age. Contradiction, whether we like it or no, is our lot. So, however, are those dialogues, still better those dramas, we might justly call history and performance.

CHAPTER 7

Stefan Herheim's *Parsifal*

I

Having staged not just one but two *Ring* cycles, Keith Warner has become something of a Wagner veteran. In an interesting and, in the best sense, provocative essay, he points out that Wagner 'almost single-handedly invented, certainly in opera', the role of director, 'almost certainly provoked into action by the work of the Duke of Saxe-Meiningen [George II] and his celebrated acting troupe's artistic director, Ludwig Chronegk', whose production of Kleist's *Der Hermannsschlacht* he had seen in 1875, the year before the first Bayreuth *Ring*, 'which Wagner chose to direct rather than conduct'.[1] It is not difficult to imagine why, on a personal level, either Wagner or a modern stage director such as Warner should wish to further the Meiningen concept not only of greater professionalism – especially noteworthy for attention paid to individual members of the crowd – but also of a single authority presiding over a production, though it is not altogether clear that Wagner was following that concept rather than working in tandem with it.[2] The directorial *Konzept*, beloved of devotees of modern *Regietheater* and detested by its opponents, stands not so very distant; although, by the same token, the Duke's insistence upon naturalistic historical verisimilitude would find favour with opponents rather than devotees. It is likewise not difficult to understand why Wagner or modern directors should wish to lessen, and preferably to abolish, the cult of 'star' performers, a key feature of the Meiningen agenda – and a *cause célèbre* for all manner of operatic 'reformers' from at least Gluck and Calzabigi onwards. Theirs is no more a 'neutral' stance than any other; nor should it be. Yet their vision, for which there may be justification to speak of in the singular, which it is no exaggeration to consider both

[1] Keith Warner, 'Gesamt Werk Kunst: A Few New Thoughts', in *The Wagner Journal*, 3/2 (2009), 55.

[2] On Duke George, the crowd, and André Antoine, see Marvin Carlson, 'Meiningen Crowd Scenes and the Theatre-Libre', in *Educational Theatre Journal*, 13 (1961), 245–9. More generally, see Ann Marie Koller, *The Theater Duke: Georg II of Saxe-Meiningen and the German Stage* (Stanford University Press: Stanford, 1984).

modern and modernistic, has held and continues to hold consequences for the understanding and experience of works both new and from the 'museum'. The same might be said about the histories we write of those works and the performances which, for many, give them life – and history.

Leaving aside the swiftly outdated naturalism of the designs for Bayreuth's first *Ring* – with which Wagner was in any case unhappy – what stands out from contemporary reports of rehearsals is, as Warner remarks, the abnormality of the composer-director's approach.[3] That encompassed 'detailed, naturalistic acting, physical and psychologically based, fleshed out through every means of expression in the actor-singer's arsenal ... decades before [perhaps a slight exaggeration in some cases] Ibsen, Antoine, Chekhov, and Stanislavsky.'[4] In the words of 'eye-witness' Heinrich Porges, 'through the performance of the *Ring*, the goal was achieved of combining the realistic style of Shakespeare with the idealistic style of antique tragedy; of bringing about an organic union between a highly stylised art, striving for a direct embodiment of the ideal, with an art rooted in fidelity to Nature (*Naturwahrheit*).'[5] However poorly that may have been achieved in practice, it remains noteworthy as an aspiration. It is, then, I hope not unduly quixotic to turn to consider matters of production as part of a tour 'after Wagner'. Given both the treatment of *Parsifal* in the first chapter, and the particular degree to which one particular (Bayreuth) production of that work has informed my thinking on the subject, it seemed appropriate to devote the present chapter to Stefan Herheim's staging of Wagner's *Bühnenweihfestspiel* and some thoughts arising.

This particular staging was first seen at Bayreuth in 2008, remaining in the repertoire until 2012. I was fortunate enough to see it in 2008, 2011, and 2012, and wrote diary reports of my experience after each performance – not, at the time, intending them to form part of this book. However, reflections following the 2012 performance led me in the direction of presenting these reports, followed by an attempted analysis of what, taken as a group, as an ongoing engagement, they might have to say about our understanding of Wagnerian and post-Wagnerian music drama and some of its political implications. I have retained the reports more or less as they stood, save for deletion of a few irrelevances, tightening up some language,

[3] Heinrich Porges, *Wagner Rehearsing the 'Ring': An Eye-Witness Account of the Stage Rehearsals of the First Bayreuth Festival*, tr. Robert L Jacobs (Cambridge University Press: Cambridge, 1983); Richard Fricke, *Wagner in Rehearsal, 1875–1876*, tr. George R. Fricke, ed. James Deaville with Evan Baker (Pendragon: Stuyvesant, NY, 1998).

[4] Warner, 'Gesamt Werk Kunst,' p. 55.

[5] Porges, *Wagner Rehearsing the 'Ring'*, pp. 4–5.

a very few elucidating additions, and the correction of odd typographical and syntactical errors, whose retention would serve no purpose than ritual humiliation of the writer. There may then be a certain degree of repetition between accounts, though not actually very much, since they tend to take their leave from each other, and I have tried to eliminate the worst; however, such repetition that remains also serves something of a cumulative function.

II

Here, first, are the thoughts arising from my first encounter with the production, on 5 August 2008, in many respects more descriptive than analytical, a balance that would tilt with further acquaintance:

Amfortas – Detlef Roth; Titurel – Diógenes Randes; Gurnemanz – Kwangchul Youn; Parsifal – Christopher Ventris; Klingsor – Thomas Jesatko; Kundry – Mihoko Fujimura; First Knight of the Grail – Arnold Bezuyen; Second Knight of the Grail – Friedemann Röhlig; First Squire – Julia Borchert; Second Squire – Ulrike Helzel; Third Squire – Clemens Bieber; Fourth Squire – Timothy Oliver; Flowermaidens – Julia Borchert, Martina Rüping, Carola Guber, Anna Korondi, Jutta Böhnert, Ulrike Helzel; Contralto solo – Simone Schröder. Stefan Herheim (director); Heike Scheele (designs); Gesine Cöllm (costumes); Alexander Meier-Dörzenbach (dramaturgy). Bayreuth Festival Chorus (chorus master: Eberhard Friedrich); Bayreuth Festival Orchestra/Daniele Gatti (conductor).

This was an outstanding production. I had greatly admired Stefan Herheim's Salzburg *Entführung*, so my expectations were high; they were nevertheless surpassed.[6] Herheim treads a difficult tightrope between presentation of his guiding *Konzept* – the *history* of *Parsifal* as a work and the world in which it has developed from the time of its first performance to that of its most recent – and recounting of the immanent *story* of Parsifal. Two stories run not so much in parallel as with mutual influence, yet without inflicting harm upon each other and without the slightest sense of contrivance. Herheim, in other words, never falls from his rope into those treacherous depths that have previously swallowed so many directors and their ideas, be they good, bad, or indifferent.

We begin in the Second Reich. So intensely dialectical and wondrously multi-layered, yet far from confusing, is Herheim's direction that we witness and hear in the first act alone the early days of post-Wagner Wahnfried, the

---

[6] This production of *Die Entführung aus dem Serail*, which I saw at the 2006 Salzburg Festival, is available on DVD: Decca B000ICL3PQ.

sickly, semi-incestuous goings-on of an impeccably *haut bourgeois* family and its nursery, that extraordinary phase of Nietzschean, Renanesque, and of course Parsifalian Christianity, the era of the oft-present Imperial eagle, and the terrifying march to war. Never have I experienced so justly ominous a tone to the outward march of the replenished – but replenished by and for what? – Grail knights as here, both musically and courtesy of the early 'patriotic' military film. The realm in which time becomes space has led us towards 1914.

It should be stressed that we miss none of the drama expected from a performance of *Parsifal*. And so, the second act begins in a field hospital, for once actually seeing those renegade knights, Sir Ferris and all, of whom Klingsor tells. The Flower-orderlies tend to them in every way they knew how: an effective tactic on the part of Klingsor as Master of Ceremonies. It is presumably this music that Henze had in mind when describing the Emperor's Buddha narration in *We Come to the River* as blossoming 'with Parsifalian luxuriance' – perhaps otherwise a rather odd comparison to make.[7] We also see Weimar Germany, the Moorish castle's owner suggestive in white tie and fishnets of Emcee himself. Maybe there is a comparison to be made between Henze's counter-tenor Emperor, Wagner's self-castrated anti-hero, and the presentation here made *en travestie*. *Cabaret's* trajectory reaches its ultimate conclusion with the end of this act, a moment for which the phrase *coup de théâtre* might have been invented. The coming of the Third Reich – Wagner's, Strauss's, Henze's, Germany's, Europe's nemesis – is signalled by the castle's destruction and the advent not only of stormtroopers and a brown-shirted, tomorrow-belonging-to-him little boy, but of swastikas too. Rarely have I experienced such a truly electric moment in the theatre. There were boos of course, from those afraid and challenged – they tended to be of conspicuously *bürgerlich* appearance – but there was louder applause for Bayreuth's belated yet brave attempt at coming to terms with its history. Self-laceration may have become tedious in some segments of German society, but the knives have been less evident near the Green Hill.

The final act opens in the garden of a bombed Wahnfried. Parsifal's coming and Good Friday offer the possibility of a reanimation, not just natural but social: a tall order, as we realise when a procession of the starved post-war population of Berlin passed across the stage. Yet Parsifal has at least enabled water to trickle forth again from the garden's fountain.

---

[7] Hans Werner Henze, *Bohemian Fifths: An Autobiography*, tr. Stewart Spencer (Faber: London, 1999), p. 339.

Amfortas's trial – in every sense – brings us from Nuremberg to the present-day Bundestag, whilst in no way detracting from the very particular agony of this very particular drama. And who says that one can peak too early? A *coup de théâtre* just as brave as that of the evocation of 1933 is offered by a video projection of the young Wagner brothers' – Wieland's and Wolfgang's – request at the 1951 reopening, that political discussion be banished from New Bayreuth. An image of Wagner himself is bricked up. Reactionaries, or at least conservatives, should have taken heart from the proportion of Wagner's stage directions followed, sometimes to the letter, but at least to the spirit. How long, for instance, is it since a production of *Parsifal* ended with the white dove hovering over the hero's head? Here, of course, the message is ambiguous. Clearly related to the eagle we have seen so many times before – and to the swan of the first act – the dove may offer hope; however, there may yet be more of the same or worse. Horace's '*Mutato nomine, de te fabula narratur*' ('Change but the name, and the tale is told of you') seems tailor-made for the video-projections in which we faced ourselves and the orchestra – a Bayreuth first in revealing the world of the covered pit.[8] We both brace ourselves and question the alleged 'openness' – hints of Norman Foster's Reichstag dome – of the new dispensation.

Daniele Gatti's reading of the score rarely drew attention to itself but contributed to the unfolding dramas in exemplary fashion. It was, I suspect, a slow reading when measured by the clock, although that says little in itself. Knappertsbusch and Boulez both have a great deal to tell us; there is no need to take sides, except against those incapable of making the score resound and cohere. The richness of the Bayreuth orchestra was ever apparent, but never more so than when it finally had our full attention, during the unstaged Prelude to Act III. That evocation of hard-won passing of time can rarely have seemed more apt than in the circumstances of this production. The gradual unfolding of the score's phrases and paragraphs was faultless. Each act was possessed both of its own character and of an array of variegation and cross-reference. And the bells sounded better than I can recall hearing them anywhere (except on the most venerable of old Bayreuth recordings).

Christopher Ventris was an excellent Parsifal. This may be less impossible a role than Siegfried or Tristan, but even so, it is a tough challenge, to which Ventris rose with great accomplishment, both as musician and as actor.

---

[8] Horace, 'Satires,' I, I, 69–70, in *Satires, Epistles, and Ars Poetica*, tr. H. Rushton Fairclough, revised edn (Harvard University Press: Cambridge, MA, 1929).

Indeed, all of the cast, with the partial exception of Mihoko Fujimura's Kundry, excelled in acting terms. Sadly, she proved no seductress, but she bought into the rest of her role and sang well enough throughout, even if her diction fell somewhat behind. (I could not help but wonder what Waltraud Meier would have made of this opportunity.) Kwangchul Youn lacked the authority of a great Gurnemanz but he proved attentive to the text, excepting one noticeable bout of poor intonation. I have heard more malevolent Klingsors than Thomas Jesatko, but there was nothing really to complain of in a well-acted performance. Detlef Roth, however, proved a triumphant Amfortas. To say that he showed himself an extremely fine singing-actor is not to detract from his considerable achievements, were his singing and acting to be considered separately; it is simply to state that such a separation would be false and that the whole was still greater than the sum of the parts. The same could be said of the superb Bayreuth Festival Chorus. And the same could be said of the entire production, which, whatever my odd reservation concerning the casting, should come to be regarded as a defining moment in the history of the Bayreuth Festival and indeed in that of the staging of Wagner's music dramas.

III

Three years later, I saw the production for a second time, on 3 August 2011:

Amfortas – Detlef Roth; Titurel – Diógenes Randes; Gurnemanz – Kwangchul Youn; Parsifal – Simon O'Neill; Klingsor – Thomas Jesatko; Kundry – Susan Maclean; First Knight of the Grail – Arnold Bezuyen; Second Knight of the Grail – Friedemann Röhlig; First Squire – Julia Borchert; Second Squire – Ulrike Helzel; Third Squire – Clemens Bieber; Fourth Squire – Willem van der Heyden; Flowermaidens – Julia Borchert, Martina Rüping, Carola Guber, Christiane Kohl, Jutta Maria Böhnert, Ulrike Helzel; Contralto solo – Simone Schröder. Stefan Herheim (director); Heike Scheele (set designs); Gesine Cöllm (costumes); Ulrich Niepel (lighting); Alexander Meier-Dörzenbach (dramaturgy); Momme Hinrichs, Torge Møller (video); Bayreuth Festival Chorus (chorus master: Eberhard Friedrich); Bayreuth Festival Orchestra/ Daniele Gatti (conductor).

Should one cross the same river twice? Could Stefan Herheim's – and Daniele Gatti's – *Parsifal* match up to my first-time experience in 2008? As with the Boulez-Chéreau 'Centenary' *Ring*, one of the few opera DVDs I find persistently engrossing, the answers proved to be 'yes' – and triumphantly so. It appears almost mandatory to voice a cavil, and I have a small one: sections of the stage direction have been relatively simplified. In most other cases, that tends to be good. Yet there had been no clutter in Herheim's *Parsifal*. Complexity, yes, but this is a complex, in many respects Hegelian, work, with an equally complex history. Herheim's achievement was and is to tell the story of both, and *that includes the score*, his musicianship and belief in music's redemptive power apparent throughout. The first half of the third act now looks for the most part surprisingly 'traditional', not that it did not incorporate and develop tradition, but I slightly regret the thinning out. (Some commentators had thought first time around that too much was going on, that Herheim should have concentrated on but a single line; that had seemed to me to miss the point.)

I do not intend to give a full account of the production, since much can already be read above. I shall instead for the most part discuss some points that especially captured my intention on this particular occasion. However, it is worth briefly mentioning the broad thrust, or rather thrusts. We witness, not so much in parallel, but inextricably interlinked, as faithful a telling of *Parsifal* as one is ever likely to find – at least for anyone interested in Wagner's meaning and dialectical thinking rather than fetishisation of incidental matters of costume – and a perceptive retelling of the course of German history from the time of the first performance until the present.

The metamorphosis of the first-act's Wahnfried into Siena Cathedral and back again is subtle and yet telling enough; but note that the pillars of both remain, transformed, in the field hospital of the Flowermaidens, as directed by Klingsor as *Cabaret* Master of Ceremonies. (Transvestite show-business is an obvious career path for the self-castrated, not unlike the *castrati* of old.) Herheim's turning the mirror on the audience is not a gimmick, but an invitation, indeed an incitement, to question everything we have thought. 'Educating Parsifal' is also 'educating *Parsifal*', is also 'educating us' – not in a didactic fashion but as part of a drama in which we should be fools not to participate. In the emotional and intellectual context Herheim has developed, as opposed to the abstraction of a mere act of reporting, it would be an unimaginative soul indeed who did not accept that invitation. Identities are blurred, or better enhanced, by the play conducted not only between these two stories but also between characters: Parsifal, at various stages from baby to old man, with Amfortas – compassion or fellow-suffering (the German, Schopenhauerian *Mitleid*, suffering *with*) indeed; and Kundry with Herzeleide, whose act of childbirth and troubled, necessarily incestuous relationship – is any act of parenting not? – is worked out in Parsifal's own education and reversion. Wagner's anticipations of Freud have never seemed so clear as in the second-act congress with Herzeleide-Kundry. The visual motif, both on stage and on film, of Kundry as Rose of Hell – Klingsor's 'Urteufelin, Höllenrose!' – guides that educative process, taking *Parsifal* beyond *Tristan*'s Nietzschean 'voluptuousness of Hell' and renewing in itself in the malevolence of Wagner's Bergian chromaticism.[9] The near-identity of Kundry and Parsifal, Christ-like, albeit Amfortas-Christ-like, at the beginning of the third act, brings us as close as we come, or indeed Wagner comes, to Christianity: help to the stricken, after the Sermon of the Mount. Those stricken in this context are the female victims of war and its after-math; that is to say, victims of the most violent struggles yet thrown up by accumulation of capital and the dialectic of Enlightenment. Visually, this is a definite *hommage* to Götz Friedrich's *Tannhäuser*: Herheim studied with Friedrich, another fine example of the musician-director.

One might have expected the electricity to wane in the second-time viewing of such *coups de théâtre* as the unfurling of swastikas at the destruction of Klingsor's castle – and of Weimar – as a brown-shirted boy, perhaps Parsifal reincarnated or perhaps not, implies, incorrectly as it would turn out, that tomorrow will belong to him. Not at all: if anything, that electricity is enhanced by expectation. (We do not, after all, stop listening to *Parsifal* once we know what 'happens next' in the plot.) The families gathered around beforehand for departure make their point chillingly.

Amfortas – and the Federal Republic – on trial in the Bundestag remains a potent, terrifying image following the third-act Transformation Music. The opening of Titurel's coffin, draped in the flag, elicits mass revulsion not only on stage but, more importantly, in the audience. (There are musical reasons for that too, to which I shall return.) The monochrome contrast, moreover, with the warmth of Ulrich Niepel's springtime lighting for the Good Friday Music, tells its own story. Christian charity has been replaced by politics, just as the post-war request of Wieland and Wolfgang Wagner, that political discussion desist on the Green Hill, shown here without comment during the Transformation Music, could not have been more of a political act had the stage been emblazoned with swastikas. Echoing, indeed quoting, their father, Siegfried's 1923 request that the German national anthem not be sung at the conclusion of *Die Meistersinger*: 'Hier gilt's der Kunst!' ('Art is what matters here!'), Wieland and Wagner's note read and reads again: 'In the interests of trouble-free progression of the Festival, we kindly request that you refrain from political debate and

---

[9] Friedrich Nietzsche, 'Ecce Homo', in *Sämtliche Werke: Kritische Studienausgabe*, ed. Giorgio Colli and Mazzino Montinari, 15 vols (De Gruyter: Berlin and New York, 1967–88), vol. 6: 'Warum ich so klug bin': §6, p. 290.

discussion on the Festival Hill. "Art is what matters here!"[10] The artwork of the future has become the artwork of another future, incorporating – sublating – artworks of a history that is our own.

That claim of depoliticisation, disingenuous in 1951, endured long past its sell-by date. Hans Peter Wild, the Mayor of Bayreuth, used it in an open letter of 1968 to Friedelind Wagner, errant sister to the Wagner brothers, Wieland recently deceased, effectively accusing her of treachery to the Festival, her hometown, and to the Federal Republic. 'The depoliticisation of the Festival remains a guiding principle of what happens on the Green Hill today,' Wild admonished her; 'you . . . effectively allied yourself with the organs of the press of the GDR.'[11] A typical ruse that: one's enemy is 'political' or 'ideological', whilst the righteous value art for its own sake. Even if Friedelind's televised allegation of a book-burning in Bayreuth were unfounded, it was, in such a situation, anything but implausible. The video wall built up during this scene around Wagner's image – perhaps also an echo of Wieland's Bayreuth wall, on whose other side lay that most awkward of Bayreuth dragons, Winifred – is the very same wall constructed every day by those who wish only to see fairy-tales of picturesque knights and dragons, wilfully deaf to the words and music of Richard Wagner, let alone to their combination in history and performance.

Some complained that Daniele Gatti's pacing, slow according to the clock but not according to the Wagnerian *melos*, worked against the dramatic urgency of Herheim's staging. My experience was quite the opposite. In allowing time for the drama to unfold, whilst upholding an unbroken musical line, Gatti presented the orchestra very much in Wagner's *Opera and Drama* image of the Greek Chorus. Moreover, there was nothing unvaried about his approach. There was violence, and a nasty violence at that, in the Flowermaidens' Music. Stage images of Weimar cabaret-turned-sour enhanced, indeed seemingly built upon, an integrated understanding of Wagner's harmony and colouring that foretold Schoenberg's Golden Calf Orgy (*Moses und Aron*). On the other hand, the luxurious decadence –Nietzschean *décadence*? – of Kundry's seduction spoke of Berg and Mahler. I mentioned above the revulsion on stage as Amfortas opened Titurel's coffin. That was almost

---

[10] 'Im Interesse einer reibungslosen Durchführung der Festspiele bitten wir, von Gesprächen und Debatten politischer Art auf dem Festspielhügel freundlichst absehen zu wollen. "Hier gilt's der Kunst!"'

[11] Quoted in Eva Rieger, *Friedelind Wagner: Richard Wagner's Rebellious Granddaughter*, tr. Chris Walton (Boydell: Woodbridge and Rochester, NY, 2013), p. 269

as nothing compared to the Mahlerian, indeed Schoenbergian (think of the *Five Orchestral Pieces*, op. 16), horror Gatti screwed up in the pit. This proved once again an exemplary collaboration between conductor and director.

What of the singers? Simon O'Neill's Parsifal was a grave disappointment. Such is the strength of Herheim's production – and Gatti's conducting – that the meaning absent from O'Neill's delivery of the text could in general be supplied elsewhere, but there was nowhere to hide when it came to O'Neill's nasal tone-production. Christopher Ventris had in 2008 been far more convincing. Susan Maclean, by contrast, proved a revelatory Kundry. I had admired Maclean in the same role before, in Leipzig (twice). Here she showed the difference between a dutiful, for the most part well-sung, yet hardly seductive, portrayal (Mihoko Fujimura last time around) and one that truly engaged with the production as living musical drama. This Kundry repelled and seduced, shrieked and consoled, provoked and served. The production might have been made for her. Thomas Jesatko remained an excellent Klingsor, revelling in his kinky sleights of hand. The agonies of Detlef Roth's Amfortas were searingly portrayed: his was a performance that made one feel not only the unsparing nature of Amfortas's wound, but the lyrical, almost Schubertian possibilities of a future that never came. We need to believe that Amfortas's life could have been different, and we did. Kwangchul Youn's Gurnemanz proved at best variable, wideness of vibrato and occasional hoarseness never compensated for by the outsize personality artists such as Sir John Tomlinson can still bring to the role. The Flowermaidens, however, were excellent: we shall doubtless hear more from many of them. And the choral singing was superlative: congratulations to the Bayreuth Festival Chorus and Eberhard Friedrich. This was not a perfect cast, then, though one could hardly have asked for more from Maclean, Jesatko, and Roth, nor from the chorus. Crucially, however, nothing detracted from the overwhelming force of Herheim's and Gatti's vision. There was no doubt, moreover, about the final redemption: it was of, for, and through Wagner's miraculous score, 'lit from behind'. Even if one thought *Parsifal* stood in no need of redemption, one realised that work and audience had been blessed.

IV

There finally came my 2012 viewing, on 11 August, prior to the production's retirement from Bayreuth at the end of that summer:

Amfortas – Detlef Roth; Titurel – Diógenes Randes; Gurnemanz – Kwangchul Youn; Parsifal – Burkhard Fritz; Klingsor – Thomas Jesatko; Kundry – Susan Maclean; First Knight of the Grail – Arnold Bezuyen; Second Knight of the Grail – Christian Tschelebiew; First Squire – Julia Borchert; Second Squire – Ulrike Helzel; Third Squire – Clemens Bieber; Fourth Squire – Willem van der Heyden; Flowermaidens – Julia Borchert, Martina Rüping, Carola Guber, Christiane Kohl, Jutta Maria Böhnert, Ulrike Helzel; Contralto solo – Simone Schröder; Stefan Herheim (director); Heike Scheele (set designs); Gesine Völlm (costumes); Ulrich Niepel (lighting); Alexander Meier-Dörzenbach (dramaturgy); Momme Hinrichs, Torge Møller (video). Bayreuth Festival Chorus (chorus master: Eberhard Friedrich); Bayreuth Festival Orchestra/ Philippe Jordan (conductor).

Having seen two previous performances, I found myself nevertheless quite taken aback by how much, especially during the first act, I fancied I was seeing for the first time. Some of it I suspect I was, for not only does the Bayreuth Festival pride itself upon its *Werkstatt* (workshop) concept, in which productions will develop from year to year, Herheim's questing, dialectical approach also especially lends itself to such reinvention. So too, of course, do Wagner's dramaturgy and compositional method, not the least of his legacies for twentieth- and twenty-first-century serialism. Convinced as I was that there had been a shift of emphasis, at least, looking back upon other early reports, I suspect that this was at least as much a matter of my approaching the staging differently, for whatever reasons: partly relative familiarity no doubt, but perhaps not just that. Herheim's multi-layered, almost geological, method is not dissimilar to Wagner's own, helping explain the 'fit' between the two artists. This production needs to be seen many times, and now, at last, it can be, since this very performance was being filmed for broadcast and DVD release.[12]

The German historical-political and *Parsifal*-reception aspects of the production are by now celebrated. If anything, I felt them underplayed during the first act, though that may, as I said, have been more a matter of my personal reception. At any rate, what most impressed on this occasion was the psychoanalytical level to the staging. Indeed, such was the overwhelming experience of the latter that I started to feel in some respects a little disappointed, protective of my earlier experiences, almost a loyalist to what I imagined, rightly or wrongly, to have been Herheim I and II, rather as if I were an Old- or even New-Bayreuth loyalist, missing my Wieland Wagner or Hans Knappertsbusch. Herheim III began to seem a meta-production, as much a re-imagining of its earlier incarnations as

[12] Alas, it seems, at least at the time of writing, that the envisaged DVD release will not materialise.

of *Parsifal* itself. Dreams and childhood come to the fore, as also, just as intriguingly, do religious experience and its psychopathology. (Remember Nietzsche and Thomas Mann?) The third scene in particular, with its priest, incense – Nietzsche's accusation of Wagner bowing before the Cross re-examined – and, most shockingly, circumcision of the infant who may or may not 'be' a young Parsifal, offer almost as much food for thought as Wagner's own Feuerbachian inversion of the elements. (That alone ought surely to question the custom, still observed in certain circles, of piously refraining from applause. This is most definitely not the *St Matthew Passion*.)

The violence of the deed of circumcision could hardly be more topical, given the contemporary legal controversy over infant genital mutilation in Germany; and yet, it also points to something older, deep-seated, and of course very much part of the *Rezeptionsgeschichte* strand: the question of whether anti-Semitism is expressed in Wagner's drama. Amfortas's cry of pain – he now seems far more central to the act, indeed to the drama as a whole, arguably more so even than Parsifal – jolts us from our complacent 'knowledge' of the work, and also anticipates Kundry's scream of laughter. Christ, whatever Wagner may have hoped, must also have undergone the procedure. Detlef Roth's commanding assumption of the role of Amfortas, still more impressive than in earlier years, undoubtedly assisted in this transformation of emphasis. What is the relationship between Amfortas and the young Parsifal, whom we see or think we see at various stages? Does the latter imagine the former, indeed the drama as a whole, in some sense? That is too easy an answer, and is complicated by the retelling of German history, but it is a questioning strand nevertheless. Notably, Gurnemanz addresses the boy Parsifal at the end of the act. Even the video despatch of young men to war (the Great War) seems as much a product of twisted familial relations – consider the inculcation of patriotism in English and German schools alike – as of great power politics.

Kundry as governess – as well, earlier and later, as Herzeleide – adds a creepy, nursery, *Turn of the Screw*-like aspect to the story, especially when, thereafter, the grown Parsifal possesses her on the bed that is both setting for and generative of so much of the action. It is there, of course, that the child is born, literally centre-stage, the delivery a powerful moment in itself, as well as intricately linked to the various stages of childhood, adolescence, adulthood, dotage, and death, both personal and political, we witness enacted. The enactment on stage of Amfortas's wounding during Gurnemanz's narration at first seems a touch literal, but psychoanalytical implications and consequences soon manifest themselves, so that one realises that such development and consideration thereof are much of the point. The late-nineteenth-century (Mann's 'bad nineteenth-century?') setting suggests, amongst other things, a family saga: *Buddenbrooks* spiced with Nietzsche.

Much of that, however, is called into question by the second act, in which the political reasserts itself with a vengeance. The delicious representation of the Flowermaidens as orderlies and flappers – is that not just what they are? – retains its dramatic power, as well as firmly putting us in the interwar period. (I say firmly, but time passes as the act does.) And yet, a reminder that the various levels of interpretation are anything but distinct is offered by a greater keenness of manipulation when it comes to Kundry's acts: above all, what she tells Parsifal. She is in turn being manipulated by Klingsor, of course, but perhaps so many of us are understandably now influenced by feminist readings, that we feel uncomplicatedly sympathetic. It is salutary to be reminded that this Rose of Hell – the rose very much part of the staging's imagery – has, despite her plight, agency of her own. That is surely more feminist than to consider her purely as a victim. And the similarity of costume between her and Klingsor, both in Weimar cross-dressing travesty, reinforces the need both have for each other, the Hegelian master–slave dialectic re-imagined. The final scene remains electric, the unfurling of swastikas and coming of Bayreuth's and Germany's darkest years truly shocking. Judging by the disgruntled noises from some members of the audience, it remains an absolute necessity too.

An interval walk around the outdoor exhibition of *Verstummte Stimmen* (the 'silenced voices' of Jews ill-treated by the Festival) reinforced the point. (Ironically, the only figure treated unjustly is Wagner himself, in which the questionable claim that anti-Semitism is expressed in the dramas is trotted out uncritically.) I could not help but think of the ongoing controversy concerning Amélie Hohmann's refusal to release correspondence between Winifred Wagner and Hitler.[13] Whatever one might think of Katharina Wagner as director, at least she seems willing to open up the Festival to necessary historical criticism.

Which leads into the third act and Herheim's attack upon the disingenuous New Bayreuth plea, signed by Wieland and Wolfgang, and displayed

---

[13] At the time of writing, Hohmann, another of Winifred Wagner's granddaughters, was refusing Katharina's requests to make public the documents left for safekeeping by Winifred. It is unclear what these documents might be, though they seem likely to include correspondence between Winifred and Hitler. Katharina threatened legal action, as part of a campaign to lead Bayreuth to greater openness concerning its role during the Third Reich.

on stage – whilst Wagner himself is hidden behind Parsifal's childhood wall – that politics be banished from the Green Hill. It was not the least astonishing aspect of this production and its history that Wolfgang, still at the helm of the Festival for the first staging, had not vetoed it. He was always, however, whatever we might think of the rest of his behaviour, a friend to directors, as so far has proved his heiress, Katharina, too. The post-war period is initially one of devastation, and improves little, if at all, whatever the mendacious ideology of the *Wirtschaftswunder*. Perhaps the point of ultimate hope comes when a star briefly appears in the sky, wonderfully touching, though what does it signify? The coming of a (false) messiah? A simple, childlike pleasure? Nothing that can be put into words? It certainly rings truer than the gaudy coloured lights that seem to signal Parsifal's descent into the realm of the (lifestyle?) guru. If anything, politics seem to stand still more starkly at the heart of the final scene. Parsifal is Lohengrin's father, though the extent to which that is a red herring may be debated. Here, however, the problematical nature of charismatic leadership seems to follow on closely, especially from Hans Neuenfels's Bayreuth production, as well as from Wagner's precedent in the character and portrayal of Siegfried.[14] It is noteworthy that Parsifal is not one of the trio we view at the end, presumably hastening us to an uncertain future; instead, we find ourselves in the hands of Gurnemanz, Kundry – no, she does not expire – and a young boy. Or is he Parsifal, and has the whole drama been a dream, or in the case of its German historical setting, the ultimate nightmare? There is certainly no solace to be gained from the despicable bickering politicians of the Bundestag, the Federal Republic's flag draping Titurel's coffin, yet Parsifal seems to have offered at best a dead-end, maybe even a touch of snake oil. Amfortas, like Siegfried, seems to have gained in dignity through death. Nihilism, as Nietzsche would doubtless have had it, or Wagner's lifelong anarchism?

Musical performances were more mixed in quality, though Roth's Amfortas continued to grow in strength. Kwangchul Youn exhibited a stronger musico-dramatic presence than previously, and an intriguingly ambiguous one at that. Who is this narrator, and is he to be trusted? Susan Maclean was perhaps a little too wild on the vocal side. It could hardly be said that her Kundry was beautiful of voice, and a little more refulgence would not at times have gone amiss, but there could be no doubting the dramatic commitment of her portrayal. Thomas Jesatko's Klingsor was by now perhaps leaning a little too much towards camp: his first 'furchtbarer

---

[14] Neuenfels's *Lohengrin* is discussed in the next chapter.

Not' sounded a little too caricatured to chill. Again, however, this is very much a stage assumption that one is unlikely to forget. (Perhaps it is just that I have become too accustomed to it.) Burkhard Fritz's Parsifal may not have been the most profound account one will hear, but his tone was secure and possessed of considerable mellifluence. Smaller parts were cast from strength: not only Diógenes Randes's unearthly Titurel but even the knights and squires shone. Choral singing, under the direction of Eberhard Friedrich, was as excellent as we have come to expect, but that achievement should never be overlooked.

The only significant drawback related to Philippe Jordan's conducting. I have heard much worse in Wagner, but this seemed a work-in-progress, particularly when considered in contrast to Daniele Gatti's work in previous years. Jordan lacked a sense of ritual, crucial to the first and third acts. That is not a matter of speed, but of steadiness, of communicating the inner pulse. Jordan seemed less an equal partner to Herheim, as Gatti certainly had done, than provider of a sound-track (ironically, given his father's appearance on Hans-Jürgen Syberberg's film, surely in many respects an honoured forerunner to this production, and in its gender politics still more adventurous[15]). There was some interesting highlighting of woodwind lines, though brass, especially during the opening Prelude, could occasionally be a little shaky. In general, though, the orchestral playing itself was superb. The interpretation seemed, however, as though it needed time and experience to settle. For instance, intriguingly Karajan-like steely moments seemed to bear little relation to the rest of what we heard. And yet, perhaps one message of this increasingly unsettling staging is that the search for perfection is not only chimerical but catastrophic.

V

What, then, might one say about those accounts taken together? Certainly Herheim's production – and, given the number of people involved, that remains a shorthand – covers something of a similar track to this book. It began – and I think it now better to invoke the past rather than present tense – with *Parsifal*, Wagner 'after Wagner', and proceeded to tell a history that led to somewhere near the present day, even turning a mirror upon the audience at one point, a moment of considerably greater theatrical

---

[15] Syberberg's 1982 film, less a production of *Parsifal* than an exploratory film that includes and expands upon Wagner's drama, has Armin Jordan, Philippe's father, both as conductor and as the actor playing the role of Amfortas. It is available on DVD: Image Entertainment 6305131112.

power than mere retelling might suggest. In metatheatrical terms, we are likely to think of Hans Neuenfels's celebrated use of an on-stage chorus to mirror the audience in his 1981 Frankfurt *Aida*.[16] Wagner's original conception of Bayreuth as a true amphitheatre, in which the audience (revolutionary or even post-revolutionary) might see itself as well as or as part of the drama, was thus intriguingly reinstated. The alleged repeated consecration of Bayreuth – in Ryan Minor's words, 'a model of administered spectatorship which brooks no opposition' – broke down or was shattered.[17] As mirrors are wont to do, one might say. The very thing brooked here was opposition, arguably truer to Wagner's revolutionary intention than Bayreuth itself had ever been. In our particular history, we might even go so far as to say that Neuenfels's Verdi and Herheim's Wagner both found themselves transformed in the historical light of Nono's use of loudspeakers, dissolving formal boundaries between chorus and audience – though of course many works, let alone productions, had previously done something similar. Bach's Passions may, again, prove just as interesting and fruitful a reference.

At any rate, the audience was not simply accused, deservedly or otherwise, but also reminded that it played a part in a drama that remained unfinished, whatever Wagner's Hegelian aspirations towards totality. It was reminded that it must interpret, shape, even write the history suggested. Far from having reached an 'end of history', we might all have become historians.[18] Such a position stands superficially close, perhaps, to post-modernism. However, given the persistence of the work concept, it is ultimately more strongly grounded in some form of object, some form of reality, than critics of history, the musical work, and the connections between them, might wish.[19] Wagner, though he might sometimes have come close to positing a false immediacy of audience response, was no proponent of art as non-reflective, non-reflexive entertainment – purveyor of the diversions opponents of interpretative stage direction more often

[16] See Clemens Risi, 'Shedding Light on the Audience: Hans Neuenfels and Peter Konwitschny Stage Verdi (and Verdians)', in *Cambridge Opera Journal*, 14 (2002), 201–10.

[17] Ryan Minor, 'Wagner's Last Chorus: Consecrating Space and Spectatorship in *Parsifal*', in *Cambridge Opera Journal*, 17 (2005), 36.

[18] See Francis Fukuyama, *The End of History and the Last Man* (Free Press: New York, 1992), and the impressive rejoinder from Jacques Derrida, *Spectres de Marx: l'état de la dette, le travail du deuil et la nouvelle Internationale* (Galilée: Paris, 1993).

[19] Cf. Richard J. Evans, *In Defence of History* (Granta: London, 1997); Carl Dahlhaus, *Foundations of Music History*, tr. J. B. Robinson (Cambridge University Press: Cambridge, 1993); Lydia Goehr, *The Imaginary Museum of Musical Works: An Essay in the Philosophy of Music* (Clarendon: Oxford, 1992).

than not wish to see enacted. 'Our theatrical public', he complained in *Opera and Drama*, 'has no *need* for the artwork; it desires *diversion* from the stage, ... well-crafted [*künstlich*] *details*, rather than the necessity of artistic [*künstlerisch*] *unity and coherence*.'[20] Miniaturism, the inability to construct a greater whole, which can be – and, in his *Essay on Conducting*, was – extended to musical as well as stage performance, is the enemy here; the attempt, even if forlorn, to achieve some form of unity of vision remains the modernistic goal.[21] Schoenberg would vigorously have nodded assent; so would Nono. Indeed, it is perhaps only Strauss who would have waved aside the question – though without necessarily waiving it.

Let us keep our sights upon Herheim for the moment, though. The matter of conducting is not irrelevant here, for whereas some of the matters of individual vocal performance mentioned in the above reviews may only be of ephemeral interest, if that, the question of coherence between 'music' and 'drama' is not. It may be of interest to read that Singer A had a less intrusive vibrato than Singer B, and if what Singer A has to offer has more of an interpretative rather than merely canary-fancying implication, then it will certainly hold at least potential for hermeneutical understanding in a fashion similar to Musicologist C's observations. More important, though, for our purposes is the way in which, at least under Daniele Gatti, one could experience the coming together of the 'work', straining towards that unity which in some sense must be possessed for the 'work concept' to retain meaning. A history largely untold in this production, and indeed this book, is of more specifically *musical* interpretation, from Hermann Levi, via Karl Muck, Siegfried Wagner, and Strauss – in 1933, immediately following the Nazi seizure of power – to Knappertsbusch, Boulez, and Gatti. Gatti's reading proved controversial; indeed, some writers dismissed it out of hand. (Much the same had happened to Boulez.) A writer in the *Frankfurter Allgemeine Zeitung* on the first revival in 2009, described the conducting as 'uninspired', with 'extremely unctuous [*sallbungsvoll*] tempi', though, in typically journalistic fashion, neglected to explain what he meant by these terms. In that respect, the reviewer concluded, there was 'no redemption.'[22]

Such, however, was not Herheim's understanding. One would hardly expect him to have been publicly critical of the conductor, though he had arguably initiated a very public controversy with Daniel Barenboim

[20] Richard Wagner, *Oper und Drama*, ed. Klaus Kropfinger (Reclam: Stuttgart, 1994), p. 388.
[21] Richard Wagner, *On Conducting*, tr. Edward Dannreuther (Dover: New York, 1989).
[22] Christian Wildhagen, *Frankfurter Allgemeine Zeitung*, Feuilleton, 5 August 2009, 'Und erlöse uns vom Erlösen.'

over *Lohengrin* in Berlin earlier that year. (Barenboim took exception to Herheim's staging of the first-act Prelude and Herheim took exception to Barenboim's absence from early rehearsals, calling him 'undisciplined'.[23]) Herheim's support for Gatti extended beyond mere courtesy. In a fascinating interview with Erling Gulbrandsen and Per-Erik Skramstad, Herheim averred that, whilst retaining some reservations concerning some choices of tempi, the experience of working together had been fruitful for both, making their collaboration far more than the sum of its parts:

> When I heard him conducting his first *Parsifal* in Rome (concert performance), I was somewhat surprised and startled: he was even slower than Toscanini – the first act alone lasted for well over two hours. Daniele was equally suspicious of my ideas, and for a while I was afraid that our different approaches wouldn't be productive and that the collaboration wouldn't work. But during the rehearsals in Bayreuth, we immediately began to communicate. Daniele saw that I felt the musical gestures totally intuitively, and that my direction corresponded with his interpretation of the score. And during the rehearsal process, I learned to understand his tempo choices and musical perspectives much better. Our collaboration turned out to be very productive, creative and we have great respect for each other.[24]

Herheim, it might usefully be added, began his career as a cellist, and offered a more unusual example than one might expect, of a director who can read the score, which he most certainly did. The issue of staging the Prelude to the first act was resolved more amicably, more fruitfully, than it would be with Barenboim in *Lohengrin*. Initially, Gatti had been sceptical, concerned that the audience might be distracted from the music. But Herheim made the excellent point in the same interview that that would suggest that, once the curtain rose, the audience need no longer concern itself with the music, continuing, 'I'm not saying that in principle the Prelude should always be staged. But if you have good reasons to portray the music in the prelude, it's just the way that it's done that you can argue against. Gatti acknowledged this and was excited about the symbiosis the staging entered into with the music.'[25] That, in a sense, restated the *echt*-Wagnerian dialectic of music drama, a more fruitful and indeed more correct understanding of the *Gesamtkunstwerk* than if one treated

[23] Manuel Brug, in *Die Welt*, 3 April 2009, 'Regisseur Herheim nennt Barenboim "disziplinlos"'.

[24] Erling E. Gulbrandsen and Per-Erik Skramstad, 'Stefan Herheim on working with Daniele Gatti, the choice of tempi and the staging of preludes', tr. Jonathan Scott-Kiddie, <http://www.wagneropera.net/Interviews/Stefan-Herheim-Gatti-Preludes.htm> (accessed 17 October 2012).

[25] Ibid.

it as mere agglomeration. The various elements – Wagner, we should remember, took great pains to stress their initial, Hegelian unity in the ancient world – gain in intensity by their interaction with one another.[26] Greater emphasis upon the staging heightened rather than lessened the effect of the orchestra, and so on.

Crucially, that enabled the emergence of an idea of the score as redeemer, *contra* the review from the *Frankfurter Allegemeine Zeitung* cited above. It was subtle, rather than thrust in one's face, unlike the undoubtedly provocative Nazi imagery of the second act. But for that reason, Herheim's candidate for an answer to Wagner's riddle of 'Redemption to the Redeemer' emerged all the more convincingly. Again, that was a possibility rather than a definitive 'solution' – but successful dramas, like successful performances, do not trade in the latter. The tale of German history, of *Parsifal* as a work throughout that history, was thereby seen and heard as requiring and receiving some form of transcendental, or at least beneficial, intervention, not so much that 'grace' discussed in the chapter on *Parsifal*, but something more immanent, arising from within, the attempted negation of the litany of negative dialectics to which history and work have been subjected. There was certainly no false mediated unity in which to rejoice or rather to wallow. However, the very possibility of hearing references such as those, so ably highlighted by Gatti, to the Second Viennese School – as much part of the work's reception as tales of performance under Furtwängler or Karajan, or indeed of staging under Berghaus or Herheim – dialectically questioned the closed nature of the musi-co-dramatic and in that very act of destabilisation granted the work new life. New life, be it noted, not a new work: this is still *Parsifal*, just as Herheim III in my typology is not a different work from Herheim I. History is not denied but rather incorporated and indeed written; it works its corrosive yet elucidating wonders.

For it is now worth returning to the question of the musical work – and to extending that question to consideration of the status of the staging of a musical drama. I mean that not so much in an ontological sense, for, as Lydia Goehr's work has shown, that variety of analytical philosophy has little light to shed here, but rather in terms of what its questioning might suggest both about itself and about the 'work itself'. As has been suggested above, the difficult yet necessary task – difficult and necessary

---

[26] See, e.g., Mark Berry, *Treacherous Bonds and Laughing Fire: Politics and Religion in Wagner's 'Ring'* (Ashgate: Aldershot and Burlington, VT, 2006), pp. 43–7.

in terms of both understanding and artistic vitality – of incorporating a stronger sense of historical purpose into work concepts will be assisted not by simply imposing something alien upon either. That has no more to do with history than it does with revealing performance. The caricature, which in certain cases has a good deal of truth to it, of modern *Regietheater*, in which, for the sake of argument, Monsalvat is arbitrarily relocated to a multi-storey car-park in Stevenage, and references to the automobile industry and 'pay and display' signs become determining features, bears no relation to the exploration of music, words, reception, and so much more offered by Herheim and other probing directors. Interestingly, Peter Konwitschny has, for very similar reasons, avowedly dissociated himself from the *Regietheater* label, not because it goes too far, but because, surface impressions apart, it really does not go far enough:

> I do not consider myself a representative of the *Regietheater*. Often, these directors present one single idea, such as for example staging *Rigoletto* in an empty swimming pool or in a slaughterhouse. These ideas are not consequentially followed through and explored, and in most cases, the singers stand next to each other on stage just as unconnected as in conventional productions.
>
> My stagings, on the other hand, aim to return to the roots: to get to the core of the pieces, through the jungle of interpretative traditions, which in most cases, have distorted the pieces. The accusation that this is 'too intellectual for the average viewer' is absurd and exposes the enemies of such theatre as opposing new insights.[27]

Indeed, the anti-intellectualism of such attacks *as such*, as opposed to perfectly justified criticisms of particular productions, reveals itself to be a strange sort of intellectual condescension. No one reading Hegel or listening to Wagner for the first time expects to 'understand' everything; nor does he mind when he 'fails' to do so. Were there a final, achievable, destination, we should then give up, having 'mastered' *Parsifal* or the *Phenomenology of Spirit*, and then move on to something else. Re-en-actment of the sort envisaged by the decriers of interpretation makes no more sense here than it does in performance; ritual, as we have seen, is in *Parsifal* and through *Parsifal* dialectically challenged from within as well as from without.

[27] Per-Erik Skramstad, Interview with Peter Konwitschny, 'I do not consider myself as a representative of the *Regietheater*,' <http://www.wagneropera.net/Interviews/Peter-Konwitschny-Interview-2009.htm> (accessed 22 October 2012). On Konwitschny, see also Frank Kämpfer (ed.), *Sehnsucht nach unentfremdeter Produktion. Der Regisseur Peter Konwitschny. Ein Materialbuch* (Zentrum für Theaterdokumentation und -information: Berlin, 1992).

Keith Warner, in the vision cited at the beginning of this chapter, clearly wishes to wrest control from the conductor, perhaps even the composer, in favour of the stage director. The elision or combination of roles in Wagner's own case blurs the boundaries, but in many other cases the shift is clearer. One can argue about whether the pendulum has swung too far, though it becomes difficult to do so without lapsing into cliché. More important remains the effort not to fall into lazy re-enactment, to pander to those Nietzsche called 'Wagnerians', the enemy not only of Wagner but of artistic vitality more generally considered: 'Behold those youths – benumbed [*erstarrt*], wan, breathless! They are Wagnerians: they understand nothing of music, – and nevertheless Wagner comes to rule over them.'[28] The question of youth may be less apposite today; the problem, the 'case', of benumbment remains.

That speaks neither of desire nor intent to throw intention out of the window. The author, the composer, the director, even the musicologist: none of them is dead, nor need any of them be. By the same token, however, intention is far from all. Those insisting upon 'respecting the composer's intentions', rarely if ever mean that; they speak of *Werktreue*, yet wish for performances, and even works, to remain truer to their own personal inclinations than to themselves, a point similar to that which Richard Taruskin has made on several occasions.[29] Perhaps, then, the experience of living with works in performance, including staging, as well as in written text, will prove one way – if certainly not the only way – of honouring the richness, as continually revealed in history, of musico-dramatic works, such as *Parsifal* and 'Herheim's *Parsifal*'.

VI

To conclude, then, *Parsifal* remains as 'different' from most products of the nineteenth-century opera house as Wagner and many of his successors have believed it to be. Wagner's various attempts to avoid the pejorative – to him – 'opera' as a description of his later works may nowadays elicit as much scepticism as blind adoration, though in simply calling *Tristan und Isolde*

[28] Friedrich Nietzsche, 'Der Fall Wagner', in *Sämtliche Werke: Kritische Studienausgabe*, ed. Giorgio Colli and Mazzino Montinari, 15 vols (De Gruyter: Berlin and New York, 1967–88), vol. 6, §8, p. 29.

[29] Richard Taruskin, *Text and Act: Essays on Music and Performance* (Oxford University Press: Oxford, 1995). Where Taruskin is more likely to go astray is when he lets this central point become distorted by his antipathy towards European modernism, on which see, e.g., Mark Berry, 'Romantic Modernism: Bach, Furtwängler, and Adorno', in *New German Critique*, 104, vol. 35, no. 2 (Spring/Summer 2008), 71–102.

'drama' (*Handlung*), he certainly captured a quality of that singular work. However, it would take a Wagnerian of extreme, unhealthy devotion not to raise at least a hint of a smile at the cumbersome *Bühnenweihfestspiel* employed for *Parsifal*. And what that term might mean has had all manner of consequences for the work's reception, even for the possibility of staging it at all, given the determination of Cosima and other Bayreuth loyalists that it remain confined to the stage it had allegedly consecrated. The surrounding aura of sanctity may seem to many repellent ('an unseemly and sacrilegious conception of art as religion and the theatre as a temple' – Stravinsky), ridiculous (Debussy, albeit continuing to honour the score alone as 'one of the loveliest monuments of sound ever raised to the serene glory of music'), or both (Nietzsche, though the greater part of his abuse would be *a priori*).[30] Moreover, the claim that *Parsifal* is in any meaningful sense a 'Christian work' as opposed to a work that treats with, amongst other things, Christianity, would find few takers today; even if the end of the first act were an invitation to receive Holy Communion, the Grail Knights' words – 'Partake of the bread, valiantly transform it into corporal strength and power' – would suggest that communion to pertain to a church or theology whose heterodoxy extended beyond the merely gnostic. That said, this tale of a 'pure fool', so ignorant that he knows not where he has come from, nor even his name, who, through Grace rather than through deeds, enlightened through compassion, rejuvenates a dying community, remains quite different from the operatic essays of any of Wagner's contemporaries and almost any of his successors. (Schoenberg may be an exception.) *Parsifal* resists assimilation to the opera house; it seems and is out of place amongst champagne, canapés, and diva-worshippers.

The signal strength of Herheim's production was that it engaged with these problems: with fraught associations, both with Bayreuth – which, for better and for worse, is also quite *different* from anywhere else – and with broader themes of German history, which the work has gathered from at least the time of its 1882 premiere. What David J. Levin analysed as the operatic conservative's – in this case, James Levine's – dread of the 'hectic stage', of 'discursive overload', turned out actually to harness such overload to fidelity in a sense all manner of opera-goers could and eventually did appreciate.[31] Indeed, as Carl Dahlhaus once wrote, 'It is

[30] Igor Stravinsky, *An Autobiography* (Simon & Schuster: New York, 1956), p. 59; Claude Debussy, 'Monsieur Croche the Dilettante Hater,' tr. B. N. Langdon Davies, in *Three Classics in the Aesthetic of Music* (Dover: New York, 1962), pp. 46–9.
[31] David J. Levin, 'Reading a Staging/Staging a Reading,' in *Cambridge Opera Journal*, 9 (1997), 57.

precisely in order to radicalise conflicts – so that "resolutions" are ruled out – that dramas are written; if not, they would be treatises.'[32] It is for precisely the same reason that we perform rather than re-enact, that we study as well as perform, that we think rather than wallow, that history enlivens rather than deadens. History, musical or otherwise, is something we write as well as make, something we think, we imagine, we perform, as well as learn; it lives on the stage as much as in the archives. For although criticism of an order Marx allotted to philosophy in an 1843 letter to Arnold Ruge – 'the *unrestrained criticism of everything established*, unrestrained not only in not fearing its own results, but even less of a conflict with whatever powers may be' – is not the only purpose of art, it remains an especially important purpose, nowhere more so than in such highly controversial 'museum' works such as Wagner's.[33]

The idea, then, of an 'artwork of the future' remains in many respects as burningly relevant as it had during the years of Wagner's Zurich exile, that is long before he started work seriously on *Parsifal* itself. An artwork that engages critically with the concerns of humanity and yet strenuously declares the (transcendental?) value of art as extending beyond mere pamphleteering, and which in form and content dramatises, problematises that tension is not simply saying something about art and its reception. It is pointing us to the deleterious consequences, as Wagner and Marx, both writing and thinking in the aftermath not only of Hegel but also of Schiller, recognised, of forced division of labour and the lack of volition experienced by the greater part of humanity in both 'work' and 'leisure'. As the tentacles of the Adornian Culture Industry have extended further, deeper, than ever, the 'haven' of an older Bayreuth, seat of the *Bühnenweihfestspiel*, as 'temple of art' may even find itself dialectically incorporated, *aufgehoben*, into the challenge of a Bayreuth not only of today but also of the future. As Ludwig Hevesi's words, inscribed upon the Vienna Secession Building, have it, 'To every age its art, to art its freedom'.[34] That need not, indeed cannot, be accomplished by all-too-easy evasion, by distancing oneself from the musical works. Herheim's dramaturgy enabled the music to emerge as its own redeemer: not in a discredited sense of 'absolute music', with the reactionary, neo-Romantic connotations that has acquired, but in a

---

[32] Carl Dahlhaus, *Ludwig van Beethoven: Approaches to his Music*, tr. Mary Whittall (Oxford University Press: Oxford, 1991), p. 13.

[33] Karl Marx, 'Letter to Ruge' (September 1843), tr. Lawrence S. Stepelevich, in Lawrence S. Stepelevich (ed.), *The Young Hegelians: An Anthology* (Cambridge University Press: Cambridge, 1983), pp. 307–8.

[34] 'Der Zeit ihre Kunst, der Kunst ihre Freiheit'.

critical sense more suited to our time, which will doubtless thereafter be subject to criticism. The immanent theology of *Parsifal* thereby renewed and reinvigorated itself.

CHAPTER 8

Staging *Lohengrin*, or Not

I

Opera-goers, at least those interested in some form of critical engagement with work and genre, have become wearily accustomed to so much of their 'experience' in the opera house standing almost diametrically opposed to their understanding and appreciation of the 'art'. It is relatively uncontroversial to say that, whatever the realities of, say, nineteenth-century *grand opéra* might have been, the worlds of corporate entertainment, advertising, fashion, and conspicuous consumption sit uneasily with Wagner, Schoenberg, Nono, *et al.*[1] Apparently without irony, the 2012 Royal Opera House programme for the *Ring* devoted its back cover to an advertisement for Barclays Wealth and Investment Management. 'Wealth. What's it to you? If wealth means being able to spend time enjoying more rarefied pursuits, we can help.'[2] To encounter such a description of *Das Rheingold* was jarring to say the least; the more apposite question might have been, 'what was "it" to Alberich?' Yet even Bayreuth has from the outset attracted and catered for audiences utterly inimical to the hopes of the creator of the artwork of the future, and even to the convenor of the gathered congregation of *Parsifal*.

Opera production, in the sense of staging, has to a certain extent, and especially in certain environments, offered opportunity for revenge, or at least for redress, although even Adorno, in an essay on *Bourgeois Opera*, was critical of the tendency towards excessive disenchantment. 'Some of the most authentic operas', amongst which he suggests *Der Freischütz*, *Die Zauberflöte*, and *Il trovatore*, have 'their true place', he writes, 'in the children's matinee and embarrass the adult, who imagines himself too sensible for them, simply because he no longer understands their pictorial language.' A child, attending a performance of *Der Freischütz*, who found 'the wolf's glen reduced to natural symbolism is right to feel

---

[1] For a different standpoint, see Nicholas Vazsonyi, *Richard Wagner: Self-Promotion and the Making of a Brand* (Cambridge University Press: Cambridge, 2010).
[2] Royal Opera House programme, *Der Ring des Nibelungen* (2012).

cheated out of the best part'.[3] Perhaps – though it seems as questionable to rule out effective use of such symbolism as to rule out effective, or indeed provocative, naturalism.

Maybe even the idea of redress is too strong, and we should adopt or adapt the admirably humane understanding of Berio, interviewed in 1980:

> my ideal public is one with many faces, all bringing different motivations to their encounter with the music. A public that is the very opposite of the one, say, that you used to find at Bayreuth, and that might take over again now that the Chereau [*sic*]-Boulez Ring Cycle has come and gone, or among the subscribers at any large opera house.[4]

At any rate, the turning of the tables may – and often does – find itself progressing no further than a tired call of *épater les bourgeois*. It is a counsel of despair really, since we seem to be exchanging Lenin's (alleged) 'the capitalists will sell us the rope with which we shall hang them', for their supplying the jokes with which we shall laugh at them: a move from *What is to be Done?* to *Arturo Ui*.[5]

Sometimes even the potential discomfort may prove enough, or at least preferable to the alternative. For, as Dallapiccola lamented in 1960:

> nowadays the performance of an opera is troublesome. If we were dealing with an audience of 'the people' – genuine people, I mean – the difficulties might be somewhat less serious. Instead, we have to contend with a certain wealthy middle class (the season-ticket holders!) Who regard the tenor's high C as just recompense for a trying day – several committee meetings in the morning, tea at five, cocktails at six-thirty – and the soprano's C as equivalent to the price of the ticket. The 'subscribers', as a rule, have no problems and don't wish to be bothered with problems. All they ask is that the evening be as carefree as possible. The administrators of our subsidised theatres [let alone their non-subsidised American counterparts] know their audience and are wary of new productions that require many rehearsals and promise uncertain receipts at the box office.[6]

3   Theodor Adorno, 'Bourgeois Opera,' tr. David J. Levin, in *Opera Through Other Eyes*, ed. David J. Levin (Stanford University Press: Stanford, 1993), pp. 26–7.
4   Luciano Berio, *Two Interviews*, with Rossana Dalmonte and Bálint András Varga, ed. and tr. David Osmond-Smith (Marion Boyars: New York and London, 1985), p. 25.
5   Scholarly opinion is divided on whether the words were actually Lenin's; some have attributed them to Stalin (though, impressionistically, the style does not seem quite right in that respect); some treat them simply as apocryphal. Vladimir Ilyich Lenin, *What is to be Done? Burning Questions of Our Movement*, revised edn (Progress Publishers: Moscow, 1964); Bertolt Brecht, *Der aufhaltsame Aufstieg des Arturo Ui* (Suhrkamp: Frankfurt, 1969).
6   Luigi Dallapiccola, 'Comments on Contemporary Opera,' in *Dallapiccola on Opera – Selected Writings of Luigi Dallapiccola: Volume One*, ed. and tr. Rudy Schackleford (Toccata Press: London, 1987), p. 105.

Such was not and is not always the case, yet we perhaps have a tendency to become too hopeful on the basis of the atypical. That said, to dispel, even to explode, such complacency, however understandable it may be in socio-economic terms, offers us a start. For one thing, the administrator's lament that 'our audience' will not like that becomes self-fulfilling; the audience will change, will broaden, if something more interesting, less pandering, is on offer. However, the search for something that lies beyond shock-value, a determination to interrogate the work, to compel at least part of the audience to think, is something rather more interesting, more productive than that.

II

The figure of La Roche in *Capriccio*, despite both the eighteenth-century setting and the precedent of and tribute to Max Reinhardt's work at the Salzburg Festival, may be seen, not unlike Wagner, to prefigure the greater importance of subsequent years ascribed to the stage director. There is perhaps an especial irony here, given La Roche's lack of sympathy for new-fangled Gluckian music drama and his nostalgia for what we might call an anticipatory conception of *bel canto*. Admittedly, La Roche is more of an impresario than most contemporary directors but that in itself reminds us that the issue of patronage, be it private, public, or state, is as vital as it was at the time of the Florentine Camerata. Clemens Krauss, when drafting the text of La Roche's great apologia for his vocation, put it thus in a letter to Strauss:

> [La Roche] should justify himself as the specialist of the theatre whose duties even embrace light music, but only where it is on an artistic level, *Singspiel*, or good comic operas and ballets ... [he] should nevertheless remain a sympathetic advocate for practical thinking in the theatre, which also supports great art out of its proceeds and so has made it possible for many a talent to come forward. His speech should finish comically and bombastically [yet affectionately, one might add], perhaps so that he blows his own trumpet and crowns himself with the halo of the art patron ... The director is the one whose mission it is from his own experience to chastise all that is bad in the theatre.[7]

Some of that remains recognisable today, yet the role of the director has clearly changed a great deal too. What has happened? A newish-found critical approach – although we should not exaggerate the novelty,

---

[7]   Quoted in Norman Del Mar, *Richard Strauss: A Commentary on his Life and Works*, 3 vols (Barrie and Rockliff: London, 1962–72), vol. 3, p. 223.

remembering the radicalism of, for instance, the Kroll Opera during the later years of Weimar Germany – is of great importance here, for better and for worse: better when taking the form of a 'critique' Adorno might have understood, worse when merely juvenile and/or uncomprehending. It is certainly not enough to justify the present by mocking the past; few things date so quickly as theatrical production styles, which observation presents an important question regarding the relationship between production and work.

For, when it comes to operatic performance, we tend to retain the 'work' concept in a very strong sense, especially when it comes to Romantic and post-Romantic works, far more so than in so-called 'straight theatre'. Handelian *opera seria* is far more likely to be cut than Wagnerian music drama, though – to many minds – pernicious 'traditional' cuts will sometimes still be made in *Tristan und Isolde*. In the latter case, however, the justification is most likely to be relief of stress upon singers' voices rather than dramatic necessity as in the case, say, of *Giulio Cesare in Egitto*. That said, there are voices, largely from without the 'traditional' opera world, who would like to disrupt the aura of the 'work' – and it is no bad thing that they should at least be heard. Frank Castorf, director of the Bayreuth *Ring* that opened in 2013, was keen to maintain his deconstructionist ways, derived from the traditions of spoken theatre, in staging Wagner. (He has served as director of the Berlin *Volksbühne* since 1992.) Castorf spoke provocatively, though not necessarily only out of a wish to shock, of wishing 'to edit Wagner together with something else', yet that proved a step too far for the Bayreuth management of Katharina Wagner and Eva Wagner-Pasquier as well as the conductor, Kyrill Petrenko.[8]

Likewise, Sebastian Baumgartner wanted to stage his Bayreuth *Tannhäuser* in 2011 without intervals and with additions of his own based upon designer Joop van Lieshour's 'obsessive Installation' as principal character (*Hauptrolle*). A compromise was reached on that occasion in that the work remained inviolate, the intervals and thus Wagner's division into acts remained, but the 'Installation' continued its work during the intervals. An irony seemingly unexplored was the very problematical nature of the work in the case of *Tannhäuser* itself. Its later, 'Paris', more strictly 'Vienna', version languishes unperformed at Bayreuth, the preference lying for what is more or less, though not quite, Wagner's

---

[8] Castorf is quoted in Anthony Tomassini, 'Adapting, Revising, Provoking', in *New York Times*, 9 March 2012. <http://www.nytimes.com/2012/03/11/arts/music/some-ground-rules-for-revising-operas-and-musicals.html?pagewanted=all&_r=0> (accessed 16 October 2012).

'Dresden' version.[9] What, however, of the undeniable truth that Wagner himself was dissatisfied with the work as it stood in any version, and shortly before his death declared to Cosima that he still owed the world a *Tannhäuser*?[10] Might one not at least consider the possibility that this is as uncompletable a work as *Moses und Aron* – and explore that thought in performance as well as writing?

The distinction that writers on the threshold of Romanticism such as Wilhelm von Humboldt and Johann Gottfried Herder drew between language and music as energetic arts, as activity (*energeia*), as opposed to supplying a product or work (*ergon*) remains worthy of consideration.[11] Yet the problem lies really in the either/or; part of the fascination of musical works, in our present case opera, and their lives in performance is of the complexity of relationship, the lack of fixity, between product and activity. Indeed, that helps enable works and performances not only to reflect, not only to comment upon, but to participate in history. An idealist or post-idealist – Hegel as much as Herder, Adorno as much as Marx – would maintain that it is only through such relationships that we can think about such matters, however those relationships may be construed, on whatever they may be based – be it language, the forces of production, relatively autonomous developments in musical technique, or most likely a complexity of relationships between them and others.

For instance, Carl Dahlhaus's *Plea for a Romantic Category*, that is, for the concept of the artwork, retains some force. As Dahlhaus wrote, originally in the 1969 *Neue Zeitschrift für Musik*, 'the idea that we are attempting to resurrect an element of Romanticism which is dead and buried misses the point. We have merely attempted to show that the category of the work of art, though it is undeniably of Romantic origin, continues to perform a function.'[12] Such functionalism is perhaps a little dubious; one might argue more strongly for the abiding presence,

[9] See, e.g., Mark Berry, 'Owing the World a *Tannhäuser*,' in Royal Opera House programme for *Tannhäuser*, December 2010, 22–6.

[10] *Cosima Wagner's Diaries*, ed. Martin Gregor-Dellin and Dietrich Mack, tr. Geoffry Skelton, 2 vols (Harcourt Brace Jovanovich: London, 1978–80), 23 January 1883, vol. 2, p. 996.

[11] See Vicki A. Spencer, *Herder's Political Thought: A Study on Language, Culture and Community* (University of Toronto Press: Toronto, 2012), p. 59; Carl Dahlhaus, 'Plea for a Romantic Category: The Concept of the Work of Art in the Newest Music,' in *Schoenberg and the New Music*, tr. Derrick Puffett and Alfred Clayton (Cambridge University Press: Cambridge, 1987), pp. 212–13.

[12] Ibid., p. 219; Dahlhaus, 'Plädoyer für eine romantische Kategorie – Der Begriff des Kunstwerks in der neuesten Musik,' in *Neue Zeitschrift für Musik*, 130 (1969), 18–22.

or better development, of such Romantic elements from a constantly adapting, even modernistic, standpoint. Dahlhaus's defence stands on shakier ground when he claims that, for the listener, 'an open, variable form seems to him to be a closed and established one because he is unable to relate the version that he is hearing at this moment to other alternatives which the performer could have chosen but did not choose'. Even when dealing with purely instrumental music, that is hardly the case; whether experiencing, say, the open forms of Boulez's Third Piano Sonata, itself of course remaining a work in progress, or objecting to a performance of the *Eroica* Symphony because it 'falls short' when mentally contrasted with Furtwängler, listeners seem perfectly capable of hearing alternatives and considering during performance some potential consequences of those alternatives. More fundamentally, however, the element of staging acts as a corrective to what Dahlhaus fears may be the 'regressive ... character' of his plea for the category of the work.[13]

We remain hesitant, then, about opening up the work concept, or at least about opening it up too far. The hesitation is not necessarily unreasonable; my point here is to suggest that it is well worth asking ourselves questions, not to demand that we disregard the concept. Moreover, that hesitation applies both to music and to words, though the issue of the latter is muddied somewhat with the controversial practice of translation. Yet many will gleefully act in more radical fashion when it comes to Wagner's oft-disregarded *Opera and Drama* concept of 'gesture' (*Gebärde*), which we may roughly align in modern terms with staging, or at least with acting.[14] The complexity of the relationship is thus fruitfully brought before our minds, indeed before our eyes and, to a lesser extent, our ears. When the dialogue between old and new, original and originary, itself becomes the stuff of the drama, as in Herheim's *Parsifal*, then the impact, even the historical truth, of the various components may be immeasurably strengthened.

Many other factors are involved too, of course, not least socio-economic matters, so integral to how one experiences the opera house and its audience, and the architectural. For instance, the alienating effect, intentional or otherwise, of experiencing Christoph Marthaler's *Katya Kabanova* at Paris's Palais Garnier, as I did in 2011, must surely have presented differences in kind from its earlier appearances at the modernist amphitheatre of the Opéra Bastille, where the greater part of the

---

[13] Dahlhaus, 'On the Decline of the Concept of the Musical Work,' p. 219.

[14] Richard Wagner, *Oper und Drama*, ed. Klaus Kropfinger, 2nd edn (Reclam: Stuttgart, 1994), p. 250.

performances given by the Opéra national de Paris now take place. At any rate, there was a stark contrast between the *mise-en-scène* and the Garnier's preposterously gilded extravagance. (Music almost seems beside the point in this monument to the style of Napoleon III and, indeed, patrons' access to comely ballerinas was often a more pressing concern at the time of construction.) A drab post-war Eastern European apartment block, as witnessed by Anna Viebrock's claustrophobic set designs, would doubtless anywhere have helped Marthaler's presentation of a closed, hypocritical moral world, choral hymn singing – in, be it noted, an addition to the text – emanating and visible from one of the flats above. Yet the sense was undeniably heightened by the venue: a dialogue between different conceptions of opera, the Garnier's selection of composers for its façade offering less than wholehearted assent to the Wagnerian artwork of the future: Rossini, Auber, Beethoven, Mozart, Spontini, Meyerbeer, and Halévy. That dialogue is not necessarily concluded, despite Marc Chagall's more inclusive ceiling, in which not only Wagner but even Stravinsky, though not Schoenberg, put in appearances. The confrontation remains pretty much unavoidable in context, even were one not to climb the celebrated staircase.

Moreover, even to participate in such dialogue is in a sense to refuse to accept the modern neo-liberal claim, a strange elision of the ontological, the epistemological, and the political, the strangeness and slipperiness at least in part witnesses to a strategy of mystification, that things need necessarily be as they are. Intelligent, provocative directors' theatre, just like any other form of intelligent, provocative performance, and indeed just like any variety of intelligent, provocative enquiry, musicological, historical or otherwise, can thus by its very nature never fail to be political.

'Wagnerians', as we have seen Nietzsche disdainfully call them, and others who wish to retreat into an illusory realm of entertainment, may not all accept that, but by the same token, some of them will if and when enthralled or at least intrigued by performance or enquiry. *Epater les bourgeois* is an understandable temptation, and in the face of the outright intimidation of booing and so forth may become inevitable, but it is unlikely in itself to persuade. Rather like Wagner himself, especially in *Parsifal* – or indeed Henze in Salzburg for *The Bassarids* – we become trapped somewhere between an open, socialist conception of theatre and the preaching to the converted of a gathered avant-gardist congregation.

There is, however, a sense in which the work concept now comes to the rescue. For all our justifiable concerns with respect to literalism, to becoming bogged down in an unchanging conception of a work that never really was, there is a parallel danger from a chaos without fixity. Unless we wish art to be confined to a series of allegedly spontaneous 'happenings' –Stockhausen's intuitive music perhaps, though no one comes to such performance with a *tabula rasa* – then we require something substantive and substantial upon which to ground ourselves. Let us briefly consider an alternative. The Maoist Cornelius Cardew – Mao was subsequently renounced for Enver Hoxha and ultimately for Stalin – would claim that only in free improvisation might music truly serve the revolutionary struggle.[15] Cardew founded the notorious Scratch Orchestra and his works included the nine-hour-long, neo-Confucian *The Great Learning*. Stockhausen, his former friend and indeed mentor, served imperialism, according to a BBC talk and subsequent article in *The Listener*. 'Elitist' music, including earlier works by Cardew himself, was tainted beyond redemption by the part they played in 'the cultural superstructure of the largest-scale system of human oppression and exploitation the world has ever known'.[16] The poverty of the results, whatever the sincerity of the aspirations, alas spoke for itself in Cardew's later music.

Performance is certainly not the only aspect of musico-dramatic life; it barely makes any sense without the existence of works and, at a more sophisticated level, the study thereof. A production of, say, *Don Giovanni* is far more likely to have something to say if those concerned – and that includes the audience as much as the performers – have done their home-work. Moreover, different people have different things to offer here: for a composer such as Berio, the best way to analyse a work was to rework the material into a new composition: 'The most profitable commentary on a symphony or an opera has always been another symphony or another opera.'[17] For someone else, a way forward might be to sing, to act, to criticise, to engage actively from the furthest recesses of the amphitheatre. Some may even try to bridge the gaps: for instance, Berio in his meta-opera, *La vera storia*. Whatever the approach or approaches adopted, they will stand in opposition to the false consciousness of false immediacy.

---

[15] On Cardew, see John Tilbury's compendious *Cornelius Cardew: A Life Unfinished* (Copula: Essex, 2008).

[16] Cornelius Cardew, 'Stockhausen Serves Imperialism,' in *Stockhausen Serves Imperialism, and Other Articles* (Latimer New Dimensions: London, 1974), p. 46.

[17] Nina Horvath, 'The "Theatre of the Ear": Analyzing Berio's Musical Documentary *A-Ronne*,' in *Musical Explorations*, 10 (2009), 73; Berio, *Two Interviews*, p. 107.

III

There remains a mixed economy in most opera houses, and certainly across the operatic world as a whole. Even houses that might be excoriated in roughly equal measure as purveyors of 'mindless traditionalism' or 'Eurotrash' will tend in practice to offer a broader range of directorial standpoints and quality than ideologues of any stripe would often admit, though it would admittedly be difficult to imagine productions that would be at home at both the New York Metropolitan Opera and the Komische Oper, Berlin. Performances that attempt to engage with the work – including the music – at a critical level are our principal concern here, having set the scene with Stefan Herheim's *Parsifal*.

Herheim's 2009 production of *Lohengrin* for the Berlin State Opera seems a good place to start, looking back to the previous chapter and forward to the work of other directors. (Again, it should be stressed that speaking of directors is in many respects shorthand for a larger group of contributors to a production, including dramaturges, designers, conductors, singers, technicians, Intendants willing to support a production, and many others too, not least – ideally – a critical audience.) It has attracted far less attention than the Bayreuth *Parsifal*, not least since the troubles discussed in the previous chapter meant that it has never been revived, and, barring an unlikely *rapprochement* between conductor and director, presumably never will be. Like that *Parsifal*, it was a multi-layered production, which would doubtless have revealed further secrets upon further acquaintance. Even upon a single viewing, an array of intricately interconnected ideas revealed themselves, whilst still – crucially – providing theatrical excitement, coherence, and engagement with the work, not least in its musical form.

The controversial staged Prelude to the first act showed Wagner both as puppet and puppeteer, an ambiguity to be revisited upon many of the characters. Apparently assumed into heaven, a similar fate – albeit with an all-important distinction – would be visited upon Lohengrin at the work's conclusion. Wagner's presence was seen on stage throughout the work, sometimes in multiple guises, both as puppets and as chorus members – frockcoat, signature *altdeutsch* cap, and all – and sometimes melding with other members of the depicted *Volk*, both changing them and being changed by them. It was difficult not to think forward to Hans Sachs's ambiguous, dialectical relationship to the crowd in *Die Meistersinger* – and thus, inevitably, to the problems of charismatic leadership and *Volksgemeinschaft* never far away in any consideration of modern German, indeed European, history. Herheim's treatment of the chorus – and the ability of the Staatsoper Chorus to rise to his apparent intentions – proved thought-provoking throughout. What might in lesser hands have degenerated into stock responses showed instead a *Volk* dangerously swayed by the ministrations of a charismatic leader and dangerous in its responses thereto. The basis of Lohengrin's power, like that of Parsifal, is charisma alone, though it is arguably more sinister here: Parsifal must discover who he is, whereas Lohengrin – it is probably better to leave to one side the red herring of Parsifal as his father – insists that none may know who he is. As members of the crowd lost their individuality, illustrated by their loss of individual modern dress, they found themselves – or rather we found them – subsumed into a bland yet fearsome force of social repression, personified by the 'Protector' of Brabant.

The scene thus shifted to an impossible, Magritte-styled Eden, followed by a make-believe world of horned helmets and other neo-mediævalisms: incorporating yet challenging the work's history, the German catastrophe again unmistakeably present. Heike Scheele's Brabantian sets and Gesine Völlm's costumes thus offered a riposte to those who claim to speak for a 'tradition' that never really was – and certainly is not now. As Dallapiccola, introducing his 1942 edition of Monteverdi's *Il ritorno d'Ulisse in patria*, put it:

> 'Tradition . . .' someone will whisper. Ferruccio Busoni – much quoted but never enough – . . . defined tradition as 'a plaster mask taken from life which, in the course of many years, and after passing through the hands of innumerable artists, leaves its resemblance to the original largely a matter of imagination.' Even those who cannot fully accept this definition would admit that tradition is an internal matter and, therefore, very difficult to define.[18]

Very difficult and doubtless futile. Lohengrin, when he arrived, apparently straight from Neuschwanstein, was the menacingly kitsch instrument of our transportation from an opera house in modern Berlin – much of Herheim's initial attention hinted at contemporary social and cultural local politics, the Herald even appearing at first as the bear of Berlin – to a world of fantasy. In that world, *Gleichschaltung* was the name of the game, just as it had been once before under another seductive leader with nothing but emptiness for a core. We could read what we wanted into him and that was part of the problem. Like his creator, Wagner, he would

---

[18] Dallapiccola, 'Monteverdi's *Il ritorno di Ulisse in Patria*: Notes on a Practical Edition,' in *Dallapiccola on Opera*, p. 231. The Busoni quotation comes from 'Sketch of a New Esthetic of Music,' in *Three Classics in the Aesthetic of Music* (Dover: New York, 1962), p. 77 n. 1.

ultimately be assumed heavenwards, but then, to seal the tragedy, come crashing back down to earth. Feuerbach, perhaps, remained.

At the heart of that tragedy, yet curiously and intriguingly decentred, stood Klaus Florian Vogt's Lohengrin, strength and siren beauty of tone brought together in an uncanny marriage of heroic and lyric tenor. There was something terrifying about the apparently deliberate emptiness of his stage delivery, which, when married to such seductive means, brought us closer than many would doubtless have liked to a profoundly serious confrontation both with ourselves and with our historical demons. Likewise, Barenboim elicited not only a golden (Lohengrin-like?) string tone but a frightening vision of madness in the brass fanfares of the third act, in which orchestra, conductor, and director worked together, even despite themselves, to the terrors of fascistic militarism, especially that with a benign face.[19]

Throughout, exterior manifestations of theatrical craft reminded the audience of instrumentalisation at work. And at the end, we saw Wagner's own celebrated words, spoken following his dissatisfaction with the first Bayreuth Festival and yet always disregarded by his would-be 'protectors' – 'Protectors'? – 'Kinder, macht neues!' After the first Bayreuth Festival, the composer had urged his followers to do it quite differently the next time. But then, what did he know? In this production, he found himself used and abused at least as much by the community here as the other way round. Was it the visible theatrical apparatus that let the hero and us down, or did it let us in on a secret? Quite rightly, there were no easy answers. For, as Adorno wisely noted in his 1963 lecture on Wagner, 'If it is true about Wagner [staging] that no matter what one does, it is wrong, the thing that is still most likely to help is to force what is false, flawed, antinomical out into the open, rather than glossing over it and generating a kind of harmony to which the most profound element in Wagner is antithetical.'[20]

---

[19] 'Fascistic' is problematical here, given the controversial nature of the question as to the extent to which National Socialism should be considered to be part of a more general European, even worldwide, movement. However, I did not wish to restrict the implications to Germany. 'Totalitarian' would have been another possibility, but that would perhaps have begged still more questions, given the question of 'equivalence' or otherwise between National Socialism and Stalinism, let alone the Popperian thesis of the 'open society' and its enemies. (See, e.g., Jacob Leib Talmon, *The Origins of Totalitarian Democracy* (Secker and Warburg: London, 1952); Karl Popper, *The Open Society and its Enemies*, 2 vols (Routledge: London, 1945).) Still, as I have tried to argue, there are worse things than the begging of questions.

[20] 'Wagner's Relevance for Today', tr. Susan H. Gillespie, in *Essays on Music*, ed. Richard Leppert (University of California Press: Berkeley, Los Angeles, and London, 2002), p. 600.

IV

Nor were there easy answers in another production, also mentioned earlier, by Hans Neuenfels for Bayreuth.[21] It has become celebrated and/ or notorious for its rats, but the important thing remains what they might mean or at least imply. Neuenfels is a celebrated figure from an earlier generation of so-called *Regietheater*, whether in spoken or musical drama. Though many visual motifs from his productions have proved highly contentious when first seen – his 1980 *Aida* for Frankfurt, resolutely contemporary in setting, with the slave girl a modern cleaner, or a highly eroticised, narcoticised *Così fan tutte* for the 2000 Salzburg Festival – a few years subsequently they will often have passed into common currency. *Der Spiegel* reported heavy booing for Neuenfels in 2010, yet by the time of my second visit in 2012, the staging seemed almost to have attained the status of a modern classic.[22] And, although it would be difficult to claim that Neuenfels engaged as closely with the music as, say, Herheim did in *Parsifal*, he did not work against it – unless one were of the opinion that rats on stage did so *ipso facto*. Shifts in the action at times certainly appeared broadly to reflect the contours of the score. I saw this *Lohengrin* twice, in 2011 and 2012. Vogt again offered his uncanny – and doubtless very different – reading on both of my visits to the Festspielhaus. Again the purity of this individual, some might say idiosyncratic, tenor delighted: coldly seductive in its (apparent) honesty, and yet chilling – an excellent fit with both work and production.

Neuenfels presented a laboratory experiment; those experimented upon were rats – or at least, they often were, for there were times when they shed much of their rat-like appearance and resembled humans. Their feet nevertheless always gave them away. Lohengrin was shown during the Prelude – opening without stage action – trying to break into the realm of experimentation. The experiment seemed at least in part political in nature – though this was never hammered home; the work made one reflect upon the staging and vice versa. Again, the darker side of *Lohengrin*, the nature of its ultra-mysterious charismatic hero and the way a crowd would follow him, was the stuff of the conflict. (That could not help but leave one asking: were Ortrud and Telramund right to resist? Were they the true rebels, revolutionaries even?) It was a pity, therefore, that we did not

---

[21] This production is also available on DVD, from BBC/Opus Arte: B007ZB7U00.
[22] Review by Werner Theurich, 'Neuer *Lohengrin* in Bayreuth: Wie man der Schwan rupft', <http://www.spiegel.de/kultur/musik/neuer-lohengrin-in-bayreuth-wie-man-den-schwan-rupft-a-708441.html> (accessed 23 October 2012).

hear the word *Führer* when Lohengrin introduced his successor, Gottfried ('Seht da den Herzog von Brabant! Zum Führer sei er euch ernannt!'). *Schützer*, the 'Protector' employed earlier for Lohengrin, was used instead.

Perhaps the abiding question with which we were left related to who was actually running the experiment? Who was on the outside? It is, in a sense, a variation upon a perennial problem of political philosophy, never more so than in Rousseau: who is the Legislator? 'A superior intelligence beholding all the passions of men without experiencing any of them would be needed.'[23] The audience, perhaps? It was certainly not the sickly, flawed, proto-Amfortas figure of King Henry the Fowler, as much a pawn as anyone else – an aspect granted added resonance when one considers the historical King Henry, founder of the Ottonian dynasty, and the Romantic as well as National Socialist view of him as father of the German nation. Wagner's twilight world between history and myth is an especially interesting feature of *Lohengrin*, fully relished here. Indeed, this shrivelled Henry found himself dragged off-stage by attendants, redolent perhaps of those enigmatic 'authorities', somehow both ominous and strangely irrelevant, to whom Don Ottavio refers in *Don Giovanni*. (We shall revisit them in the next chapter.) The two characters who briefly managed to throw off the shackles of supervision were Ortrud and Lohengrin, at a time when arguably both of them are at the height of their powers, during the second act. So perhaps no authority was absolute though whatever this was behind the experiment – Fate? the near-omnipotent surveillance of late capitalism? The illusion of the *Gesamtkunstwerk*? Nothing at all? – would in both cases manage to reassert itself, before bringing forth the fragile infant figure of Gottfried from an egg. Leaders, such as they be, were clearly to be moulded, nurtured, not born: a typical, eminently understandable, German preoccupation. The Protector/*Führer* needed protecting too.

V

It was as the *Führer* that he was definitely hailed in Peter Konwitschny's staging. This production was first seen in Hamburg in 1998, but travelled across Europe, taking in other houses such as Copenhagen and Barcelona (where it was filmed), before Konwitschny decided to stage it once again in Wagner's home town of Leipzig.[24] The director had recently been

---

[23] Jean-Jacques Rousseau, *The Social Contract and Discourses*, tr. G. D. H. Cole, revised J. H. Brumfett, John C. Hall, and P. D. Jimack (Dent: London, 1993), p. 213.
[24] The Barcelona performance may be seen on EuroArts B000Q7ZKVQ, though it suffers

made director of productions at the Leipzig Opera, itself possessed of a fascinating if fraught relationship with the city's greatest son. Following the Second World War, a new house was necessary, opening in 1960 with *Die Meistersinger*, the Wagner work whose populist aspects, or at least readings, most appealed to the East German authorities, Joachim Herz's staging apparently even having delighted Walter Ulbricht, though not the party commissars. A Nuremberg of old, including Hans Sachs, Albrecht Dürer, and Veit Stoß, could be understood as a 'good' forerunner of the GDR, more recent Nuremberg connotations being left to the West.[25] Herz's Leipzig *Ring* (1973–6) is now widely acknowledged as a milestone in political interpretation, overshadowed in (relatively) popular consciousness by the subsequent Chéreau production, partly on account of the latter's wider availability, not least on television and video, but much more than a mere forerunner. Konwitschny had partly been welcomed to Leipzig as the son of his father, Franz, who had from 1949 to 1962 been Principal Conductor of the Leipzig Gewandhaus Orchestra, which, like many German orchestras, plays both for the city's concert series and for the opera – with, in this case, the added responsibility of playing for the services in Bach's Thomaskirche. Multifarious historical resonances abound, then, even prior to discussion of the production itself.

Konwitschny's travelling production became celebrated for its schoolroom setting, much as that of Neuenfels did for its rats. I attended Leipzig's opening night, on 18 December 2009. It had many strengths – despite sections, especially earlier on during the third act, which transferred less well to the schoolroom setting. Issues of leadership, exclusion, (forbidden) sexual politics, and of course (forbidden) knowledge relating to Elsa's question – who *is* Lohengrin? – were nevertheless illuminated. The setting brought to mind the fickle mob violence – how Telramund and Ortrud were turned upon – and unthinking obedience portrayed in William Golding's *Lord of the Flies*.[26] Helmut Brade's designs and costumes, the latter in collaboration with Inga von Bredow, successfully evoked both conformity and individual characterisation, the dialectic between the latter having been reported upon as a strength in Herz's *Meistersinger* –

---

from a barking tenor, whose less than mellifluous tone could hardly stand more distant from Vogt's performances.

[25] See Patrick Carnegy, *Wagner and the Art of the Theatre* (Yale University Press: New Haven and London, 2006), pp. 320–3, 419, n. 34, the latter referring to a letter of 2 September 2000 from Herz to Carnegy; Joachim Herz, *Theater – Kunst des erfüllten Augenblicks*, ed. Ilse Kobán (Henschelverlag: Berlin, 1989).

[26] William Golding, *Lord of the Flies* (Edward Arnold: London, 1970).

certainly the case in Herheim's and Neuenfels's stagings too. Historical preoccupation with what might bring individuals, good, bad, or neutral, to follow and to obey charismatic leaders is never far away in modern German, indeed European, artistic consciousness.

Here, as much as in both of the preceding productions, any black-and-white sense of 'rightness' concerning Lohengrin's cause was rendered untenable. Lohengrin's charismatic power emerged more potently than, to employ Max Weber's distinctions, the traditional, legal forms pertaining to King Henry. However, that power by its very nature was to prove inherently unstable, Weber's classic distinctions held and dramatically extended. The road to 1933 was clearly one of Konwitschny's concerns, there being something undeniably chilling in this context to hear Lohengrin introduce Gottfried, as he should: 'Seht da den Herzog von Brabant! Zum Führer sei er euch ernannt!' Whether the appearance of a boy with a machine gun went 'too far' would doubtless depend on taste and inclination; there would perhaps be more subtle ways of portraying the problem, though arguably subtlety is not what is required here. However, almost irrespective of intention, one began to ask what alternatives there might have been. Ortrud and her paganism, for instance? Hardly an appetising prospect for a Marxist such as Konwitschny, or indeed for many others, and arguably as resonant of National Socialism as Lohengrin or Gottfried.

VI

By contrast, one performance and recording project explicitly disavowed the theatre for the alleged purity of the concert hall. Marek Janowski, conducting the entire Wagner dramatic corpus from *The Flying Dutchman* onwards, explicitly signalled his disdain for modern *Regietheater* by insisting upon performing them in concert.[27] This project, recorded by Pentatone, offered on the face of it the prospect of interpretative 'neutrality'; it began, however, to take on a more starkly ideological hue when considered in the light of the booklets accompanying the recordings. For instance, that to *Lohengrin* contained, as did the rest of the series, an encomium from Norbert Lammert, Christian Democrat President of the Bundestag, who wrote, 'The concept between the cycle is so disarmingly simple as to be a stroke of genius: here it is only about what Wagner has to say, no one else. There is no drama on stage to compete with the flow of the music, no direction to support or ruin Wagner's poetry.' It is not

---

[27] My review of the *Lohengrin* recording may be seen in *Opera*, 63 (2012), 1425–6.

difficult to imagine that the writer thought 'ruin' more frequent than 'support'. He continued, 'whereas many opera houses nowadays are inclined to a superabundance of ideas from the director, Marek Janowski does the complete opposite: no distracting images. Instead of this, he invites a clear reflection of the essentials, of the music.'[28] Such, it need hardly be pointed out, is quite a different conception from that of the symbiosis Herheim and Gatti believed they had achieved in *Parsifal*.

In Lammert's words, the ideological intent, whatever one may think of it, at least verges upon the explicit. Under the guise of alleged historical facts, however, the booklet note by Steffen Georgi, the Berlin Radio Symphony Orchestra's dramaturge, attempted to shore up such a position by denying Wagner's politics, rather as we have seen Wieland and Wolfgang Wagner attempt following the Second World War. Georgi thus wrote under the (mocking) heading, 'Wagner – a revolutionary?':

> When compared with the social upheavals conceptualised by Karl Marx and Friedrich Engels, the theatre reformer Richard Wagner pales, from today's standpoint in the best case a tin-pot revolutionary (*Westentaschenrevolutionär*). He jumped aboard the great revolutionary train with his 'artistic revolutionary' interests, though perhaps he conflates, in his 'action hero' zeal, his 'revolution' from above with that which is monarchical, beholden to authority, and undemocratic, and thus, in the sense of the revolution, reactionary. Heinrich and Thomas Mann would later emphasise those oppressive characteristics in Wagner.
> . . .
> Wagner's real, world-altering revolution took place in the territory of music – which interested no government of the time.[29]

To say that music interested no government of the time is straightforwardly untrue, as the writer must surely have known. The Thomas Mann referred to would presumably be the same writer who outraged Nazi and conservative opinion – as we have seen, Strauss included – by presenting Wagner as a 'cultural Bolshevist'.[30] Moreover, whatever one thinks of Wagner's revolutionary activities, even in the circumscribed sense accorded them here, he placed himself in considerable personal danger and would be exiled

---

[28] 'A Word of Greeting in Connection with the Wagner Cycle Recordings by the Rundfunk-Sinfonieorchester Berlin,' in booklet to Pentatone PTC 5186 403, *Lohengrin*, p. 42.
[29] Steffen Georgi, 'Mein lieber Schwan,' in ibid., pp. 30–1. There is an English translation in the booklet but, presumably unwittingly, it misrepresents Georgi. For instance, it has him speak of social upheavals 'instigated' rather than 'projected', 'conceptualised', or even 'planned' (*entworfenen*), by Marx and Engels.
[30] Thomas Mann, 'Sufferings and Greatness of Richard Wagner,' in *Essays of Three Decades*, tr. H. T. Lowe-Porter (Knopf: New York, 1976), p. 352.

from the German Confederation until 1860, still longer from Saxony.

More important still, one would only have to dignify Wagner's works, dramatic and theoretical, with the most cursory of glances – at, for instance, the torrential catechism, *Die Revolution*, for instance – to realise that Wagner was anything but a mere 'artistic revolutionary'. That 1849 piece for the revolutionary *Volksblätter* hymned the 'sublime goddess *Revolution*', the 'ever-rejuvenating mother of mankind', who prophesies a new Feuerbachian world of love, in which '*all* as brothers', echoing and yet extending Beethoven's Ninth Symphony, would be '*free* in their desires, *free* in their deeds, *free* in their pleasures'.[31]

The greater point, however, is not so much how inaccurate and mis-leading Georgi's claims may have been, but that Wagner has continued to be fought over for political ends: in a concert performance just as much as in cases of alleged directorial excess. After all, there has never been a more profoundly ideological, thoroughly historical concept than that of 'absolute music' – and that deserves to be a cause for celebration of historical and æsthetic richness, not for censure.[32]

---

[31] Richard Wagner, 'Die Revolution', in *Sämtliche Schriften und Dichtungen*, ed. Richard Sternfeld and Hans von Wolzogen, 16 vols in 10 (Breitkopf und Härtel: Leipzig, 1912–14), vol. 12, pp. 245, 251.

[32] Cf. Carl Dahlhaus, *The Idea of Absolute Music*, tr. Roger Lustig (University of Chicago Press: Chicago and London, 1989); Daniel Chua, *Absolute Music and the Construction of Meaning* (Cambridge University Press: Cambridge, 1999).

CHAPTER 9

From Wagner to Nono

I

When dealing with operatic performance 'after Wagner' it does not seem unreasonable to have devoted considerable space to *Parsifal* and to *Lohengrin*. However, it would have been unduly restrictive to leave matters there. The Wagnerian legacy of the 'director' extends far beyond his own works – and did so when he was alive too; one may even trace it back, as here, beyond the visit of the Duke of Meiningen's troupe. It certainly holds interesting implications for our understanding of the artwork and its conceptual stability.

It is not difficult to imagine Wagner's reaction had conductors, directors, singers, or anyone else questioned the aspirant totality of his own works. Konwitschny's Hamburg 2002 *Meistersinger*, in which the final scene is interrupted by a discussion as to whether one can or should proceed in the light of preceding – or should that be succeeding? – German history would surely have met with an angry response. Nevertheless, Konwitschny's breaking down of boundaries between stage and audience, rupturing the aura of the work, had Romantic precedent, for instance in the deconstructionism of Ludwig Tieck's *Puss in Boots*, which has roles for authors, actors, audience, and stagehands, and would itself most likely exert some influence over the communal idea of the 'artwork of the future'.[1] Porges, in his report upon the *Ring* rehearsals, described Wagner's aim as having been:

> to imbue the company of artists as one organic entity with that complete freedom of expression which as a rule is exercised only be a single personality. In order to achieve this artistic freedom the performers must from the outset subordinate themselves without reservation to the creator of the work, and thereby acquire that gift of self-abandonment (*Selbstentäusserung*) which, in his penetrating essay, 'On Actors and Singers', Wagner singled out as the basis of all dramatic talent.[2]

[1] Ludwig Tieck, *Der gestiefelte Kater*, ed. Gerald Gillespie (Edinburgh University Press: Edinburgh, 1974).
[2] Heinrich Porges, *Wagner Rehearsing the 'Ring': An Eye-Witness Account of the Stage*

Maybe that was indeed Wagner's aim, though we need not necessarily conflate Porges and Wagner. However, even if Porges is correct, Wagner provides alternative examples and the act of 'subordination' cannot but help incite insubordination, some at least of it potentially fruitful.

One of Wagner's alternative examples may be found in his Dresden performances of other composers' operas during the 1840s. His 1847 production of Gluck's *Iphigénie en Aulide*, 'wherein I had to prove myself as a stage director as well; indeed, I was even obliged to lend the most urgent aid to the scene-painters and the machinists', revealed Wagner not only as conductor but as imaginative editor and composer, a musicologist of sorts, whatever his subsequently dismissive attitude towards dusty academics.[3] Gluck's opera was presented in a new edition, for which Wagner provided preludes, postludes, and transitions, in order, as he saw it, to aid the dramatic flow of a number opera, also bringing Gluck's orchestration the advantages or otherwise of a mid-nineteenth-century hue. Wagner additionally attempted a quasi-modern-'authentic' return beyond Racine to Euripides by altering the ending, ridding Gluck's work of its conventional concluding marriage between Iphigénie and Achille. (Advocacy of Mozart in Strauss's version of *Idomeneo*, the *Frau ohne Schatten*-like interpolation included, may be understood partly in that light.) Work upon *Iphigénie*, or rather *Iphigenia*, since the work was performed in German, was sufficient in scale and importance to delay progress on *Lohengrin*. 'I had to find new ways', Wagner would recall, 'to enliven the staging, for the problem seemed to me to lie largely in the conventional treatment of such scenes prevailing at the Paris Opera during Gluck's time.' Indeed, in a development that once again might seem to have presaged modern theatrical practice, 'even the management' of the Dresden Court Opera 'was sufficiently amazed at this exceptionally popular success of a Gluck opera to take the initiative and add my name to posters from the second performance onwards as the author of this adaptation.'[4] Wagner would certainly be today excoriated as a purveyor of 'Eurotrash' in some quarters, those very quarters that would 'protect' his works. So is Konwitschny, one of whose unfulfilled Leipzig projects

---

Rehearsals of the First Bayreuth Festival, tr. Robert L Jacobs (Cambridge University Press: Cambridge, 1983), pp. 2–3; Richard Wagner, 'Über Schauspieler und Sänger,' in *Sämtliche Schriften und Dichtungen*, ed. Richard Sternfeld and Hans von Wolzogen, 16 vols in 10 (Breitkopf und Härtel: Leipzig, 1912–14), vol. 9, p. 230.

[3] Richard Wagner, *My Life*, tr. Andrew Gray, ed. Mary Whittall (Cambridge: Cambridge University Press, 1983), p. 338.

[4] Ibid., p. 338.

was to present a 'Leipzig *Ring*' for the 2013 bicentenary of Wagner's birth: avoiding the problems of casting and overexposure attendant to every major world opera house in performing Wagner by instead presenting a 'ring' of Gluck's six reform operas. Gluck the progressive, the musical dramatist foe of crowd-pleasing *opera seria*, was clearly being presented by Wagner as of contemporary concern, a John the Baptist reforming figure, with few guesses required as to who might emerge Christ-like from the experience.

Wagner's version long enjoyed popularity in the German-speaking world, though the age of 'authenticity' has not looked kindly upon it. Mahler, for instance, would use it for his 1907 Vienna performances, and may have chosen the work on account of Wagner's advocacy; Mahler even extended tradition by adding a few transitional bars of his own.[5] More surprisingly, Wagner's 'new' ending, recently found an unlikely champion in a conductor, who, whilst having no truck with the 'authenticity' of period instruments, has long stood as an advocate of 'fidelity' to the score, especially in nineteenth-century Italian opera. Riccardo Muti, whose refusal to countenance 'traditional' vocal embellishments in Donizetti and Verdi – high Cs and the like – which suggests in him a kindred, slightly puritanical, spirit to the reformist Gluck, opted to employ Wagner's alternative ending, if not his other revisions, both at La Scala in 2003 and at the Rome Opera in 2009. Dramatic credibility, or at least the perception of such, trumped textual fidelity.

'Fidelity' after Wagner, then, can take many forms, comfortable neither for those who would take a literalist approach to stage direction, nor for apostles of 'authenticity'. The latter naturally tend also to loathe his meddling with Beethoven, let alone Wagner's metaphysical understanding of his predecessor. How very much of its time now seems Ernest Newman's claim: 'To-day no one would dream of questioning Wagner's reading of the [Gluck] overture,' though Newman makes the good point, often missed, that Wagner ignored the then-popular Berlin version, which included Gaspare Spontini's emendations, instead returning to – if also adding to – Gluck's own score for Paris.[6] It would indeed be a brave musician who were even to consider a (post-)Wagnerian reading.

Now if only someone might uncover Wagner's lost Zurich 1850 revision of *Don Giovanni*, the cat might truly be set amongst the pigeons. He

---

[5]   Henry-Louis de La Grange, *Gustav Mahler: Volume 3. Vienna: Triumph and Disillusion (1904–1907)* (Oxford University Press: Oxford, 1999), p. 592.
[6]   Ernest Newman, *The Life of Richard Wagner*, 4 vols (Cambridge University Press: Cambridge, 1976), vol. 1, p. 427. See also Wagner, *My Life*, p. 337.

describes it as a *Bearbeitung* in a letter from early that year to Theodor Uhlig, and speaks of having 'carefully nuanced' (*sorgfältig nüancirt*) the orchestra, made a new translation, and various other changes, which, without a score, it is not always easy fully to understand. That is, of course, if we take what he has to say not only at face value – there is no particular reason we should not – but also as his final thoughts on a work he would conduct eight months later. In any case, Wagner ends that particularly discussion with the playful, 'Now, enough of this patchwork maintenance!'[7] There are extant, tantalisingly, a fragment, discovered in the late 1990s, comprising nine bars of off-stage trumpet cues, plus dialogue cues, and another fragment of just two bars held by the University of Leipzig. Chris Walton speculates that Wagner's revisions were less radical than might have been implied, perhaps exaggerated as part of a marketing ploy. At present, however, we might with equal justification speculate otherwise.[8] We simply do not know. Perhaps, however, we might hope that an imaginative composer would dare enter the mediated realm of re-imagining Wagner's re-imagining – aided by a sympathetic director and cast.

II

For all our latter-day reverence for the musico-dramatic work concept, *Don Giovanni* has experienced a chequered history in that respect. Indeed, more often than not conductors and/or directors will even today, in a climate of near-maniacal 'authenticity', opt for a conflation of Mozart's versions for Prague and Vienna: largely, one fears, a matter of bowing to singers' – and audiences' – demands for extra arias rather than out of genuine dramatic conviction. It is, of course, a bitter pill to swallow, to lose one of Donna Elvira's arias and one of Don Ottavio's; the Vienna duet between Zerlina and Leporello is generally considered no great loss. However, there has yet to be mounted a dramatic, as opposed to pragmatic, justification for offering the now commonplace succession of arias in the second act. (One might hazard a possible explanation, as Devil's Advocate, in the guise of heightening the elements of *opera seria* display, striking a blow against Wagnerian notions of dramatic cohesion and continuity, but that case remains to be made.)

---

[7] Letter to Theodor Uhlig of February (?) 1852, in Richard Wagner, *Sämtliche Briefe*, ed. Gertrud Strobel, Werner Wolf, Hans-Joachim Bauer, Johannes Forner, *et al.* (VEB Deutscher Verlag für Musik/Breitkopf und Härtel: Leipzig, 1967–), vol. 4, pp. 298–9.

[8] Chris Walton, *Richard Wagner's Zurich: The Muse of Place* (Camden House: Woodbridge and Rochester, NY, 2007), p. 168.

More extreme measures, however, were taken in the more distant past. Berlioz, writing of an 1834 Paris staging, was moved to lament:

> It is a pity that it was considered necessary to take various dances, extended, lopped off, reordered, and orchestrated according to the method which seems to me so inimical to musical sense and the interests of art, from other works of Mozart, and insert them into *Don Giovanni*; without these additions the absolutely pure style of this sublime score, boldly breaking the public habits of the last eight or ten years, might have completed this important revolution.[9]

Moreover, a reference to the Stone Guest scene, 'the trombones, which have been silent for some time', suggests that, in contravention of the score, they had been heard earlier – though, given Mozart's reorchestrations of Handel, dismay might be misplaced.[10]

There persisted, furthermore, a Romantic tradition of omitting the final scene. For the Mozart year of 1906, Mahler in Vienna not only altered some of the orchestration, made cuts both of complete arias and ensembles and also within certain numbers, and interpolated the finale to Mozart's Divertimento in B-flat major, KV 287/271*h*. In a practice that was already being questioned, he and his director, Alfred Roller – the latter, of course, also a crucial figure in the history of Wagner staging – concluded with Don Giovanni's descent into Hell.[11] Whereas to many modern audiences the final sextet introduces a note of bracing, almost Brechtian alienation, framing the action in a sense that both harks back to more ancient traditions as well as looking forwards beyond Romanticism, there was for Mahler and Roller nothing more to say at this point, notwithstanding the oddness of what therefore became the final cadence. However, as Henry-Louis de La Grange notes, many other recent productions of *Don Giovanni* had included it, notably that given by Ernst von Possart in Munich.[12] (Possart was the actor for whom Strauss wrote his 1897 melodrama, *Enoch Arden*.)

The 'tradition' seemed to have died out; Furtwängler, whom, amongst post-war conductors, some might have suspected of harbouring such tendencies, did not continue it. And then, Claus Guth staged the work as part of a Da Ponte trilogy for the Salzburg Festival, *Don Giovanni* first

---

[9] *Journal des Débats*, 15 November 1835, translated in Julian Rushton, *W.A. Mozart: Don Giovanni* (Cambridge University Press: Cambridge, 1981), p. 133.

[10] Ibid., p. 134.

[11] La Grange, *Gustav Mahler: Volume 3*, pp. 287, 299.

[12] Ibid., p. 299, n. 67; Christof Bitter, *Wandlungen in den Inszenierungsformen des Don Giovanni, 1787–1928* (Bosse: Regensburg, 1961), p. 118.

seen in 2008 – a little more than a century after Mahler, and thus almost as distant from him as he was from Mozart – and revived in 2010.[13] (Note the transition from speaking of Mahler's or Furtwängler's *Don Giovanni* to the director's.) The premise, as revealed in a brief programme discussion, was that:

> Mozart tried to deal with all of our lives in the three hours he had for this opera. But what if he managed to compress everything that moves and occupies us into this framework? We must die. What do we do with our lifetime? Do we conform and subordinate ourselves, do we break out, do we try to fit in or break loose, cut our ties?[14]

Interesting enough so far; the problem was that Guth's realisation failed to live up to the promise. What it boiled down to on stage seemed closer to a reality television programme: how would someone with three hours left to live decide to spend those three hours? By taking drugs and trying – unsuccessfully – to have sex with a number of women in a forest, all with the help of a slightly subordinate friend. I say 'slightly subordinate', since it was not at all clear what the social relationship between the protagonists might be. Blithely casting aside distinctions of order was one thing, but Guth offered no adequate substitute.

The setting itself intrigued: a landscape akin to the Salzburg Mönchsberg or Hampstead Heath. There was certainly more than a hint of the cruising ground here, though the action remained strictly heterosexual: perhaps a missed opportunity, which would be taken up by a more daring re-imagining for Heaven, the London gay nightclub, in 2012. Nevertheless, though absorbing enough in a modern filmic sort of way, Guth's *Don Giovanni* was not a patch upon his brilliant 2006 rethinking of *Le nozze di Figaro*, in which the near-impossible had been accomplished, transforming *convincingly* the sparkle of Mozartian *opera buffa* into a joyless Strindberg-like world of suffocation. (There the relationship between the Count and Figaro had been thought through, hints of a sado-masochistic master–servant/ slave relationship surfacing in chilling fashion.) The problem was not that too much had been altered, but that not enough had been rethought, leaving the production stranded in a no-man's-land between work and performance. Who, for instance, was the Commendatore supposed to be at the end? A ghost seemed rather at odds with the setting; had he just come back to life? No one seemed to know – nor, sadly, to care.

---

[13] The production has since been seen also at La Scala and at the Berlin State Opera.

[14] In conversation with Peter Schneeburger, in Salzburg Festival programme for *Don Giovanni*, 2010, p. 25.

The familiar conflation of the score was employed, barring the Leporello and Zerlina duet. (It seems to have been included in 2008, then cut in 2010.) I found myself quite unprepared for the absence of the final scene, not having been made aware beforehand. Yes, expectations were confounded, which can sometimes be a good thing in itself, and yes of course there was the Romantic-Mahlerian tradition to which to appeal. In context, however, the feeling of straightforward incompletion was jarring rather than fruitful. It was difficult to avoid the suspicion that Guth had simply misunderstood the nature of the sextet. Its alienation effect might have rendered both work and production more interesting; without it, we veered dangerously close to melodrama, especially odd given the general tone of the production. The problem was not the decision as such, but its placing and indeed the director's reasoning. Guth claimed that Mozart was 'bowing to convention', yet throughout the work Mozart had come close to destroying any such concept; the finale could be understood to be still more radical in this context, inevitably to us suggesting Stravinsky and beyond: the neo-Classicism of *The Rake's Progress* or at least of *Neue Sachlichkeit*. Oliver Knussen understands this very well in his fantasy opera (1984–5, revised 1999), *Higglety Pigglety Pop!* Both *Higglety* and *Don Giovanni* end 'outside' their dramas, in bright if tarnished D major – and the Mother Goose World Theatre surely pays tribute to Stravinsky's work too. The repetitions of *Higglety*'s closing-scene gala performance, no mere convention but the time-honoured tradition of a play within a play, unsettle as they should. What do they mean? When will they stop? That is a more radical rethinking than simply not knowing how to conclude. For, in performance, Mozart's score begged for completion. It did not chillingly come to a halt, after *Wozzeck*; it seemed rather just to stop, awkwardly. Although it was interesting, then, to hear an accidental revival of this venerable 'version', in practice, however, the inappropriate context served principally to confirm discrediting of the tradition. Here was an instructive case of a director who, unlike Herheim or Konwitschny, seemed to have too little knowledge of, or indeed interest in, the score; 'respect' for the work would have expanded rather than lessened performative options.

III

The production, or rather reworking, for Heaven proved a different matter entirely. It could not boast the Salzburg Festival, nor a starry cast, nor the Vienna Philharmonic Orchestra; indeed, it had to employ a much-reduced orchestration (four violins, viola, cello, double bass, oboe, clarinet, bassoon). There were even a few singers who were not 'classically' trained. Skilfully executed by Tony Burke and Ken Roberts, the performing version also cut the score to a little more than half its length. Not only was it cut; it was translated, or rather adapted – with wit and flair by Ranjit Bolt. Leo's Catalogue Aria, for instance, transferred its attention, for instance, to Hampstead Heath, Clapham Common, the lavatories at Heaven, etc. There was even a club remix by Vince Clarke, formerly of Erasure and Depeche Mode, of the dance music from the final scene of the first act. Nevertheless, this *Don Giovanni* captured a re-creative spirit lacking in Salzburg.

There were oddities: for instance, the title, *Don Giovanni: The Opera*, to which one might well have responded: 'as opposed to "Don Giovanni: The …"?' However, the central conceit was pursued not only coherently, but with far more, at least so it seemed, of an ear to the drama of Mozart's score which had ensnared Berlioz, Wagner, Mahler, and so many others. All of the names were changed and, with the exception of Don (no longer Don Giovanni), a Soho club owner, each of the roles underwent gender reversal. Leporello became Leo, Don's personal assistant. Elvira was transformed into an older, rather tiresome gay man, Eddie, deluded in his belief that he had ever been 'with' Don in the first place, just as captivated as Da Ponte's Elvira. Donna Anna became Alan, with Olivia (Don Ottavio) his fag hag accomplice; Alan had – as many of us, post-E. T. A. Hoffmann, suspect in Donna Anna's case – consented quite willingly to Don's advances, yet wished to pretend otherwise. Zerlina and Masetto were Zac and Marina, a working-class couple about to marry, yet with the former interested in exploring his repressed sexual orientation before it was too late.[15] The Commendatore, wittily, became Petra; what one lost in vocal transposition, one almost regained in the smile provoked by the stony choice of name. An additional Everyman's provision of cocaine added fuel to the kinetic energy of production and score, and brought back memories of Calixto Bieito's production for the English National Opera.

One great strength of Dominic Gray's production, again in contrast to so many other stagings, was its appreciation and reinterpretation of societal distinctions. They were not, admittedly, as subtle as those Mozart and Da Ponte crafted, but that was in part a reflection of the new setting. In 1787, a society of orders stood upon the brink of revolutionary upheaval – indeed, Joseph II was unleashing such forces 'from above' in

[15] See E. T. A. Hoffmann, 'Don Juan,' in *Sämtliche Werke*, 10 vols (series never completed), ed. Georg von Maassen (Müller: Munich and Leipzig, 1908–28), pp. 62–73.

the Habsburg Monarchy – whereas in 1987, the year of updating, class, despite the claims of the Conservative government, remained very much an operative concept. The attraction Zac felt towards Don was above all sexual in nature, but that was reinforced by, and partly a product of, the glaring contrast between Don's riches – in one sense, he was a victor of the Thatcher years – and Zac's poverty: on the night before their wedding, he could only stretch to taking Marina to a Wimpy Bar.

Gray's setting of 1980s hedonism, liberation, and, crucially, repression, seemed ideal for the work. A perfect example would be the final scene's presentation of a properly Foucauldian sense of the social construction of madness or indeed disease more generally: Hell for modernity? Was a straitjacketed Don insane, stricken by HIV/AIDS, or perhaps both? He was certainly held captive by the neo-Hobbesian ideology of Thatcherism. (Those who relate the latter to Locke have often missed the point, or at least part of the point; the strength of the state, those 'authorities' to which Don Ottavio refers, was always crucial to Thatcherism and modern 'conservatism' in general.) The staging's particular resonance was the notorious Section 28 of the 1988 Local Government Act, which prohibited 'promotion' by local authorities of homosexuality. Perhaps the much-lauded 'Essex Man', England's response to the 'Reagan Democrat', was obliquely deconstructed in the portrayal of Zac. For libertarianism, we were reminded, was never really a Thatcherite characteristic at all. However, libertinism has, since the writings of the Marquis de Sade, contemporary to Mozart and Da Ponte, proved an abidingly political issue; here it appeared to gain truer modern relevance, fidelity to the work expressed through an imaginative degree of infidelity.

In an unlikely setting, it was possible once again to ask oneself what would Wagner have done; indeed, what did he do? We do not know; the historical record, as we have seen, is frustratingly and yet also suggestively incomplete. Yet the prospect, via Wagner and perhaps Mahler too, of a *Don Giovanni* of our own age, even if never realised, or even realisable, might at least heighten dramatic – even musical? – possibilities for the future.

IV

Another opera, in almost every sense post-Wagnerian, offering potential in performance for interrogation of the work concept is Berg's *Lulu. Lulu* also offers social criticism, though many stage directors seem strangely reluctant to acknowledge that, favouring the imprecision of existentialism. Like *Moses und Aron*, *Lulu* remains unfinished, though to a lesser extent in every sense. There is certainly no reason to believe that the composer could not have completed it, nor that its lack of completion is bound up with the antinomies explored in the case of Schoenberg. Even in the case of the incomplete third act, it was only eighty-seven bars that required addition of voices, both stage and orchestral, though the greater part of the act as left by Berg remains in short score. One cannot help but wonder what might have become of the work had Schoenberg accepted the invitation of Berg's widow, Helene, to complete it, although, by the same token, it was always unlikely; fantasy is probably here more interesting than whatever the reality in an alternative history might have been. In any case, as is well known, *Lulu* became known to the world in two acts, as first performed in Zurich in 1937; Helene's unwillingness to permit completion by another composer's – or musicologist's – hand deepened. Even after her death in 1976, when the fruits of Friedrich Cerha's work on the sketches and score could be shown, the Alban Berg Foundation issued a legal challenge to Cerha's three-act version; its failure enabled the 1979 premiere in Paris from the Bayreuth team of Boulez and Chéreau.

Cerha's work is lauded by most and rightly so. There is nevertheless no reason why alternatives should not be attempted, though it seems almost pointlessly puritanical to continue with the 'Zurich version'. A particularly odd case, interesting from our point of view, if ultimately a failure, was presented by a 2012 so-called *Berliner Fassung*, presented at the Berlin State Opera. Its origins lay not in dissatisfaction with Cerha, nor in a desire only to present what Berg himself wrote, but instead in rather confused dramaturgical criticism by the stage director, Andrea Breth, criticism unlikely to have proceeded very far had it not been for the problematical yet unrelated nature of the work's incompletion.

The choice of stage director was that of the Music Director, Daniel Barenboim, who, impressed by a collaboration at the Salzburg Festival for *Eugene Onegin*, invited Breth to Berlin, to direct both *Wozzeck* and *Lulu*. The former was performed in 2011 to widespread acclaim, apparently auguring well for the latter, which Barenboim, though something of a *Wozzeck* veteran, was to conduct for the first time. Breth, however, had decided that the first scene of the third act was 'impossible to stage', quite why remaining unclear; it was nevertheless made clear that her participation was conditional upon its excision.[16] Protective of the work as generally understood, Universal Edition, publisher of Cerha's completion and

---

[16] That was confirmed in a talk given by Breth and Barenboim during the April 2012 Berlin *Festtage*.

facilitator of his initial, clandestine work on the score, refused to permit a truncated performance. An alternative version of the final scene had therefore to be prepared, in this case, at Barenboim's invitation, by David Robert Coleman, a composer and assistant conductor at the Staatsoper.

That background emerged in my case only after the performance, so I was taken aback, to say the least, by the absence of this part of the drama, just as I had been by the absence of the Prologue, which should frame so beautifully what we are about to see and to hear, the whole world in this blackest of comedies a stage or rather a circus: a mirror image, in a sense, of the *Don Giovanni* sextet. Instead, at the very opening, we saw an actor horizontal on the stage, who proceeded to read excerpts from Kierkegaard, followed by Lulu's third-act scream.

Once past the surprise at disruption of the work's aura, what, then, was the problem? However enigmatic or inchoate Breth's rejection of the Paris Scene might have been, something intriguing might possibly have come from an alternative version of its London counterpart and from the reminders of the instability of the work concept. That, alas, nevertheless depended on the task being accomplished well. Both Coleman's version and Breth's direction failed to do so, entailing widespread bewilderment and annoyance, with nothing discernible in the way of countervailing challenge. First, Coleman's sketchy orchestration sounded more akin to a first, jejune attempt to look through Berg's manuscripts than a finished 'version', let alone a competitor to Cerha. Steel drums appeared at one point, allegedly as an intimation of an early juke-box, though it seemed highly unlikely anyone would have guessed that without the aid of the programme. Necessity of sorts may have prescribed the general course of action, but no virtue was made of it. Berg's harmonisation of the hurdy-gurdy *Lautenlied*, 'Konfession', the melody Wedekind's own, was tossed aside in favour of a manifestly inferior if 'original' version by Wedekind.[17] That was not simply a matter of a less interesting harmonisation, but also of having missed the tune's first appearance in the excised Paris Scene; Berg's dodecaphonic writing and method were thereby undermined. There was, sadly, no recompense for the violence done to Berg's symmetries, dramatic and musical.

Breth's direction might have offered some salvation, but it made matters worse. Fatally, what we saw evinced no interest in Berg's structural concerns, substituting for them a play of actors and mimed actions. Infidelity

[17] See Douglas Jarman, *The Music of Alban Berg* (University of California Press: Berkeley and Los Angeles, 1979) pp. 209, 246.

may be fruitful, but perhaps it requires at least an implicit fidelity to be meaningful. The setting resembled a cross between a Beckett parody and a 1980s pop video: a grim warehouse with a crashed car and a great deal of scaffolding. (The latter actually provided a degree of relief; one could imagine in its structures some Bauhaus-like, Adornian counterpoint to the constructivism, if not the Romanticism, of Berg's score.) A great deal went on, but relatively little seemed to have anything to do with the opera 'itself', nor indeed with the 'characters' who sang in this production. Instead of a film of Lulu's trial – given a general enthusiasm to use film at any and every opportunity, many contemporary directors are oddly reluctant to 'respect' the prescribed visual counterpoint to Berg's palindrome – we simply saw a couple of filmed eyes, maybe Lulu's, maybe not. One extra, meanwhile, tipped another extra out of a wheelbarrow, put her back in again, and wheeled her off. The quasi-Beckettian atmosphere might or might not have illuminated the work; the real problem was that no discernible attempt was made to fit the two together, nor even provocatively to set them against each other. Nor was there any change of scenery, despite the clear dramatic necessity to shift from one milieu to another, the sameness airising seemingly by default rather than a positive decision. If the idea were to excise supposed misogyny and perhaps other uncomfortably drawn characters – which begs the question, why is it so difficult to distinguish between attitudes voiced by characters and those voiced by creators? – then the achievement was more to neuter, indeed almost to obliterate, the drama.

The truly odd thing was that Barenboim conducted the remaining torso of Berg's score in excellent fashion, so much so that one could almost, especially if one knew the score, fill in the gaps. Despite the ruptures, there seemed to be a true understanding of both dramatic and musical flow and the generative nature of Berg's twelve-note writing. Allied to a dark-hued, traditionally 'old German' Staatskapelle Berlin on fine form – 'authentic' in the best sense – there was a frustrating sense of what might have been, the work and/or other versions of the work reasserting itself or themselves. Much of the singing impressed too. In the title role, Mojca Erdmann sang for the most part as well as she acted, adopting a credible doll-like approach that permitted all manner of coloratura parallels – for instance, Offenbach's *Tales of Hoffmann* Olympia – to be drawn. Deborah Polaski offered an unusually forthright performance as Countess Geschwitz. Stephan Rügamer was compelled to perform a distinctly odd, questionably caricatured Negro dance, surely more offensive than anything alleged to be found in the opera itself, yet nevertheless emerged with credit, as did

Georg Nigl's Athlete, who, thanks to Breth's *Konzept*, also had to perform a great deal of background shadow-boxing (literally). Performances can contribute so much, but they could not in this case salvage a dramaturgical and musicological mess. As, then, with Guth's *Don Giovanni*, we found ourselves almost by default in the world of Levin's 'weak enactment', as discussed in the Introduction, or at least veering towards it, although such was surely never the intention.

V

By contrast, a difficulty concerning 'versions' of *Lulu* had worked itself out rather well two years earlier, at the 2010 Salzburg Festival. On this occasion, the 'problem' had originated with the originally intended conductor, Nikolaus Harnoncourt, who had wished to perform the work, in the tradition of Zurich – a house with which he held a lengthy association – as a two-act torso. Questionable, one might think; but again, it might have made one think about the work, completion, and so forth. Harnoncourt withdrew, however, and his replacement, Marc Albrecht, wished to restore the third act, requiring the swift provision of additional scenes. In difficult circumstances, the director, Vera Nemirova, a Konwitschny protégée, coped rather well. If the staging of the third act bore certain signs of haste and did not necessarily mesh quite so well with what had gone before, that in itself had its own story to tell. Several audience members were heard to say that they were able to discern the 'different style' of Cerha as opposed to Berg; whether 'objectively' true or otherwise, reflection upon the work concept had resulted in reflection upon it. The reinstated Paris Scene, swiftly imagined by virtue of necessity, proved a provocative triumph. Indeed, it seemed as though Nemirova, liberated by the relatively short notice of staging, had relied upon theatrical instinct to extend her performative idea of metatheatricality, doubtless suggested by the Animal Tamer's Prologue, omitted in Berlin. Earlier scenes had had mirrors reveal conductor, orchestra, and the audience, but the *coup de théâtre* was for this act to open with end-of-interval toasts from within the audience, members of whom were revealed actually to be characters in the opera. (It took no wild leap of imagination to imagine figures dressed in evening tails and ball-gowns as members of a Salzburg audience.) The action was thereafter played out in a space that blurred, if not quite obliterated, the boundary between 'performance' and the world beyond. It was hardly a novel concept in itself; the question was whether it worked, and it did. Lulu's (Patricia Petibon's) emergence down the steps of the Felsenreitschule in a slinky, stylish gown – Klaus Noack's costume design especially telling here – enhanced her classic 'star' quality, in retrospect all the more poignant, all the more an indictment of capitalist society, on account of its brevity.

Animal masks donned by her retinue both emphasised inhumanity and harked back to that metatheatrical Prologue. All the world, or at least all the riding school, was a stage. The audience, senses heightened by such direct 'involvement', was given the opportunity to feel responsibility for the capitalist world of shareholding boom-and-bust that would in short succession elevate and destroy the (anti-)heroine. Shares in Jungfrau – the English translation, 'Virgin', offers a splendid contemporary irony – might have been held, or short-sold, by almost anyone present. Likewise, Lulu's refusal to accept the Marquis's offer of an opportunity in a Cairo brothel, that refusal resulting in his reporting her to the police and thus her flight to London, might have been her refusal to any or indeed to all of us. Even in a production that largely rejected the temporality of which Berg's score speaks so evocatively, the political was teasingly yet defiantly reinstated, rendering social and economic structures at least as guilty as sexual politics.

VI

Meanwhile, back in (East) Berlin, the Komische Oper, traditionally the most 'radical' of the city's houses and truest to an idealised sense of its Marxist dramaturgical heritage, presented in October 2012 the Austrian composer Olga Neuwirth's *American Lulu*, composed over the preceding six years. This new/old 'work' has already received a good number of performances elsewhere, including an Opera Group presentation at London's Young Vic theatre in September 2013, Neuwirth's version billed then as a 'new interpretation'.

In a work lasting about half the time of the original, Neuwirth and Helga Utz adapt, including reorchestration, the first two acts; Neuwirth writes her own third act, both text and music. With Berg's – admittedly, selectively employed – jazz-influenced scoring in mind, Neuwirth's reorchestration and composition alike make their move to New Orleans via a wind-dominated ensemble, Berg's voluptuous strings put in their place and now heard through an aural filter of Brecht-Weill. More contentious, perhaps, is the inclusion of more popular music 'proper', especially Eleanor's (our new Geschwitz's) blues music, into the score. Its incorporation, presumably intentionally so – though, as we know, intention is far from all – is oddly uncritical, as if the consequence of a curious evasion of Adorno, typical of a good deal of post-modernist cultural criticism. It seems to be suggested that Berg's opera stands in need of criticism, but that of an allegedly purer popular culture does not. The new version of the film music – and we actually saw a film at the Young Vic, in John Fulljames's production – is brought to us, like the 'jazz band' music, via a recording of a Wonder Morton organ: evocative, contemporaneous, and yet also, rightly for a new work, somewhat oblique in its relationship to the 'original'. The third act of *Lulu* proper, which Neuwirth regards as 'unsatisfactory' – 'after great trials and tribulations, two women are simply slaughtered by a serial killer; and that is that' – becomes instead 'an unresolved murder case'. Neuwirth, however strongly we may disagree with her assessment of the 'original', is inspired to offer her own music, clearly flowing from that of Berg, still more from that of Berg-Neuwirth, and yet which takes on a life of its own: a twenty-first-century re-imagination of post-expresssionist music. There are coloratura vocal leaps; there is vocal seduction; there is a hard-edged, yet sinuous quality: in line with, yet not to be identified with, Berg's own.

What of the new setting? In lieu of Berg's Prologue, we start at the end, in 1970s New York, when Clarence (Schigolch) asks Lulu why, when she is now so wealthy, she is no more satisfied, prompting her to look back at her life, beginning in 1950s New Orleans. A photographer with whom she is living is soon supplanted by Dr Bloom, purchaser of the pictures; Lulu dances in Bloom's club, music written for her by his son, Jimmy. Some of Berg's intricate parallelism falls by the wayside as Neuwirth's drama takes on a different trajectory, yet there are compensations of sorts. The 'new' drama is punctuated by reminders of the Civil Rights Movement: words from Martin Luther King, and sounds, in Eleanor's final song, of 'We shall overcome'. It is not subtle, and it is perhaps all too easy to retort, 'that is the point', but it helps us appreciate more fully the balancing-act between existential and social – far too often tilted on stage in favour of the former – in Berg's opera.

Should we consider *American Lulu* in reference to Berg's work, or as a work in itself? That depends, of course, on who 'we' are. Either we know the original or we do not, but a question that permits neither 'yes' or 'no' as a 'straight' answer is a good question for Neuwirth to be asking audiences, steeped in all-too-often unreflective notions of *Werktreue*. It is certainly not the case that *Lulu* stands in 'need' of such attention as Gluck's *Iphigénie* seems to have done in Wagner's Dresden, but that should not disqualify Neuwirth's attempt, far more successful than a great deal of negative critical opinion permitted. Adding a further twist of work-problematisation, not only the Young Vic, but the Komische Oper, a house that has, since the days of its creator Walter Felsenstein, prided itself upon opera in the (German) vernacular, gave the work in English. Work and political implications alike continue to develop.

VII

Nono considered *Lulu*, even in its 'incomplete' form, to be one of the two greatest operas of the twentieth century, the other being Schoenberg's *Die glückliche Hand*.[18] In many ways, it would have been fitting to draw towards a close by considering performances of *Intolleranza 1960*, and indeed Henze's *Natascha Ungeheuer*. Alas, during my time at work on this book I have been unable to attend any – and if stagings of the former are rare enough, those of the latter seem non-existent. However, it seems equally fitting to take the story on from *Intolleranza*, in order to consider Nono's second music drama, *Al gran sole carico d'amore*, especially when the principal staging addressed has strong connections with a house and a director prominent in our story so far. Moreover, a staging which deals in a strong sense with the work concept, imparting what is perhaps an 'unfaithful' yet fruitful unity to Nono's multivalent work, helps bring together in one sense or another not only most of the histories recounted in this chapter, but a good number of those explored in this book.

Al gran sole, composed between 1972 and 1974, and premiered in Milan in 1975, was first directed by Yuri Lyubimov, head of Moscow's Taganka Theatre. Lyubimov was already a specialist from stagings of repertoire works in many of the techniques he and Nono, as joint librettists, drawing upon a vast assemblage of other writers, would employ in *Al gran sole*: montage: simultaneity, representation of one character – insofar as 'character' does not mislead – by several actors or singers. Those 'laterna magika' techniques familiar from *Intolleranza* may thereby be understood to have been rejuvenated and extended. The historical scenes presented in this *azione scenica* – Nono by now rejected entirely the term 'opera', though so of course had Wagner – are told from different perspectives, albeit with a privileged place, allotted to women and their often unspoken, let alone unsung, histories, inverting the 'normal' order of things. (In a sense, though not necessarily in the same sense, Neuwirth would attempt something similar in *American Lulu*.) Differing perspectives all serve to focus attention back upon the present, always a construct rather than a given, a state of affairs dramatically heightened by the productive tension between Nono's

[18] Luigi Nono, 'Gespräch mit Martine Cadieu [I]', in *Texte: Studien zu seiner Musik*, ed. Jürg Stenzl (Atlantis: Zurich, 1975), p. 181.

present and our own. Texts originate – in alphabetical order, so as not to imply priority – with Brecht, Tania Bunke (the Argentine-East German 'Tania the Guerilla', who fought in the Bolivian insurgency alongside Che Guevara), Fidel Castro, Che Guevara, the Bulgarian Communist Georgi Dimitrov, Gorki, Gramsci, Lenin, Marx, the Paris Communard Louise Michel (herself a 'character' in the action), Cesare Pavese, Rimbaud, and the Cuban revolutionaries Celia Sánchez and Haydée Santamaria, as well as other popular sources, such as the Internationale and two Russian revolutionary songs. Those sources are in themselves indicative; one would hardly expect that gathering of writers to be transformed into a paean to American militarism and consumer capitalism.

By the same token, however, the specific nature of the assemblage, just as in Berio's *Sinfonia* – or, for that matter, Bach's music for the Mass in B minor – is the thing. Three European societies are visited in the throes of revolution or would-be revolution. We observe, construct, participate in the 1871 Paris Commune, the Russia of 1905, and the industrial travails of post-Second World War Turin ('around 1950'). Nono's and Italy's own Cold War(s) find themselves situated both within that broader revolutionary context and within specific conflicts of Christian Democracy against Italian Communism, and – recalling *Intolleranza* – the problem of migration, in this case Italian workers from the south seeking work in the richer north, more specifically those car factories to which Nono took his music and to which friends such as Pollini and Abbado took theirs.

European history is for Nono now understood through the prism of recent developments such as the Chilean coup that had overthrown Salvador Allende in 1973 – a setback that had sent shockwaves through the European Left, ensuring that Allende's government and the succeeding terror under Augusto Pinochet would retain emblematic status for decades to come – and the American invasion of Vietnam. Nono's collage-like vision also encompasses conflicts in the Third World, as it was still called: Cuba, Bolivia, and Vietnam.[19] Revolutionary situations are thus brought into contact with each other, workers of the world uniting, that dialectic

---

[19] Nono would most likely have rejected the term 'collage'. He certainly spoke unfavourably of it in his 1959 Darmstadt lecture, 'Geschichte und Gegenwart der Musik von Heute', though it is not entirely clear whether he intended this as a general critique or in specific reference to Cage: 'The collage-method has its origin in colonialist thought, and there is no functional difference between a hollow Indian incantation drum, which serves in a European household as a dustbin, and the orientalisms which are used by an occidental culture to make its aesthetical tinkering with material more attractive.' (*Texte*, p. 38.)

of engagement standing at the very heart of Nono's understanding. For instance, following a prelude in which we hear words from Guevara, Michel, and Marx, the first scene has Tania Bunke question – such questioning being crucial to Nono's and indeed to our critical framework – Brecht on the Paris Communards. The expression and expressive form of that questioning is entrusted, as the score has it, to 'chorus and orchestra'. As in *Moses und Aron*, only more so, we might understand, with the composer's warrant, the principal protagonist to be the chorus; yet behind it there lies, consciously or otherwise, another chorus: Wagner's Greek Chorus of the orchestra.

The year 2009 marked something of a red-letter day for *Al gran sole*, Europe witnessing two major stagings. The first was at the Salzburg Festival, directed by Katie Mitchell. Peter Konwitschny brought his production, originally seen in Hamburg, to Leipzig later that year. Konwitschny's short-lived appointment as director of productions at Oper Leipzig was an important factor in this case, enabling him to bring to his new house an already-existing production, which would nevertheless be modified in context, as Nono would have hoped. Likewise, in Salzburg, Jürgen Flimm's artistic directorship was crucial. He had also produced the work before, for Frankfurt in 1978, his first opera production and the premiere of Nono's revised version of the work. Although, on this occasion, Flimm ceded that role to Katie Mitchell, the role of individual champions should not be underestimated.

Despite the obvious attractions and relevance to the work of Mitchell's overtly metatheatrical approach, Konwitschny's attempt to elicit more of a conventional revolutionary narrative actually cohered better in practice. Mitchell's framing of the artwork and its production – in the ordinary as well as the theatrical sense – seems often to work better when applied to a work that does not already contain so much of its metatheatrical apparatus to begin with. For instance, her 2009 *After Dido*, for the English National Opera at the Young Vic theatre, 'a live music and film performance inspired by Purcell's *Dido and Aeneas*', at whose core stood a performance of Purcell's opera, was able to go beyond the work to tell, in the words of the publicity material, 'three contemporary urban stories of grief, lost love, departure, and death', which unfolded in self-contained locations on different sections of the stage. Yet *After Dido* was also to be found in 'the making of' these stories, unfolding before our eyes and ears. That 'making of' was not so much a story in itself, after the manner of the Prologue to *Ariadne auf Naxos*; nevertheless, it acquired a dramatic thrust of its own, not least since it was with those 'workings' that the piece opened, as the prologue to a radio broadcast, during which we heard recorded snatches of other theatre music by Purcell. (*Dido's* own Prologue is, of course missing, the missing parts of the work having in the past offered a spur to composer-conductors such as Britten, as well as to directors such as Mitchell.[20]) Applying similar techniques to *Al gran sole* seemed less necessary and, for all the technical prowess involved, did not entirely silence suspicions that a 'one size fits all' metatheatricality was being imposed upon the work. Konwitschny's more 'operatic' approach came across as the more radical, even the more interventionist, and also the more dramatically and politically fruitful.

It was both heartening and instructive to witness the warmth of the reception and the size of the house for the last night of Konwitschny's *Al gran sole*. The immediacy of the almost 'operatic' experience came as quite a contrast after the familiar Mitchell on-stage screening and re-screening of scenes – and not solely in terms of staging. For an interesting and commendable aspect of both productions was how closely integrated staging and musical performance seemed to be. Whereas Konwitschny, aided once again by Helmut Brade's designs, took one very much into the heart of Nono's revolutionary 'provocations' of which Nono spoke as being the origins of all his work, the Salzburg performance had tended to look back at such matters as more a thing of the past, presenting a more æstheticised experience.

Much doubtless depends upon how relevant today one considers the writings and experiences of the men and women involved; or, to put it another way, how ripe one considers the time for a more sober, historical, even distanced assessment of concerns, which, following the events of 1989, might no longer be considered to be our own. In addition, there is a strong ideological impetus to claim those concerns as of little relevance, not least from the standpoint of the apparent 'victors' of German uni-fication, on either side of the erstwhile Iron Curtain. Oddly, or perhaps not so oddly, such an impetus seems at least as strong on the so-called Left as the Right; indeed, one of the more striking aspects of thoughtful

---

[20] Britten did not go so far as to compose new music for *Dido and Aeneas*. However, in the edition he made with Imogen Holst – less far-reaching in its interventions than for the more problematical semi-opera, *The Fairy Queen* – he added at the end of the second act a trio for the Sorceress and witches, borrowing music from *The Indian Queen*, a chorus from the 1687 *Welcome Song*, Z. 335, and a dance from the Overture to the play, *Sir Anthony Love or, The Rambling Lady*. He also went beyond additions of dynamic markings, phrasing, and articulation to realise the harpsichord continuo part. The Britten version, conducted by the (new) composer, may be heard in a 1959 BBC studio recording on CD (BBC Legends BBCB 8003–2).

right-wing commentary on the financial crisis has been its willingness to look to Marx.

In any case, more direct revolutionary experience, as opposed to the concerns of modern-day political economy, was granted heightened relevance by the location, Leipzig, where, as the production team pointed out, there was no need to ask whether the audience would understand the barrage of revolutionary texts presented, at least when it came to Marx, Lenin, Brecht, and Gorki.[21] Or perhaps there actually was every reason in 2009 to question that belief; old revolutionaries have a tendency to forget that the world has 'moved on'. At any rate, the timing of the premiere on 8 October would have made its point to some at least in the specific audience: the eve of the twentieth anniversary of what was the largest protest to date in the GDR's history, 75,000 demonstrators attending the Leipzig Monday Peace Prayers, bravely defying a regime that had just congratulated its Chinese counterpart for its 'success' in dealing with demonstrators in Tiananmen Square.[22] In little more than a week, Erich Honecker would have resigned. The role assumed by the then *Gewandhauskapellmeister*, Kurt Masur, in the events of 1989 is well known. Many in the orchestra would have played under him; some of the audience would have heard him conduct at the Gewandhaus, just on the other side of the Karl-Marx-Platz – now, once again, the Augustusplatz – from the Opera.

There were concrete settings: the Paris Commune for the first part and Turin for the second part's industrial unrest, although that did not prevent additional voices – and faces – from participating. Lenin as chorus leader was a witty touch, likewise the Punch and Judy politicians' act of Adolphe Thiers and Bismarck. The latter pair, even in the original 'text', if one can speak of such a thing, veered still more closely to the 'operatic' or even to the *commedia dell'arte*. But it was with the Gorki-Brecht tale of the Mother – did Nono here have an echo of the *Prigioniero* Mother in his mind? – and Pavese's prostitute Deola, that Konwitschny went for the jugular, particularly with respect to the factory strike. Malevolence was brought to vivid theatrical life, not only on the part of the factory owner – though there was something splendidly agitprop about him and

21 Alexander von Maravić, 'Post scriptum Leipzig 2009,' to 'Die Liebe – vom Leben beladen. Zu Stück und Aufführung. Helmut Brade, Johannes Harneit und Peter Konwitschny im Gespräch mit Albrecht Puhlmann in Hannover 2004,' in Oper Leipzig programme to Luigi Nono, *Unter der großen Sonne von Liebe beladen/Al gran sole carico d'amore* (2009), p. 37.
22 Dirk Philipsen, *We Were the People: Voices from East Germany's Revolutionary Autumn of 1989* (Duke University Press: Durham, NC, 1993), p. 200.

about the worker who betrayed his comrades – but also, more crucially, with respect to the entire mode of production upon which such structures were based. Nevertheless, an almost traditional evocation of theatrical or *Parsifal*-like compassion, true in spirit to Nono's own responses, won out with respect to the workers hemmed in by the walls of Brade's designs. There was anger, of course, but the human spirit came first, recalling Dallapiccola, especially in the defiance of the Mother's son, Pavel, a martyr and true hero to the socialist cause.

Every member of the cast contributed wholeheartedly and it would be more than typically invidious to single out anyone in particular. Iris Vermillion's mother provoked, however, perhaps the most powerful emotional response, through the human dignity of a lonely yet true contralto voice: quintessential Nono, one might say, in thought and in practice. Tuomas Pursio's Pavel was just as impressive: an angry young man who could so easily have gone off the rails, he was in a sense saved by the desperation of the situation: his finest hour. Pursio exhibited a sense of dangerous attraction, which could finally be focused rather than dissipated. Perhaps though there was also a warning (from Konwitschny, if not from Nono), of how revolutionaries might go astray, the erstwhile GDR proffering an obvious example. Moreover, in the context of the relationships explored above of both Henze and Nono with their home and quasi-adoptive countries, the intervention of an Italian composer in a 'German' matter offers another standpoint from which one might consider such questions.

Neither librettist nor composer left any stage directions – an interesting case from our standpoint. Were the vigilantes of 'fidelity' to the work to come across this, who knows what they might make of it? It is unlikely, however, given that their energies appear concentrated more or less entirely upon 'standard repertoire', a telling point in itself.

VIII

Nono's works of the 1980s are more commonly understood to be enigmatic, requiring the listener to find his own path, symbolised by a thirteenth-century inscription he came across in Toledo in 1985, 'Caminantes, no hay caminos, hay que caminar' ('Travellers, there are no paths, only travelling itself'). The 1987 memorial piece for Tarkovsky, *No hay caminos, hay que caminar... Andrei Tarkovskiji*, would offer something of a testament in retrospect to the composer's 'late', allegedly more internalised, preoccupations, Nono's third and final music drama, *Promoteo*, included. Yet already in *Al gran sole*, Nono had demonstrated his belief that the revolutionary pilgrim must act similarly, find his or her pathway, construct the necessary history and respond accordingly. Every performance, every production will be different, not only or even principally from æsthetic necessity, but because the provocations to which it will respond, and which it might in return propose, will always be different. To put it another, perhaps better, way, æsthetic necessity is political necessity; alternatively, there can no more be 'absolute' music than 'absolute' politics. 'Every musician,' and we might say by extension, every listener, 'chooses in the contemporary world his own standpoint and every choice is political.'[23] Just as *Al gran sole* invokes a choice we might consider existentialist in addition to its overtly 'political' content, so would one of the late companion pieces to *No hay caminos*, *Caminantes Ayacucho*, explicitly reinstate political commitment, invoking the southern Peruvian city of Ayacucho, scene of a rebellion against the Spanish in the early nineteenth century and of severe social unrest ever since, up to and including that involving the Maoist Shining Path guerillas.[24]

No more than for Wagner, then, was there a straightforward progression or regression from revolution to metaphysical withdrawal. We do not know how Nono, who died on 8 May 1990, would have reacted to the longer-term aftermath and consequences of the revolutions of 1989, to claims of the 'end of history' and so forth, though his 1982 *Quando stanno morendo, Diario polacco no. 2* had already offered something of a 'J'accuse' against Leonid Brezhnev's USSR. Brezhnev's *sozialistische Bruderkuß* with Honecker had perhaps already lost whatever currency it might once have held. However, there is no more reason to think that Nono's world-view would have collapsed than to claim that the experience of exile 150 years earlier should have led Wagner to turn his back upon the revolution in which he had fought and which he would then set out to chronicle, to criticise, to memorialise, to relive. Witness ceases neither after the event nor beyond the grave; indeed, it often proves to be then and only then that Minerva will bid her choicest owls take flight.

Or, as Wagner put it in a letter to Theodor Uhlig, in which we earlier saw outlined the necessity for *post*-revolutionary performance of the *Ring*:

[23] Nono, 'Gespräch mit Martine Cadieu [II], in ibid., p. 188.
[24] See Jayme Patricia Heilman, *Before the Shining Path: Politics in Rural Ayacucho 1895–1980* (Stanford University Press: Stanford, 2010); Cynthia McClintock, 'Peru's Sendero Luminoso Rebellion: Origins and Trajectory,' in *Power and Popular Protest: Latin American Social Movements*, ed. Susan Eckstein, 2nd edn (University of California Press: Berkeley and Los Angeles, 2001), pp. 61–101.

However extravagant this plan may be, it is nevertheless the only one upon which I can wager my life, my writing, my energies. Should I witness its achievement, so shall I have lived gloriously; if not, so shall I have died for the sake of something beautiful. Only this [idea] can still cheer me. –

Leb wohl![25]

[25] Letter to Theodor Uhlig of 12 November 1851, in Wagner, *Sämtliche Briefe*, vol. 4, p. 176

BIBLIOGRAPHY

Abbado, Claudio, 'My Silent Friend: Remembering Luigi Nono,' in *Contemporary Music Review*, 18 (1999), 3–5

Abbado, Claudio and representatives of the Berlin Philharmonic Orchestra, concert programme declaration from 9/10 December 1992, printed in the accompanying booklet to the CD release of Abbado's live Berlin recording of *Il canto sospeso*, Sony CD SK 53360

Abbate, Carolyn, *In Search of Opera* (Princeton University Press: Princeton, 2001)

Abbate, Carolyn, 'Music – Drastic or Gnostic?' in *Critical Inquiry*, 30 (2004), 505–36

Adlington, Robert, *Louis Andriessen: De Staat* (Ashgate: Aldershot and Burlington, VT, 2004)

Adorno, Theodor Wiesengrund, 'Bourgeois Opera,' tr. David J. Levin, in *Opera Through Other Eyes*, ed. Levin, pp. 25–43

Adorno, Theodor Wiesengrund, *Essays on Music*, ed. Richard Leppert (University of California Press: Berkeley, Los Angeles, and London, 2002)

Adorno, Theodor Wiesengrund, *In Search of Wagner*, tr. Rodney Livingstone (Verso: London and New York, 1981)

Adorno, Theodor Wiesengrund, *Moments musicaux: Neu gedruckte Aufsätze 1928–1962* (Suhrkamp: Frankfurt am Main, 1964)

Adorno, Theodor Wiesengrund, *Prisms*, tr. Samuel and Sherry Weber (MIT Press: Cambridge, MA, 1981)

Adorno, Theodor Wiesengrund, *Quasi una Fantasia: Essays on Modern Music*, tr. Rodney Livingstone (Verso: London and New York, 1998)

Adorno, Theodor Wiesengrund, *Sound Figures*, tr. Rodney Livingstone (Stanford University Press: Stanford, 1999)

Adorno, Theodor Wiesengrund, *Versuch über Wagner* (Suhrkamp: Frankfurt, 1981)

Adorno, Theodor Wiesengrund, 'What Does Coming to Terms with the Past Mean?' in *Bitburg in Moral and Political Perspective*, ed. Geoffrey Hartman (Indiana University Press: Bloomington, 1986), pp. 114–29

Adorno, Theodor Wiesengrund, and Horkheimer, Max, *Dialectic of Enlightenment*, tr. John Cumming (Verso: London and New York, 1997)

Æschylus, 'Agamemnon', tr. Richmond Lattimore, in *Greek Tragedies*, ed. Grene and Lattimore (Chicago University Press: Chicago and London, 1991–), vol. 1, pp. 1–60

Albright, Daniel, 'Butchering Moses', in *The Opera Quarterly*, 23 (2007), 441–54

Alegant, Brian, *The Twelve-Note Music of Luigi Dallapiccola* (University of Rochester Press: Rochester, NY, 2010)

Alleg, Henri, *La Gangrène* (Minuit: Lausanne, 1959)

Alleg, Henri, *La Question*, with introduction by Jean-Paul Sartre (La Cité: Lausanne, 1958)

Allen, Roger, '"All is here music": Houston Stewart Chamberlain and *Der Ring des Nibelungen*', *wagnerspectrum*, 3 (2006), 155–68

Allen, Roger, '*Die Weihe des Hauses*: Houston Stewart Chamberlain and the Early Reception of *Parsifal*', in *A Companion to Wagner's Parsifal*, ed. Kinderman and Syer, pp. 245–76

Andriessen, Louis, 'Komponieren für *Die Massnahme*', in *Brechts Modell der Lehrstücke: Zeugnisse, Diskussion, Erfahrungen*, ed. Steinweg, pp. 362–82

Andriessen, Louis, note to *De Staat* (Boosey and Hawkes: New York and London, 1994)

Applegate, Celia, and Potter, Pamela (eds), *Music and German National Identity* (University of Chicago Press: Chicago, 2002)

Ashby, Arved (ed.), *The Pleasure of Modernist Music: Listening, Meaning, Intention, Ideology* (University of Rochester Press: Rochester, NY, and Woodbridge, 2004)

Auner, Joseph, 'Schoenberg as Moses and Aron', in *The Opera Quarterly*, 23 (2007), 373–84

Bachmann, Ingeborg, *Werke*, 4 vols, ed. Christine Koschel, Clemens Münster, and Inge von Weidenbaum (Piper: Munich and Zurich, 1993)

Bachmann, Ingeborg, *Zwei Hörspiele: Die Zikaden, Der gute Gott von Manhattan* (Oldenbourg: Munich, 1969)

Bailey, Walter (ed.), *The Schoenberg Companion* (Greenwood Press: Westport, Conn. and London, 1998)

Balzac, Honoré de, *Séraphita*, tr. Clara Bell (Dedalus: Sawtry and New York, 1989)

Baransky, Zygmunt G., and West, Rebecca G. (eds), *The Cambridge Companion to Modern Italian Culture* (Cambridge University Press: Cambridge, 2001)

Barone, Anthony, 'Richard Wagner's *Parsifal* and the Theory of Late Style,' in *Cambridge Opera Journal*, 7 (1995), 37–54

Barthes, Roland, 'Le Discours de l'histoire,' in *Information sur les sciences sociales*, 4 (1976), 65–75

Beales, Derek, *Prosperity and Plunder: European Catholic Monasteries in the Age of Revolution, 1650–1815* (Cambridge University Press: Cambridge, 2003)

Beckett, Lucy, *Parsifal* (Cambridge University Press: Cambridge, 1981)

Beiser, Frederick (ed.), *The Early Political Writings of the German Romantics*, tr. Frederick Beiser (Cambridge University Press: Cambridge, 1996)

Benedictis, Angela Ida de, and Mosch, Ulrich (eds), *Alla ricerca di luce e chiarezza: L'epistolario Helmut Lachenmann – Luigi Nono (1957–1990)*

Benjamin, Walter, *Illuminations*, tr. Harry Zohn, ed. Hannah Arendt (Harcourt: New York, 1969)

Benjamin, Walter, *Selected Writings*, ed. Michael W. Jennings *et al.*, 4 vols (Harvard University Press: Cambridge, MA, 1996–2003)

Benjamin, Walter, 'Theses on the Philosophy of History,' tr. Harry Zohn, in *German 20th Century Philosophy: The Frankfurt School*, ed. Schirmacher, pp. 71–80

Berio, Luciano, *Two Interviews*, with Rossana Dalmonte and Bálint András Varga, ed. and tr. David Osmond-Smith (Marion Boyars: New York and London, 1985)

Berman, Russell A., 'The Subjects of Community: Aspiration, Memory, Resistance 1918–1945,' in *Philosophy and German Literature, 1700–1990*, ed. Saul, pp. 197–244

Berry, Mark, 'Owing the World a *Tannhäuser*,' in Royal Opera House programme for *Tannhäuser*, December 2010, 22–6

Berry, Mark, Review in *Opera*, 63 (2012), 1425–6

Berry, Mark, 'Richard Wagner and the Politics of Music Drama,' in *Historical Journal*, 47 (2004), 663–83

Berry, Mark, 'Romantic Modernism: Bach, Furtwängler, and Adorno,' in *New German Critique*, 104, vol. 35, no. 2 (Spring/Summer 2008), 71–102

Berry, Mark, *Treacherous Bonds and Laughing Fire: Politics and Religion in Wagner's 'Ring'* (Ashgate: Aldershot and Burlington, VT, 2006)

Berry, Mark, 'Wagner Rescued from the Opera House?' in *The Wagner Journal*, 7/3 (2013), 3

Berry, Mark, 'Where it all Began: Fairies in Leipzig,' in *The Wagner Journal*, 7/3 (2013), 57–60

Biess, Frank, *Homecomings: Returning POWs and the Legacies of Defeat in Postwar Germany* (Princeton University Press: Princeton, 2006)

Bitter, Christof, *Wandlungen in den Inszenierungsformen des Don Giovanni, 1787–1928* (Bosse: Regensburg, 1961)

Blanning, Tim, 'Richard Wagner and Max Weber,' in *wagnerspectrum*, 2 (2005), 93–110

Blanning, Tim, 'The Enlightenment in Catholic Germany,' in *The Enlightenment in National Context*, ed. Roy Porter and Teich, pp. 118–26

Bloch, Ernst, *Geist der Utopie*, 2nd edn (Suhrkamp: Frankfurt am Main, 1980)

Bokina, John, *Opera and Politics from Monteverdi to Henze* (Yale University Press: New Haven and London, 1997)

Borchmeyer, Dieter, *Drama and the World of Richard Wagner*, tr. Daphne Ellis (Princeton University Press: Princeton, 2003)

Borio, Gianmorio, 'Nono, Luigi,' *Grove Music Online. Oxford Music Online*. Oxford University Press. Web. 15 March 2012. <http://www.oxfordmusiconline.com/subscriber/article/grove/music/20044>

Botstein, Leon, 'The Enigmas of Richard Strauss: A Revisionist View,' in *Richard Strauss and his World*, ed. Gilliam, pp. 3–32

Boulez, Pierre, 'Boulez on Schoenberg's "Moses und Aron". An Interview with Wolfgang Schaufler,' tr. Stewart Spencer, in booklet accompanying Deutsche Grammophon CD 449 174-2

Boulez, Pierre, *Conversations with Célestin Deliège*, tr. Robert Wangermée (Eulenburg: London, 1976)

Boulez, Pierre, *Orientations: Collected Writings*, ed. Jean-Jacques Nattiez, tr. Martin Cooper (Faber: London and Boston, 1986)

Boulez, Pierre, *Relevés d'apprenti*, ed. Paule Thévenin (Seuil: Paris, 1966)

Boulez, Pierre, and Chéreau, Patrice, 'Commentaires sur "Mythologie et idéologie",' in *Programmhefte der Bayreuther Festspiele*, 1977, no. 6, 1–19, 86–102

Boulez, Pierre, and Liebermann, Rolf, '"Opera Houses? – Blow them up!" Pierre Boulez versus Rolf Liebermann,' in *Opera*, 19 (1968), 440–50

Bowie, Andrew, *Music, Philosophy, and Modernity* (Cambridge University Press: Cambridge, 2009)

Brand, Juliane, Hailey, Christopher, and Harris, Donald (eds), *The Berg-Schoenberg Correspondence* (Macmillan: Basingstoke, 1987)

Brecht, Bertolt, *Der aufhaltsame Aufstieg des Arturo Ui* (Suhrkamp: Frankfurt, 1969)

Brecht, Bertolt, *Gesammelte Werke*, 20 vols (Suhrkamp: Frankfurt, 1967)

Brecht, Bertolt, 'Sonnet über Kleists Stück "Prinz von Homburg",' reprinted with commentary by Walter Benjamin, in 'Commentary on Poems by Brecht', tr. Edmund Jephcott, in Benjamin, *Selected Writings*, vol. 4, pp. 237–8

Breckmann, Warren, 'Politics in a Symbolic Key: Pierre Leroux, Romantic Socialism, and the Schelling Affair', in *Modern Intellectual History*, 2 (2005), 61–86

Brindle, Reginald Smith, *The New Music: The Avant-garde Since 1945*, 2nd edn (Oxford University Press: Oxford, 1987)

Brug, Manuel, 'Regisseur Herheim nennt Barenboim "disziplinlos"', in *Die Welt*, 3 April 2009

Busoni, Ferruccio, *Selected Letters*, tr. and ed. Anthony Beaumont (Columbia University Press: New York, 1987)

Busoni, Ferruccio, 'Sketch of a New Esthetic of Music', in *Three Classics in the Aesthetic of Music* (Dover: New York, 1962), tr. Theodore Baker, pp. 73–102

Cahn, Steven J., 'The Artist as Modern Prophet: A Study of Historical Consciousness and its expression in Schoenberg's "Vorgefühl," Op. 22 no. 4', in *Schoenberg and Words: The Modernist Years*, ed. Cross and Berman, pp. 243–71

Cardew, Cornelius, *Stockhausen Serves Imperialism, and Other Articles* (Latimer New Dimensions: London, 1974)

Carlson, Marvin, 'Meiningen Crowd Scenes and the Theatre-Libre', in *Educational Theatre Journal*, 13 (1961), 245–9

Carnegy, Patrick, *Wagner and the Art of the Theatre* (Yale University Press: New Haven and London, 2006)

Carr, Edward Hallett, *What is History?* (Penguin: Harmondsworth, 2008)

Certeau, Michel de, *L'Ecriture de l'histoire* (Gallimard: Paris, 1975)

Chamberlain, Houston Stewart, 'Notes sur *Parsifal*', in *Revue wagnérienne*, 2 (1886–7), 220–6

Cherlin, Michael, 'Dialectical Opposition in Schoenberg's Music and Thought', in *Music Theory Spectrum*, 22 (2000), 157–76

Christiansen, Rupert, 'Boulez and the Blight of Opera', in *The Daily Telegraph*, 7 September 1996

Christensen, Jean, 'The Spiritual and the Material in Schoenberg's Thinking', in *Music and Letters*, 65 (1984), 337–44

Chua, Daniel, *Absolute Music and the Construction of Meaning* (Cambridge University Press: Cambridge, 1999)

Cicora, Mary A., 'Medievalism and Metaphysics: the Literary Background of *Parsifal*', in *A Companion to Wagner's Parsifal*, ed. Kinderman and Syer, pp. 29–53

Cieszkowski August von, *Prolegomena zur Historiosophie* (Veit: Berlin, 1838)

Clark, Christopher, *Iron Kingdom: The Rise and Downfall of Prussia, 1600–1947* (Allen Lane: London, 2006)

Cohen, Josh, *Interrupting Auschwitz: Art, Religion, Philosophy* (Continuum: New York and London, 2003)

Covach, John, 'The Sources of Schoenberg's Aesthetic Theology,' in *19th-Century Music*, 19 (1996), 252–62

Craft, Robert, *Stravinsky: Chronicle of a Friendship* (Knopf: New York, 1973)

Cross, Charlotte M., and Berman, Russell A. (eds), *Political and Religious Ideas in the Works of Arnold Schoenberg* (Garland: New York and London, 2000)

Cross, Charlotte M., and Berman, Russell A. (eds), *Schoenberg and Words: The Modernist Years* (Garland: New York and London, 2000)

Dahlhaus, Carl, *Foundations of Music History*, tr. J. B. Robinson (Cambridge University Press: Cambridge, 1993)

Dahlhaus, Carl, *Ludwig van Beethoven: Approaches to his Music*, tr. Mary Whittall (Oxford University Press: Oxford, 1991)

Dahlhaus, Carl, 'Plädoyer für eine romantische Kategorie – Der Begriff des Kunstwerks in der neuesten Musik,' in *Neue Zeitschrift für Musik*, 130 (1969), 18–22

Dahlhaus, Carl, *Richard Wagner's Music Dramas*, tr. Mary Whittall (Cambridge University Press: Cambridge, 1979)

Dahlhaus, Carl, *Schoenberg and the New Music*, tr. Derrick Puffett and Alfred Clayton (Cambridge University Press: Cambridge, 1987)

Dahlhaus, Carl, *The Idea of Absolute Music*, tr. Roger Lustig (University of Chicago Press: Chicago and London, 1989)

Dallapiccola, Luigi, *Dallapiccola on Opera – Selected Writings of Luigi Dallapiccola: Volume One*, ed. and tr. Rudy Shackleford (Toccata Press: London, 1987)

Dallapiccola, Luigi, 'Meeting with Webern (Pages from a Diary),' tr. John C. G. Waterhouse, in *Tempo*, New Series, 99 (1972), 2–7

Dallapiccola, Luigi, *Saggi, Testimonianze, Carteggio, Biografia e Bibliografia*, ed. Fiamma Nicolodi (Suvini Zerboni: Milan, 1975)

Dangerfield, George, *The Strange Death of Liberal England* (Harrison Smith and Robert Haas: New York, 1935)

Daub, Adrian, '"Taceat Muller in Theatro": Guntram, Schopenhauer, and the Female Voice,' in *Opera Quarterly*, 25 (2009), 230–46

Deathridge, John, and Döge, Klaus (eds), 'Dokumente und Texte zu "Lohengrin",' in Wagner, *Sämtliche Werke*, vol. 26

Debussy, Claude, 'Monsieur Croche the Dilettante Hater', tr. B. N. Langdon Davies, in *Three Classics in the Aesthetic of Music* (Dover: New York, 1962), pp. 1–71

De Felice, Renzo, *Il fascismo: Le interpretazioni dei contemporanei e degli storici* (Laterza: Rome, 1970)

Del Mar, Norman, *Richard Strauss: A Commentary on his Life and Works*, 3 vols (Barrie and Rockliff: London, 1962–72)

Derrida, Jacques, *Spectres de Marx: l'état de la dette, le travail du deuil et la nouvelle Internationale* (Galilée: Paris, 1993)

Dineen, Murray, 'Modernism and Words: Schoenberg, Adorno, Moses', in *Schoenberg and Words*, ed. Cross and Berman, pp. 347–66

Downes, Stephen, *Hans Werner Henze: Tristan (1973)* (Ashgate: Aldershot and Burlington, VT, 2011)

Dunn, James D. G., *Romans 1–8* (Thomas Nelson: Dallas, 1988)

Dunn, John, *Political Obligation in Its Historical Context: Essays in Political Theory* (Cambridge University Press: Cambridge, 1980)

Earle, Ben, 'Dallapiccola and the Politics of Commitment: Re-Reading *Il prigioniero*', in *Radical Musicology*, 2 (2007)

Earle, Ben, 'The Avant-Garde Artist as Superman: Aesthetics and Politics in Dallapiccola's *Volo di notte*', in *Italian Music During the Fascist Period*, ed. Illiano, pp. 657–716.

Earle, Ben, 'The Politics of the New Music', in *Music and Letters*, 94 (2013), 664–71

Eckstein, Susan (ed.), *Power and Popular Protest: Latin American Social Movements*, 2nd edn (University of California Press: Berkeley and Los Angeles, 2001)

Ehrhardt, Bettina (director), *A Trail on the Water*, TDK DVD DVWW-DOCNONO

Eliot, T. S., *Collected Poems 1909–1962* (Faber: London, 1963)

Eluard, Paul, *Œuvres complètes*, ed. Marcelle Dumas and Lucien Scheller (Gallimard: Paris, 1968)

Evans, Richard J., *In Defence of History* (Granta: London, 1997)

Falck, Robert, 'Emancipation of the Dissonance', *Journal of the Arnold Schoenberg Institute*, 6 (1982), 106–11

Fearn, Raymond, *The Music of Luigi Dallapiccola* (University of Rochester Press: Rochester, NY, and Woodbridge, 2003)

Feuerbach, Ludwig, *The Essence of Christianity*, tr. George Eliot (Prometheus: Buffalo, NY, 1989)

Fichte, Johann Gottlieb, *Sämtliche Werke*, 10 vols, ed. I. H. Fichte (Viet: Bonn and Berlin, 1834–46)

Forkel, Johann Nikolai, *Über Johann Sebastian Bachs Leben, Kunst und Kunstwerke*, ed. Claudia Maria Knipsel (Henschel: Berlin, 2000)

Forte, Allen, *The Structure of Atonal Music* (Yale University Press: New Haven, 1973)

Frei, Norbert, *Adenauer's Germany and the Nazi Past: The Politics of Amnesty and Integration* (Columbia University Press: New York, 2002)

Freud, Sigmund, *The Origins of Religion. Totem and Taboo, Moses and Monotheism, and Other Works*, tr. James Strachey *et al.*, ed. Albert Dickson (Penguin: Harmondsworth, 1985)

Fricke, Richard, *Wagner in Rehearsal, 1875–1876*, tr. George R. Fricke, ed. James Deaville with Evan Baker (Pendragon: Stuyvesant, NY, 1998)

Friedrich, Sven, 'Ambivalenz der Leidenschaft – Thomas Mann und Richard Wagner. Zum 125. Geburtstag Thomas Manns,' in *Programmhefte der Bayreuther Festspiele* (2000), 134–42

Fučik, Julius, *Reportage unter dem Strang geschrieben*, tr. Felix Rausch (Pahl-Rugenstein: Cologne, 2000)

Fukuyama, Francis, *The End of History and the Last Man* (Free Press: New York, 1992)

Gasca, Alberto, *Da Cimarosa a Stravinsky* (De Santis: Rome, 1939)

Gavin, Barrie (director), *Hans Werner Henze: Memoirs of an Outsider*, Arthaus Musik DVD 100360

Geck, Martin, and Voss, Egon (eds), 'Dokumente zur Entstehung und ersten Aufführung des Bühnenweihfestspiels "Parsifal",' in Wagner, *Sämtliche Werke*, vol. 30

Georgi, Steffen, 'Mein lieber Schwan,' in booklet to Pentatone PTC 5186 403, *Lohengrin*, 18–40

Gibbons, Tom H., 'Cubism and "The Fourth Dimension" in the Context of the Late Nineteenth-Century and Early Twentieth-Century Revival of Occult Idealism,' in *Journal of the Warburg and Courtauld Institutes*, 44 (1981), 130–47

Gilliam, Bryan (ed.), *Richard Strauss and his World* (Princeton University Press: Princeton, 1992)

Gilliam, Bryan, *The Life of Richard Strauss* (Cambridge University Press: Cambridge, 1999)

Goehr, Alexander, *Finding the Key: Selected Writings of Alexander Goehr*, ed. Derrick Puffett (Faber: London, 1998)

Goehr, Lydia, *The Imaginary Museum of Musical Works: An Essay in the Philosophy of Music* (Clarendon: Oxford, 1992)

Goethe, Johann Wolfgang von, *Faust: eine Tragödie*, ed. Erich Trunz (Beck: Munich, 1999)

Goethe, Johann Wolfgang von, *Sämtliche Werke, Tagebücher und Gespräche*, 39 vols in 43, ed. Dieter Borchmeyer *et al.* (Deutsche Klassiker: Frankfurt am Main, 1985–99)

Goethe, Johann Wolfgang von, *Werke*, 9th edn, ed. Erich Trunz, 14 vols (Beck: Munich, 1981)

Golding, William, *Lord of the Flies* (Edward Arnold: London, 1970)

Goldstein, Bluma, 'Schoenberg's "Moses und Aron": A Vanishing Biblical Nation,' in *Political and Religious Ideas*, ed. Cross and Berman, pp. 159–92

Gorodecki, Michael, 'Strands in 20th-Century Italian Music: 1 – Luigi Nono: A History of Belief,' in *The Musical Times*, 1787 (1992), 10–17

Gramsci, Antonio, *Selections from Cultural Writings*, tr. William Boelhower, ed. David Forgacs and Geoffrey Nowell-Smith (Lawrence and Wishart: London, 1985)

Gramsci, Antonio, *Selections from the Prison Notebooks*, ed. and tr. Quintin Hoare and Geoffrey Nowell Smith (Lawrence and Wishart: London, 1971)

Grene, David, and Richmond Lattimore, *Greek Tragedies* (Chicago University Press: Chicago and London, 1991–)

Griffiths, Paul, Review in *The Musical Times*, 114 (1973), 803

Gulbrandsen, Erling E., and Skramstad, Per-Erik, 'Stefan Herheim on working with Daniele Gatti, the choice of tempi and the staging of preludes,' tr. Jonathan Scott-Kiddie, http://www.wagneropera.net/Interviews/Stefan-Herheim-Gatti-Preludes.htm

Guth, Claus, conversation with Peter Schneeburger in Salzburg Festival programme for *Don Giovanni*, 2010

Haimo, Ethan, 'Schoenberg, Numerology, and *Moses und Aron*,' in *The Opera Quarterly*, 23 (2007), 385–94

Haimo, Ethan, *Schoenberg's Serial Odyssey: The Evolution of his Twelve-Tone Method, 1914–1928* (Oxford University Press: Oxford, 1990)

Haimo, Ethan, 'The Evolution of the Twelve-Note Method,' in *The Schoenberg Companion*, ed. Walter Bailey (Greenwood Press: Westport, CT, and London, 1998), pp. 101–28

Hamao, Fusako, 'The Origin and Development of Schoenberg's Twelve-Tone Method' (Ph.D. dissertation, Yale University, 1988)

Hamp, Anton, *Ein Blick in die Geisterwerkstatt Richard Wagners: Von einem alten geistlichen Freunde des Meisters von Bayreuth zur Erinnerung an dessen Schwanengesang – den 'Parzival'* (Berlin, 1904)

Harper-Scott, Paul, *The Quilting Points of Musical Modernism* (Cambridge University Press: Cambridge and New York, 2012)

Hartmann, Rudolph, *Richard Strauss: The Staging of his Operas and Ballets* (Phaidon: Oxford, 1982)

Harvey, David, *A Brief History of Neoliberalism* (Oxford University Press: Oxford, 2005)

Häusler, Josef, *Spiegel der neuen Musik, Donaueschingen: Chronik, Tendenzen, Werkbesprechungen* (Bärenreiter: Kassel, 1996)

Hegel, Georg Friedrich Wilhelm, *Werke*, ed. Eva Moldenhauer and Karl Markus Michel, 20 vols (Suhrkamp: Frankfurt am Main, 1969–72)

Heilman, Jayme Patricia, *Before the Shining Path: Politics in Rural Ayacucho 1895–1980* (Stanford University Press: Stanford, 2010)

Heine, Heinrich, *Sämtliche Werke*, ed. Oscar Walzel, 10 vols (Insel: Leipzig, 1911–15)

Helm, Everett, 'Luigi Dallapiccola in einem unveröffentlichten Gespräch,' in *Melos/Neue Zeitschrift für Musik*, 6 (1976), 469–71

Henze, Hans Werner, *Bohemian Fifths: An Autobiography*, tr. Stewart Spencer (Faber: London, 1999)

Henze, Hans Werner, Interview with Alan Blyth, in *Gramophone*, 49 (1972), 1690

Henze, Hans Werner, Interview with Ivan Hewett, *Daily Telegraph*, 7 January 2010

Henze, Hans Werner, *L'Upupa. Nachtstücke aus dem Morgenland: Autobiographische Mitteilungen* (Propyläen: Berlin, 2003)

Henze, Hans Werner, *Music and Politics: Collected Writings 1953–81*, tr. Peter Labanyi (Faber: London, 1982)

Henze, Hans Werner, and Ruzicka, Peter, 'Conversation between Hans Werner Henze and Peter Ruzicka,' 20 October 1999, tr. Steven Lindberg, in booklet note to Wergo CD WER 6637 2, pp. 18–26

Herz, Joachim, *Theater – Kunst des erfüllten Augenblicks*, ed. Ilse Kobán (Henschelverlag: Berlin, 1989)

Hess, Moses, *Philosophische und sozialistische Schriften 1837–1850*, ed. August Cornu and Wolfgang Mönke (Akademie-Verlag: Berlin, 1961)

Heyworth, Peter, 'The Gilded Cage,' in *Encounter*, 22 (1964), 74–8

Hockenos, Paul, *Joschka Fischer and the Making of the Berlin Republic: An Alternative History of Postwar Germany* (Oxford University Press: Oxford, 2008)

Hoffmann, E. T. A., *Sämtliche Werke*, 10 vols, ed. Georg von Maassen (Müller: Munich and Leipzig, 1908–28)

Holloway, Robin, 'Motif, Memory and Meaning in "Twilight of the Gods",' in *Twilight of the Gods / Götterdämmerung*, ed. John, pp. 13–38

Holub, Renate, *Antonio Gramsci: Beyond Marxism and Postmodernism* (Routledge: London and New York, 1992)

Honour, Hugh, *Romanticism* (Harper and Row: New York, 1979)

Horace, *Satires, Epistles, and Ars Poetica*, tr. H. Rushton Fairclough, revised edn (Harvard University Press: Cambridge, MA, 1929)

Horvath, Nina, 'The "Theatre of the Ear": Analyzing Berio's Musical Documentary *A-Ronne*,' in *Musical Explorations*, 10 (2009), 73–103

Illiano, Roberto (ed.), *Italian Music During the Fascist Period* (Brepols: Turnhout, 2004)

Jameson, Fredric, *Brecht and Method* (Verso: New York and London, 1998)

Jarman, Douglas, *The Music of Alban Berg* (University of California Press: Berkeley and Los Angeles, 1979)

John, Nicholas (ed.), *Twilight of the Gods / Götterdämmerung* (John Calder: London and New York, 1985)

Johnson, Julian, *Webern and the Transformation of Nature* (Cambridge University Press: Cambridge, 1999)

Jones, Ernest, *Sigmund Freud Life and Work, Volume Three: The Last Phase 1919–1939* (Hogarth Press: London, 1957)

Jünger, Ernst, *In Stahlgewittern* (Klett-Cotta: Stuttgart, 2007)

Kain, Philip J., *Schiller, Hegel, and Marx: State, Society, and the Aesthetic Ideal of Ancient Greece* (McGill-Queen's University Press: Kingston and Montreal, 1982)

Kämper, Dietrich, *Gefangenschaft und Freiheit: Leben und Werk des Komponisten Luigi Dallapiccola* (Gitarre und Laute: Cologne, 1984)

Kämpfer, Frank (ed.), *Sehnsucht nach unentfremdeter Produktion. Der Regisseur Peter Konwitschny. Ein Materialbuch* (Zentrum für Theaterdokumentation und -information: Berlin, 1992)

Kandinsky, Vasily, and Marc, Franz (eds), Der blaue Reiter (Piper: Munich, 1912)

Kant, Immanuel, *Critique of Judgment*, tr. Werner S. Pluhar (Hackett: Indianapolis, 1987)

Kant, Immanuel, *Critique of Pure Reason*, tr. Norman Kemp Smith (Palgrave Macmillan: Basingstoke and New York, 2003)

Kant, Immanuel, *Political Writings*, tr. H. B. Nisbet, ed. Hans Reiss (Cambridge University Press: Cambridge, 1970)

Kater, Michael H., *Composers of the Nazi Era: Eight Portraits* (Oxford University Press: Oxford, 1999)

Kienzle, Ulrike, '*Parsifal* and Religion: A Christian Music Drama?' tr. Mary A. Cicora, in *Companion to Wagner's 'Parsifal'*, ed. Kinderman and Syer, pp. 81–130

Kinderman, William, 'The Third-Act Prelude of Wagner's *Parsifal*: Genesis, Form, and Dramatic Meaning,' in *19th-Century Music*, 29 (2005–6), 161–84

Kinderman, William, *Wagner's 'Parsifal'* (Oxford University Press: New York, 2013)

Kinderman, William, 'Wagner's *Parsifal*: Musical Form and the Drama of Redemption,' in *The Journal of Musicology*, 4 (1985), 431–46

Kinderman, William, and Syer, Katherine R. (eds), *A Companion to Wagner's Parsifal* (Boydell and Brewer: Woodbridge, 2005)

Kleist, Heinrich von, *Prinz Friedrich von Homburg* (Echo Library: Teddington, 2007)

Klemperer, Otto, *Meine Erinnerungen an Gustav Mahler* (Atlantis: Zurich, 1960)

Koller, Ann Marie, *The Theater Duke: Georg II of Saxe-Meiningen and the German Stage* (Stanford University Press: Stanford, 1984)

Kordes, Gesa, 'Darmstadt, Postwar Experimentation, and the West German Search for a New Musical Identity,' in *Music and German National Identity*, ed. Applegate and Potter, pp. 205–17

Korngold, Julius, Review of 'Der Rosenkavalier,' *Neue Freie Presse*, 9 April 1911 (16750)

Krämer, Dieter, *Kreuzberg 1968–2013: Abbruch, Aufburch, Umbruch* (Nicolai: Berlin, 2013)

Kramer, Lawrence, *Opera and Modern Culture: Wagner and Strauss* (University of California Press: Berkeley, Los Angeles, and London, 2004)

Kraus, Karl, 'Kulturpleite,' in *Die Fackel*, 649–56 (June 1924), 52–6

Krenek, Ernst, *Music Here and Now* trans. Barthold Fles (Norton: New York, 1939)

Küng, Hans, '*Wagner's Parsifal: a Theology for our Time,*' in *Michigan Quarterly Review*, 23 (1984), 311–33

Küppers, Kurt, 'Richard Wagner und der christliche Gottesdienst,' in *Forum katholische Theologie*, 8 (1992), 38–59

Lachenmann, Helmut, 'Open Letter to Hans Werner Henze,' tr. Jeffrey Stadelmann, in *Perspectives of New Music*, 35 (1997), 189–200

Lachenmann, Helmut, 'Touched by Nono,' in *Contemporary Music Review*, 18 (1999), 17–30

La Grange, Henry Louis de, *Gustav Mahler: Volume 3. Vienna: Triumph and Disillusion (1904–1907)* (Oxford University Press: Oxford, 1999)

Lammert, Norbert, 'A Word of Greeting in Connection with the Wagner Cycle Recordings by the Rundfunk-Sinfonieorchester Berlin,' in booklet to Pentatone PTC 5186 403, *Lohengrin*, p. 42.

Large, David Clay, *Germans to the Front: West German Rearmament in the Adenauer Era* (University of North Carolina Press: Chapel Hill, 1996)

Larner, Gerald, Review, in *The Musical Times*, 112 (1971), 1096

Latham, Edward, 'The Prophet and the Pitchman: Dramatic Structure and its Musical Elucidation in "Moses und Aron," Act 1, Scene 2,' in *Political and Religious Ideas in the Works of Arnold Schoenberg*, ed. Cross and Berman, pp. 131–58

Lenin, Vladimir Ilyich, *What is to be Done? Burning Questions of Our Movement*, revised edn (Progress Publishers: Moscow, 1964)

Levi, Erik, *Mozart and the Nazis: How the Third Reich Abused a Cultural Icon* (Yale University Press: New Haven and London, 2010)

Levi, Erik, *Music in the Third Reich* (Macmillan: Basingstoke, 1994)

Levin, David J. (ed.), *Opera Through Other Eyes* (Stanford University Press: Stanford, 1993)

Levin, David J, 'Reading a Staging/Staging a Reading,' in *Cambridge Opera Journal*, 9 (1997), 47–71

Lewin, David, 'Moses und Aron: Some General Remarks, and Analytic Notes for Act I, Scene I,' in *Perspectives of New Music*, 6 (1967), 1–17

Lindenberger, Herbert, 'Arnold Schoenberg's "Der Biblische Weg" and "Moses und Aron": On the Transactions of Aesthetics and Politics,' in *Modern Judaism*, 9 (1989), 55–70

Loos, Alfred, *Sämtliche Schriften*, ed. Franz Glück, 2 vols (Herold: Vienna and Munich, 1962)

Lorenz, Alfred, *Das Geheimnis der Form bei Richard Wagner*, 4 vols (Hesse: Berlin, 1924–33)

Lorenz-Gotha, Alfred, 'Parsifal als Übermensch,' in *Die Musik*, 1 (1901–2), 1876–82

Lourié, Arthur, *Sergei Koussevitsky and his Epoch* (Knopf: New York, 1931)

Lovejoy, Arthur, 'The Meaning of Romanticism for the Historian of Ideas,' in *Journal of the History of Ideas*, 2 (1941), 257–78

Lubac, Henri de, *The Drama of Atheist Humanism*, tr. Edith M. Riley (Sheed & Ward: London, 1949)

Lutyens, Elisabeth, Henze, Hans Werner, and Wood, Hugh, 'Tributes to Dallapiccola,' in *Tempo*, 108 (March 1974), 15–18

Macdonald, Malcolm, *Schoenberg* (Oxford University Press: New York, 2008)

Mach, Ernst, *The Analysis of Sensations and the Relation of the Physical to the Psychical*, tr. Sydney Waterlow (London: Routledge/Thoemmes, 1996)

Maconie, Robin, *Other Planets: The Music of Karlheinz Stockhausen* (Scarecrow Press: Lanham, MD, Toronto, and Oxford, 2005)

Mahler, Alma, *Gustav Mahler: Memories and Letters*, tr. Basil Creighton, ed. Donald Mitchell, 3rd edn (John Murray: London, 1973)

Majakowski, Wladimir, *Werke*, ed. Leonhard Kossuth, 10 vols (Insel: Frankfurt, 1966–73)

Manig, Bert-Oliver. *Die Politik der Ehre. Die Rehabilitierung der Berufs-soldaten in der fruehen Bundesrepublik* (Wallstein: Göttingen, 2004)

Mann, Thomas, *Doctor Faustus: The Life of the German Composer Adrian Leverkühn as Told by a Friend*, tr. John E. Woods (Vintage: New York, 1999)

Mann, Thomas, Essays of Three Decades, tr. H. T. Lowe-Porter (Knopf: New York, 1976)

Maravić, Alexander von, 'Post scriptum Leipzig 2009,' to 'Die Liebe – vom Leben beladen . Zu Stück und Aufführung. Helmut Brade, Johannes Harneit und Peter Konwitschny im Gespräch mit Albrecht Puhlmann in Hannover 2004,' in Oper Leipzig programme to Luigi Nono, *Unter der großen Sonne von Liebe beladen/Al gran sole carico d'amore* (2009), 32–7

Marcuse, Herbert, *The Aesthetic Dimension: Toward a Critique of Marxist Aesthetics*, tr. Herbert Marcuse and Erica Sherover (Macmillan: Basingstoke and London, 1979)

Marx, Karl, *Die Frühschriften*, ed. Siegfried Landshut (Kröner: Stuttgart, 1971)

Marx, Karl, *Grundrisse: Foundations of the Critique of Political Economy*, tr. Martin Nicolaus (Penguin: Harmondsworth, 1993)

Marx, Karl, 'Letter to Ruge' (September 1843), in *The Young Hegelians*, ed. Stepelevich, pp. 307–9

Marx, Karl, and Engels, Friedrich, *Marx-Engels Gesamtausgabe*, ed. various (Dietz: Berlin, 1972–)

Marx, Karl, and Engels, Friedrich, *Selected Works*, 3 vols (Progress: Moscow, 1969–70)

McClatchie, Stephen, *Analyzing Wagner's Operas: Alfred Lorenz and German Nationalist Ideology* (University of Rochester Press: Rochester, NY, 1998)

McClintock, Cynthia, 'Peru's Sendero Luminoso Rebellion: Origins and Trajectory,' in *Power and Popular Protest*, ed. Eckstein, pp. 61–101

Meinecke, Friedrich, *The German Catastrophe: Reflections and Recollections*, tr. Sidney Bradshaw Fay (Harvard University Press: Harvard, 1950).

Melograni, Piero, 'The Cult of the Duce in Mussolini's Italy,' in *Journal of Contemporary History*, 11 (1976), 221–37

Michel, Pierre, *Luigi Dallapiccola* (Contrechamps: Geneva, 1996)

Millington, Barry, 'Parsifal: Facing the Contradictions,' in *Musical Times*, 124 (1983), 97–8

Minor, Ryan, 'Wagner's Last Chorus: Consecrating Space and Spectatorship in *Parsifal*,' in *Cambridge Opera Journal*, 17 (2005), 1–36

Moeller, Robert G., *War Stories: The Search for a Useable Past in the Federal Republic* (University of California Press: Berkeley and Los Angeles, 2001)

Morgan, Robert, 'Dissonant Prolongation: Theoretical and Compositional Precedents,' *Journal of Music Theory*, 20 (1976), 62–72

Morris, Christopher, *Reading Opera Between the Lines: Orchestral Interludes and Cultural Meaning from Wagner to Berg* (Cambridge University Press: Cambridge, 2002)

Nathan, Hans, 'The Twelve-note Compositions of Luigi Dallapiccola,' in *The Musical Quarterly*, 44 (1958), 289–310

Neighbour, O. W., 'Schoenberg, Arnold,' *Grove Music Online. Oxford Music Online*. 8 December 2009 <http://www.oxfordmusiconline. com/subscriber/article/grove/music/25024>

Newman, Ernest, *The Life of Richard Wagner*, 4 vols (Cambridge University Press: Cambridge, 1976)

Nietzsche, Friedrich, *Sämtliche Werke: Kritische Studienausgabe*, ed. Giorgio Colli and Mazzino Montinari, 15 vols (De Gruyter: Berlin and New York, 1967–88)

Nono, Luigi, *Autori Vari*, ed. Enzo Restagno (EDT musica: Turin, 1987)

Nono, Luigi, *Texte: Studien zu seiner Musik*, ed. Jürg Stenzl (Atlantis: Zurich, 1975)

Novalis, 'Pollen,' in *The Early Political Writings of the German Romantics*, tr. Frederick Beiser, pp. 7–31

Nutt, Harry, Review of Christopher Clark, *Iron Kingdom*, Frankfurter Rundschau, 21 March 2007

Nyman, Michael, *Experimental Music: Cage and Beyond*, 2nd edn (Cambridge University Press: Cambridge, 1999)

Osborne, Richard, *Herbert von Karajan: A Life in Music* (Chatto & Windus: London, 1998)

Payne, Stanley G., *A History of Fascism 1914–45* (Routledge: London, 1995)

Perle, George, *Serial Composition and Atonality: An Introduction to the Music of Schoenberg, Berg, and Webern*, 6th edn (University of California Press: Berkeley and Los Angeles, 1991)

Perotti, Sandro, *Iri de Iri: Analisi della musica strumentale di Dallapiccola* (Guerini: Milan, 1988)

Petrassi, Goffredo, Martino, Donald, Perkins, John, and Sessions, Roger, 'In Memoriam,' in *Perspectives of New Music*, 13/1 (Autumn-Winter, 1974), 240–5

Philipsen, Dirk, *We Were the People: Voices from East Germany's Revolutionary Autumn of 1989* (Duke University Press: Durham, NC, 1993),

Plaskitt, James, '"The Language of Passion": Wagner and Romanticism,' in *Wagner 1976: A Celebration of the Bayreuth Festival*, ed. Spencer, pp. 156–65

Poizat, Michel, *The Angel's Cry: Beyond the Pleasure Principle in Opera*, tr. Arthur Denner (Cornell University Press: Ithaca, 1992)

Popper, Karl, *The Open Society and its Enemies*, 2 vols (Routledge: London, 1945)

Porges, Heinrich, *Wagner Rehearsing the 'Ring': An Eye-Witness Account of the Stage Rehearsals of the First Bayreuth Festival*, tr. Robert L Jacobs (Cambridge University Press: Cambridge, 1983)

Porter, Andrew, 'Henze's "Young Lord",' in *The Musical Times*, 110 (1969), 1028–30

Porter, Roy, and Teich, Mikulás (eds), *The Enlightenment in National Context* (Cambridge University Press: Cambridge, 1981)

Potter, Pamela M., 'The Politicization of Handel and his Oratorios in the Weimar Republic, the Third Reich, and the Early Years of the German Democratic Republic,' in *The Musical Quarterly*, 85 (2001), 311–41

Pratella, Francesco Balilla, *Manifesto futurist* (Spes-Salimbeni: Florence, 1980)

Ranke, Leopold von, *Sämtliche Werke*, 54 vols (Duncker and Humblot: Leipzig, 1867–90)

Renan, Ernest, *The Life of Jesus*, tr. unknown (Black: London, 1904)

Reich, Willi, *Schoenberg: A Critical Biography*, tr. Leo Black (Praeger: London, 1971)

Rieger, Eva, *Friedelind Wagner: Richard Wagner's Rebellious Granddaughter*, tr. Chris Walton (Boydell: Woodbridge and Rochester, NY, 2013)

Ringer, Alexander, *Arnold Schoenberg: The Composer as Jew* (Oxford University Press: Oxford, 1990)

Risi, Clemens, 'Shedding Light on the Audience: Hans Neuenfels and Peter Konwitschny Stage Verdi (and Verdians),' in *Cambridge Opera Journal*, 14 (2002), 201–10

Ritter, Alexander, *Verfall und Reform. Eine Schilderung deutscher Theater-Zustände nebst einem Vorschlag zur Reorganisation der Provinzial-Bühnen* (Stuber: Würzburg, 1864).

Ross, Alex, 'The Last Emperor: Richard Strauss,' in *The New Yorker*, 20 December 1999, 93–4

Ross, Alex, *The Rest is Noise: Listening to the Twentieth Century* (Fourth Estate: London, 2008)

Rousseau, Jean-Jacques, *The Social Contract and Discourses*, tr. G. D. H. Cole, revised J. H. Brumfett, John C. Hall, and P. D. Jimack (Dent: London, 1993)

Rumsfeld, Donald, and Myers, Richard, 'United States Department of Defense News Briefing,' 12 February 2002

Ruprecht, Erich, and Bänsch, Dieter, *Literarische Manifeste der Jahrhundertwende, 1890–1910* (J. B. Metzler: Stuttgart, 1970)

Rushton, Julian, *W. A. Mozart: Don Giovanni* (Cambridge University Press: Cambridge, 1981)

Russolo, Luigi, *L'arte dei rumori* (Carucci: Rome, 1975)

Rzewski, Frederic, *Nonsequiturs: Writings and Lectures on Improvisation, Composition, and Interpretation*, ed. Gisela Gronemeyer and Reinhard Oehlschlagel (Edition MusikTexte: Cologne, 2007)

Santi, Piero, 'Luciano Berio,' in *Die Reihe*, 4 (1958), 98–102

Sartre, Jean-Paul, *Un Théâtre de situations*, ed. Michel Contat and Michel Rybalka (Gallimard: Paris, 1972)

Sartre, Jean-Paul, *Was ist Literatur?: ein Essay*, tr. Hans Georg Brenner (Rohwolt: Hamburg, 1958)

Saul, Nicholas (ed.), *Philosophy and German Literature, 1700–1990* (Cambridge University Press: Cambridge, 2002)

Scherzinger, Martin, 'In Memory of a Receding Dialectic: The Political Relevance of Autonomy and Formalism in Modernist Musical Aesthetics,' in *The Pleasure of Modernist Music: Listening, Meaning, Intention, Ideology*, ed. Ashby, pp. 68–100

Schiller, Johann Christoph Friedrich von, *Don Carlos: Infant von Spanien* (Göschen: Leipzig, 1804)

Schiller, Johann Christoph Friedrich von, *On the Aesthetic Education of Man*, tr. Elizabeth M. Wilkinson and L. A. Willoughby (Oxford University Press: Oxford, 1967)

Schirmacher, Wolfgang (ed.), *German 20th Century Philosophy: The Frankfurt School* (Continuum: New York, 2000)

Schmidt, Felix, and Hohmeyer, Jürgen, Interview with Pierre Boulez, 'Sprengt die Opernhäuser in die Luft!,' in *Der Spiegel*, 40 (25 September 1967), 166–74

Schmidt, James (ed.), *What is Enlightenment? Eighteenth-Century Answers and Twentieth-Century Questions* (University of California

Press: Berkeley and Los Angeles, 1996)

Schmitz, Eugen, *Emil Naumanns Illustrierte Musikgeschichte von den Anfängen der Tonkunst bis zur Gegenwart, neu gestaltet* (Union Deutsche Verlagsgesellschaft: Stuttgart, 1934)

Schoenberg, Arnold, *Briefe*, ed. Erwin Stein (Schott: Mainz, 1958)

Schoenberg, Arnold, 'Das Verhältnis zum Text,' in Der blaue Reiter, ed. Kandinsky and Marc, pp. 60–75

Schoenberg, Arnold, 'Der biblische Weg,' with English translation by Moshe Lazar, *Journal of the Arnold Schoenberg Institute*, 17 (1994), 162–330

Schoenberg, Arnold, 'Four-Point Programme for Jewry,' in *Journal of the Arnold Schoenberg Institute*, 3 (1979), 51–2

Schoenberg, Arnold, *Letters*, ed. Erwin Stein, tr. Eithne Wilkins and Ernst Kaiser (Faber: London and Boston, 1964)

Schoenberg, Arnold, *Style and Idea: Selected Writings*, ed. Leonard Stein, with translations by Leo Black (Faber: London, 1975)

Schoenberg, Arnold, *Zusammenhang, Kontrapunkt, Instrumentation, Formenlehre*, ed. Severine Neff, tr. Charlotte M. Cross and Severine Neff (University of Nebraska Press: Lincoln, 1994)

Schopenhauer, Arthur, *Die Welt als Wille und Vorstellung*, 2 vols (Deutscher Taschenbuch: Munich, 2002)

Schopenhauer, Arthur, *Parerga and Paralipomena*, tr. E. F. J. Payne (Oxford University Press: Oxford, 1974)

Schuh, Willi (ed.), *A Confidential Matter: The Letters of Richard Strauss and Stefan Zweig, 1931–1935*, tr. Max Knight (University of California Press: Berkeley and Los Angeles, 1977)

Scruton, Roger, 'A Quest for Truth,' in *Literary Review*, April 2006, 14–15

Scruton, Roger, *Death-Devoted Heart: Sex and the Sacred in Wagner's 'Tristan and Isolde'* (Oxford University Press: Oxford and New York, 2004)

Shaw, George Bernard, *The Perfect Wagnerite: A Commentary on the Niblung's Ring*, 4th edn (Dover: New York, 1967)

Shaw, Jennifer, 'Androgyny and the Eternal Feminine in *Die Jakobsleiter*,' in *Political and Religious Ideas in the Works of Arnold Schoenberg*, ed. Cross and Berman, pp. 61–76

Simms, Bryan A., *The Atonal Music of Arnold Schoenberg* (Oxford University Press: Oxford, 2000)

Skinner, Quentin, 'Meaning and Understanding in the History of Ideas,' in *History and Theory*, 8 (1969), 1–53

Skramstad, Per-Erik, Interview with Peter Konwitschny, 'I do not consider myself as a representative of the *Regietheater*, <http://www.wagnerop-era.net/Interviews/Peter-Konwitschny-Interview-2009.htm>.

Spencer, Stewart (ed.), *Wagner 1976: A Celebration of the Bayreuth Festival* (Wagner Society: London, 1976)

Spencer, Stewart, and Millington, Barry (eds), *Selected Letters of Richard Wagner*, tr. Stewart Spencer (Dent: London, 1987)

Spencer, Vicki A., *Herder's Political Thought: A Study on Language, Culture and Community* (University of Toronto Press: Toronto, 2012)

Spotts, Frederic, *Bayreuth: A History of the Wagner Festival* (Yale University Press: New Haven and London, 1996)

Steinberg, Michael P., 'Richard Strauss and the Question,' in *Richard Strauss and his World*, ed. Gilliam, pp. 164–89

Steinweg, Reiner (ed.), *Brechts Modell der Lehrstücke: Zeugnisse, Diskussion, Erfahrungen* (Suhrkamp: Frankfurt, 1976)

Stenzl, Jürg, 'Luigi Nono und Cesare Pavese,' in Nono, *Texte: Studien zu seiner Musik*, pp. 409–33

Stenzl, Jürg, *Von Puccini zu Luigi Nono. Italienische Musik 1922–1952: Faschismus–Resistenza–Republik* (Fritz Knuf: Buren. 1990)

Stepelevich, Lawrence S. (ed.), *The Young Hegelians: An Anthology* (Cambridge University Press: Cambridge, 1983)

Stephan, Rudolph, 'Editor's Preface,' to Arnold Schoenberg, *Die Jakobsleiter*, ed. Winfried Zillig, revised ed. Rudolph Stephan (Universal Edition: Vienna, 1980)

Stephan, Rudolph, 'Hans Werner Henze,' in *Die Reihe*, 4 (1960), 29–35

Steuermann, Clara, 'From the Archives: Schoenberg's Library Catalogue,' in *Journal of the Arnold Schoenberg Institute*, 3 (1979), 203–18

Stewart, Suzanne R., 'The Theft of the Operatic Voice: Masochistic Seduction in Wagner's *Parsifal*,' in *Musical Quarterly*, 80 (1996), 597–628

Stirner, Max, *The Ego and its Own*, tr. Steven Byington, ed. David Leopold (Cambridge University Press: Cambridge, 1995)

Stockhausen, Karlheinz, 'Music and Speech,' in *Die Reihe*, 6 (1964), 40–64

Stone, Marla, 'Staging Fascism: The Exhibition of the Fascist Revolution,' in *Journal of Contemporary History*, 28 (1993), 215–43

Strauss, David Friedrich, *Das Leben Jesu, kritisch bearbeitet*, 2 vols (C. F. Osiander: Tübingen, 1835–6)

Strauss, Richard, *Recollections and Reflections*, ed. Willi Schuh, tr. L. J. Lawrence (Boosey and Hawkes: London, 1953)

Stravinsky, Igor, *An Autobiography* (Simon & Schuster: New York, 1956)

Stravinsky, Igor, and Craft, Robert, *Conversations with Igor Stravinsky* (Faber: London, 1959)

Stravinsky, Igor, and Craft, Robert, *Expositions and Developments* (Faber: London, 1962)

Syer, Katherine, '"It left me no Peace": From Carlo Gozzi's *La donna serpente* to Wagner's *Parsifal*,' in *The Musical Quarterly*, 94 (2011), 325–80

Talmon, Jacob Leib, *The Origins of Totalitarian Democracy* (Secker and Warburg: London, 1952)

Tanner, Michael, *Wagner* (HarperCollins: London, 1996)

Taruskin, Richard, *Defining Russia Musically: Historical and Hermeneutical Essays* (Princeton University Press: Princeton, 1997)

Taruskin, Richard, *Text and Act: Essays on Music and Performance* (Oxford University Press: Oxford, 1995)

Taruskin, Richard, *The Oxford History of Western Music*, 5 vols (Oxford University Press: New York, 2010)

Taylor A. J. P., *The Course of German History: A Survey of the Development of German History since 1815* (Hamish Hamilton: London, 1961)

Taylor, Charles, *Hegel* (Cambridge University Press: Cambridge, 1975)

Taylor, Charles, *Hegel and Modern Society* (Cambridge University Press: Cambridge, 1979)

Terry, Ken, 'Frederic Rzewski and the Improvising Avant Garde,' in *Down Beat*, 46 (1979), 20–1

Theurich, Werner, 'Neuer *Lohengrin* in Bayreuth: Wie man der Schwan rupft,' <http://www.spiegel.de/kultur/musik/neuer-lohengrin-in-bayreuth-wie-man-den-schwan-rupft-a-708441.html>.

Thomas, Nick, *Protest Movements in 1960s West Germany: A Social History of Dissent and Democracy* (Berg: Oxford and New York, 2003)

Tieck, Ludwig, *Der gestiefelte Kater*, ed. Gerald Gillespie (Edinburgh University Press: Edinburgh, 1974)

Tilbury, John, *Cornelius Cardew: A Life Unfinished* (Copula: Essex, 2008)

Till, Nicholas (ed.), *The Cambridge Companion to Opera Studies* (Cambridge University Press: Cambridge, 2012)

Till, Nicholas, 'The Operatic Work: Texts, Performances, Repetitions, and Repertories,' in *The Cambridge Companion to Opera Studies*, ed. Till, pp. 225–49

Togliatti, Palmera, *Sul fascismo*, ed. Giuseppe Vacca (Laterza: Rome, 2004)

Tomassini, Anthony, 'Adapting, Revising, Provoking,' in *New York Times*, 9 March 2012

Tomlinson, Gary, *Metaphysical Song: An Essay on Opera* (Princeton University Press: Princeton, 1999)

Tooze, Adam, 'Reassessing the Moral Economy of Post-war Reconstruction: The Terms of the West German Settlement in 1952,' in *Past and Present*, 210 (2011), 47–70

Treadwell, James, 'Reading and Staging Again,' in *Cambridge Opera Journal*, 10 (1998), 205–20

Treitschke, Heinrich von, *History of Germany in the Nineteenth Century*, tr. Eden and Cedar Paul, 7 vols (Jarrold: London, 1915–19)

Ungeheuer, Natascha, *Ölbilder* (Ararat: Berlin, 1985)

Varga, Bálint András, *Conversations with Iannis Xenakis* (Faber: London, 1996)

Vazsonyi, Nicholas, *Richard Wagner: Self-Promotion and the Making of a Brand* (Cambridge University Press: Cambridge, 2010)

Vermeil, Jean, *Conversations with Pierre Boulez: Thoughts on Conducting*, tr. Camille Naish (Amadeus: Portland, 1996)

Voltaire, *Œuvres completes*, vol. 15, 'Romans' (Hachette: Paris, 1859–62)

Vries, Hent de, *Minimal Theologies: Critiques of Secular Religion in Adorno and Levinas*, tr. Geoffrey Hale (Johns Hopkins University Press: Baltimore, MD, and London, 2005)

Wagner, Cosima, *Cosima Wagner's Diaries*, ed. M. Gregor-Dellin and D. Mack, tr. G. Skelton, 2 vols (Harcourt Brace Jovanovich: London, 1978–80)

Wagner, Cosima, *Die Tagebücher*, 2 vols (Piper: Munich and Zurich, 1976–7)

Wagner, Richard, *My Life*, tr. Andrew Gray, ed. Mary Whittall (Cambridge University Press: Cambridge, 1983)

Wagner, Richard, *On Conducting*, tr. Edward Dannreuther (Dover, New York, 1989)

Wagner, Richard, *Oper und Drama*, ed. Klaus Kropfinger (Reclam: Stuttgart, 1994)

Wagner, Richard, *Sämtliche Briefe*, ed. Gertrud Strobel, Werner Wolf, Hans-Joachim Bauer, Johannes Forner, *et al.* (VEB Deutscher Verlag für Musik/Breitkopf und Härtel: Leipzig, 1967–)

Wagner, Richard, *Sämtliche Schriften und Dichtungen*, ed. Richard Sternfeld and Hans von Wolzogen, 16 vols in 10 (Breitkopf und Härtel: Leipzig, 1912–14)

Wagner, Richard, *Sämtliche Werke*, ed. Carl Dahlhaus, Egon Voss, and others (Schott: Mainz, 1970–)

Wagner, Richard, *The Diary of Richard Wagner 1865–1882: The Brown Book*, ed. Joachim Bergfeld, tr. George Bird (Cambridge University Press: London, 1980)

Walton, Chris, *Richard Wagner's Zurich: The Muse of Place* (Camden House: Woodbridge and Rochester, NY, 2007)

Wapnewski, Peter, *Der traurige Gott: Richard Wagner in seinen Helden* (Beck: Munich, 1978)

Warner, Keith, 'Gesamt Werk Kunst: A Few New Thoughts,' in *The Wagner Journal*, 3/2 (2009), 49–61

Warrack, John, 'Henze's "Der Prinz von Homburg" at Hamburg,' in *Opera*, 11 (1960), 460

Waterhouse, John C. G., 'Since Verdi: Italian Serious Music 1860–1995,' in *The Cambridge Companion to Modern Italian Culture*, ed. Baranski and West, pp. 311–24

Watkins, Holly, 'Schoenberg's Interior Designs,' in *Journal of the American Musicological Society*, 61 (2008), 123–206

Webern, Anton, *The Path to the New Music*, ed. Willi Reich, tr. Leo Black (Presser: London, 1963)

Werfel, Franz, contribution to *Arnold Schönberg zum 60. Geburtstag, 13. September 1934* (Universal Edition: Vienna, 1934)

White, Hayden, *Metahistory: The Historical Imagination in Nineteenth-Century Europe* (Johns Hopkins University Press: Baltimore, MD, 1973)

White, Pamela C., *Schoenberg and the God-Idea: The Opera 'Moses und Aron'* (University of Michigan Press: Ann Arbor, 1985),

Whittall, Arnold, 'The Music,' in *Parsifal*, ed. Beckett, pp. 61–86

Whittall, Arnold, 'Schoenberg: "Erwartung", etc.,' in booklet accompanying EMI CDC 55212 2, pp. 4–8

Wildhagen, Christian, 'Und erlöse uns vom Erlösen,' in *Frankfurter Allgemeine Zeitung*, Feuilleton, 5 August 2009

Wunberg, Gotthard, ed., *Die Wiener Moderne: Literatur, Kunst und Musick zwischen 1890 und 1910* (Reclam: Stuttgart, 2000)

Youmans, Charles, *Richard Strauss's Orchestral Music and the German Intellectual Tradition: The Philosophical Roots of Musical Modernism* (Indiana University Press: Bloomington and Indianopolis, 2005)

Zenck, Martin, 'Zur Aneignung Händels in der nationalen Literaturgeschichtsschreibung des 19. Jahrhunderts,' in *Bericht über den internationalen musikwissenschaftlichen Kongreß Stuttgart 1985* (Bärenreiter: Kassel, 1987), pp. 273–80

Zöllner, Johann Carl Friedrich, *Die transcendentale Physik und die sogenannte Philosophie: eine deutsche Antwort auf eine 'sogenannte wissenschaftliche Frage'* (Staackmann: Leipzig, 1879)

Zuckerkandl, Bertha, 'Hermann Bahr, Ernst Mach und Emil Zuckerkandl im Gespräch,' in *Die Wiener Moderne*, ed. Wunberg, pp. 171–7

INDEX

Abbado, Claudio 125, 149, 161, 163, 169, 267
Abbate, Carolyn 8–9
'absolute' music 23, 250, 272
Abyssinia, Italian invasion of 131–2
Achilles 35
Adam, the first man 45
Adenauer, Konrad 182, 203
Adorno, Theodor Wiesengrund 3, 4, 6, 13, 17, 18, 19, 29, 36, 38, 39–40, 52, 62, 81, 84–5, 89, 90, 95–6, 99, 102, 110, 120, 133 n.20, 134, 142, 162, 178, 181, 186, 190, 194, 195, 232, 234, 237, 238, 244, 262, 264
 critique of Wagner 6, 29, 38, 133 n.20, 244
 Dialectic of Enlightenment (with Max Horkheimer) 60, 61–2, 142, 217
 Henze on 178, 181–2 n.31
Æschylus 106
 Agamemnon 13
agitprop 74, 163, 166
Alba, Third Duke of, Fernando Álvarez de Toledo 139
Albrecht, Marc 263
Albright, Daniel 65 n.4
Alegant, Brian 138
Algeria, War of Independence 151, 159, 165, 166
Alleg, Henri 161, 165
Allende, Salvador 145, 198, 267
Altenberg, Peter 73
Amnesty International 144
Amsterdam 10, 77
anarchism 36, 42, 67, 104–5, 155
Andersch, Alfred 160
Andriessen, Louis 14–15
 De Staat 14–15
androgyny 70
anti-Semitism 65, 73–4, 109, 161, 167, 173, 221, 222

Antoine, André 211
APO (Außerparlemantarische Opposition) 196
Apollo 186
Aquinas, St Thomas 97
Arden of Faversham 119
Areopagus 12
army 116, 136, 165, 166, 182–3, 185, 187, 189, 197
Arnold Schoenberg Center 24
Aryans 73, 109, 174
atheism 67, 107
Athens 12, 13, 33, 56
 See also tragedy, Greek
atom bomb 167
atonality 52, 64, 68, 93
Auber, Daniel-François-Esprit 240
Auden, Wystan Hugh 175, 191, 202
Augustinianism 63
Auner, Joseph 85
Auschwitz 116, 197
Austria-Hungary 111 n.33, 127–8
avant-garde 131, 153–6, 177–82, 198, 240
 American 154
 post-war European 131, 153–6, 177–82;
 See also 'Darmstadt School'
Ayacucho 272

Baader, Andreas 194
Bach, Johann Sebastian 68, 77–9, 94, 95–6, 138, 140, 174, 193, 203, 225, 247
 Art of Fugue 79
 Mass in B minor 267
 Musical Offering 96, 140
 Passion settings 77–8, 163–4, 221, 225
 Prelude and Fugue in E-flat major, 'St Anne' BWV 552 96